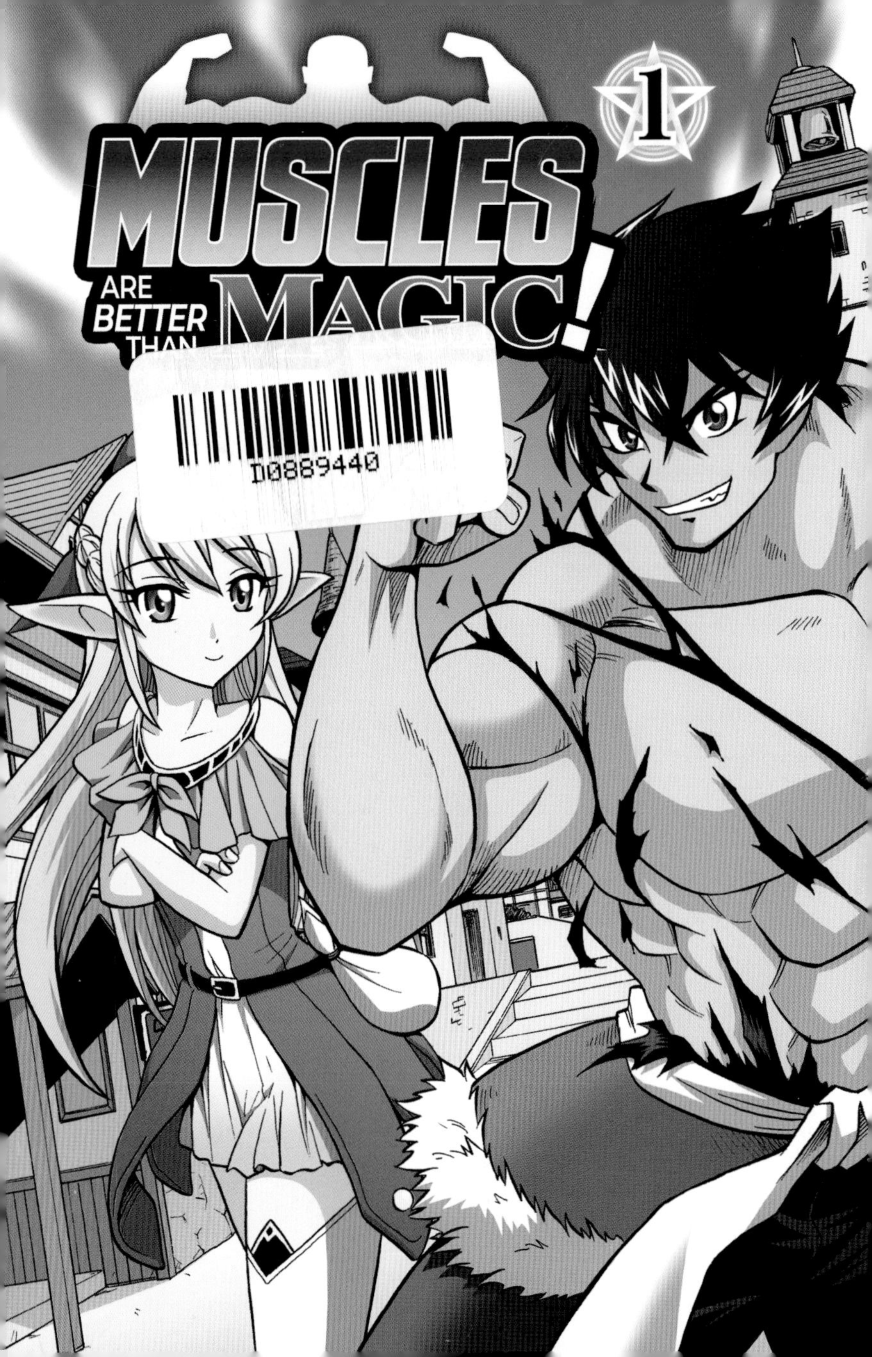
1
MUSCLES
ARE BETTER THAN MAGIC!

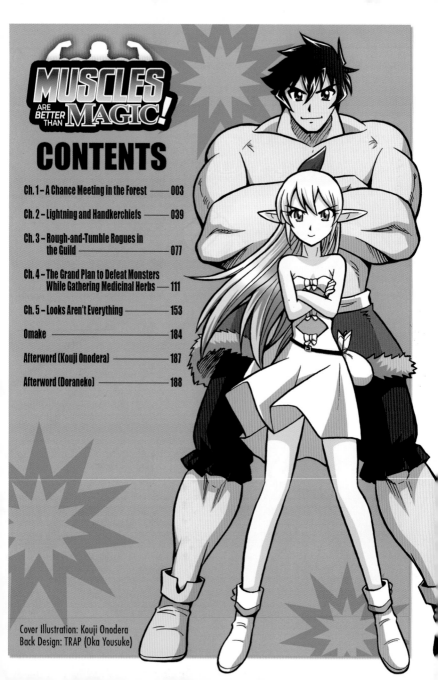

MUSCLES ARE BETTER THAN MAGIC!

CONTENTS

Cover Illustration: Kouji Onodera
Back Design: TRAP (Oka Yousuke)

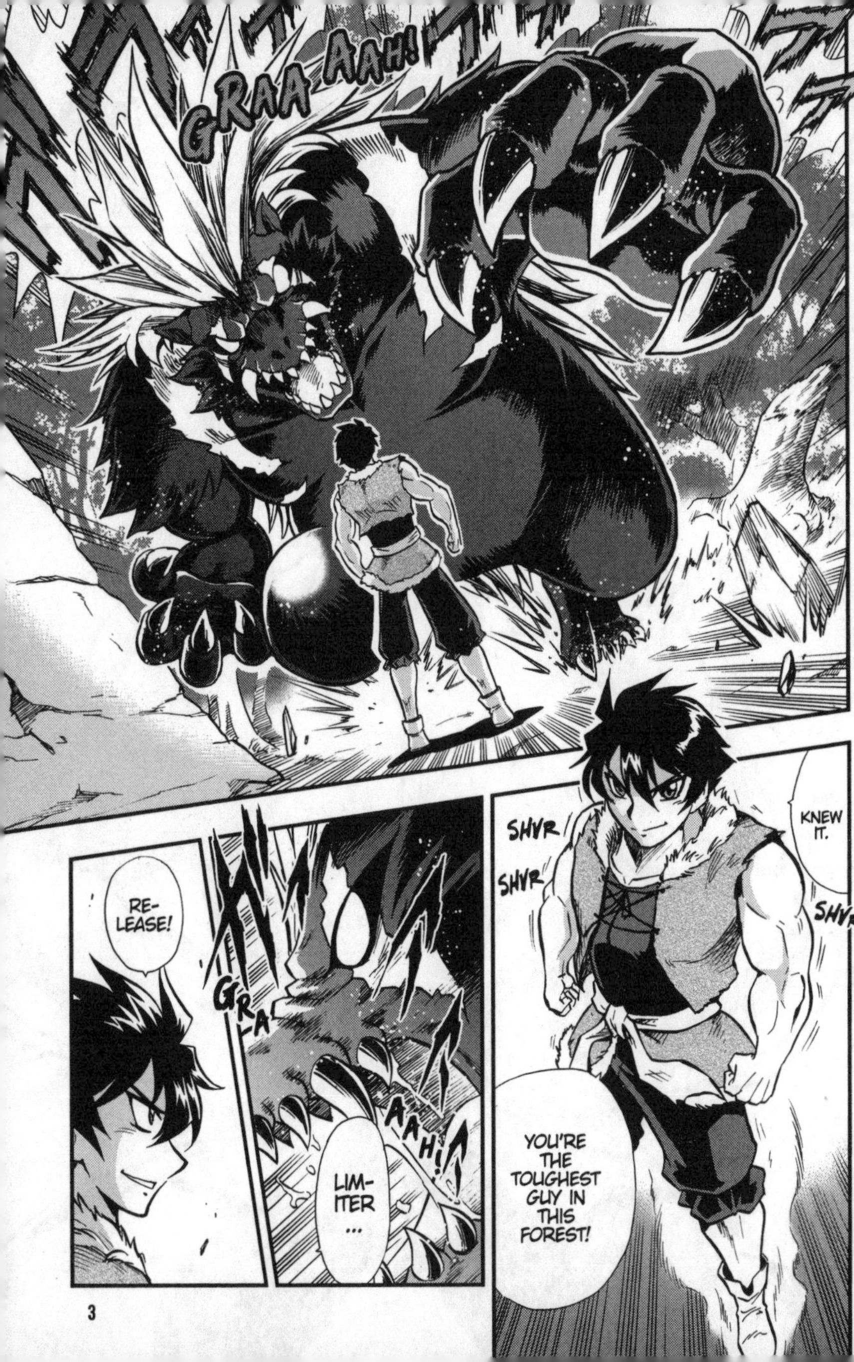
GRAA AAH!
KNEW IT.
SHVR
SHVR
SHVR
YOU'RE THE TOUGHEST GUY IN THIS FOREST!
GRAAAH!
LIMITER ...
RE-LEASE!

CHAPTER 1
A Chance Meeting in the Forest

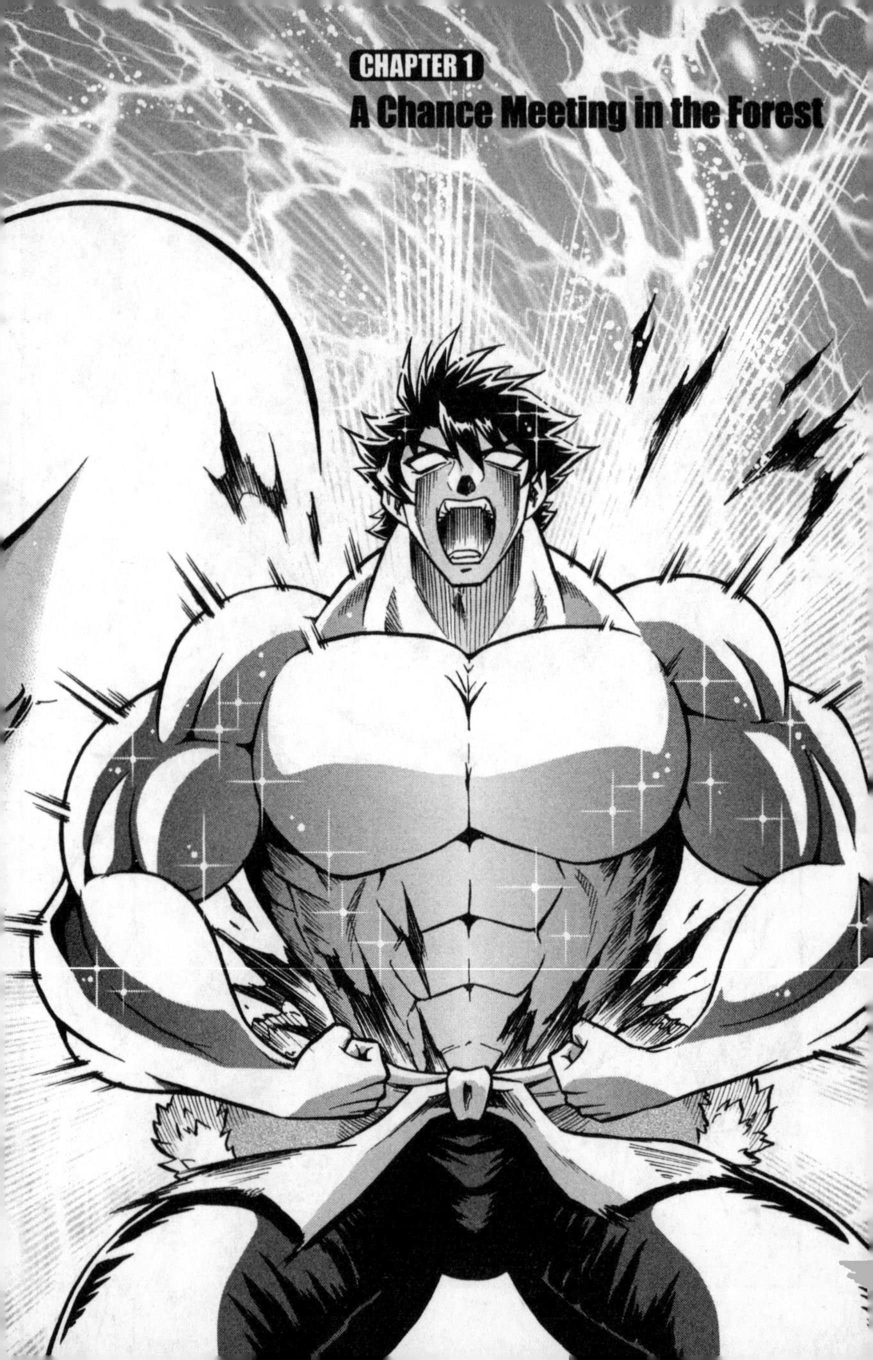

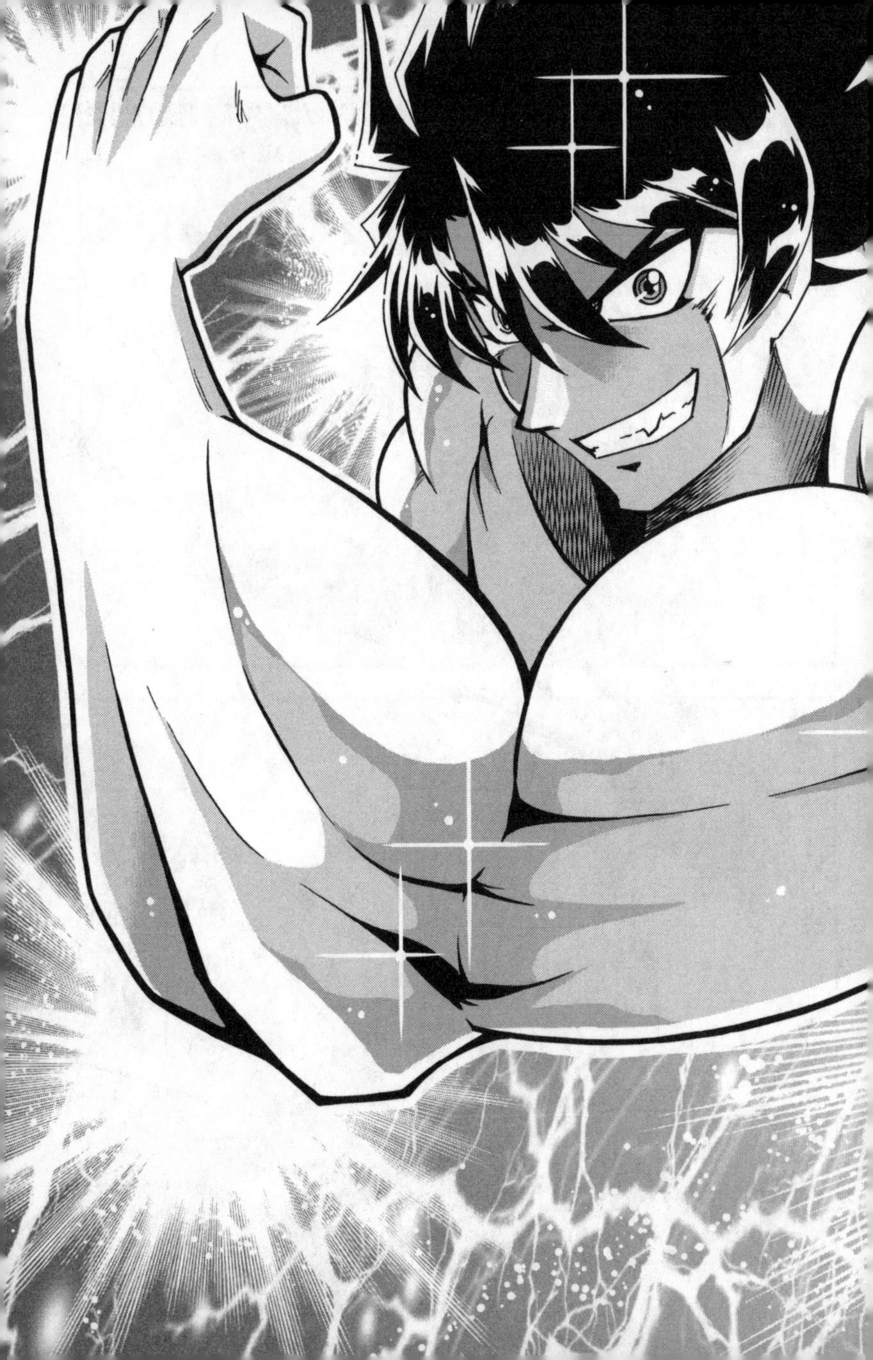

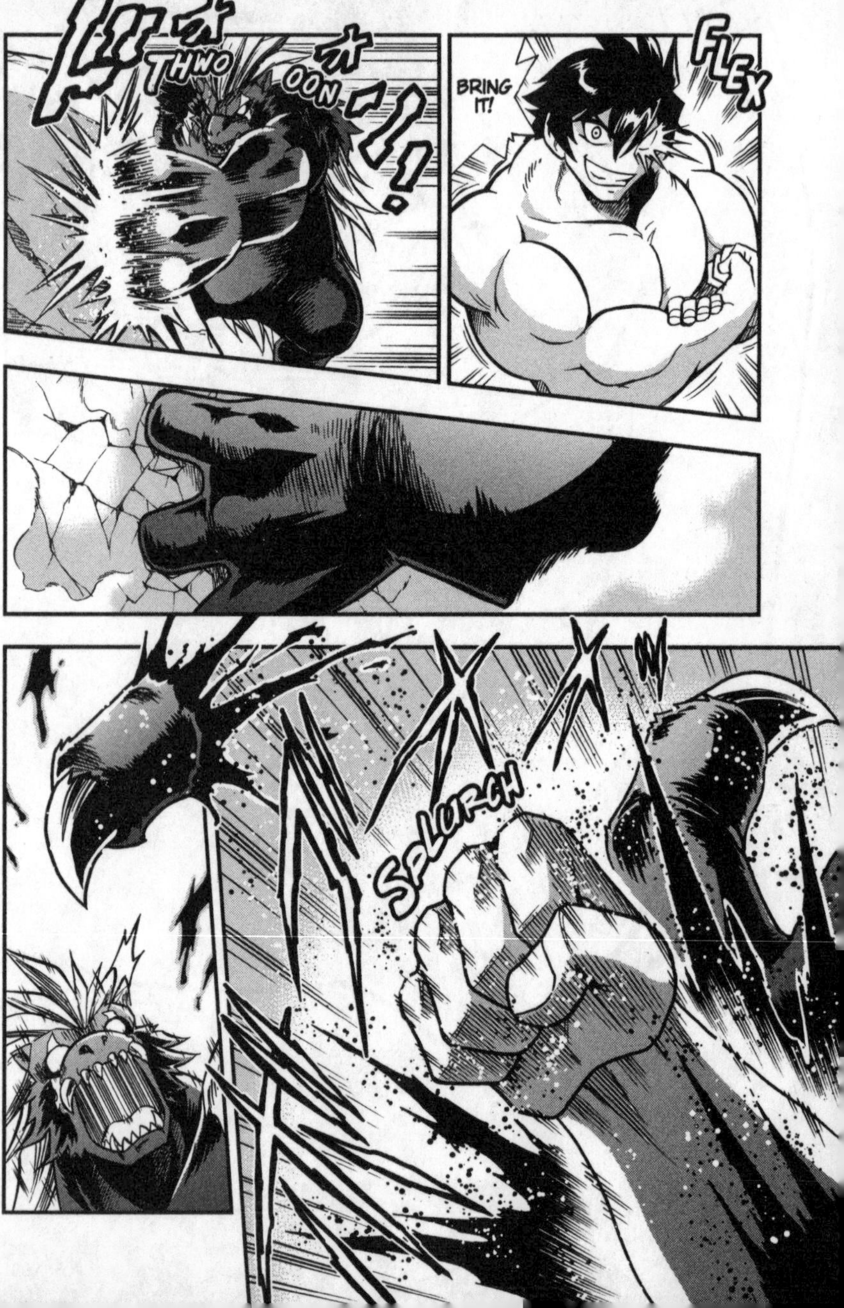
FLEX
BRING IT!
THWOOON
SPLURCH

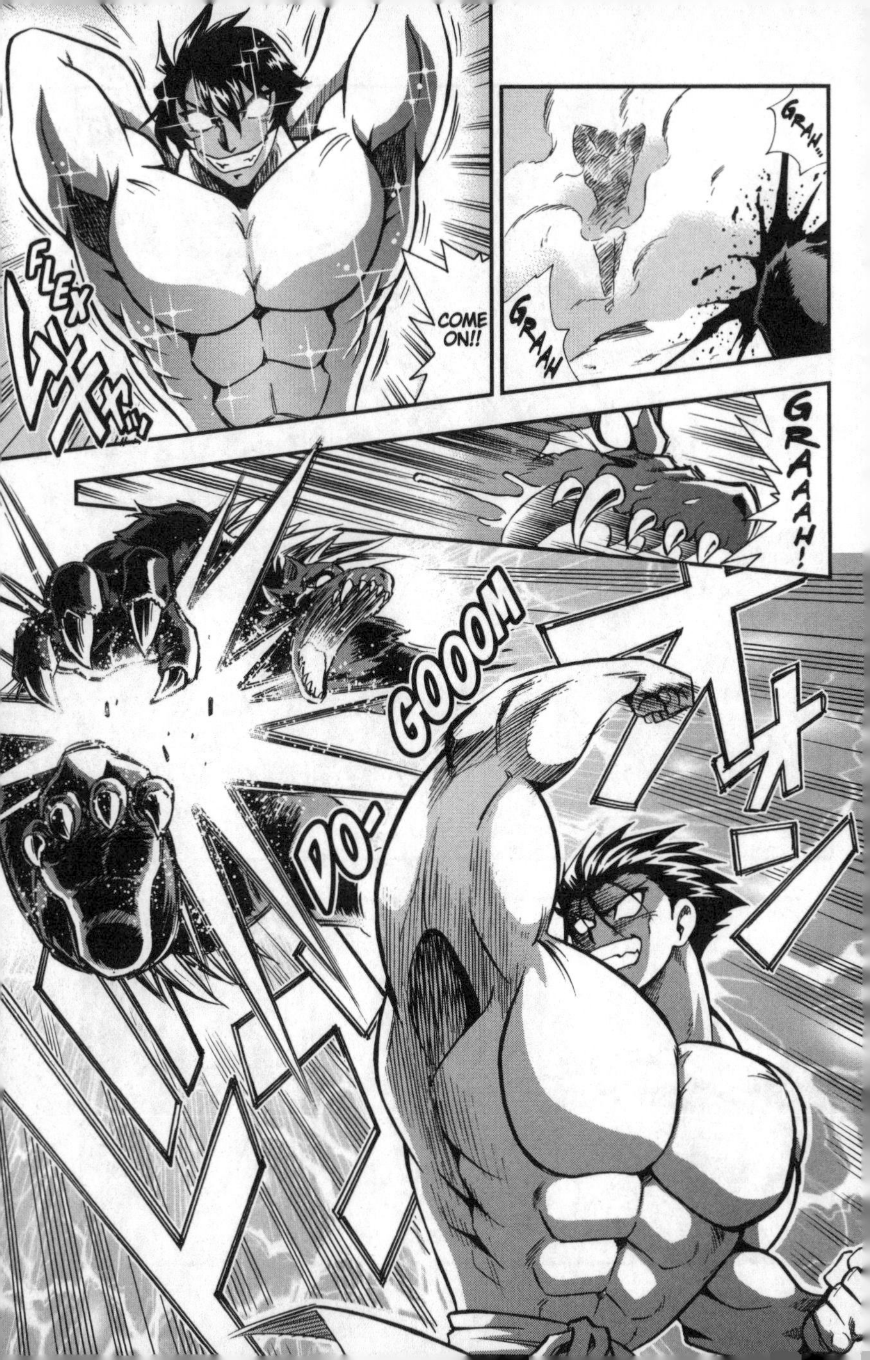
GRAH...
GRAAH
FLEX
COME ON!!
GRAAAAH!
DO-GOOOM

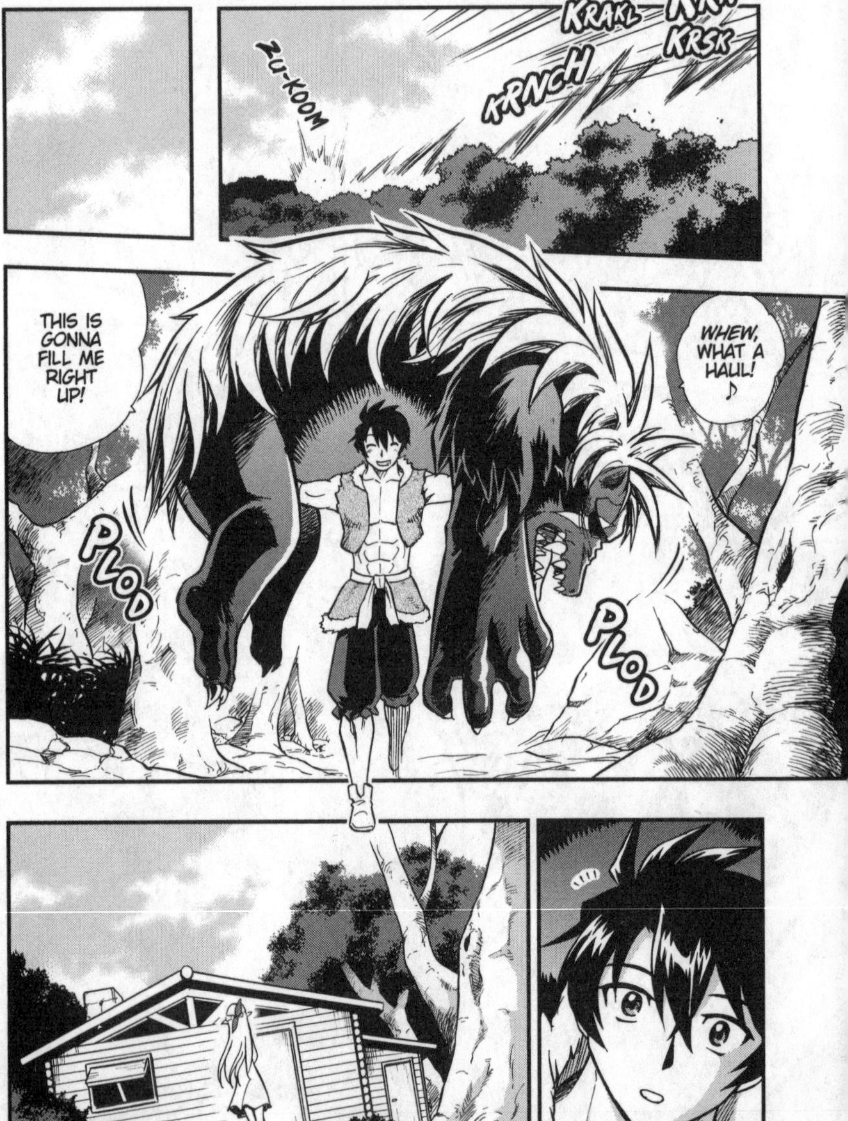
KRK
KRSK
KRAKL
KRNCH
ZU-KOOM
WHEW, WHAT A HAUL! ♪
THIS IS GONNA FILL ME RIGHT UP!
PLOD
PLOD

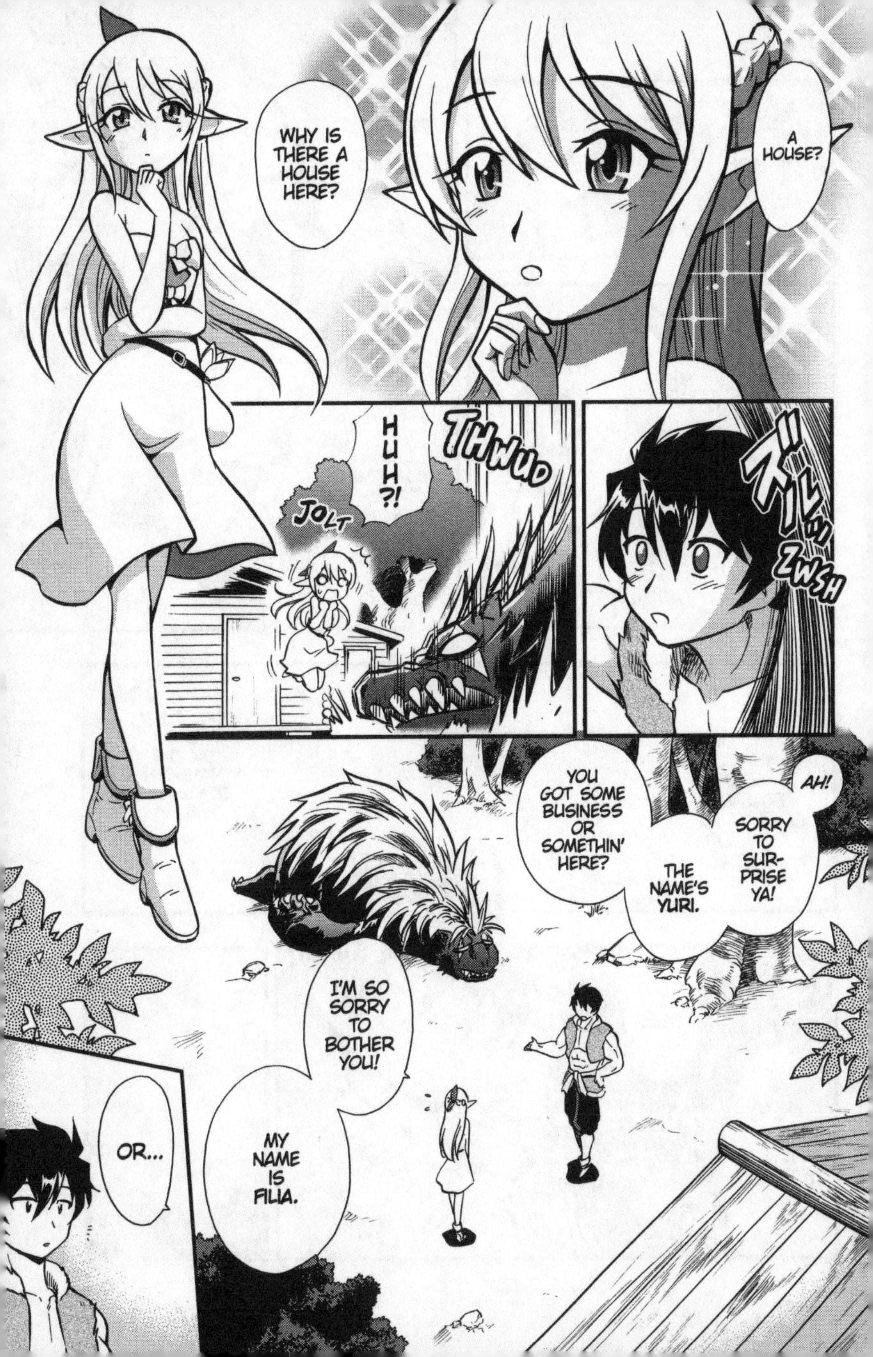
A HOUSE?
WHY IS THERE A HOUSE HERE?
ZWSH
THWUD
HUH?!
JOLT
AH!
SORRY TO SUR-PRISE YA!
THE NAME'S YURI.
YOU GOT SOME BUSINESS OR SOMETHIN' HERE?
I'M SO SORRY TO BOTHER YOU!
MY NAME IS FILIA.
OR...

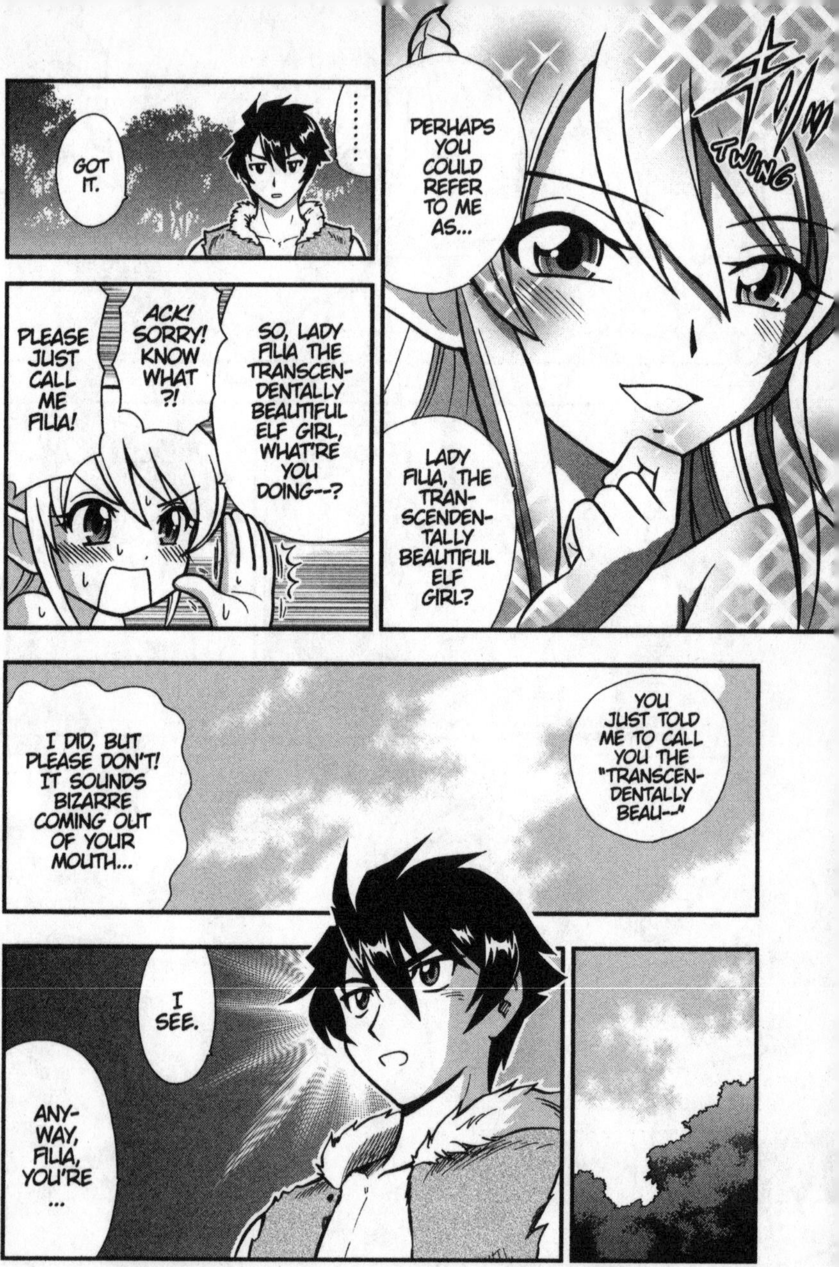

TWING
PERHAPS YOU COULD REFER TO ME AS...
LADY FILIA, THE TRAN-SCENDEN-TALLY BEAUTIFUL ELF GIRL?
......
GOT IT.
SO, LADY FILIA THE TRANSCEN-DENTALLY BEAUTIFUL ELF GIRL, WHAT'RE YOU DOING--?
ACK! SORRY! KNOW WHAT?!
PLEASE JUST CALL ME FILIA!
YOU JUST TOLD ME TO CALL YOU THE "TRANSCEN-DENTALLY BEAU--"
I DID, BUT PLEASE DON'T! IT SOUNDS BIZARRE COMING OUT OF YOUR MOUTH...
I SEE.
ANY-WAY, FILIA, YOU'RE ...

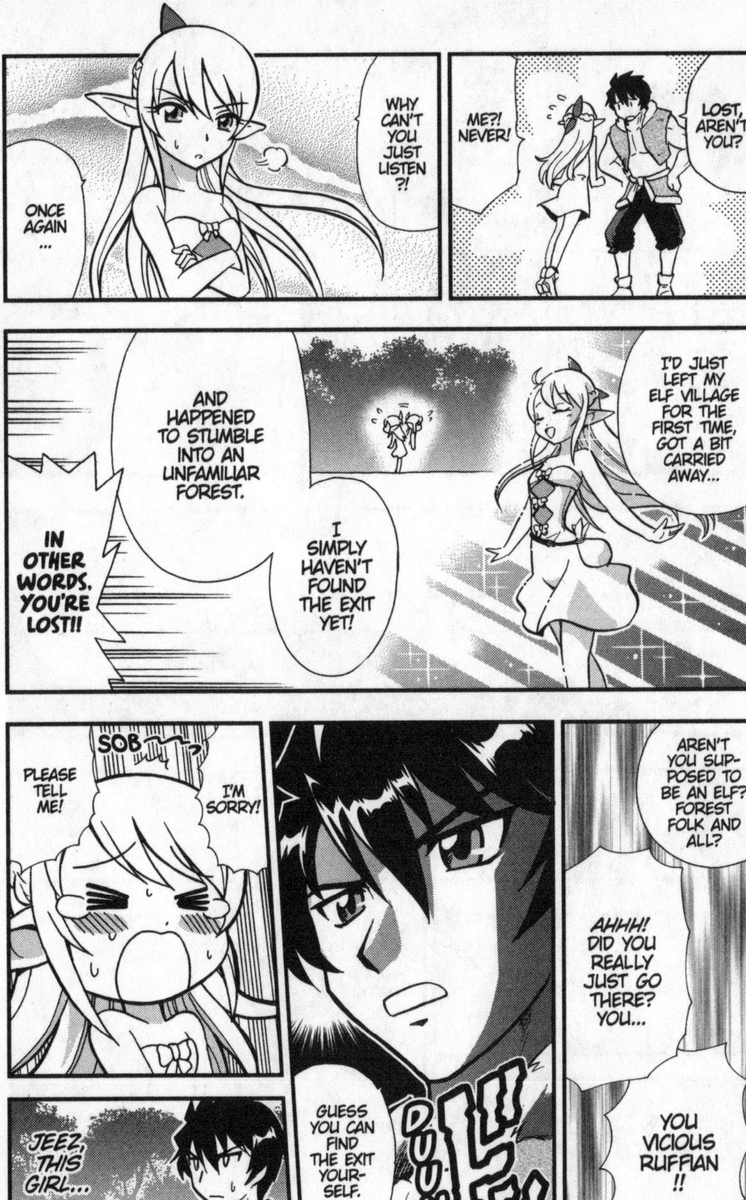
LOST, AREN'T YOU?
ME?! NEVER!
WHY CAN'T YOU JUST LISTEN?!
ONCE AGAIN...
I'D JUST LEFT MY ELF VILLAGE FOR THE FIRST TIME, GOT A BIT CARRIED AWAY...
AND HAPPENED TO STUMBLE INTO AN UNFAMILIAR FOREST.
I SIMPLY HAVEN'T FOUND THE EXIT YET!
IN OTHER WORDS, YOU'RE LOST!!
AREN'T YOU SUP-POSED TO BE AN ELF? FOREST FOLK AND ALL?
AHHH! DID YOU REALLY JUST GO THERE? YOU...
YOU VICIOUS RUFFIAN!!
GUESS YOU CAN FIND THE EXIT YOUR-SELF.
DUUN
SOB
I'M SORRY!
PLEASE TELL ME!
JEEZ, THIS GIRL...

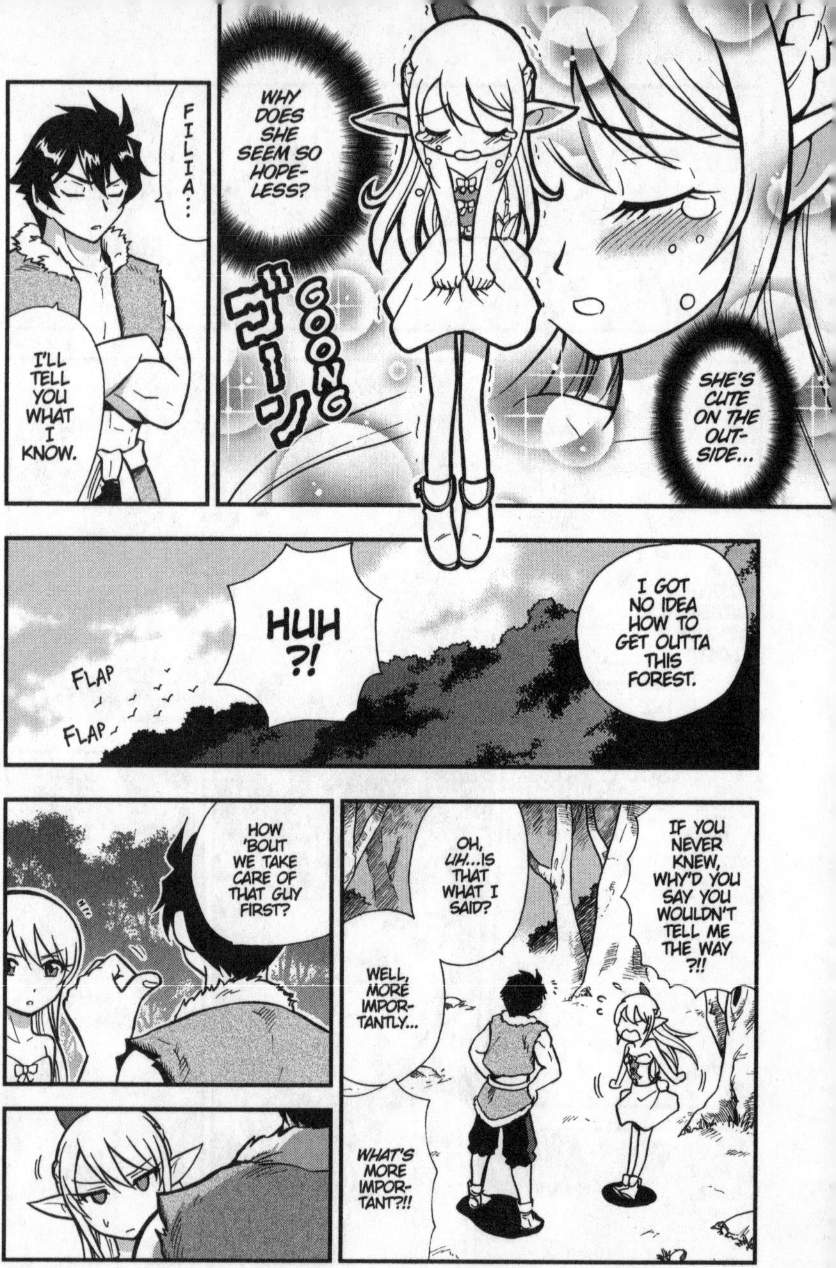
SHE'S CUTE ON THE OUT-SIDE...
WHY DOES SHE SEEM SO HOPE-LESS?
GOONG
FILIA...
I'LL TELL YOU WHAT I KNOW.
I GOT NO IDEA HOW TO GET OUTTA THIS FOREST.
HUH?!
FLAP
FLAP
IF YOU NEVER KNEW, WHY'D YOU SAY YOU WOULDN'T TELL ME THE WAY?!!
OH, UH...IS THAT WHAT I SAID?
WELL, MORE IMPOR-TANTLY...
WHAT'S MORE IMPOR-TANT?!!
HOW 'BOUT WE TAKE CARE OF THAT GUY FIRST?

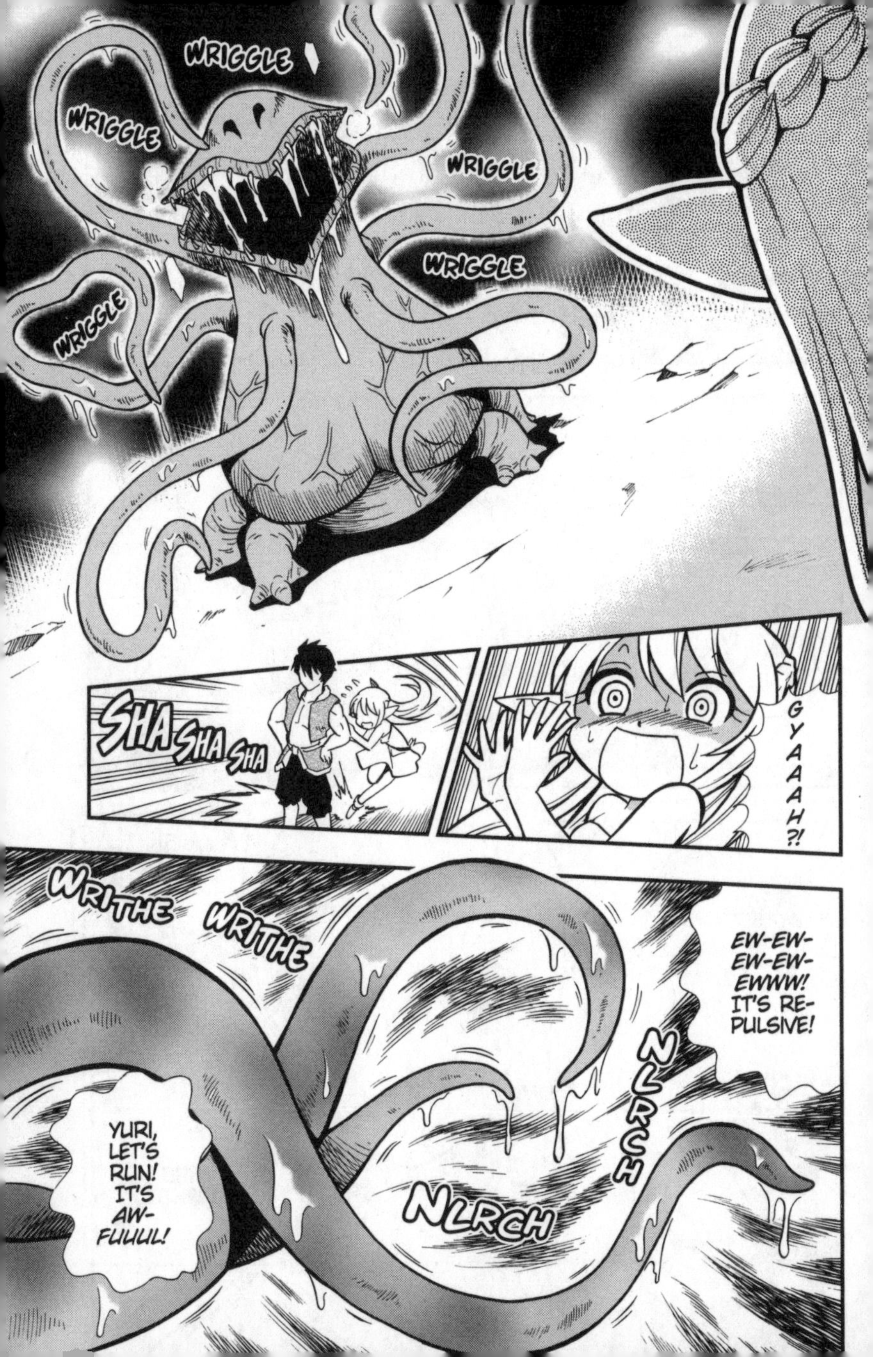
WRIGGLE
WRIGGLE
WRIGGLE
WRIGGLE
WRIGGLE
GYAAAAH?!
SHA SHA SHA
EW-EW-EW-EW-EWWW! IT'S RE-PULSIVE!
NLRCH
WRITHE WRITHE
NLRCH
YURI, LET'S RUN! IT'S AW-FUUUL!

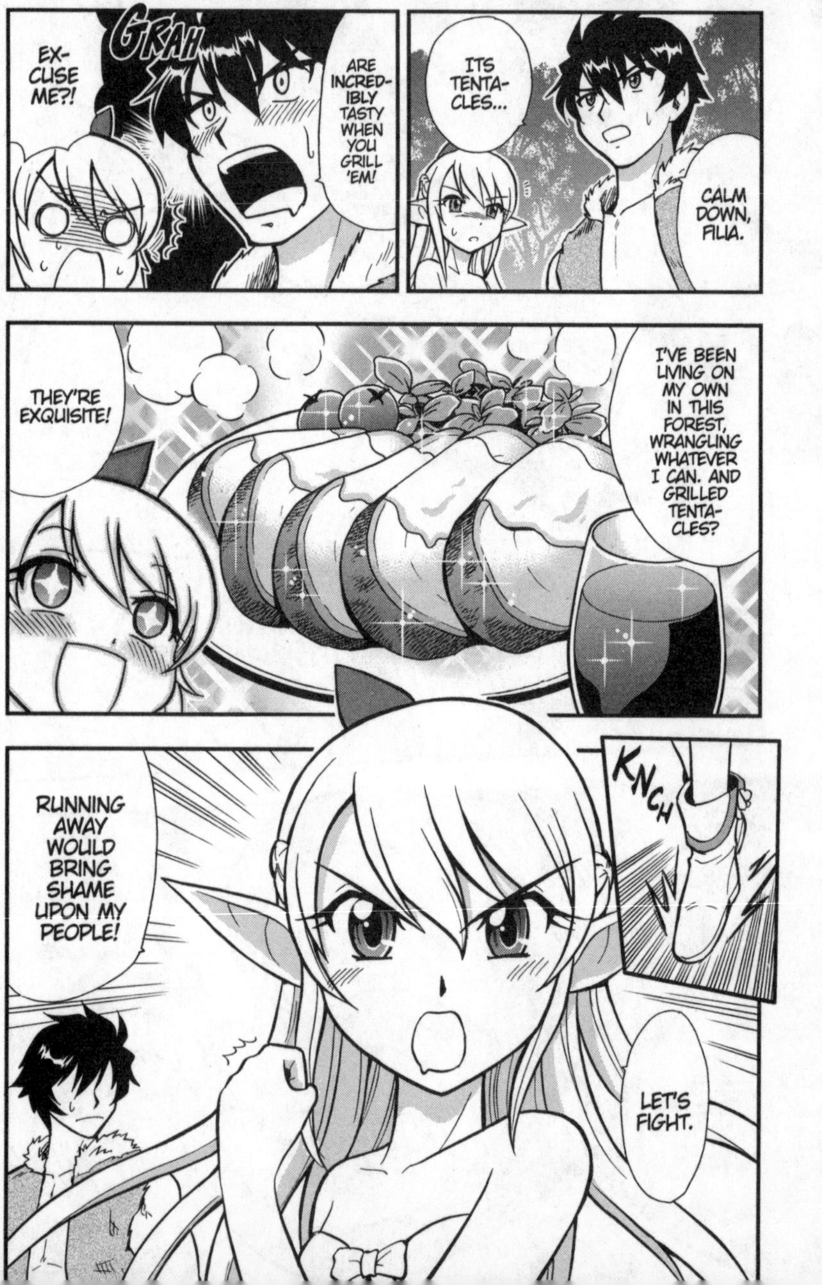
ITS TENTACLES...
CALM DOWN, FILIA.
ARE INCREDIBLY TASTY WHEN YOU GRILL 'EM!
GRAH
EXCUSE ME?!
I'VE BEEN LIVING ON MY OWN IN THIS FOREST, WRANGLING WHATEVER I CAN. AND GRILLED TENTACLES?
THEY'RE EXQUISITE!
KNCH
RUNNING AWAY WOULD BRING SHAME UPON MY PEOPLE!
LET'S FIGHT.

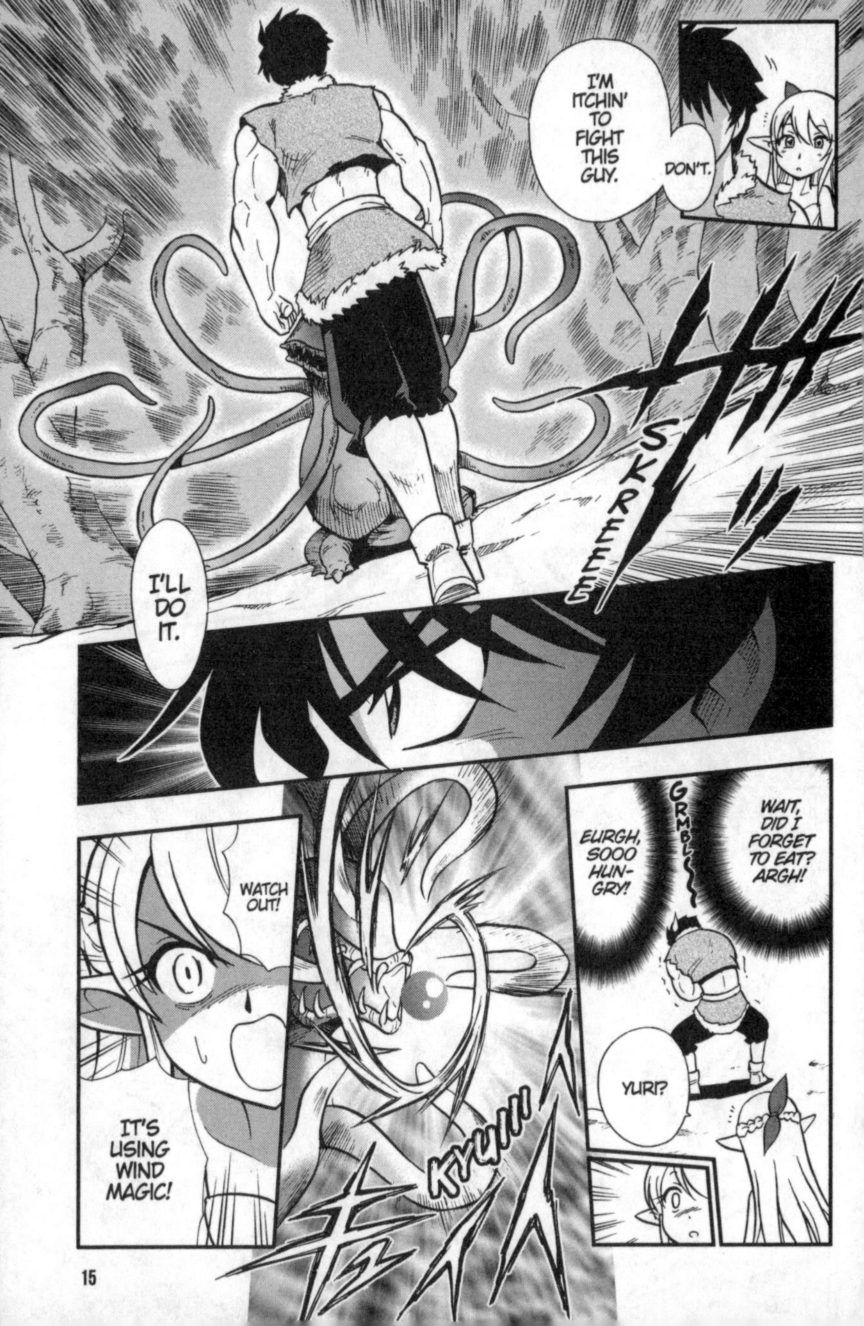
I'M ITCHIN' TO FIGHT THIS GUY.
DON'T.
I'LL DO IT.
SKREEEE
WAIT, DID I FORGET TO EAT? ARGH!
GRMBL~
EURGH, SOOO HUN-GRY!
YURI?
WATCH OUT!
IT'S USING WIND MAGIC!
KYUIII

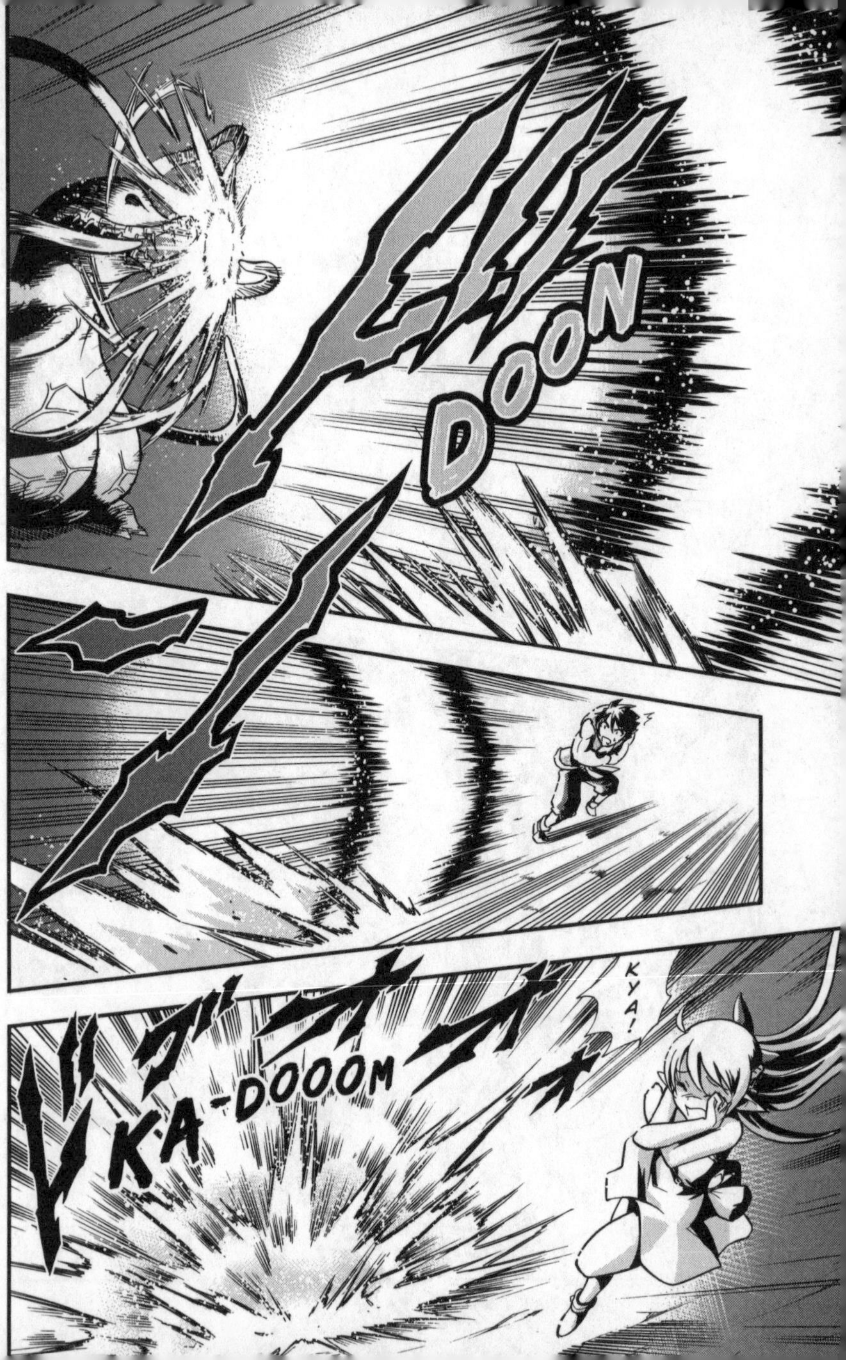
DOOON
KYA!
KA-DOOOM

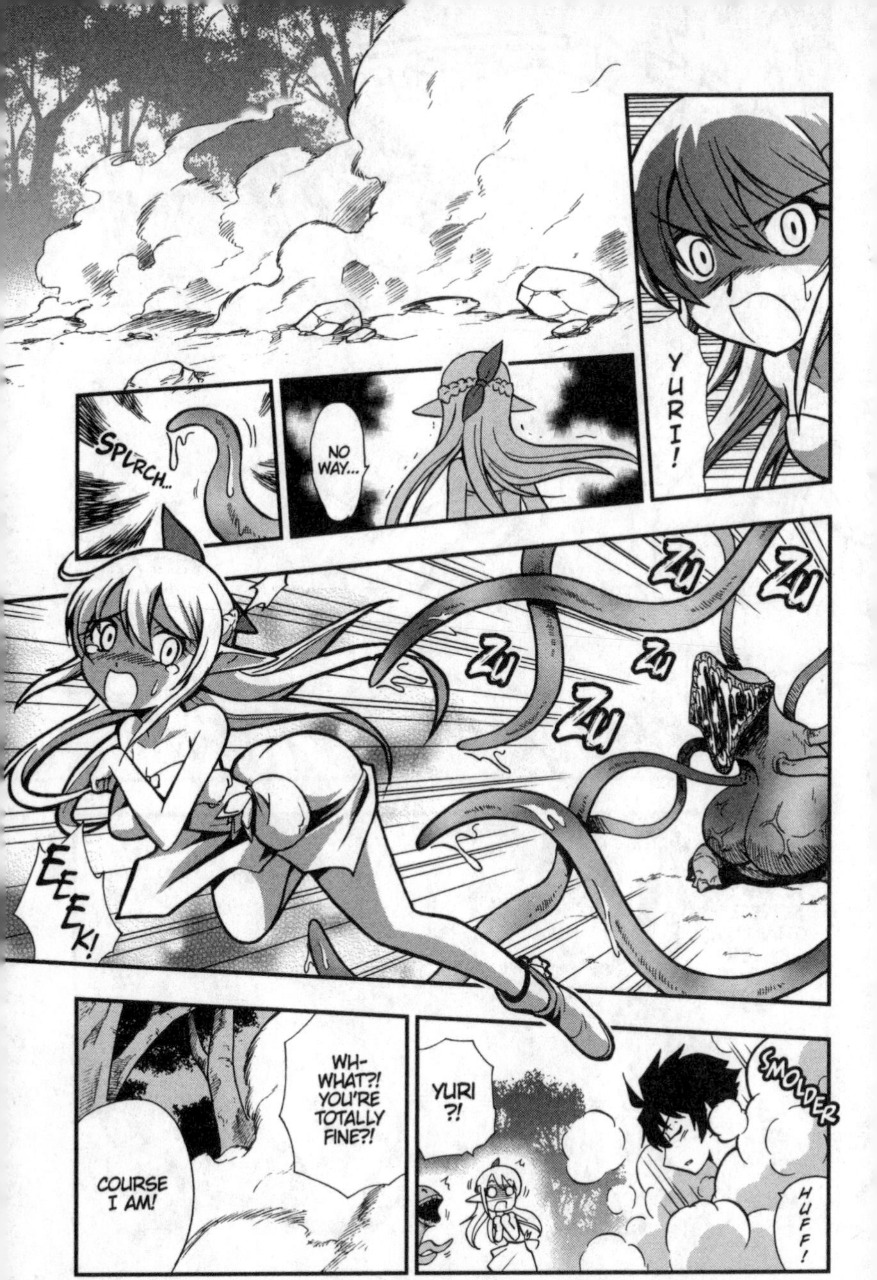

YURI!
NO WAY...
SPLRCH...
ZU
ZU
ZU
ZU
ZU
EEEEK!
SMOLDER
HUFF!
YURI ?!
WH-WHAT?! YOU'RE TOTALLY FINE?!
COURSE I AM!

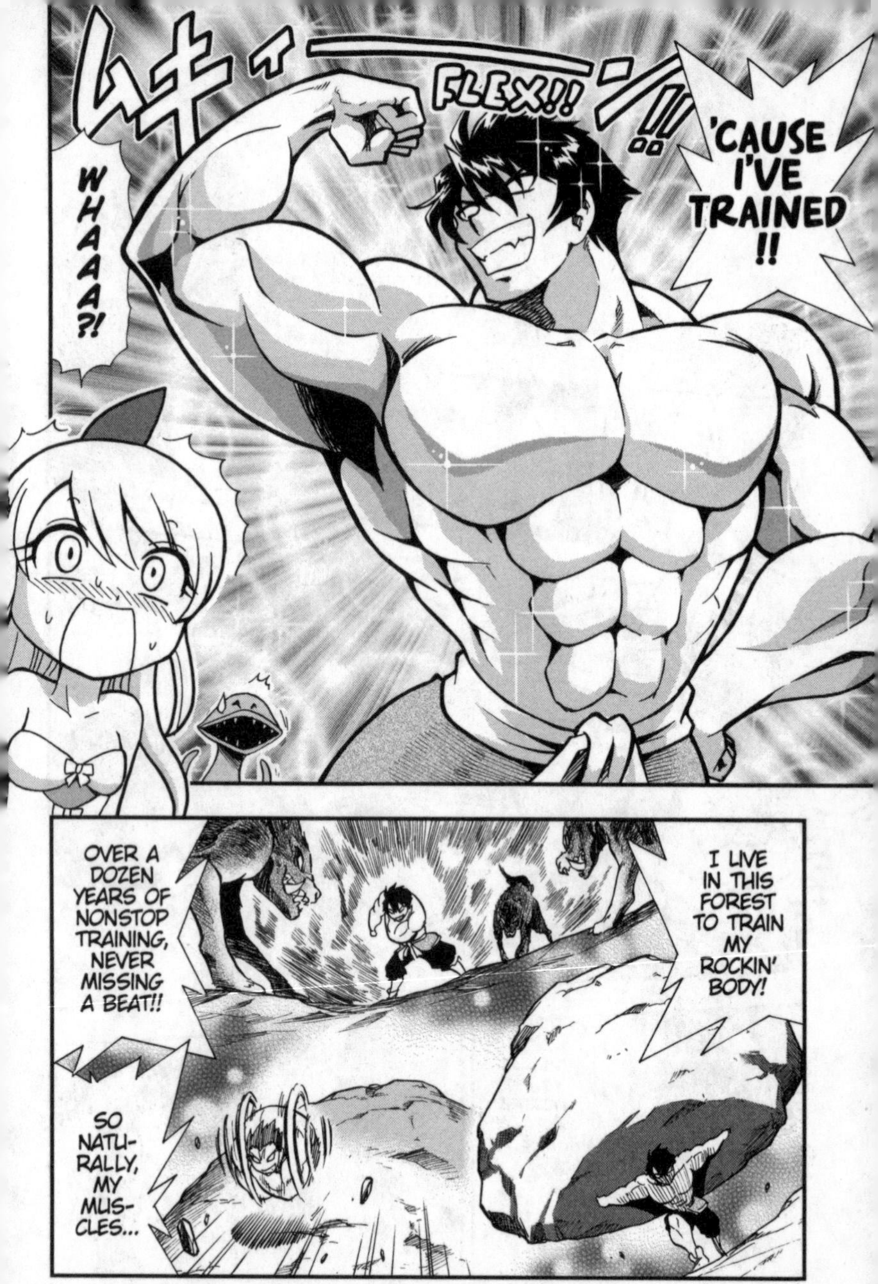

ムキィーーン!!
FLEX!!
'CAUSE I'VE TRAINED!!
WHAAAAA?!
I LIVE IN THIS FOREST TO TRAIN MY ROCKIN' BODY!
OVER A DOZEN YEARS OF NONSTOP TRAINING, NEVER MISSING A BEAT!!
SO NATU-RALLY, MY MUS-CLES...

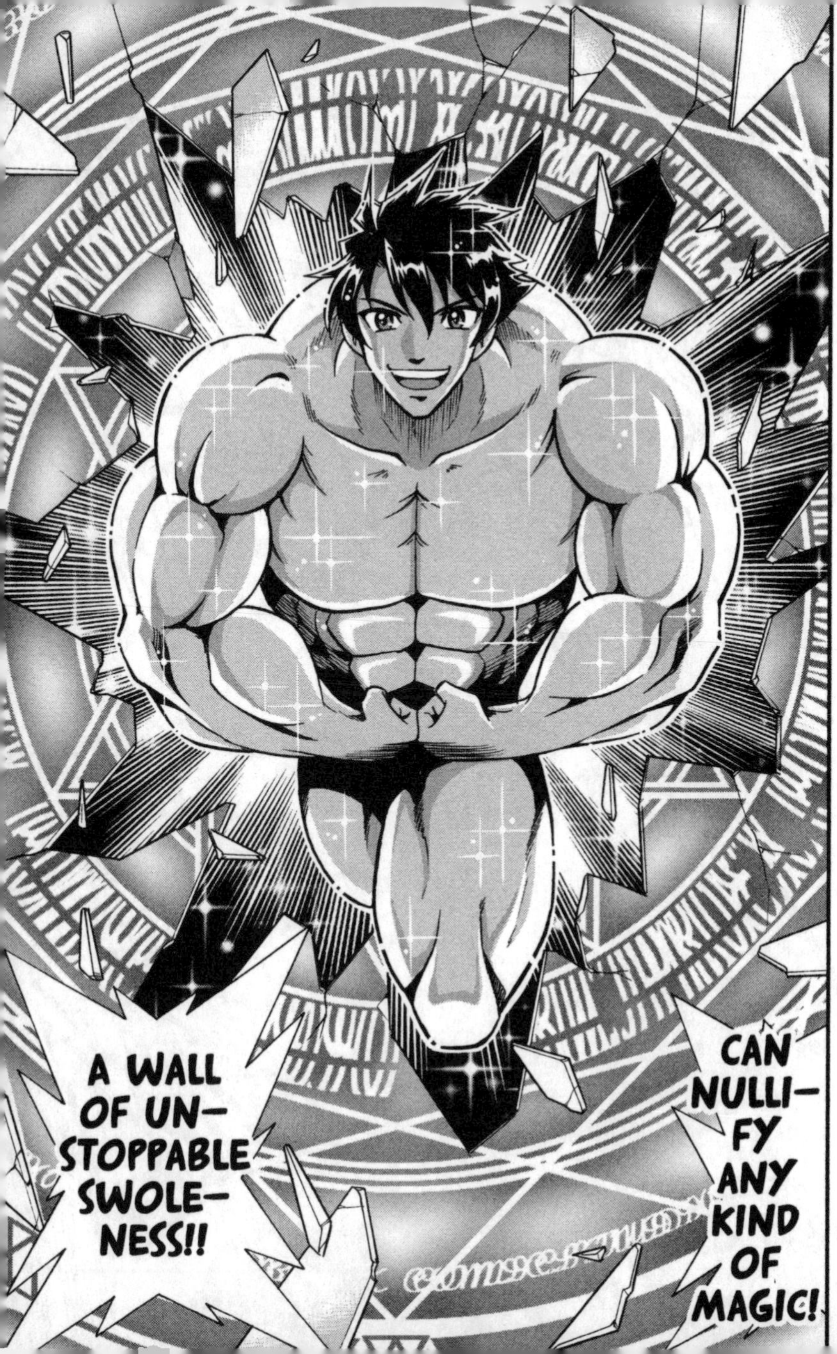
CAN NULLI-FY ANY KIND OF MAGIC!
A WALL OF UN-STOPPABLE SWOLE-NESS!!

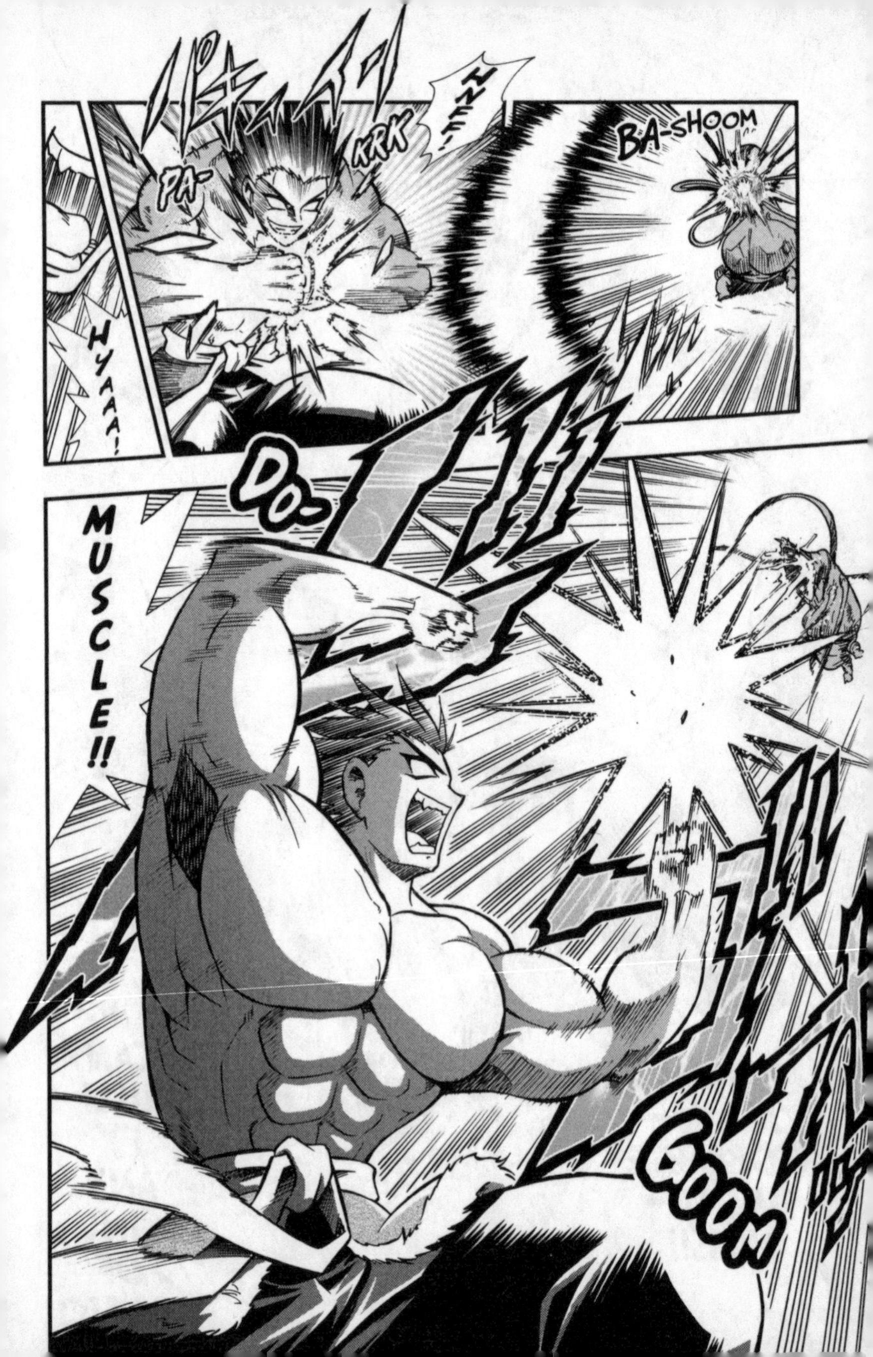
BA-SHOOM
HNEF!
KRK
PA-
HYAAA!
DO-
MUSCLE!!
GOOM

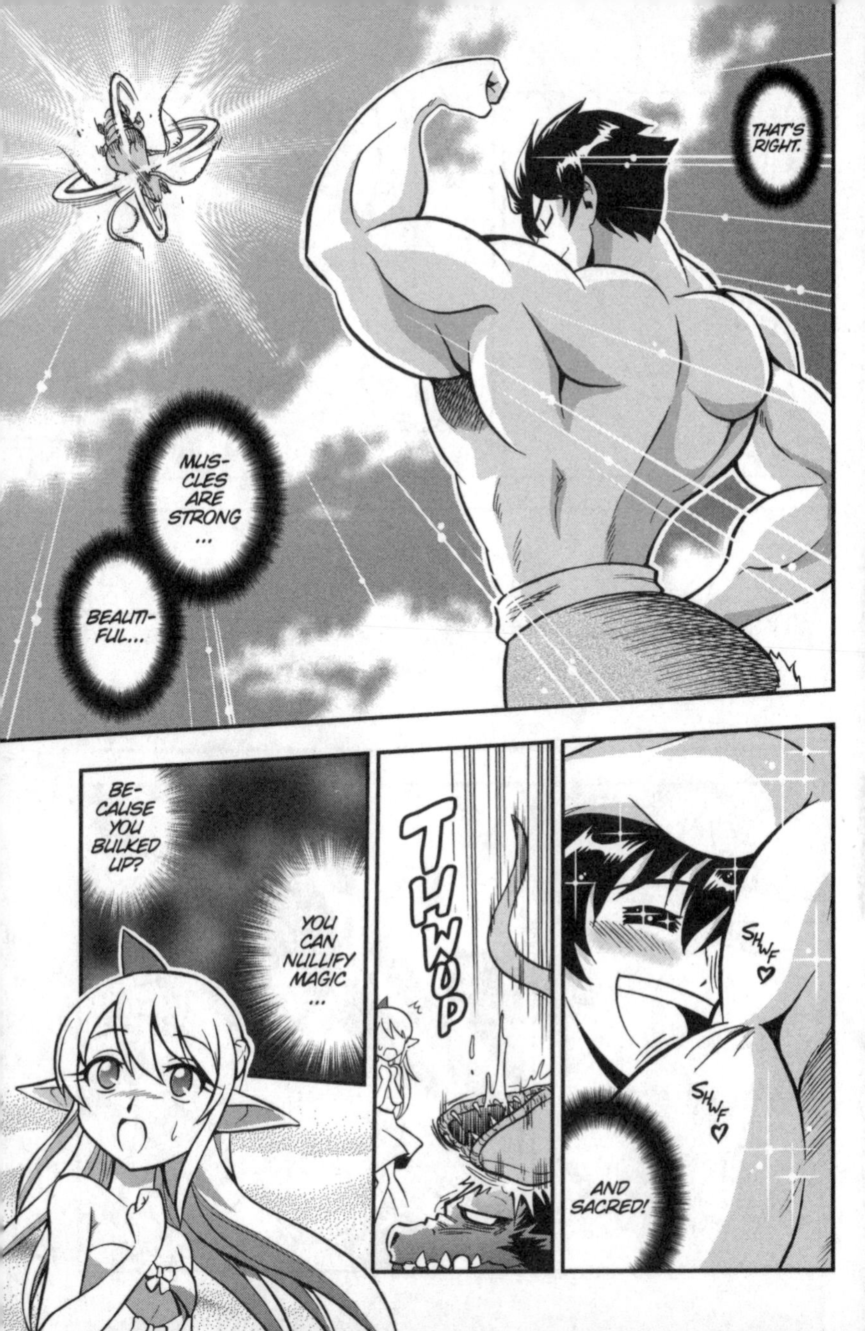
THAT'S RIGHT.
MUS-CLES ARE STRONG...
BEAUTI-FUL...
SHWF ♡
SHWF ♡
AND SACRED!
THWOOP
BE-CAUSE YOU BULKED UP?
YOU CAN NULLIFY MAGIC...

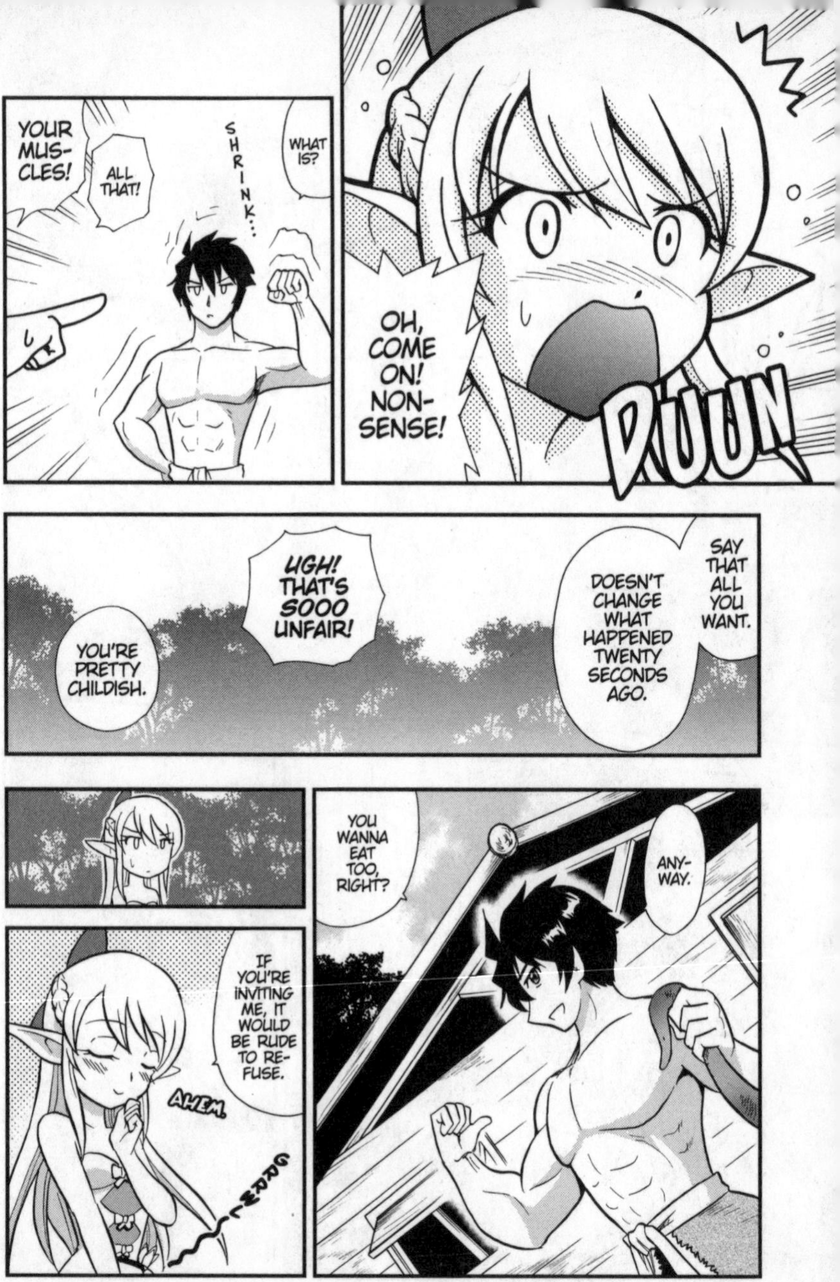
OH, COME ON! NON-SENSE!
DUUN!
WHAT IS?
SHRINK...
YOUR MUS-CLES!
ALL THAT!
SAY THAT ALL YOU WANT.
DOESN'T CHANGE WHAT HAPPENED TWENTY SECONDS AGO.
UGH! THAT'S SOOO UNFAIR!
YOU'RE PRETTY CHILDISH.
ANY-WAY.
YOU WANNA EAT TOO, RIGHT?
IF YOU'RE INVITING ME, IT WOULD BE RUDE TO RE-FUSE.
AHEM.

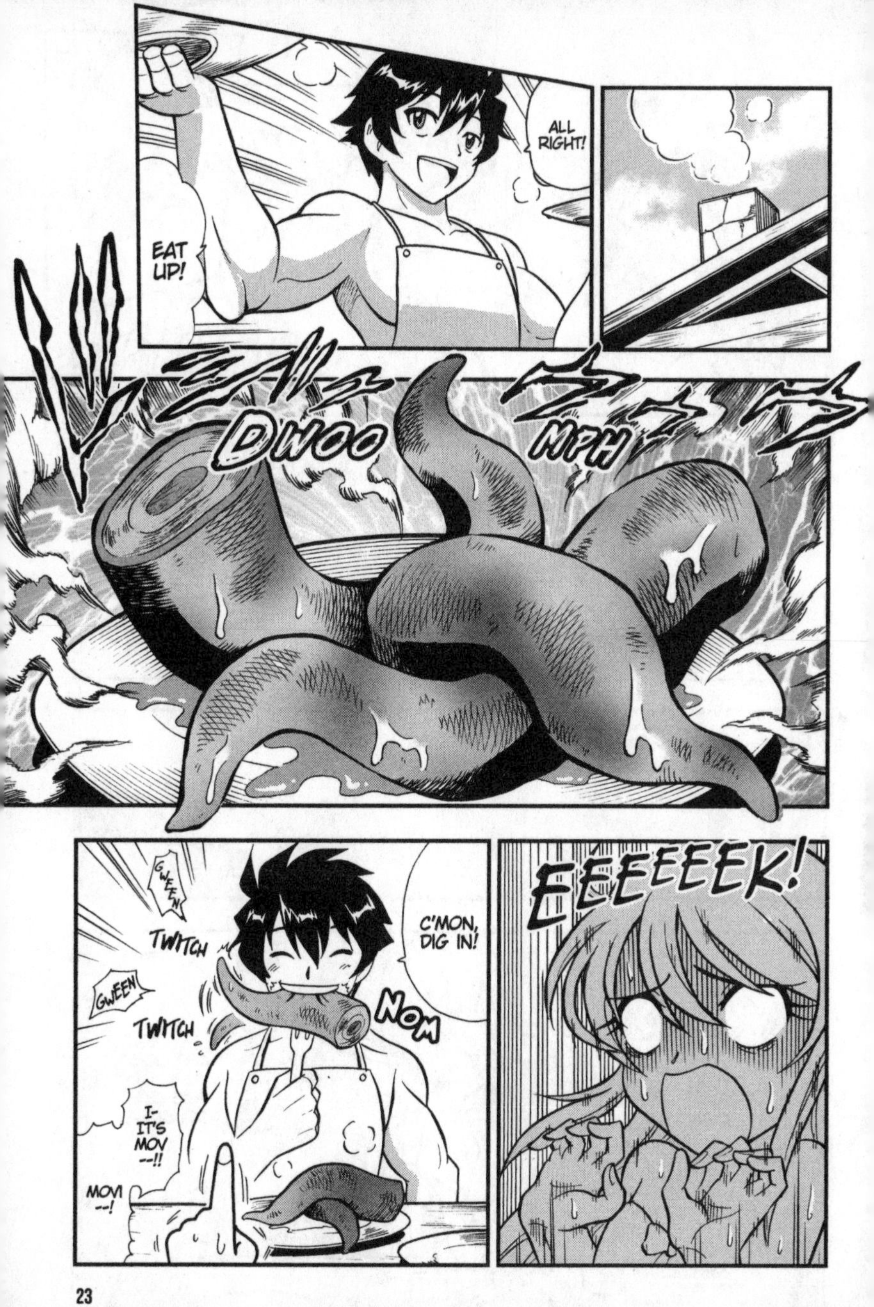
ALL RIGHT!
EAT UP!
DWOO
MPH
EEEEEEEK!
C'MON, DIG IN!
GWEEN
TWITCH
NOM
GWEEN
TWITCH
I- IT'S MOV--!!
MOVI --!

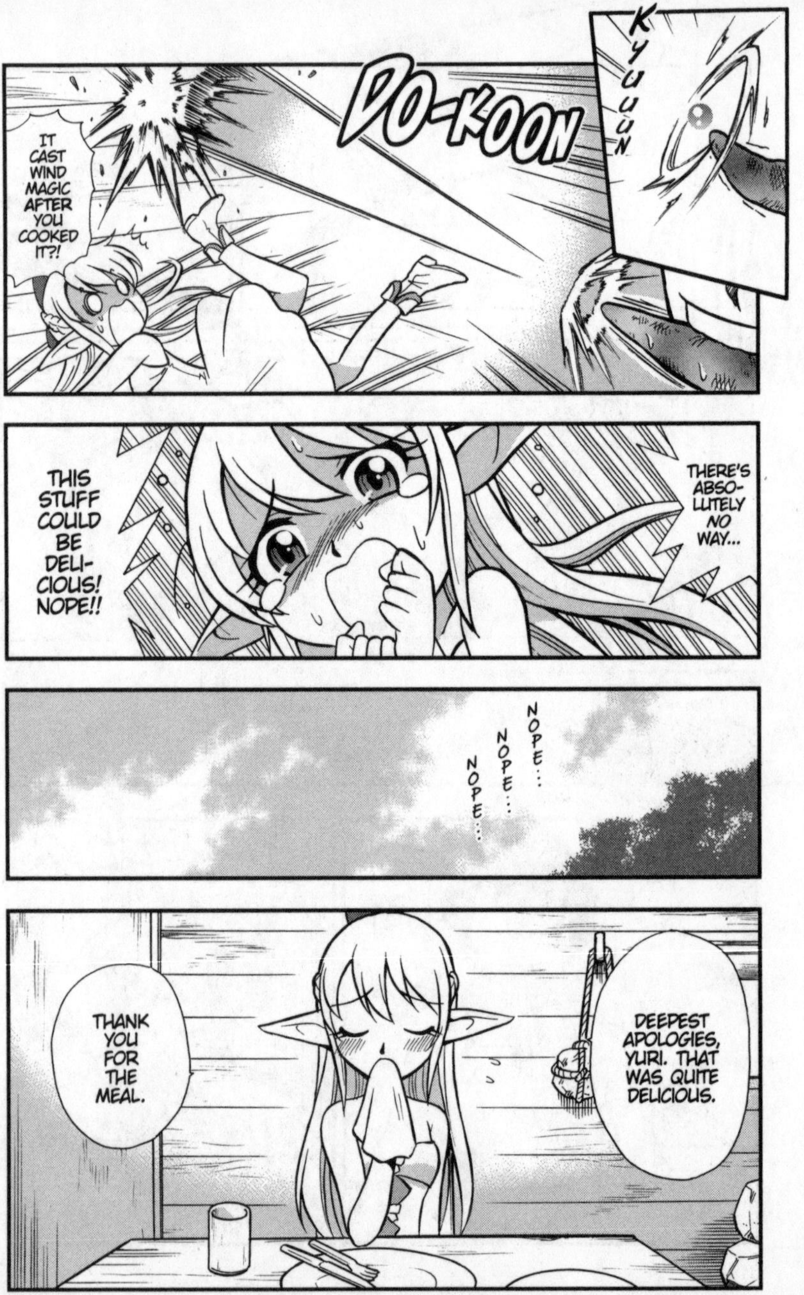
KYUUUUN
DO-KOON
IT CAST WIND MAGIC AFTER YOU COOKED IT?!
THERE'S ABSO-LUTELY NO WAY...
THIS STUFF COULD BE DELI-CIOUS! NOPE!!
NOPE...
NOPE...
NOPE...
DEEPEST APOLOGIES, YURI. THAT WAS QUITE DELICIOUS.
THANK YOU FOR THE MEAL.

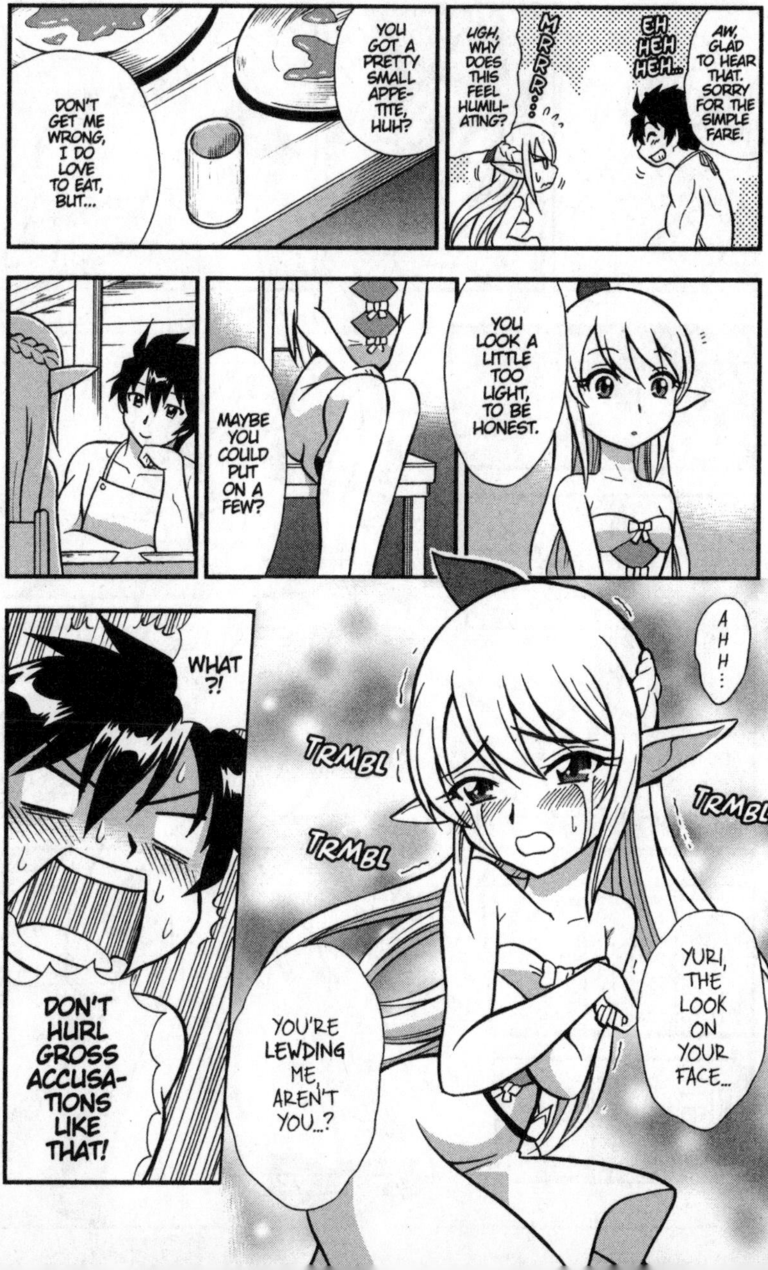
AW, GLAD TO HEAR THAT. SORRY FOR THE SIMPLE FARE.
EH HEH HEH...
MRRR...
UGH, WHY DOES THIS FEEL HUMILIATING?
YOU GOT A PRETTY SMALL APPETITE, HUH?
DON'T GET ME WRONG, I DO LOVE TO EAT, BUT...
YOU LOOK A LITTLE TOO LIGHT, TO BE HONEST.
MAYBE YOU COULD PUT ON A FEW?
AHH...
TRMBL
TRMBL
TRMBL
YURI, THE LOOK ON YOUR FACE...
YOU'RE LEWDING ME, AREN'T YOU...?
WHAT?!
DON'T HURL GROSS ACCUSATIONS LIKE THAT!

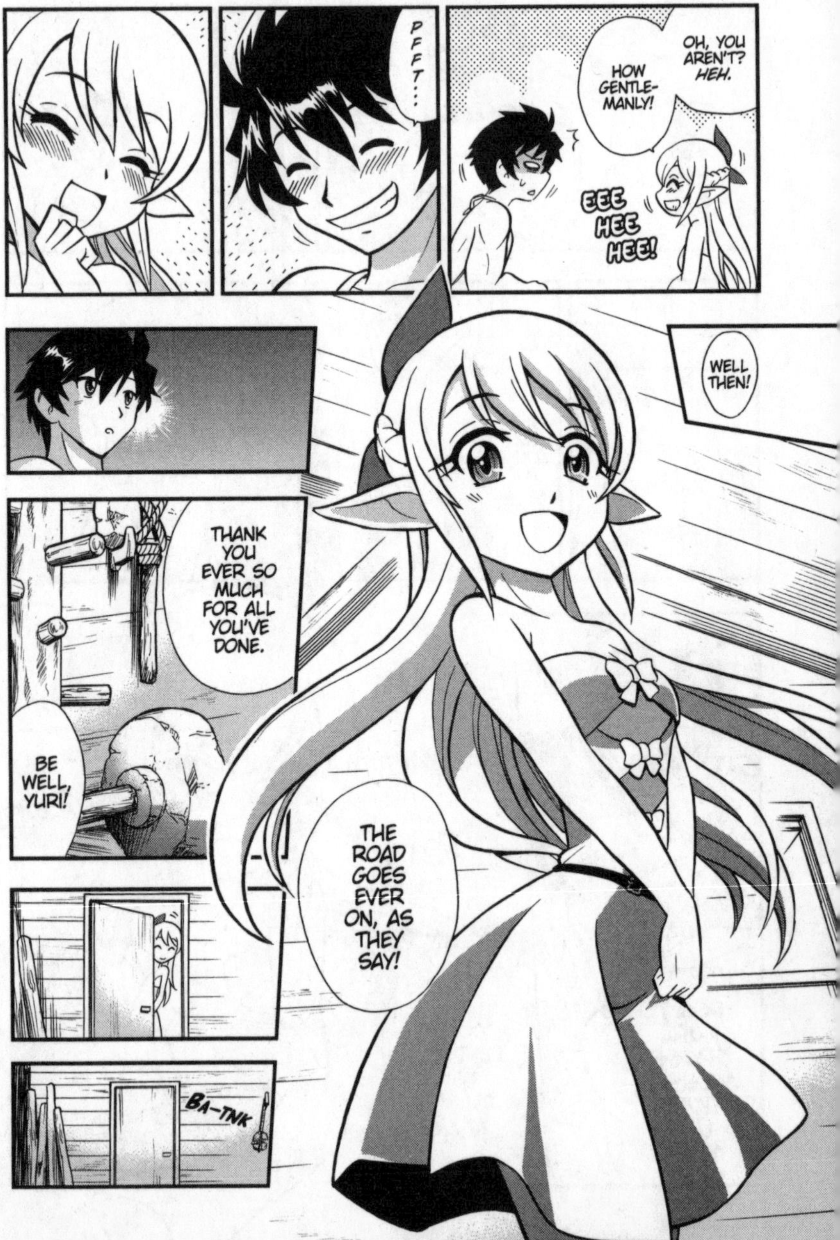
OH, YOU AREN'T? HEH.
HOW GENTLE-MANLY!
EEE HEE HEE!
PFFT...
WELL THEN!
THE ROAD GOES EVER ON, AS THEY SAY!
THANK YOU EVER SO MUCH FOR ALL YOU'VE DONE.
BE WELL, YURI!
BA-TNK

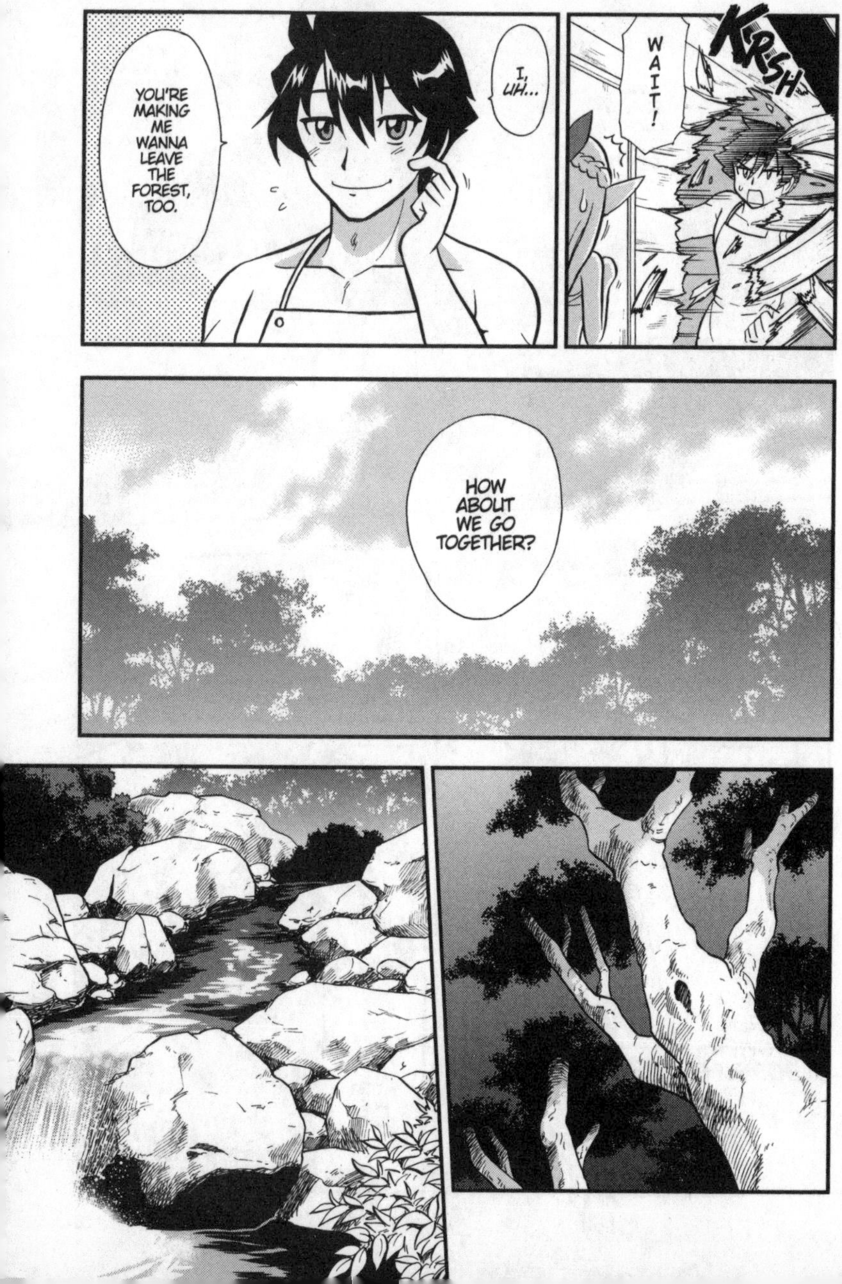
KRSH
WAIT!
I, UH...
YOU'RE MAKING ME WANNA LEAVE THE FOREST, TOO.
HOW ABOUT WE GO TOGETHER?

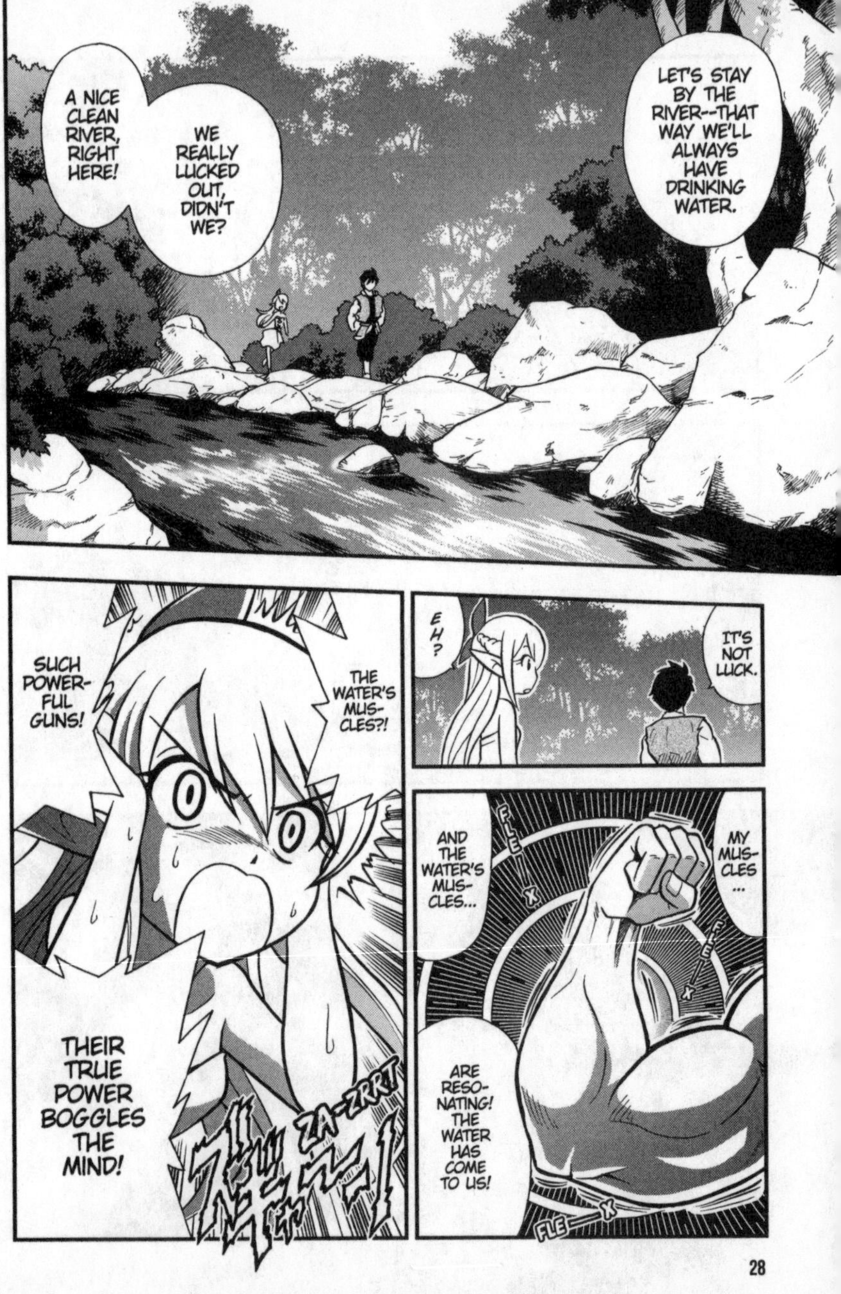
LET'S STAY BY THE RIVER--THAT WAY WE'LL ALWAYS HAVE DRINKING WATER.
WE REALLY LUCKED OUT, DIDN'T WE?
A NICE CLEAN RIVER, RIGHT HERE!
IT'S NOT LUCK.
EH?
MY MUSCLES...
FLE--X
AND THE WATER'S MUSCLES...
FLE--X
ARE RESONATING! THE WATER HAS COME TO US!
FLE--X
THE WATER'S MUSCLES?!
SUCH POWERFUL GUNS!
ZA-ZRRT
THEIR TRUE POWER BOGGLES THE MIND!

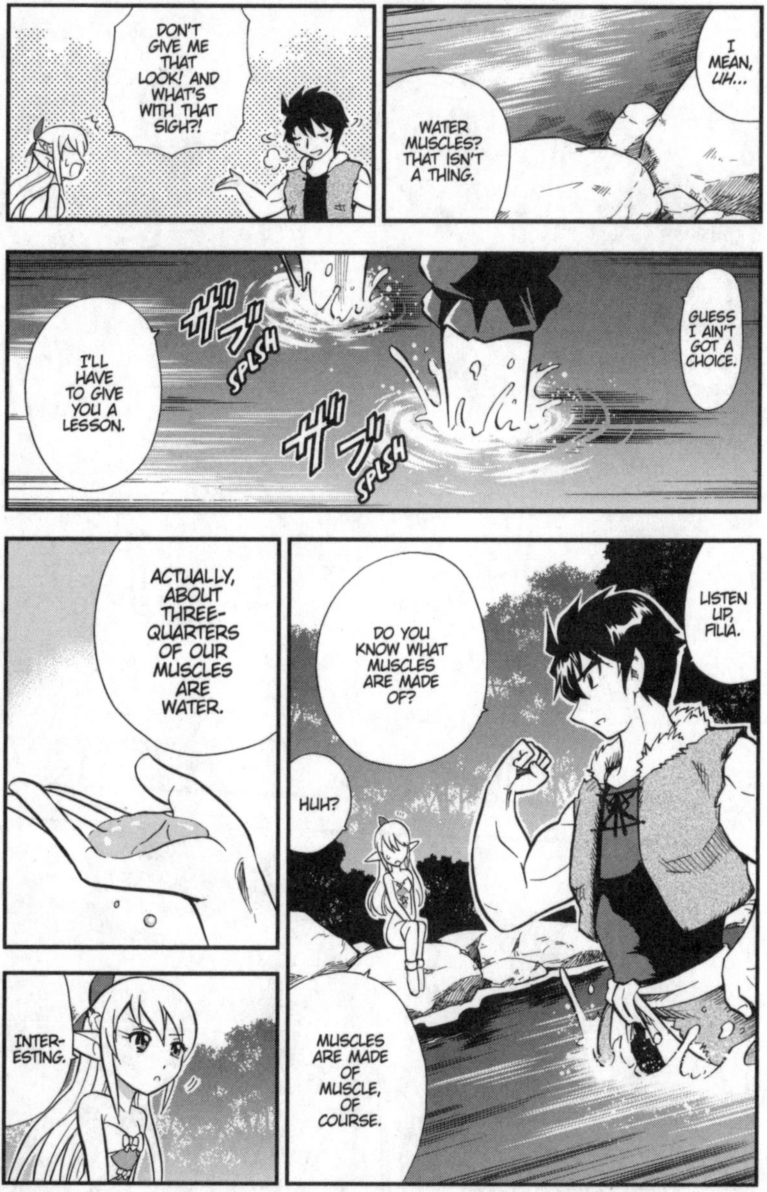
I MEAN, UH...
WATER MUSCLES? THAT ISN'T A THING.
DON'T GIVE ME THAT LOOK! AND WHAT'S WITH THAT SIGH?!
GUESS I AIN'T GOT A CHOICE.
ザブ
SPLSH
ザブ
SPLSH
I'LL HAVE TO GIVE YOU A LESSON.
LISTEN UP, FILIA.
DO YOU KNOW WHAT MUSCLES ARE MADE OF?
HUH?
MUSCLES ARE MADE OF MUSCLE, OF COURSE.
ACTUALLY, ABOUT THREE-QUARTERS OF OUR MUSCLES ARE WATER.
INTER-ESTING.

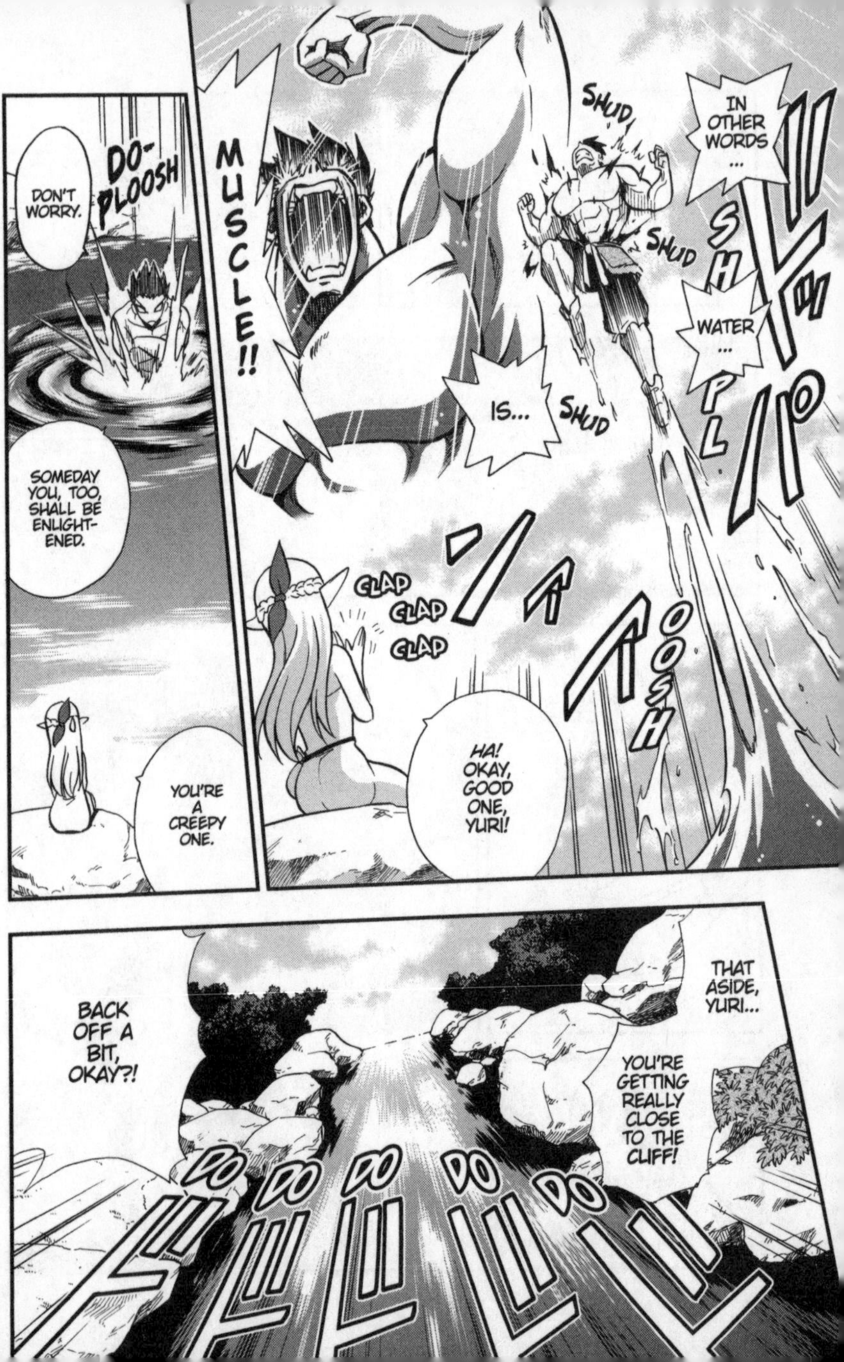
IN OTHER WORDS ...
SHUD
SHUD
WATER ...
IS...
SHUD
MUSCLE!!
CLAP
CLAP
CLAP
HA! OKAY, GOOD ONE, YURI!
DO-PLOOSH
DON'T WORRY.
SOMEDAY YOU, TOO, SHALL BE ENLIGHT-ENED.
YOU'RE A CREEPY ONE.
THAT ASIDE, YURI...
YOU'RE GETTING REALLY CLOSE TO THE CLIFF!
BACK OFF A BIT, OKAY?!
DO DO DO DO DO

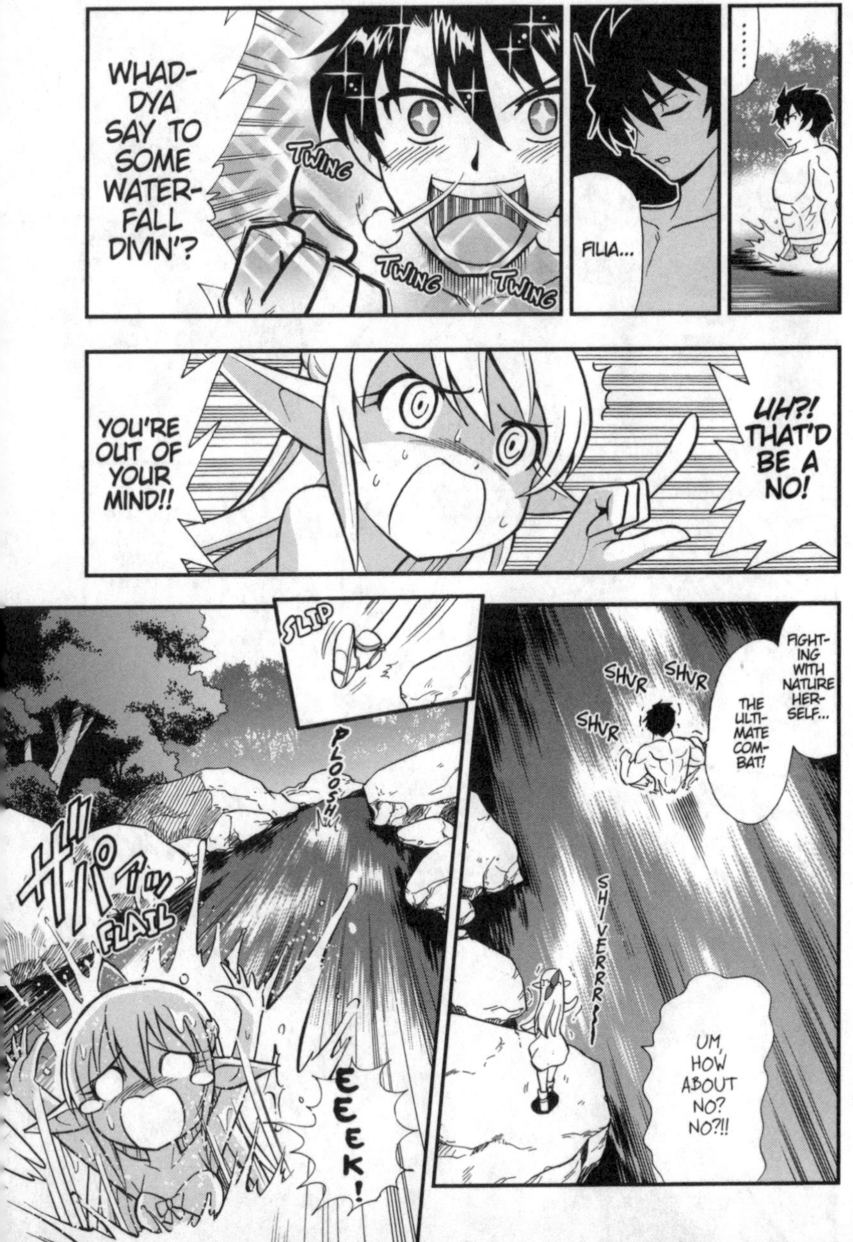
......
FILIA...
WHAD-DYA SAY TO SOME WATER-FALL DIVIN'?
TWING
TWING
TWING
UH?! THAT'D BE A NO!
YOU'RE OUT OF YOUR MIND!!
FIGHT-ING WITH NATURE HER-SELF...
THE ULTI-MATE COM-BAT!
SHVR
SHVR
SHVR
SHIVERRR~
UM, HOW ABOUT NO? NO?!!
SLIP
PLOOSH
FLAIL
EEEK!

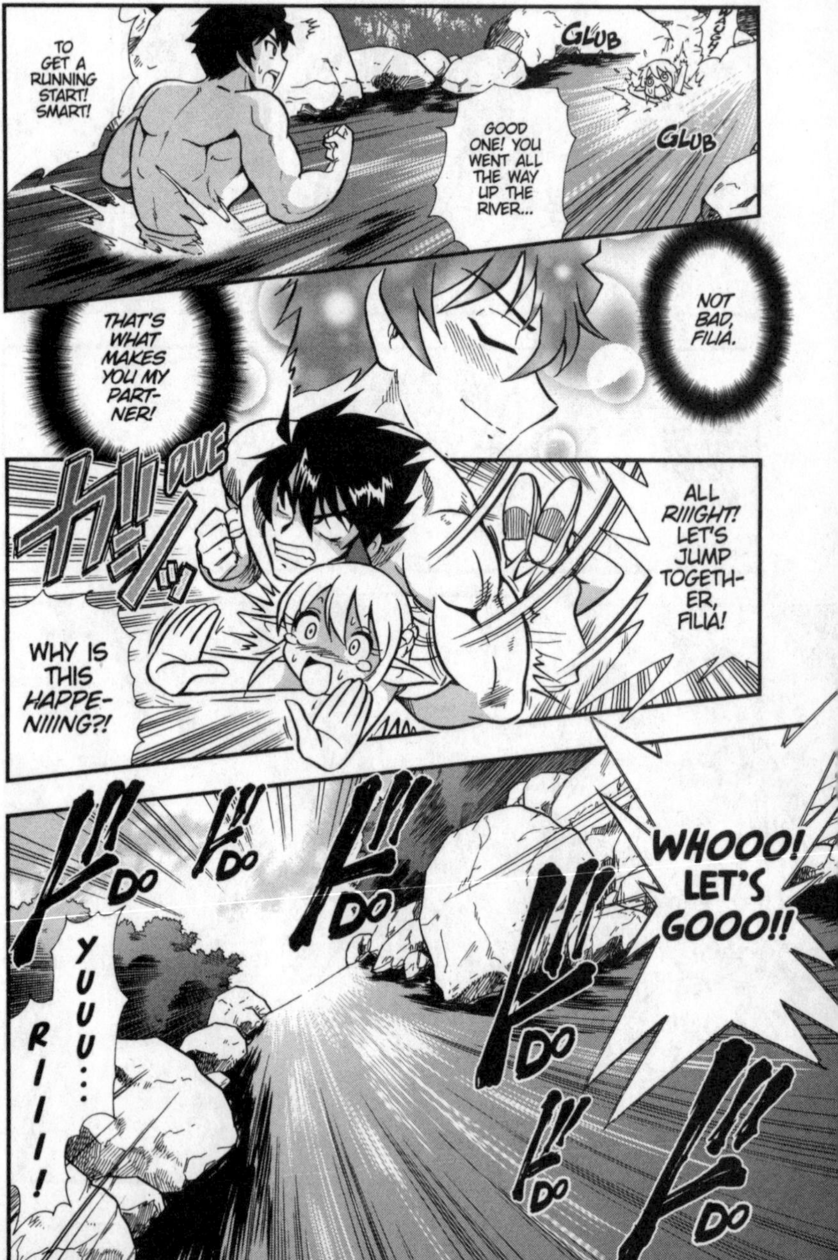
GLUB
GLUB
GOOD ONE! YOU WENT ALL THE WAY UP THE RIVER...
TO GET A RUNNING START! SMART!
NOT BAD, FILIA.
THAT'S WHAT MAKES YOU MY PART-NER!
ALL RIIIGHT! LET'S JUMP TOGETH-ER, FILIA!
DIVE
WHY IS THIS HAPPE-NIIING?!
WHOOO! LET'S GOOO!!
DO
DO
DO
DO
DO
DO
DO
YUUU... RIIII!

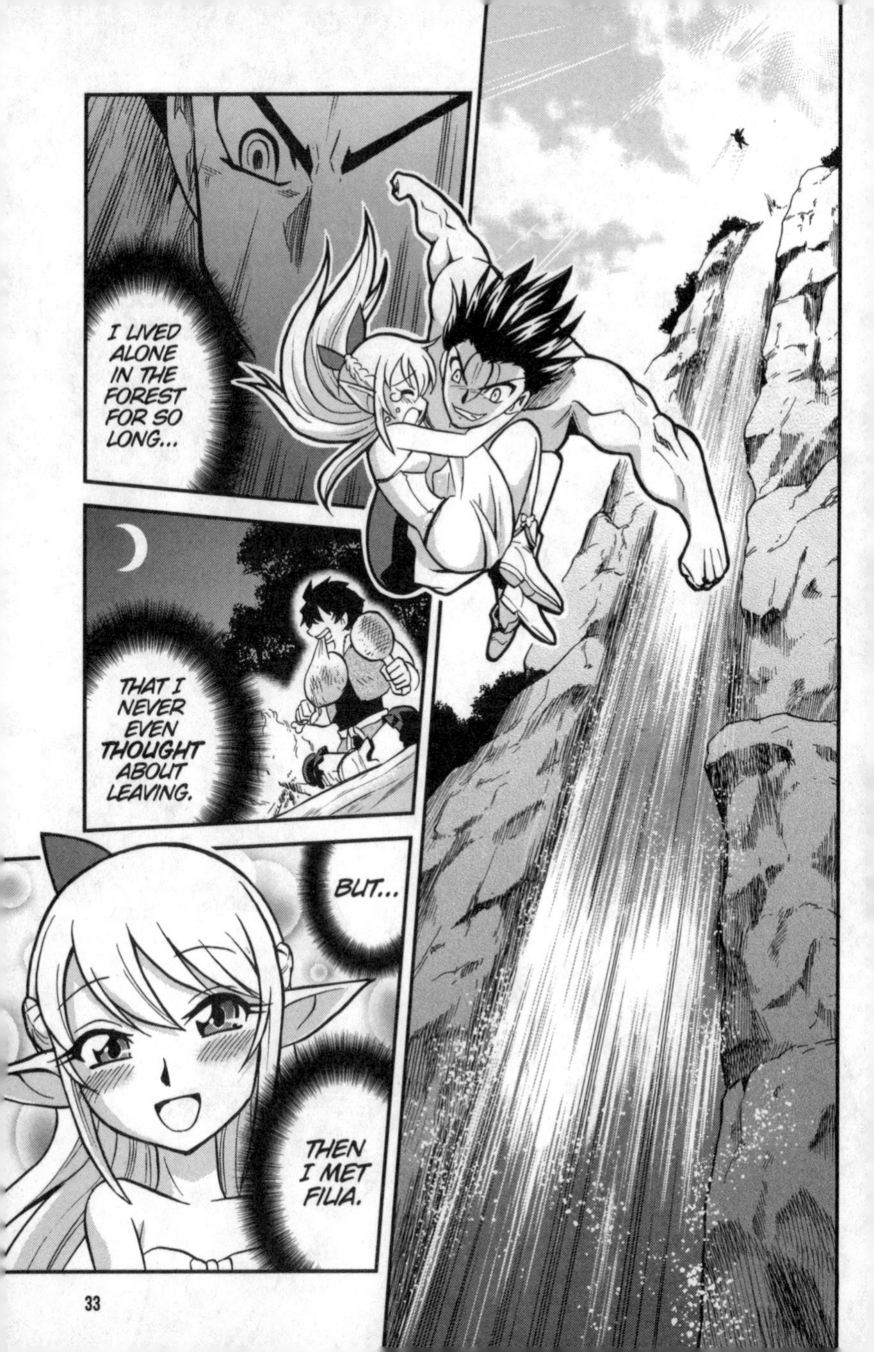
I LIVED ALONE IN THE FOREST FOR SO LONG...
THAT I NEVER EVEN THOUGHT ABOUT LEAVING.
BUT...
THEN I MET FILIA.

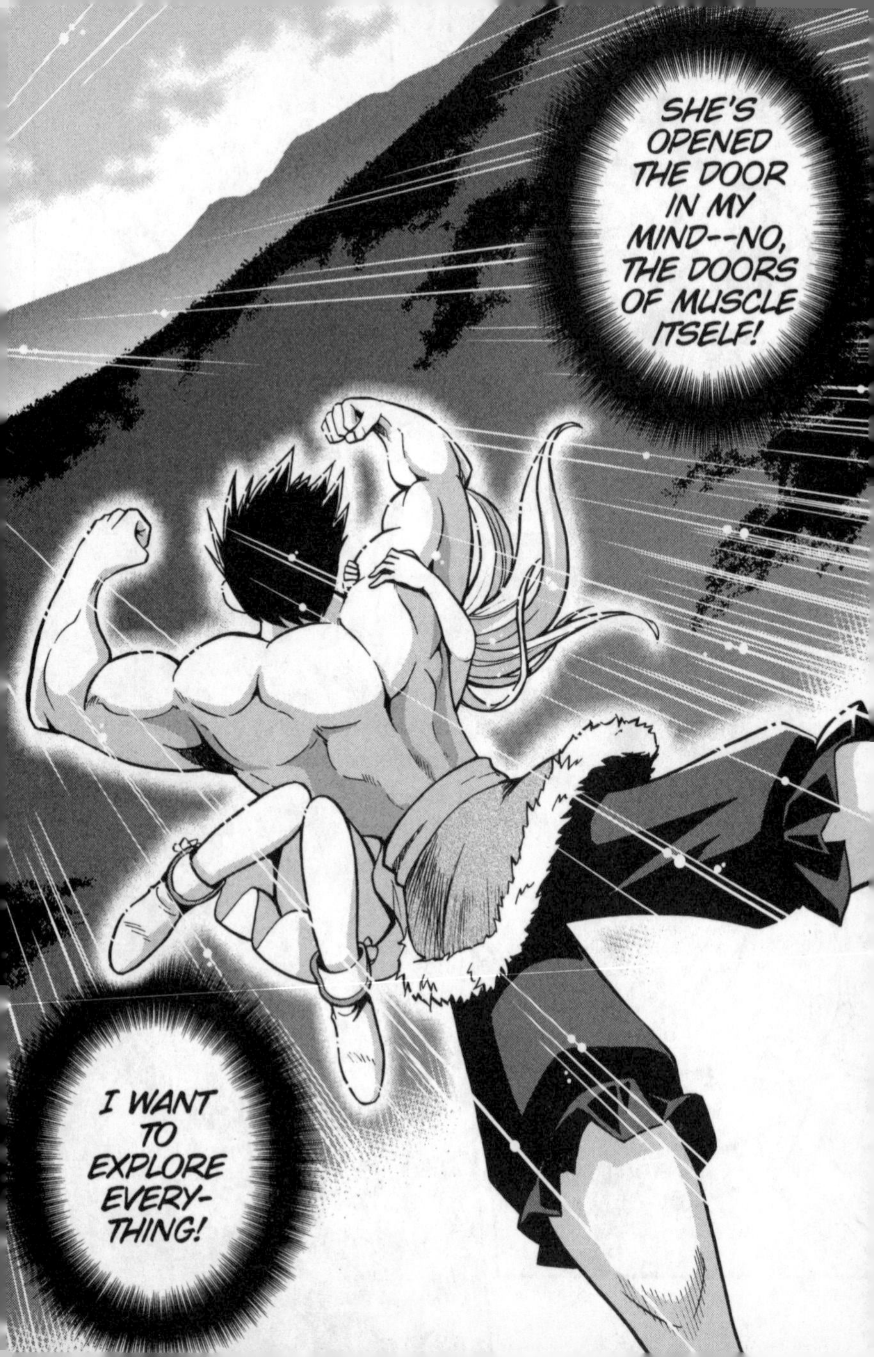
SHE'S OPENED THE DOOR IN MY MIND--NO, THE DOORS OF MUSCLE ITSELF!
I WANT TO EXPLORE EVERY-THING!

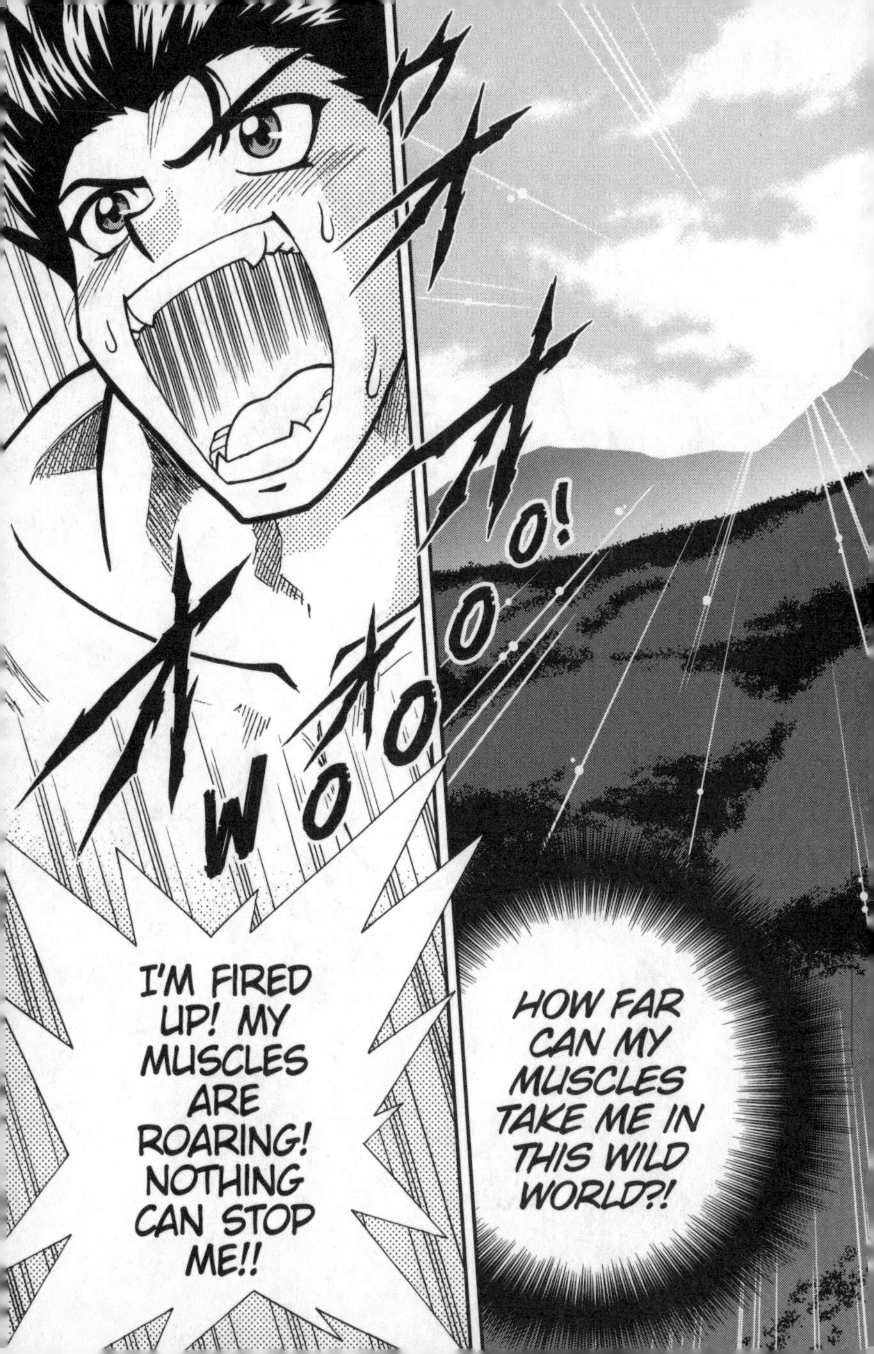
HOW FAR CAN MY MUSCLES TAKE ME IN THIS WILD WORLD?!
WOOOOO!
I'M FIRED UP! MY MUSCLES ARE ROARING! NOTHING CAN STOP ME!!

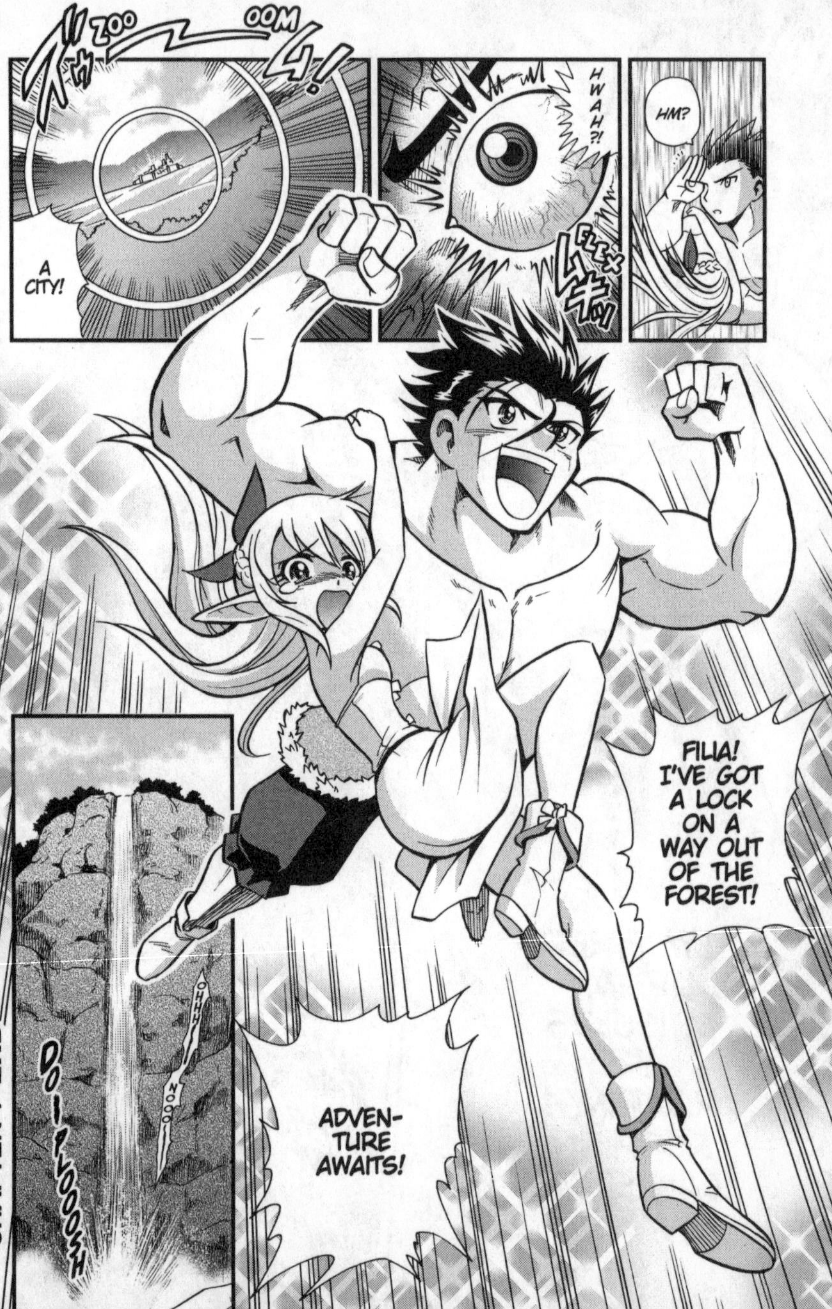
HM?
HWAH?!
FLEX
ZOO—OOM!
A CITY!
FILIA! I'VE GOT A LOCK ON A WAY OUT OF THE FOREST!
ADVENTURE AWAITS!
OHHH NOOO
DO-PLOOOSH
CHAPTER 1 = END

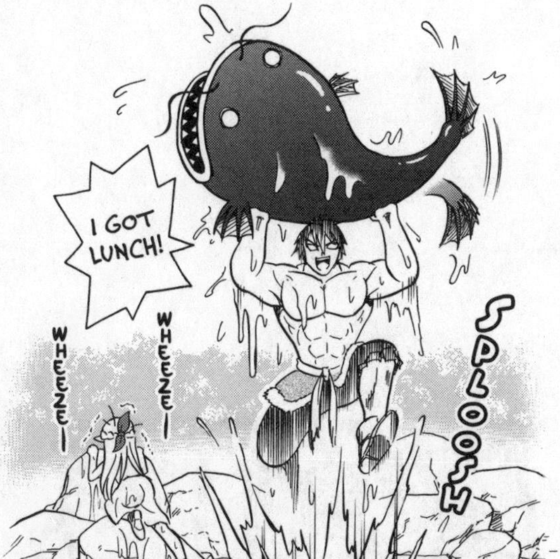
I GOT LUNCH!
SPLOOSH
WHEEZE
WHEEZE

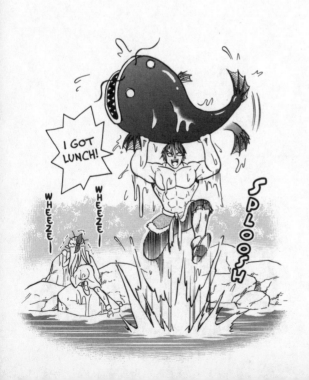

MUSCLES ARE BETTER THAN MAGIC!

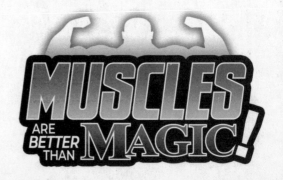

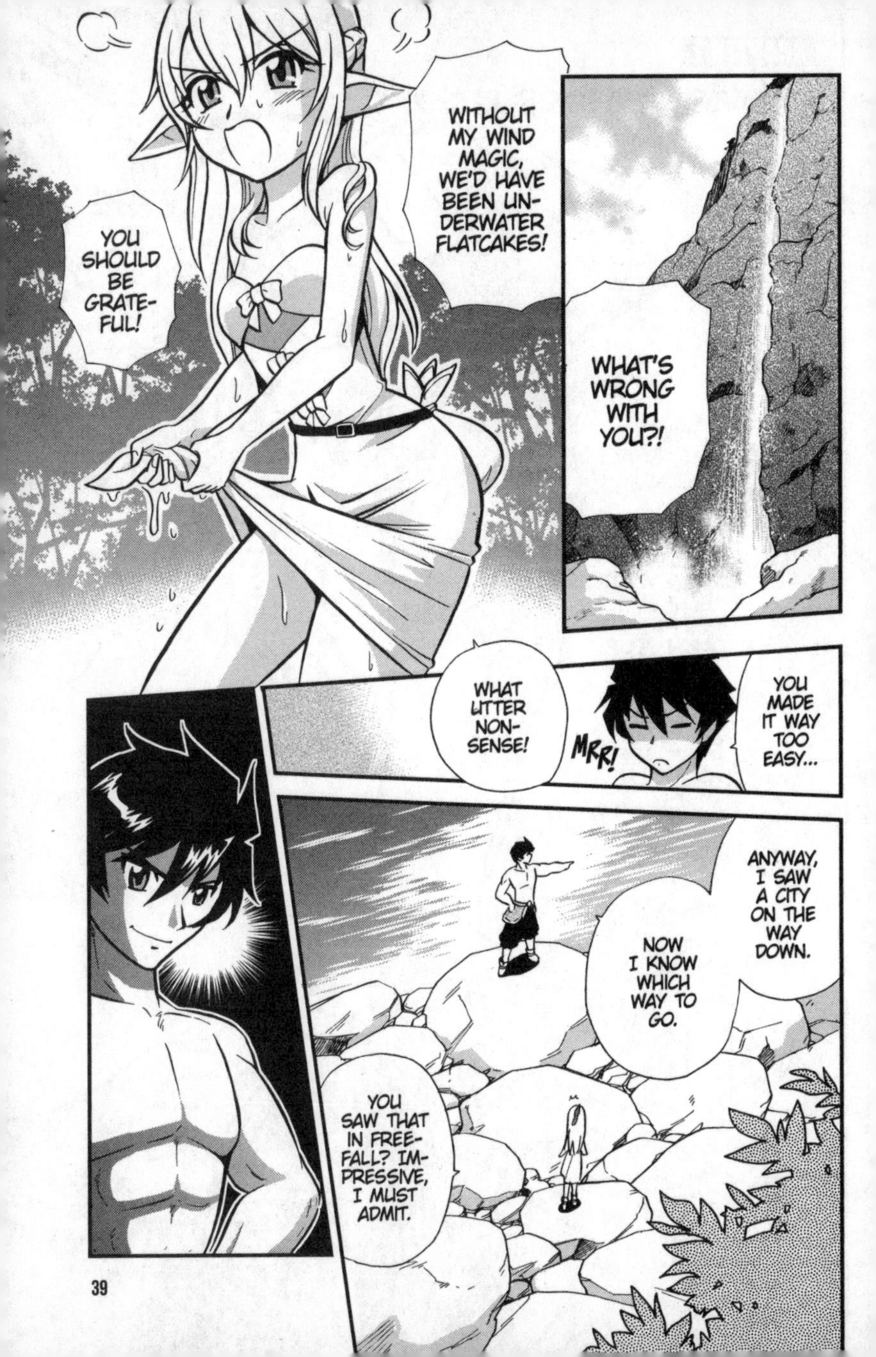
WHAT'S WRONG WITH YOU?!
WITHOUT MY WIND MAGIC, WE'D HAVE BEEN UN-DERWATER FLATCAKES!
YOU SHOULD BE GRATE-FUL!
YOU MADE IT WAY TOO EASY...
MRR!
WHAT UTTER NON-SENSE!
ANYWAY, I SAW A CITY ON THE WAY DOWN.
NOW I KNOW WHICH WAY TO GO.
YOU SAW THAT IN FREE-FALL? IM-PRESSIVE, I MUST ADMIT.

CHAPTER 2
Lightning and Handkerchiefs

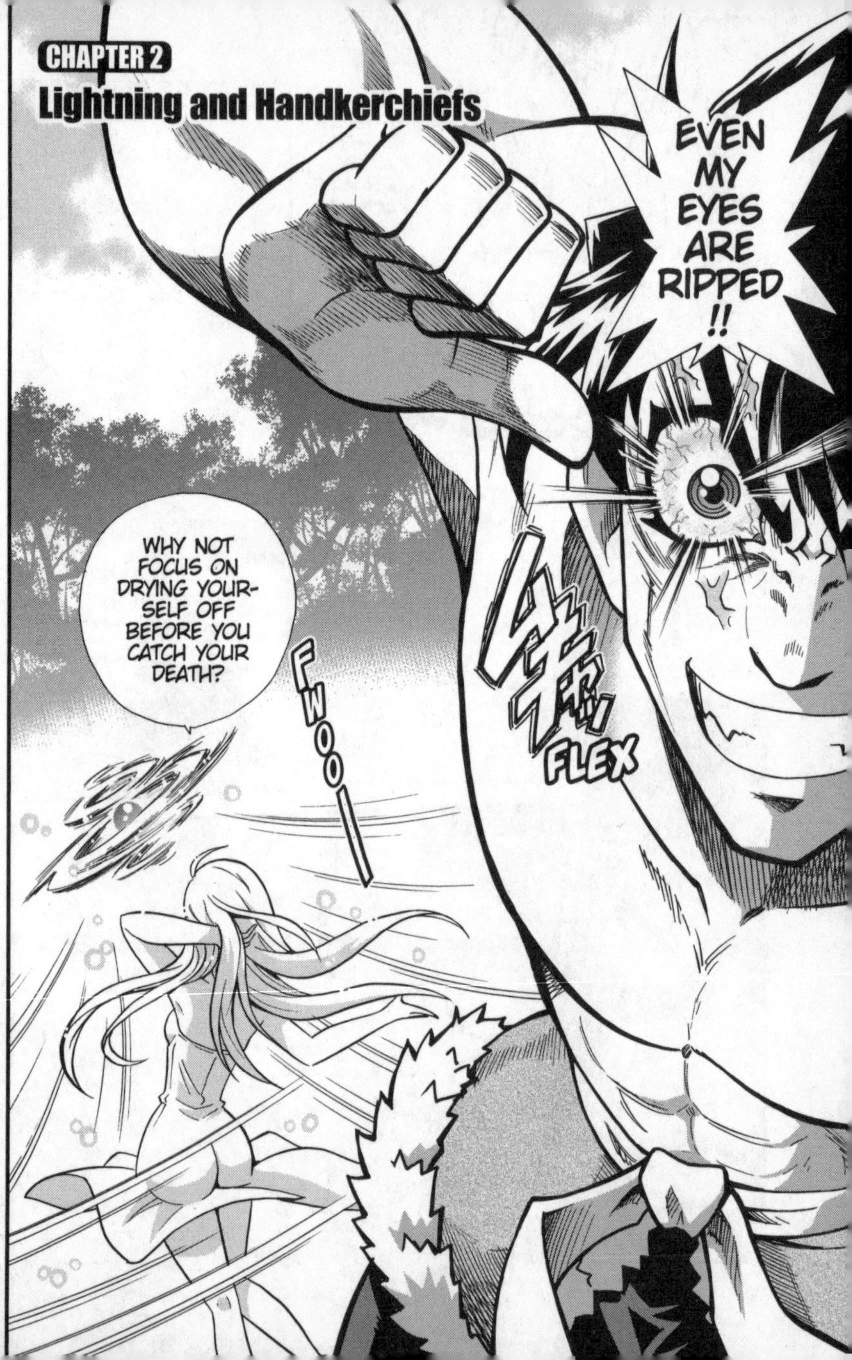
EVEN MY EYES ARE RIPPED!!
FLEX
FWOO—
WHY NOT FOCUS ON DRYING YOUR-SELF OFF BEFORE YOU CATCH YOUR DEATH?

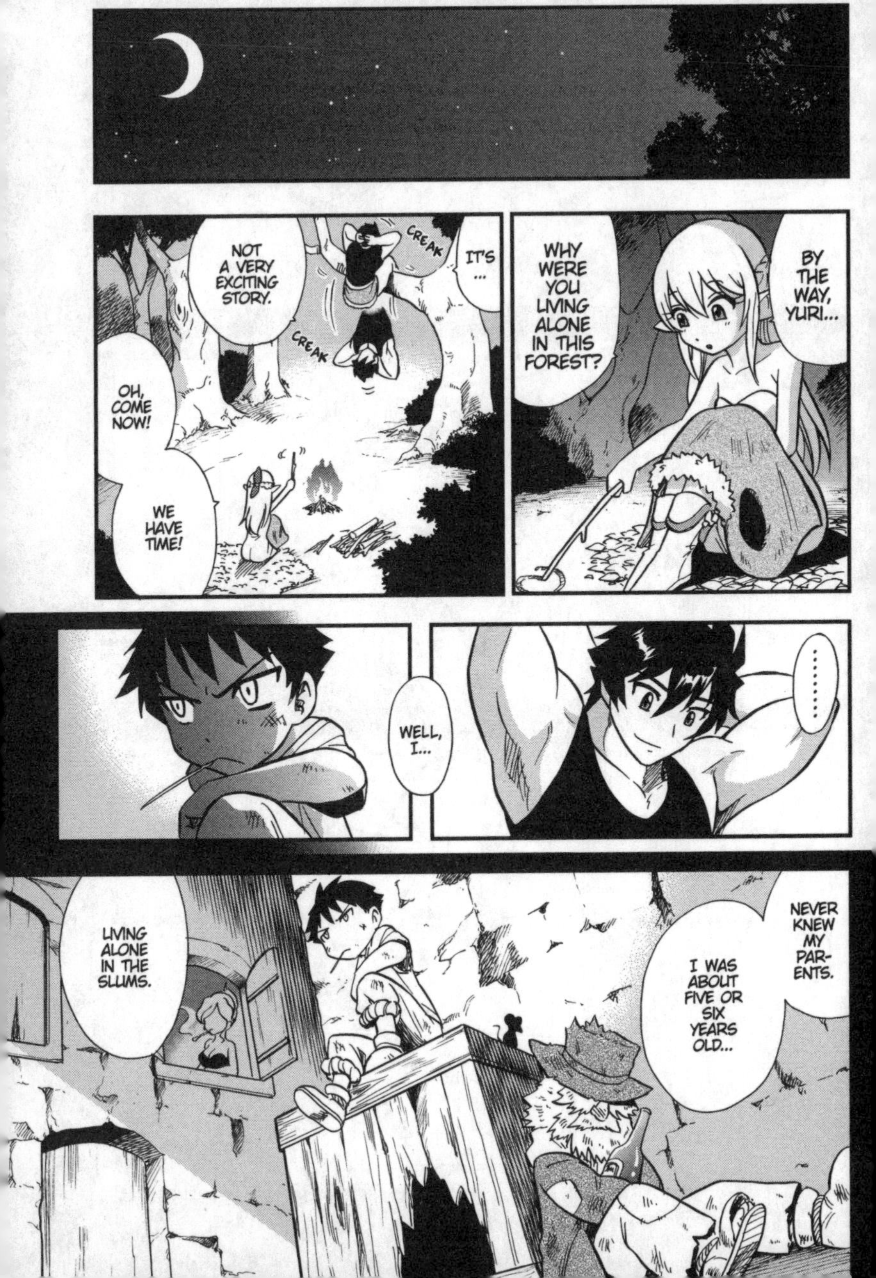
BY THE WAY, YURI...
WHY WERE YOU LIVING ALONE IN THIS FOREST?
IT'S ...
CREAK
NOT A VERY EXCITING STORY.
CREAK
OH, COME NOW!
WE HAVE TIME!
......
WELL, I...
NEVER KNEW MY PAR-ENTS.
I WAS ABOUT FIVE OR SIX YEARS OLD...
LIVING ALONE IN THE SLUMS.

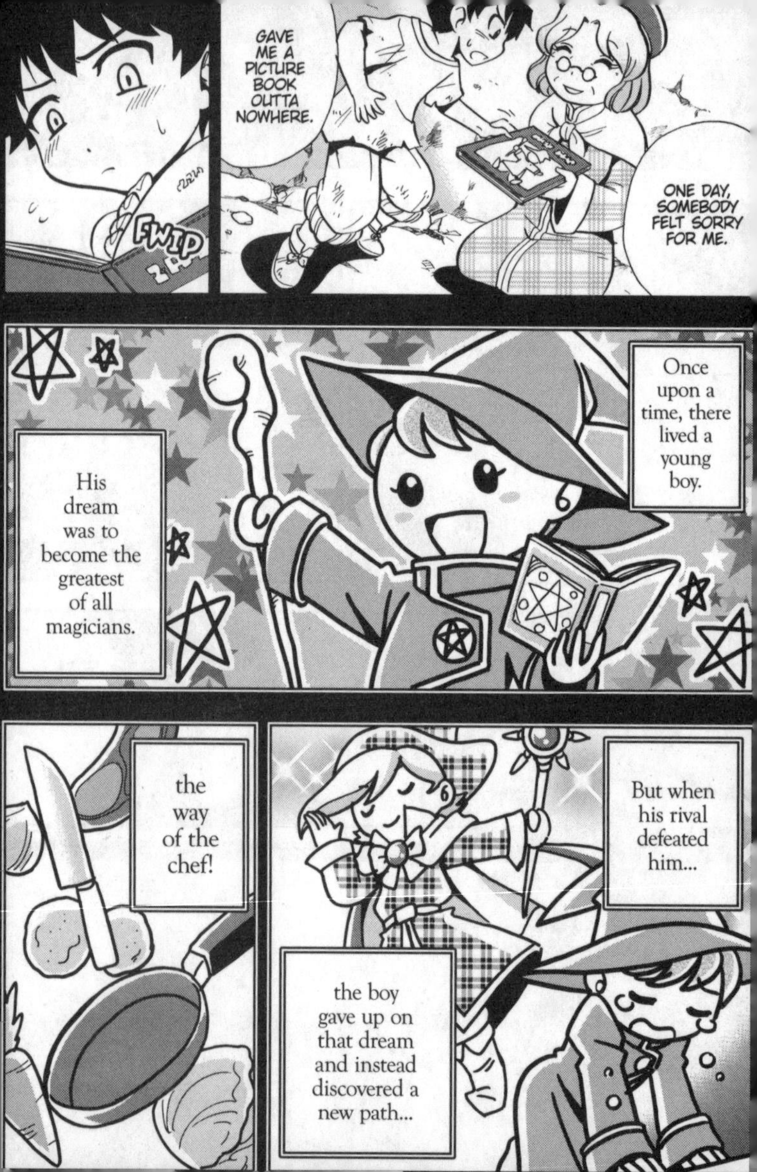
ONE DAY, SOMEBODY FELT SORRY FOR ME.
GAVE ME A PICTURE BOOK OUTTA NOWHERE.
FWIP
Once upon a time, there lived a young boy.
His dream was to become the greatest of all magicians.
But when his rival defeated him...
the boy gave up on that dream and instead discovered a new path...
the way of the chef!

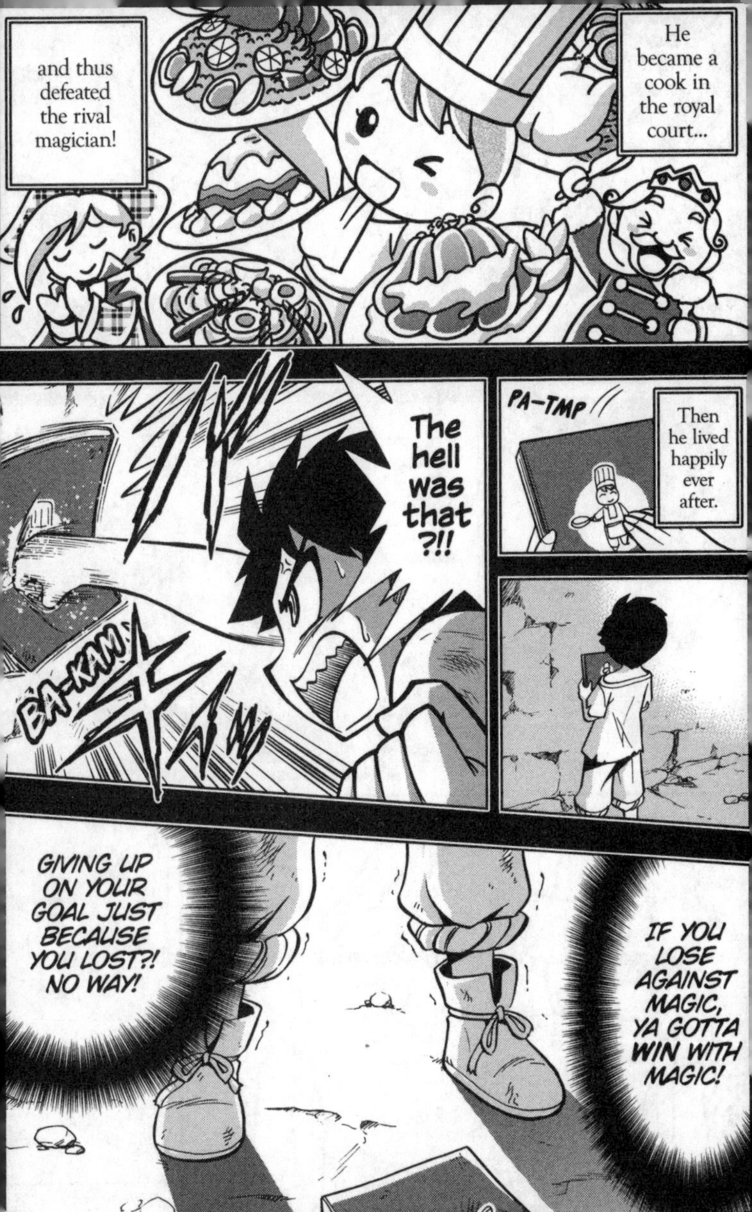
He became a cook in the royal court...
and thus defeated the rival magician!
PA-TMP
Then he lived happily ever after.
The hell was that?!!
BA-KAM
IF YOU LOSE AGAINST MAGIC, YA GOTTA WIN WITH MAGIC!
GIVING UP ON YOUR GOAL JUST BECAUSE YOU LOST?! NO WAY!

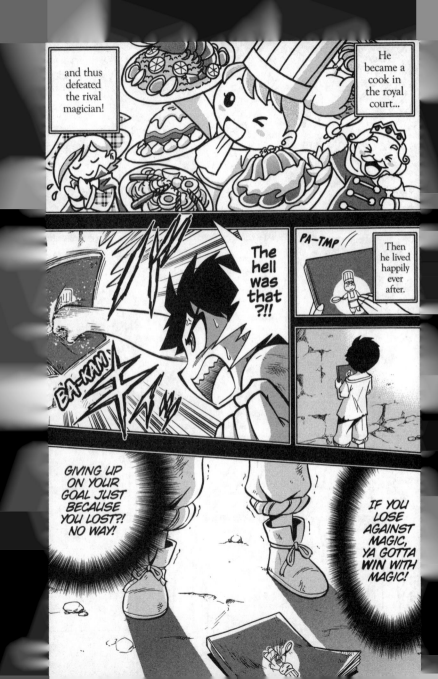

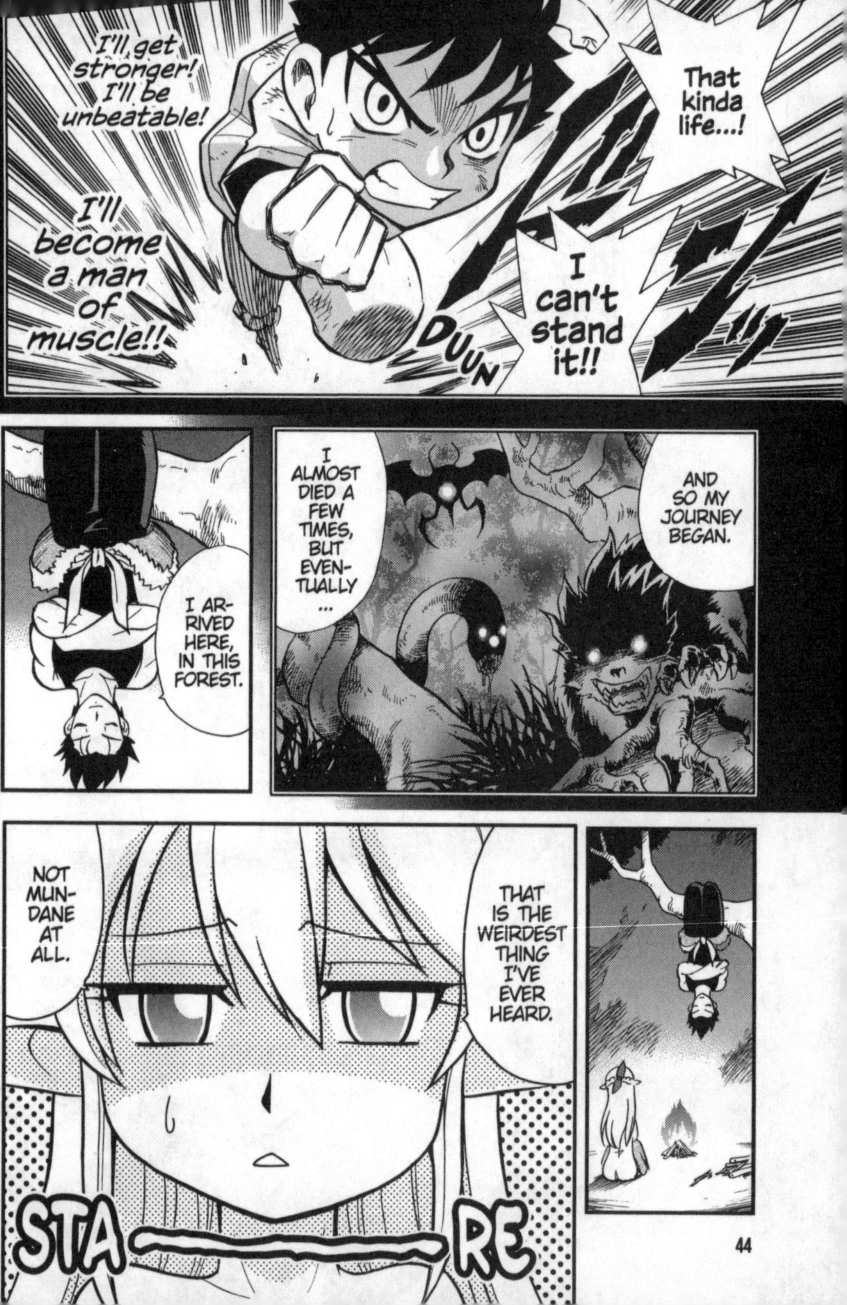
That kinda life...!
I can't stand it!!
DUUN
I'll get stronger! I'll be unbeatable!
I'll become a man of muscle!!
AND SO MY JOURNEY BEGAN.
I ALMOST DIED A FEW TIMES, BUT EVENTUALLY...
I ARRIVED HERE, IN THIS FOREST.
THAT IS THE WEIRDEST THING I'VE EVER HEARD.
NOT MUNDANE AT ALL.
STA——RE

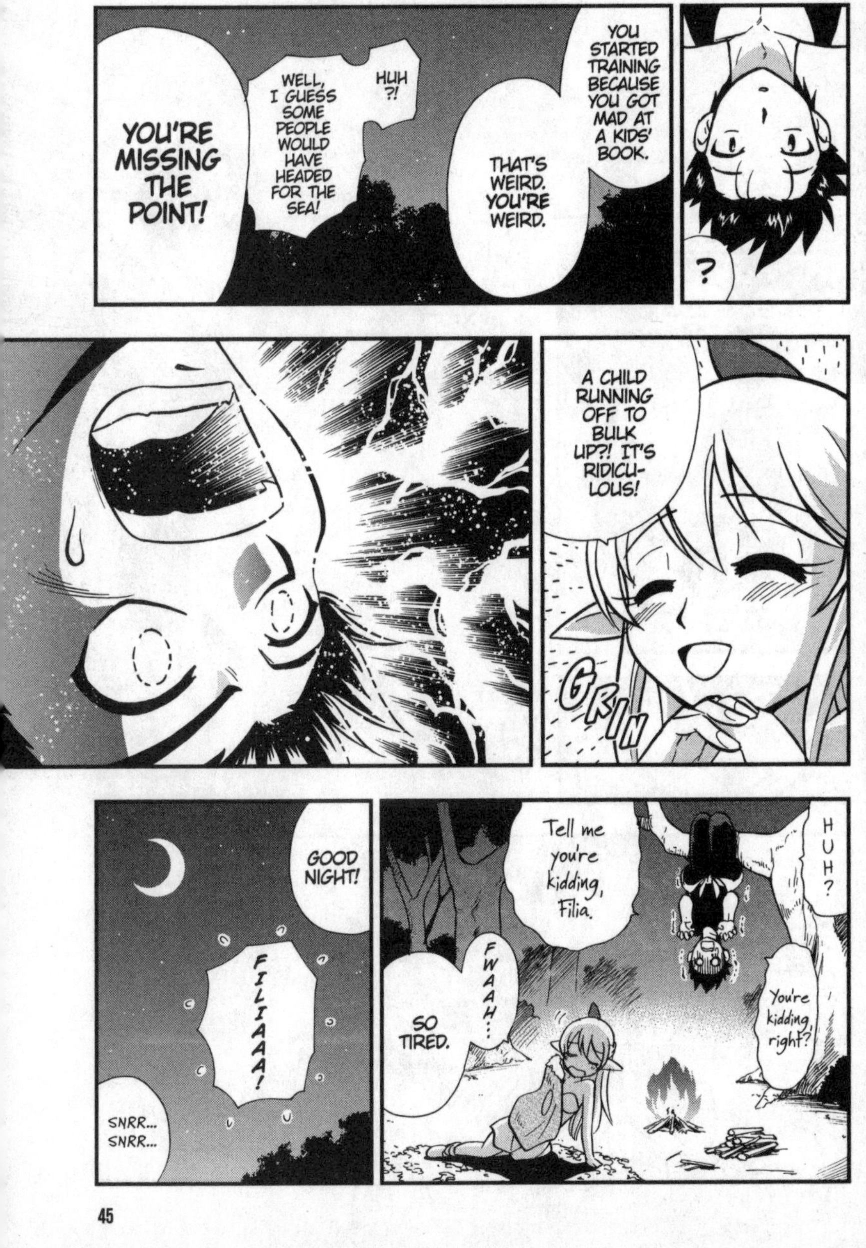
?
YOU STARTED TRAINING BECAUSE YOU GOT MAD AT A KIDS' BOOK.
THAT'S WEIRD. YOU'RE WEIRD.
HUH?!
WELL, I GUESS SOME PEOPLE WOULD HAVE HEADED FOR THE SEA!
YOU'RE MISSING THE POINT!
A CHILD RUNNING OFF TO BULK UP?! IT'S RIDICULOUS!
GRIN
HUH?
Tell me you're kidding, Filia.
You're kidding, right?
FWAAAH...
SO TIRED.
GOOD NIGHT!
FILIAAA!
SNRR... SNRR...

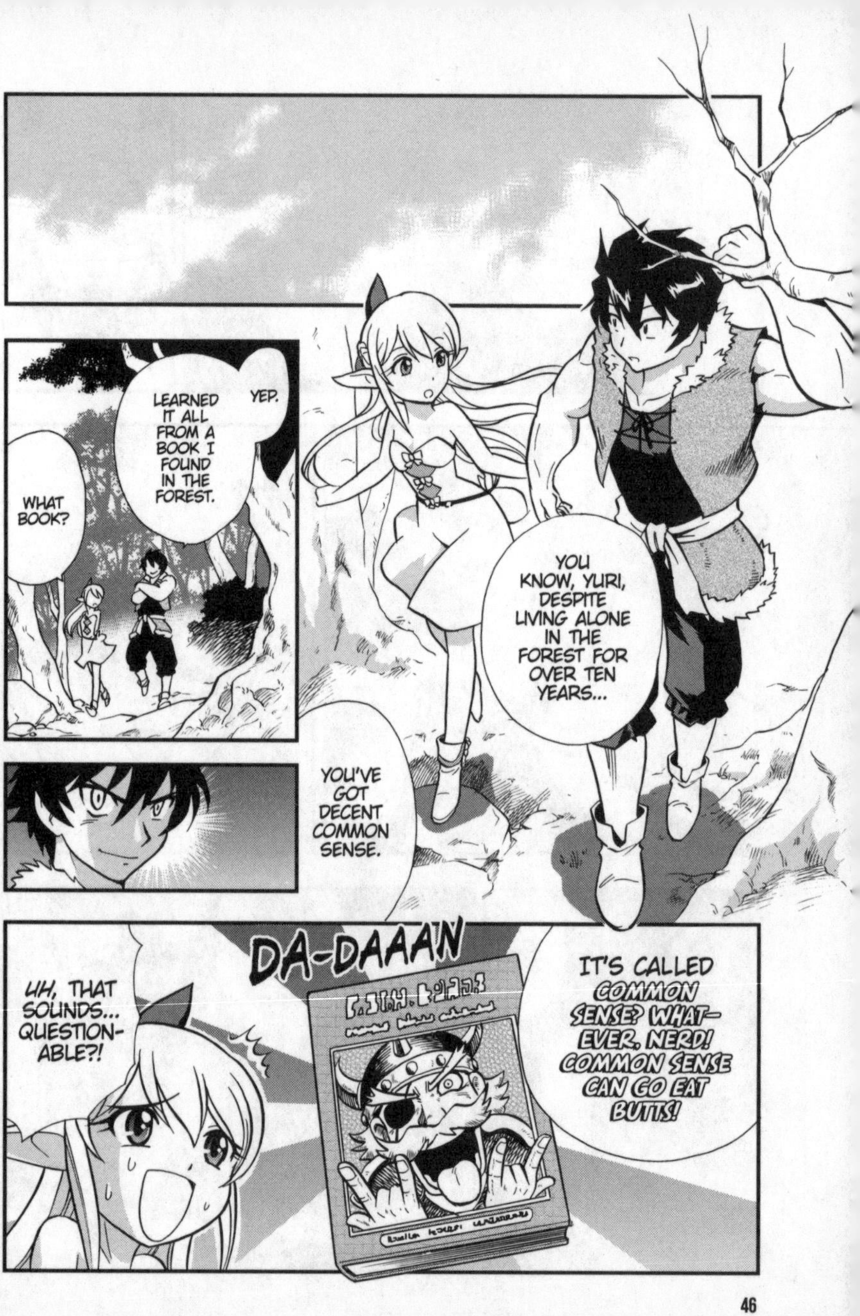
YOU KNOW, YURI, DESPITE LIVING ALONE IN THE FOREST FOR OVER TEN YEARS...
YOU'VE GOT DECENT COMMON SENSE.
YEP.
LEARNED IT ALL FROM A BOOK I FOUND IN THE FOREST.
WHAT BOOK?
IT'S CALLED COMMON SENSE? WHAT-EVER, NERD! COMMON SENSE CAN GO EAT BUTTS!
DA-DAAAN
UH, THAT SOUNDS... QUESTION-ABLE?!

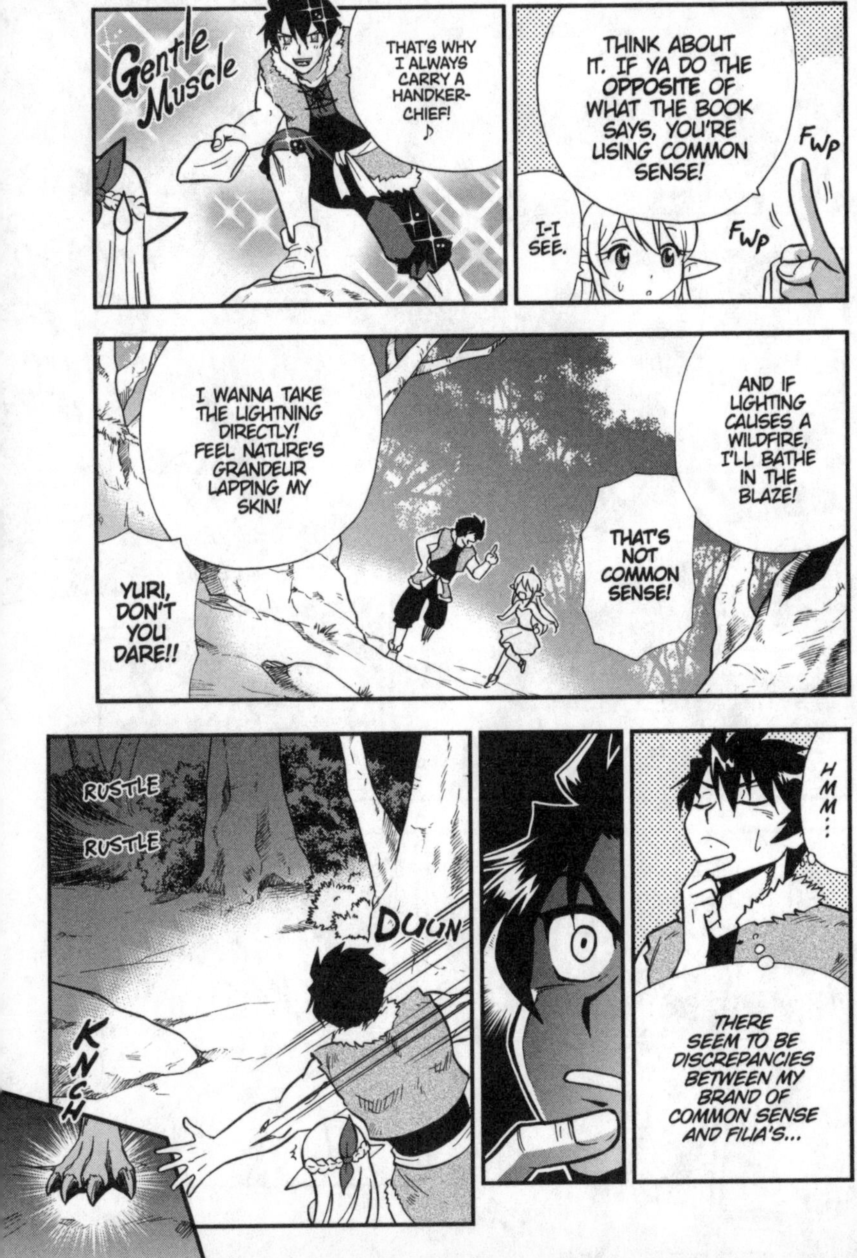
THINK ABOUT IT. IF YA DO THE OPPOSITE OF WHAT THE BOOK SAYS, YOU'RE USING COMMON SENSE!
FWP
FWP
I-I SEE.
THAT'S WHY I ALWAYS CARRY A HANDKER-CHIEF! ♪
Gentle Muscle
AND IF LIGHTING CAUSES A WILDFIRE, I'LL BATHE IN THE BLAZE!
THAT'S NOT COMMON SENSE!
I WANNA TAKE THE LIGHTNING DIRECTLY! FEEL NATURE'S GRANDEUR LAPPING MY SKIN!
YURI, DON'T YOU DARE!!
HMM...
THERE SEEM TO BE DISCREPANCIES BETWEEN MY BRAND OF COMMON SENSE AND FILIA'S...
RUSTLE
RUSTLE
DUUN
KNCH

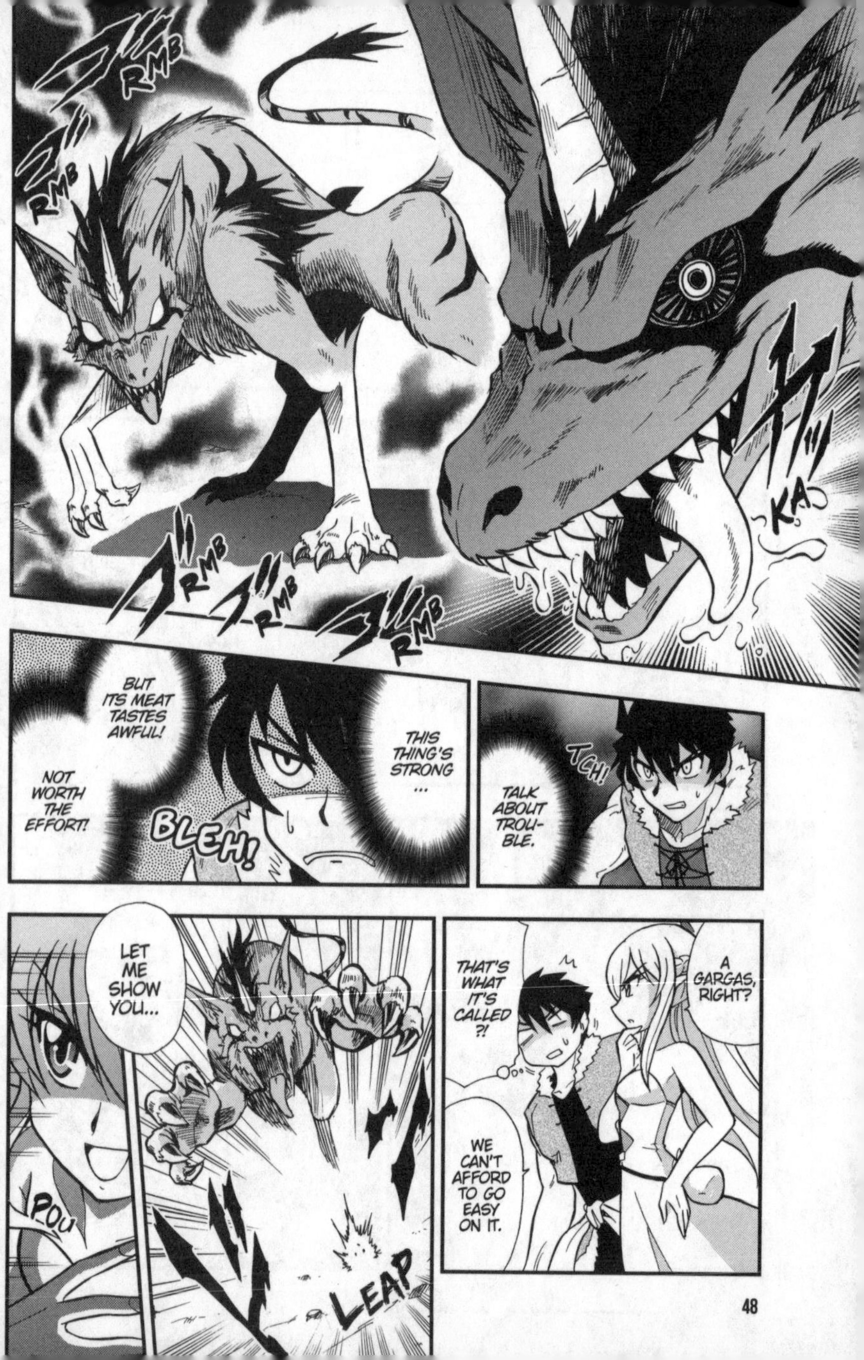
RMB
RMB
KA
RMB
RMB
RMB
TCH!
TALK ABOUT TROUBLE.
THIS THING'S STRONG ...
BUT ITS MEAT TASTES AWFUL!
NOT WORTH THE EFFORT!
BLEH!
A GARGAS, RIGHT?
THAT'S WHAT IT'S CALLED ?!
WE CAN'T AFFORD TO GO EASY ON IT.
LET ME SHOW YOU...
POU
LEAP

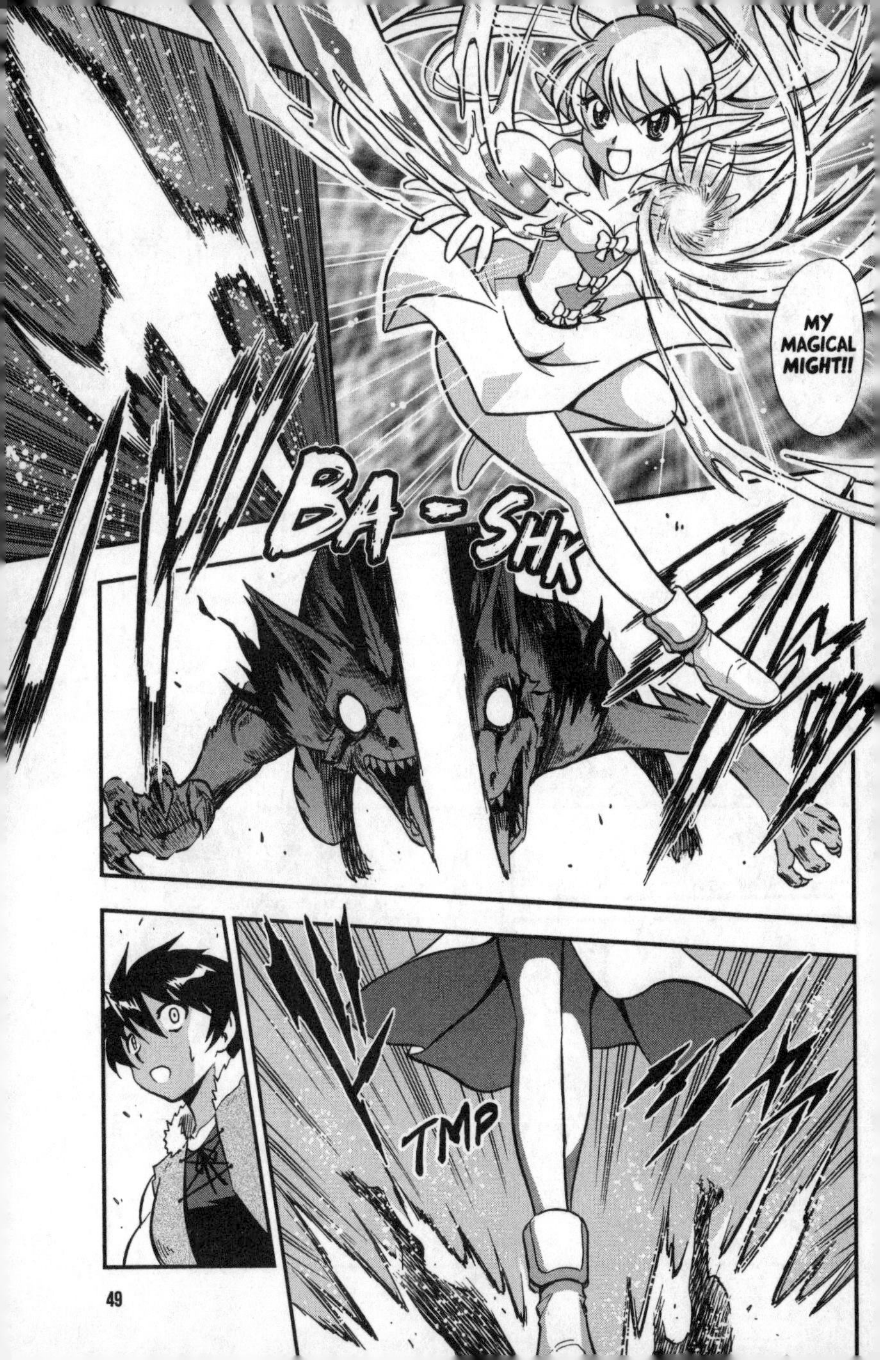
MY MAGICAL MIGHT!!
BA-SHK
TMP

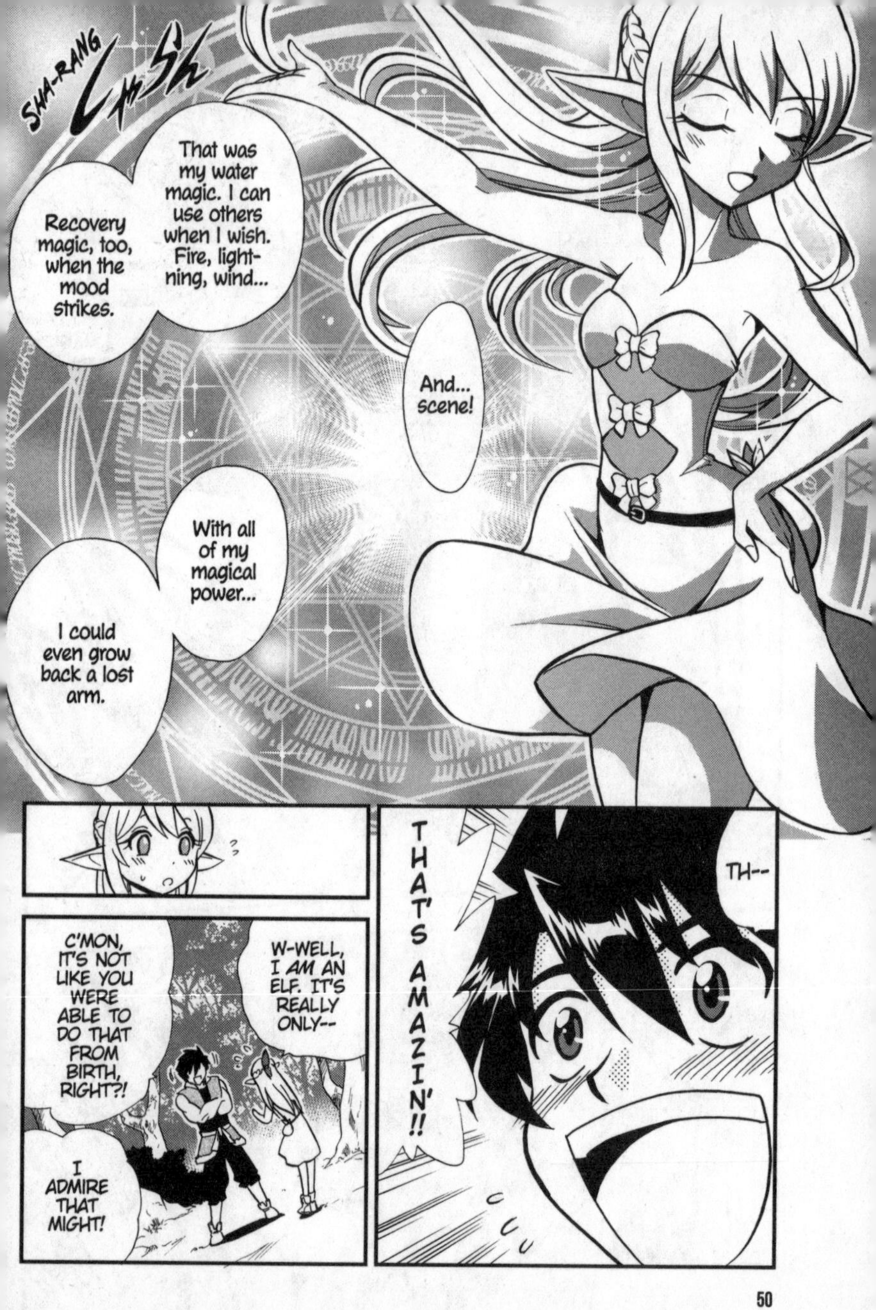
SHA-RANG
That was my water magic. I can use others when I wish. Fire, lightning, wind...
Recovery magic, too, when the mood strikes.
And... scene!
With all of my magical power...
I could even grow back a lost arm.
TH--
THAT'S AMAZIN'!!
W-WELL, I *AM* AN ELF. IT'S REALLY ONLY--
C'MON, IT'S NOT LIKE YOU WERE ABLE TO DO THAT FROM BIRTH, RIGHT?!
I ADMIRE THAT MIGHT!

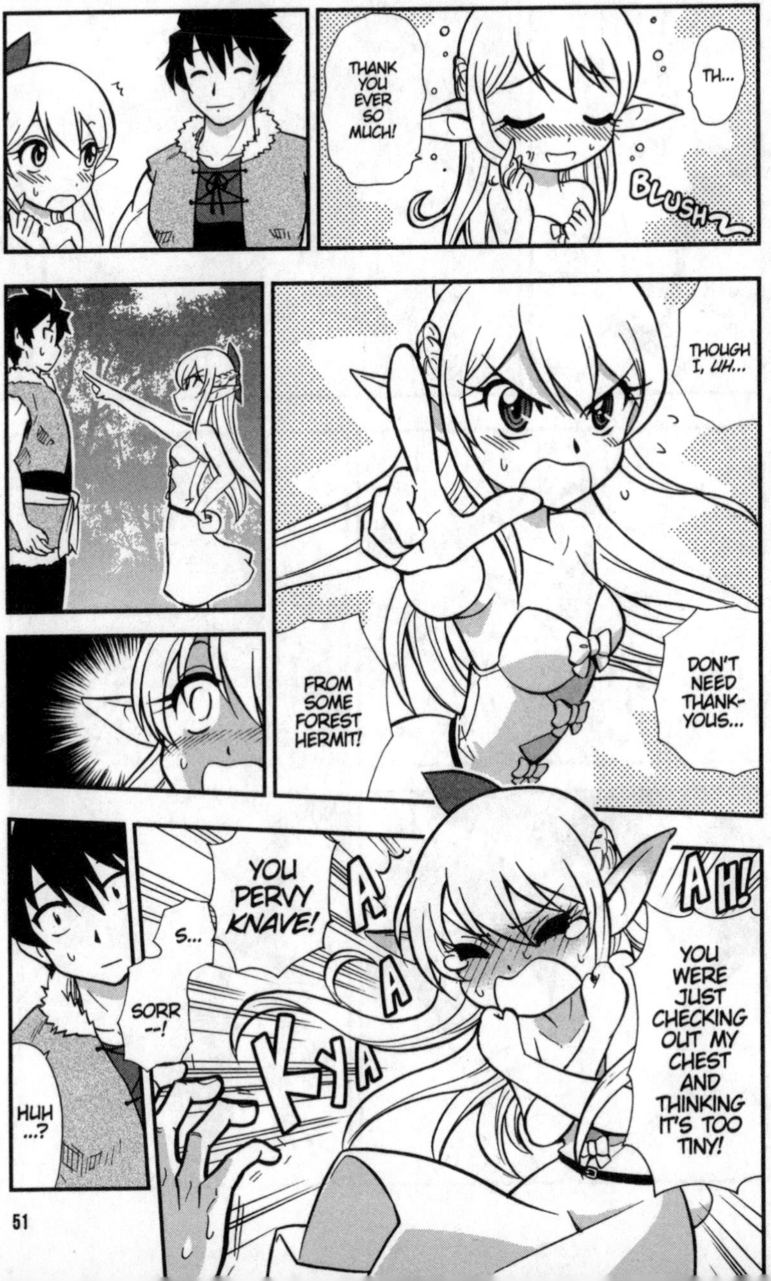
TH...
THANK YOU EVER SO MUCH!
BLUSH
THOUGH I, UH...
DON'T NEED THANK-YOUS...
FROM SOME FOREST HERMIT!
AH!
YOU WERE JUST CHECKING OUT MY CHEST AND THINKING IT'S TOO TINY!
A
A
YOU PERVY KNAVE!
S...
SORR--!
HUH...?

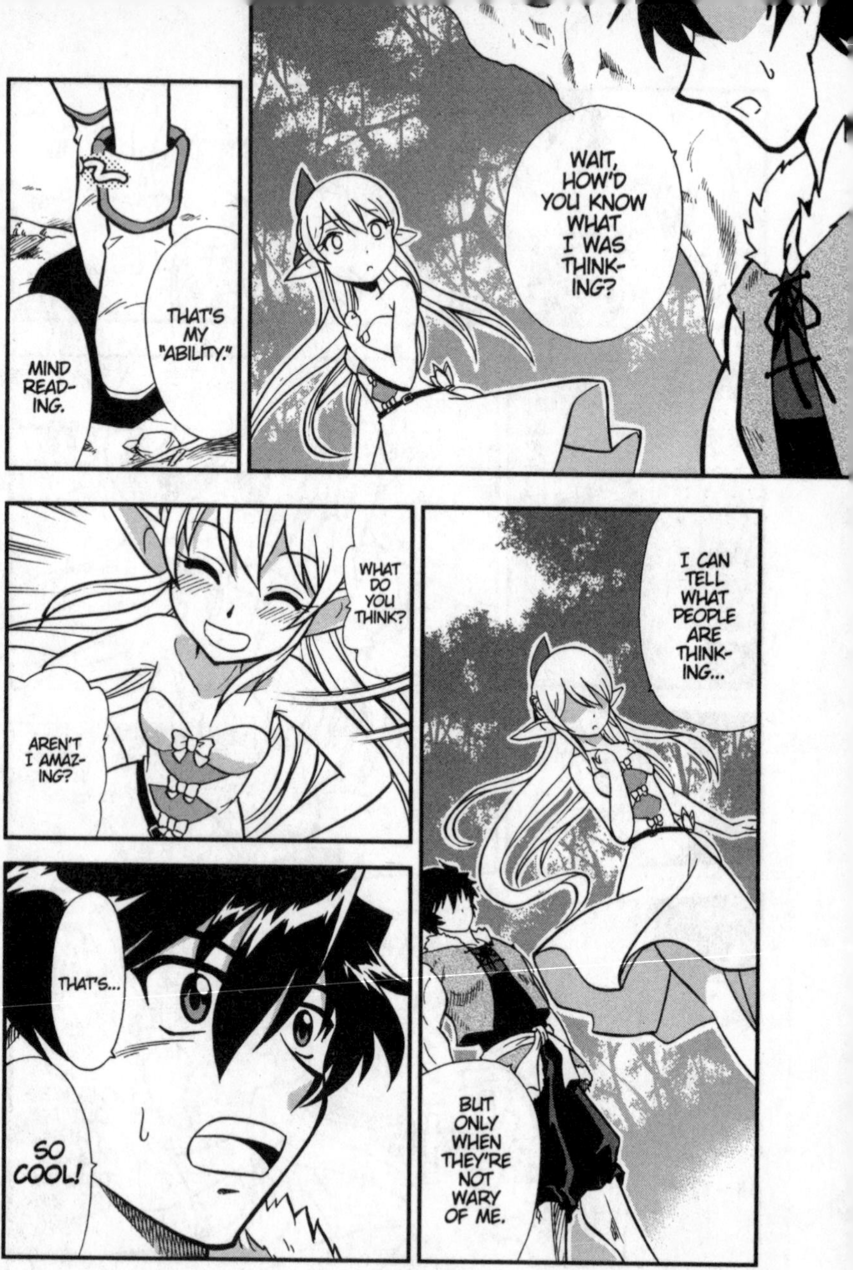
WAIT, HOW'D YOU KNOW WHAT I WAS THINKING?
THAT'S MY "ABILITY."
MIND READING.
I CAN TELL WHAT PEOPLE ARE THINKING...
BUT ONLY WHEN THEY'RE NOT WARY OF ME.
WHAT DO YOU THINK?
AREN'T I AMAZING?
THAT'S...
SO COOL!

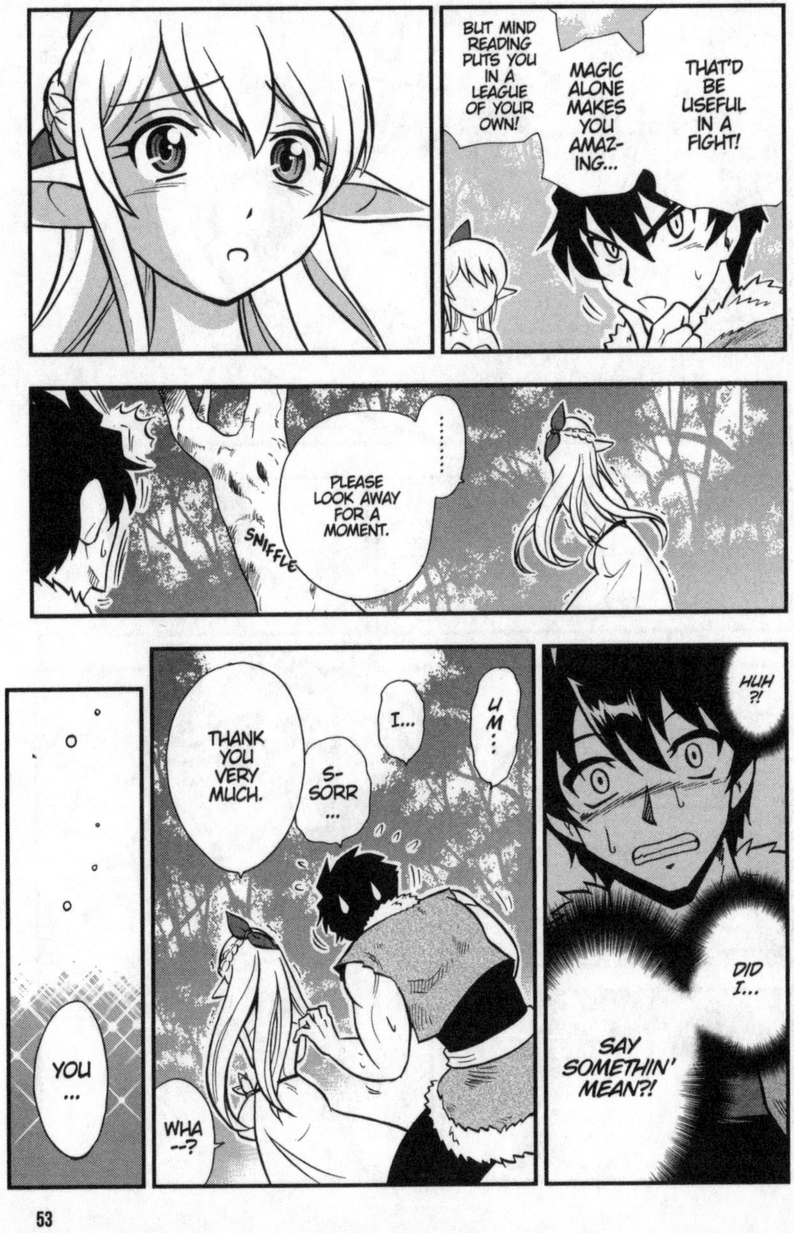
THAT'D BE USEFUL IN A FIGHT!
MAGIC ALONE MAKES YOU AMAZ-ING...
BUT MIND READING PUTS YOU IN A LEAGUE OF YOUR OWN!
......
PLEASE LOOK AWAY FOR A MOMENT.
SNIFFLE
HUH?!
DID I...
SAY SOMETHIN' MEAN?!
UM...
I...
S-SORR...
THANK YOU VERY MUCH.
WHA--?
YOU...

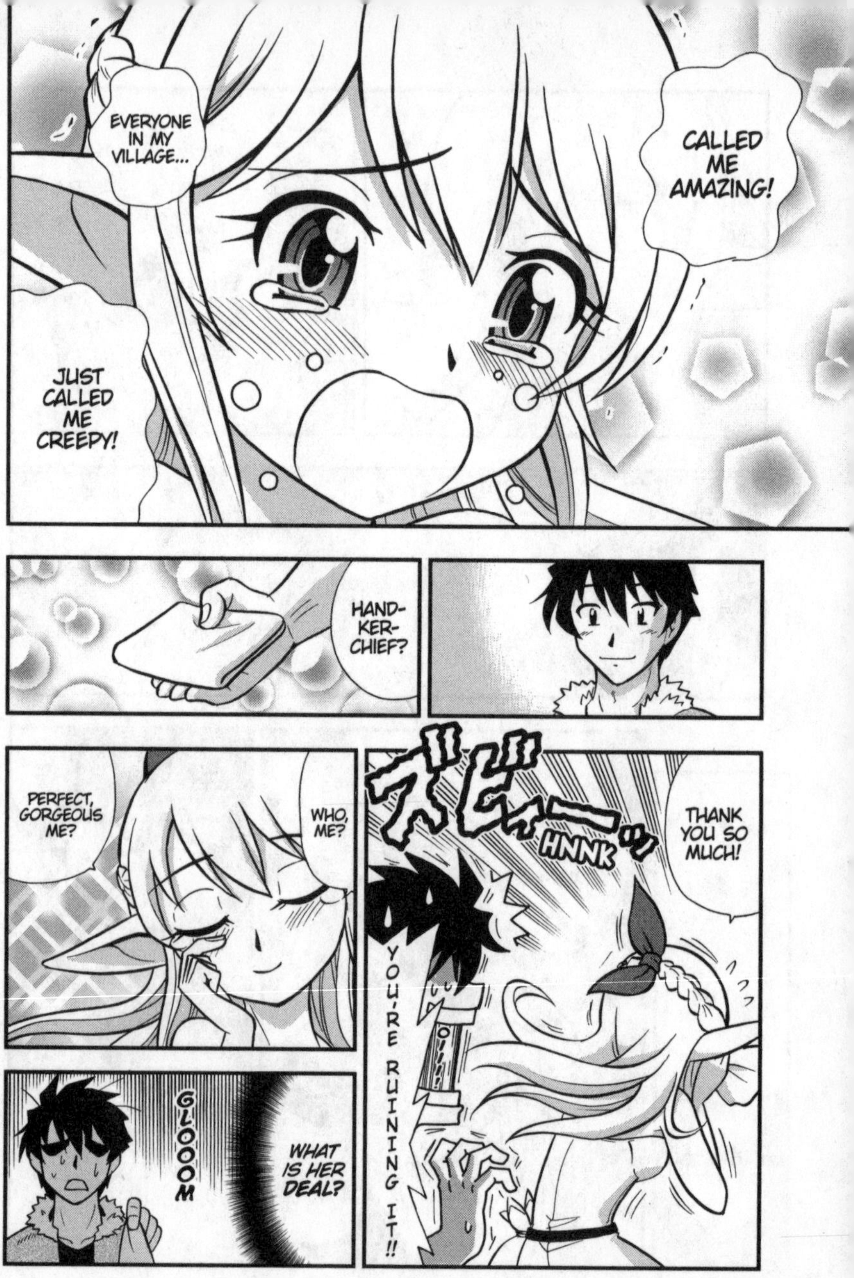
CALLED ME AMAZING!
EVERYONE IN MY VILLAGE...
JUST CALLED ME CREEPY!
HAND-KER-CHIEF?
THANK YOU SO MUCH!
HNNK
YOU'RE RUINING IT!!
WHO, ME?
PERFECT, GORGEOUS ME?
WHAT IS HER DEAL?
GLOOOOM

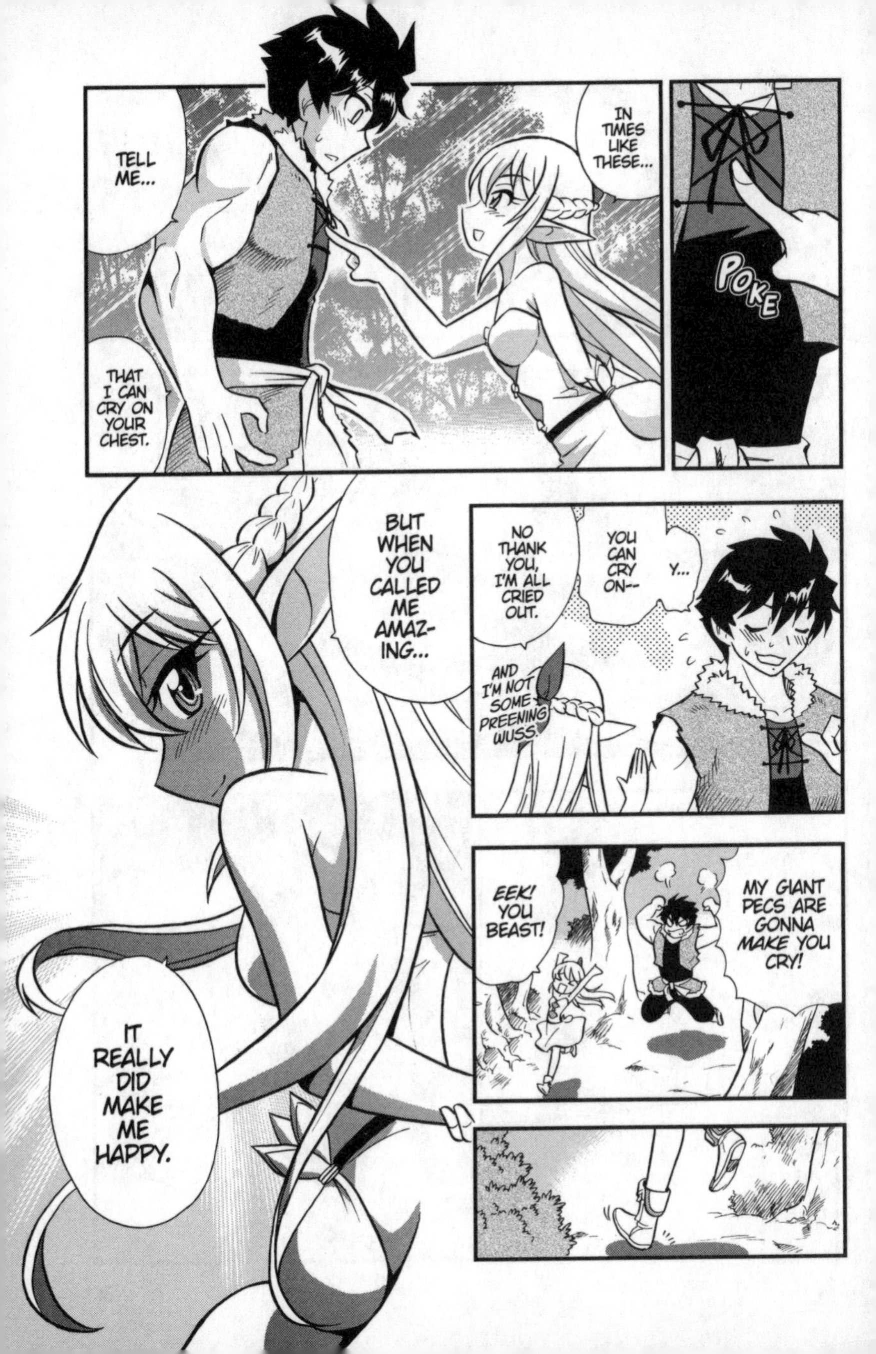
POKE
IN TIMES LIKE THESE...
TELL ME...
THAT I CAN CRY ON YOUR CHEST.
Y...
YOU CAN CRY ON--
NO THANK YOU, I'M ALL CRIED OUT.
AND I'M NOT SOME PREENING WUSS.
MY GIANT PECS ARE GONNA MAKE YOU CRY!
EEK! YOU BEAST!
BUT WHEN YOU CALLED ME AMAZING...
IT REALLY DID MAKE ME HAPPY.

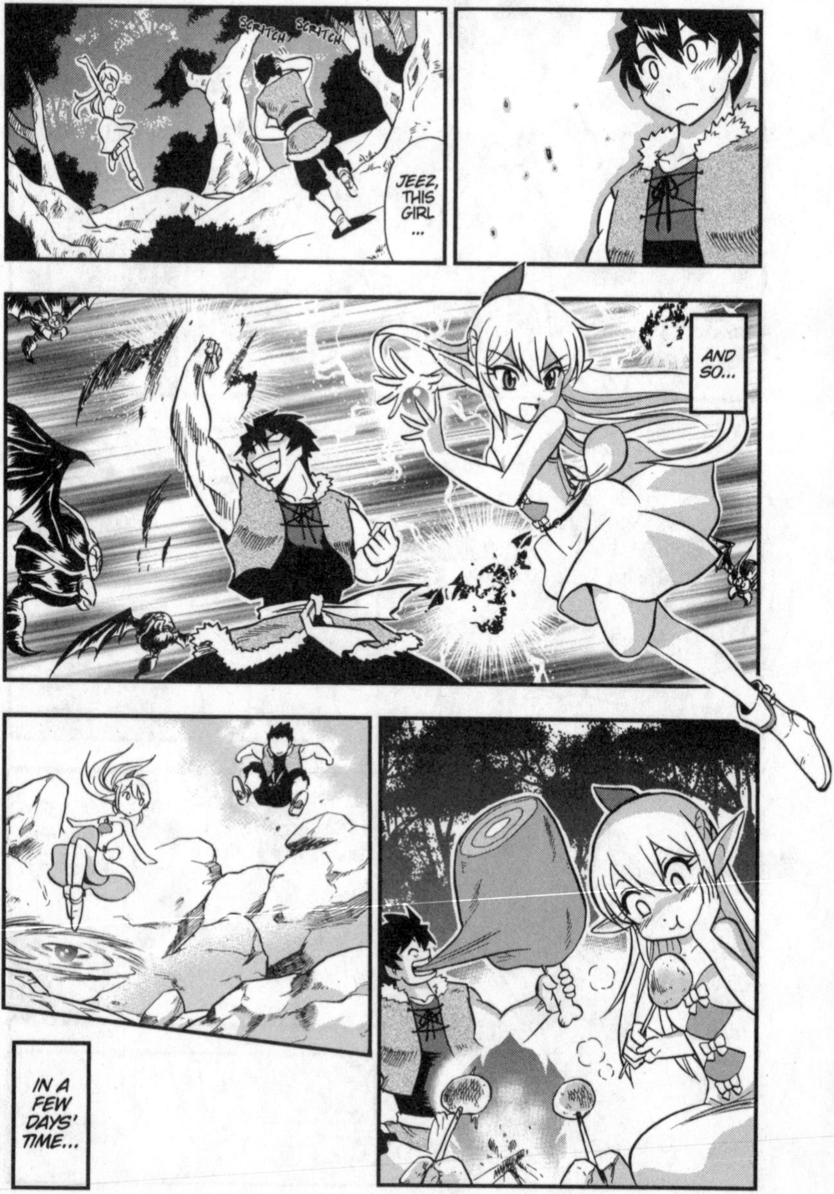

SCRITCH SCRITCH
JEEZ, THIS GIRL ...
AND SO...
IN A FEW DAYS' TIME...

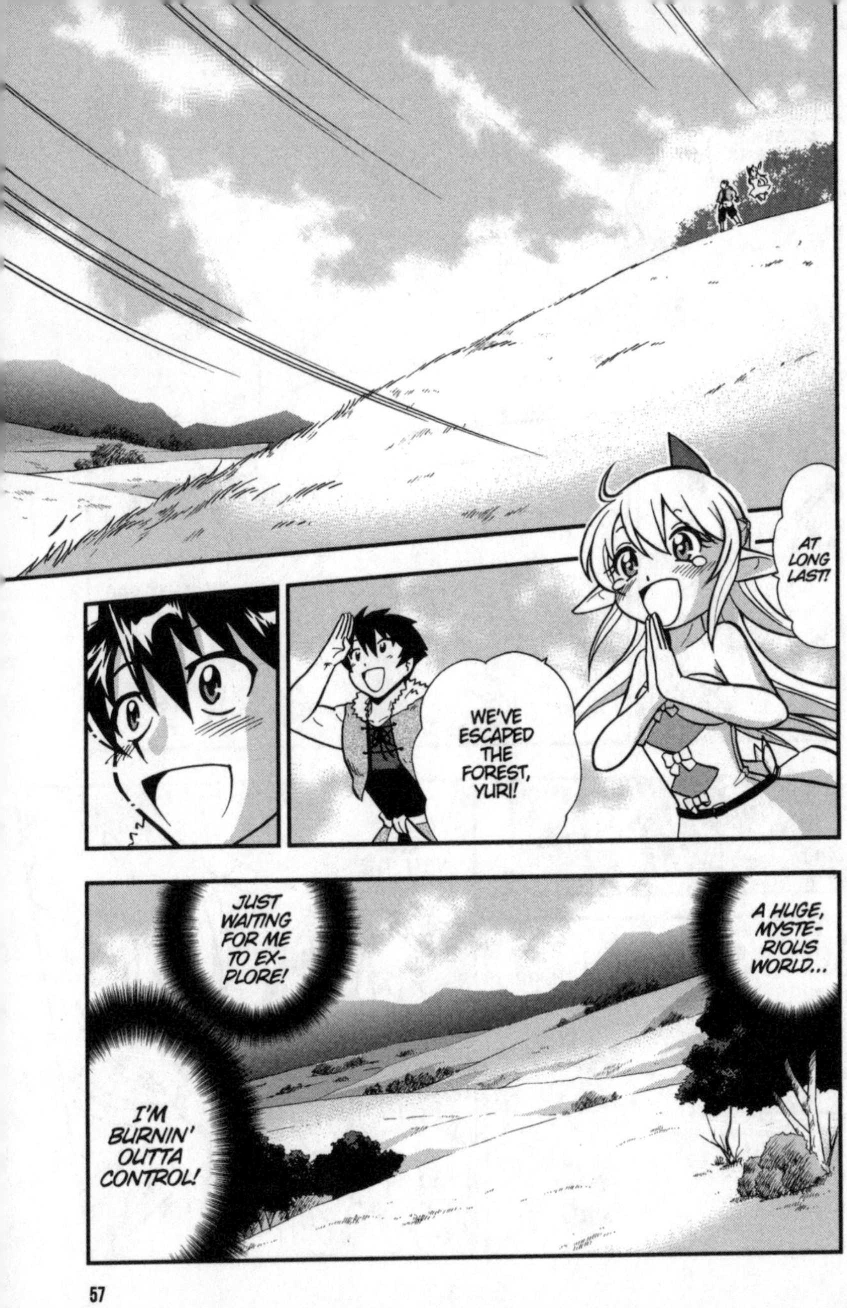
AT LONG LAST!
WE'VE ESCAPED THE FOREST, YURI!
A HUGE, MYSTERIOUS WORLD...
JUST WAITING FOR ME TO EXPLORE!
I'M BURNIN' OUTTA CONTROL!

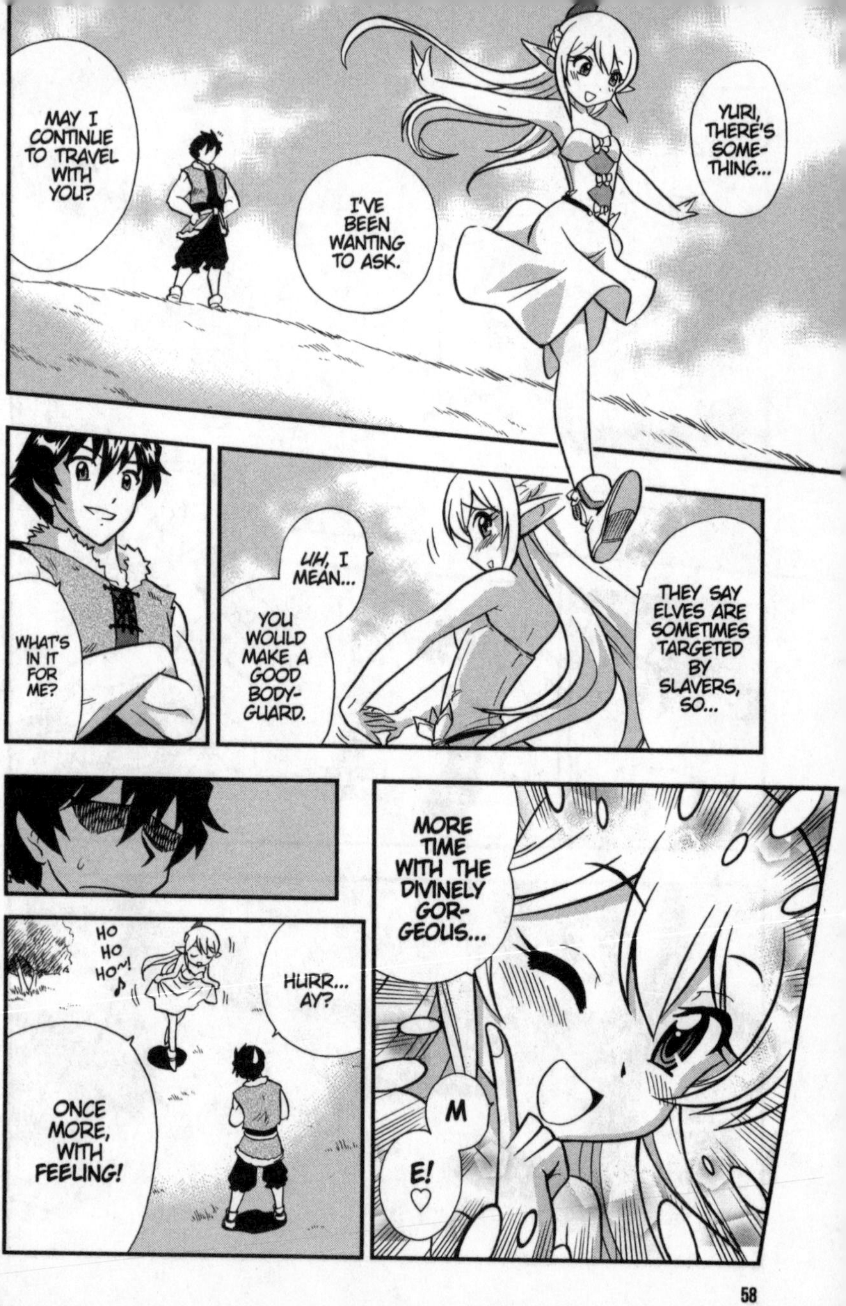
YURI, THERE'S SOME-THING...
I'VE BEEN WANTING TO ASK.
MAY I CONTINUE TO TRAVEL WITH YOU?
THEY SAY ELVES ARE SOMETIMES TARGETED BY SLAVERS, SO...
UH, I MEAN...
YOU WOULD MAKE A GOOD BODY-GUARD.
WHAT'S IN IT FOR ME?
MORE TIME WITH THE DIVINELY GOR-GEOUS...
M
E! ♡
HO HO HO~! ♪
HURR... AY?
ONCE MORE, WITH FEELING!

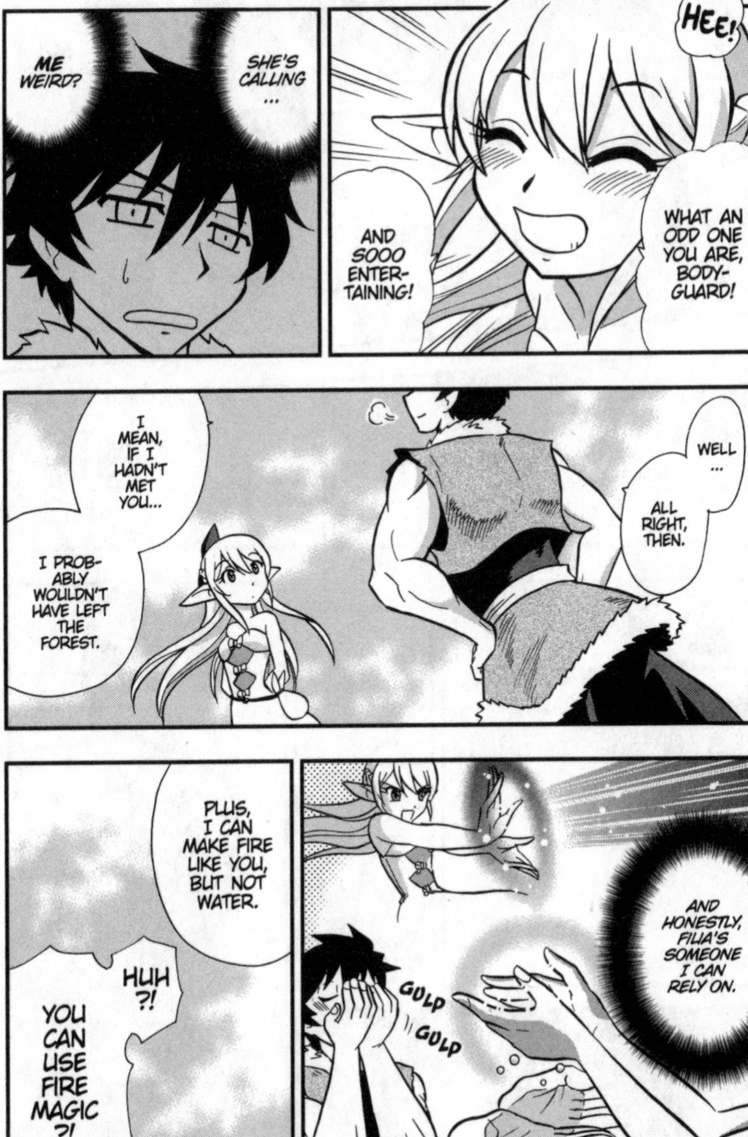
HEE!
WHAT AN ODD ONE YOU ARE, BODY-GUARD!
AND SOOO ENTER-TAINING!
SHE'S CALLING ...
ME WEIRD?
WELL ...
ALL RIGHT, THEN.
I MEAN, IF I HADN'T MET YOU...
I PROB-ABLY WOULDN'T HAVE LEFT THE FOREST.
AND HONESTLY, FILIA'S SOMEONE I CAN RELY ON.
GULP
GULP
PLUS, I CAN MAKE FIRE LIKE YOU, BUT NOT WATER.
HUH ?!
YOU CAN USE FIRE MAGIC ?!

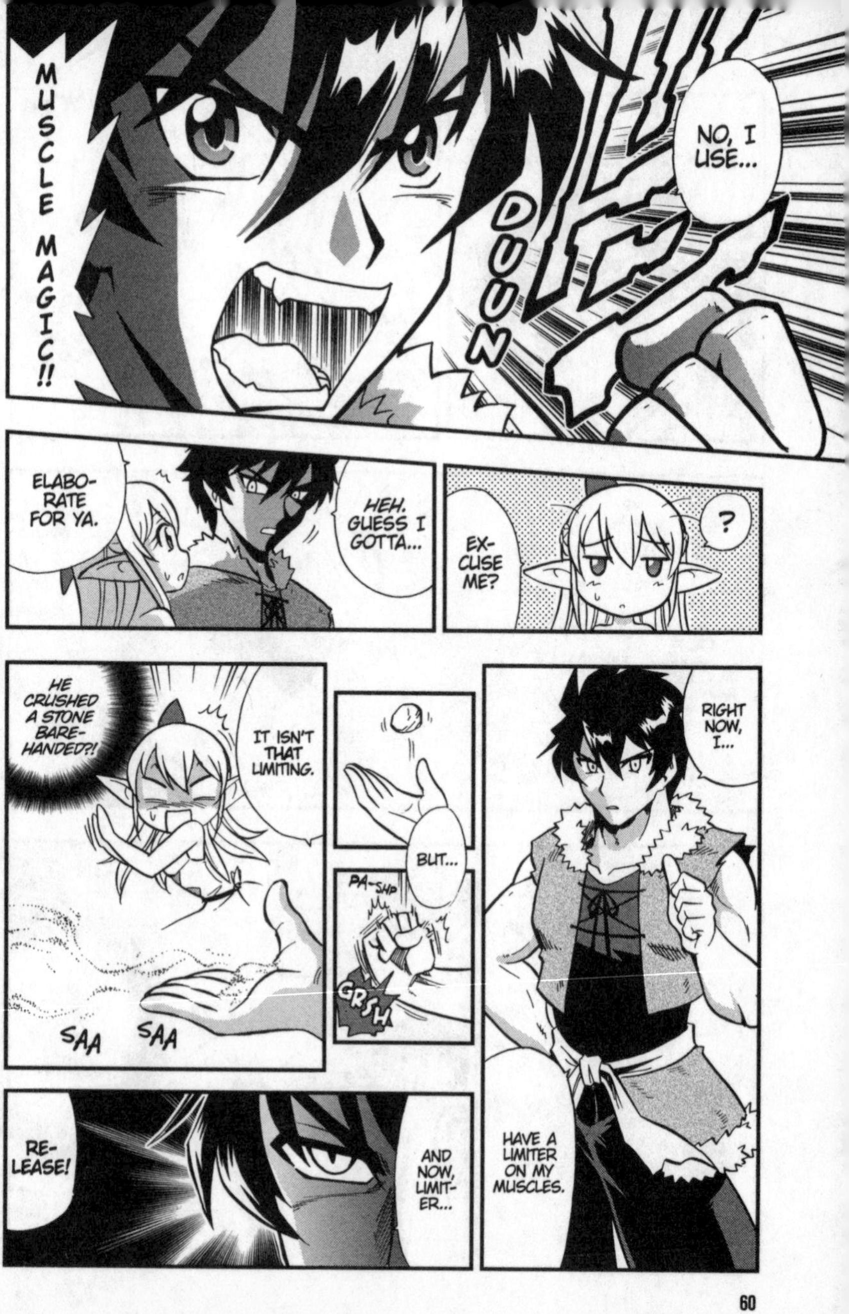
NO, I USE...
DUUN
MUSCLE MAGIC!!
?
EX-CUSE ME?
HEH. GUESS I GOTTA...
ELABO-RATE FOR YA.
RIGHT NOW, I...
HAVE A LIMITER ON MY MUSCLES.
BUT...
PA-SHP
GRSH
IT ISN'T THAT LIMITING.
HE CRUSHED A STONE BARE-HANDED?!
SAA
SAA
AND NOW, LIMIT-ER...
RE-LEASE!

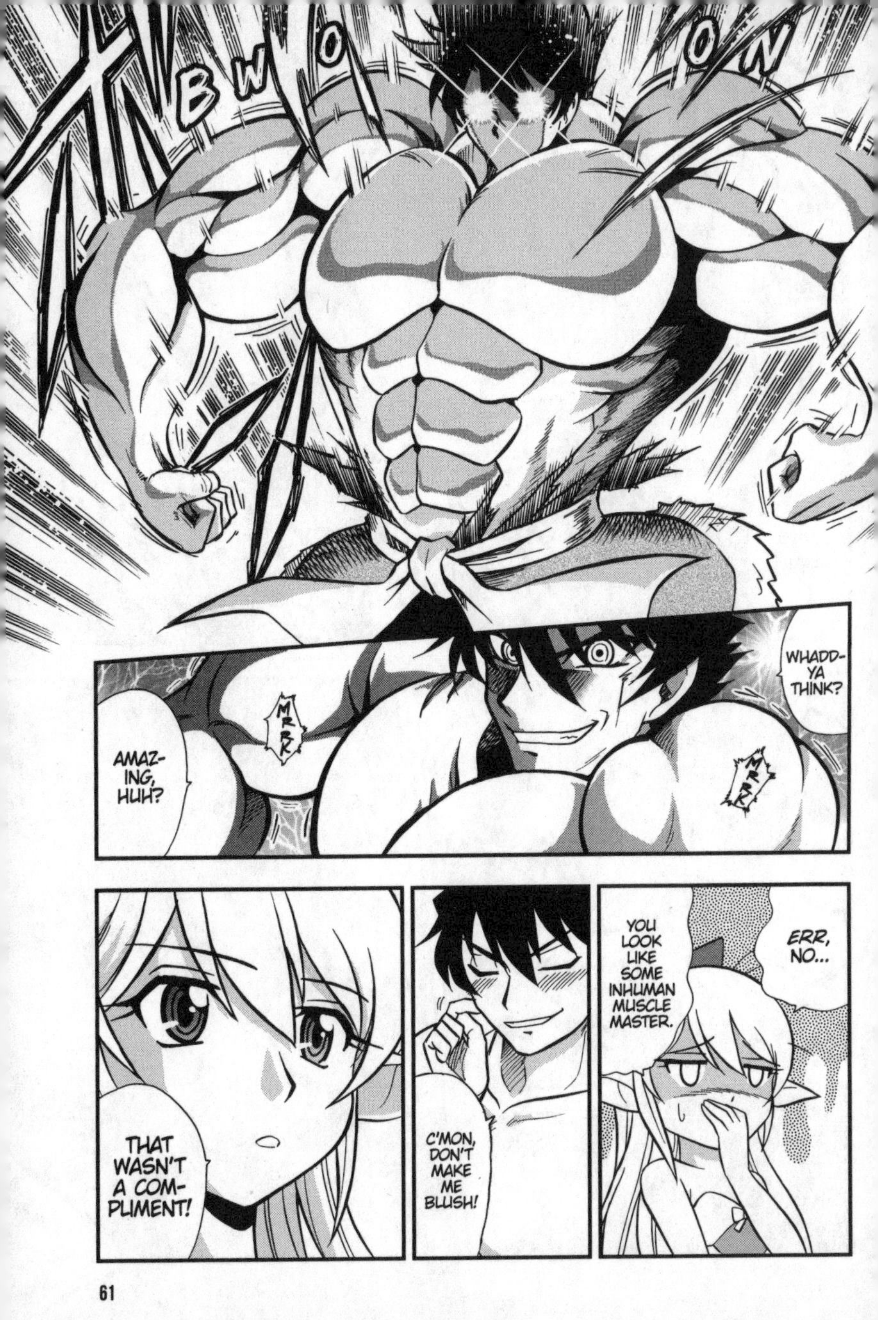
BWOOON
WHADD-YA THINK?
MRRK
MRRK
AMAZ-ING, HUH?
ERR, NO...
YOU LOOK LIKE SOME INHUMAN MUSCLE MASTER.
C'MON, DON'T MAKE ME BLUSH!
THAT WASN'T A COM-PLIMENT!

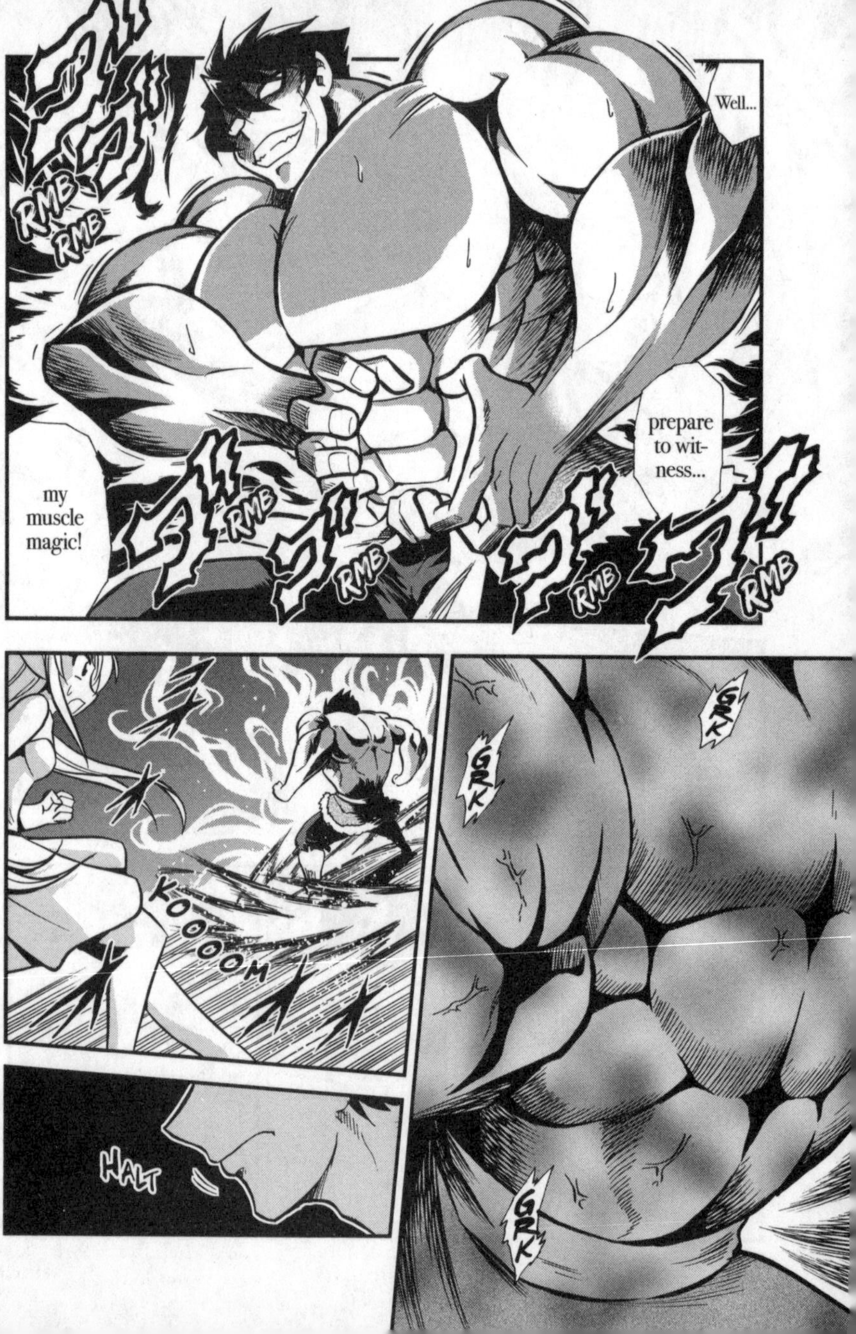
Well...
prepare to wit-ness...
RMB
RMB
RMB
RMB
RMB
RMB
my muscle magic!
GRK
GRK
GRK
KOOOOM
HALT

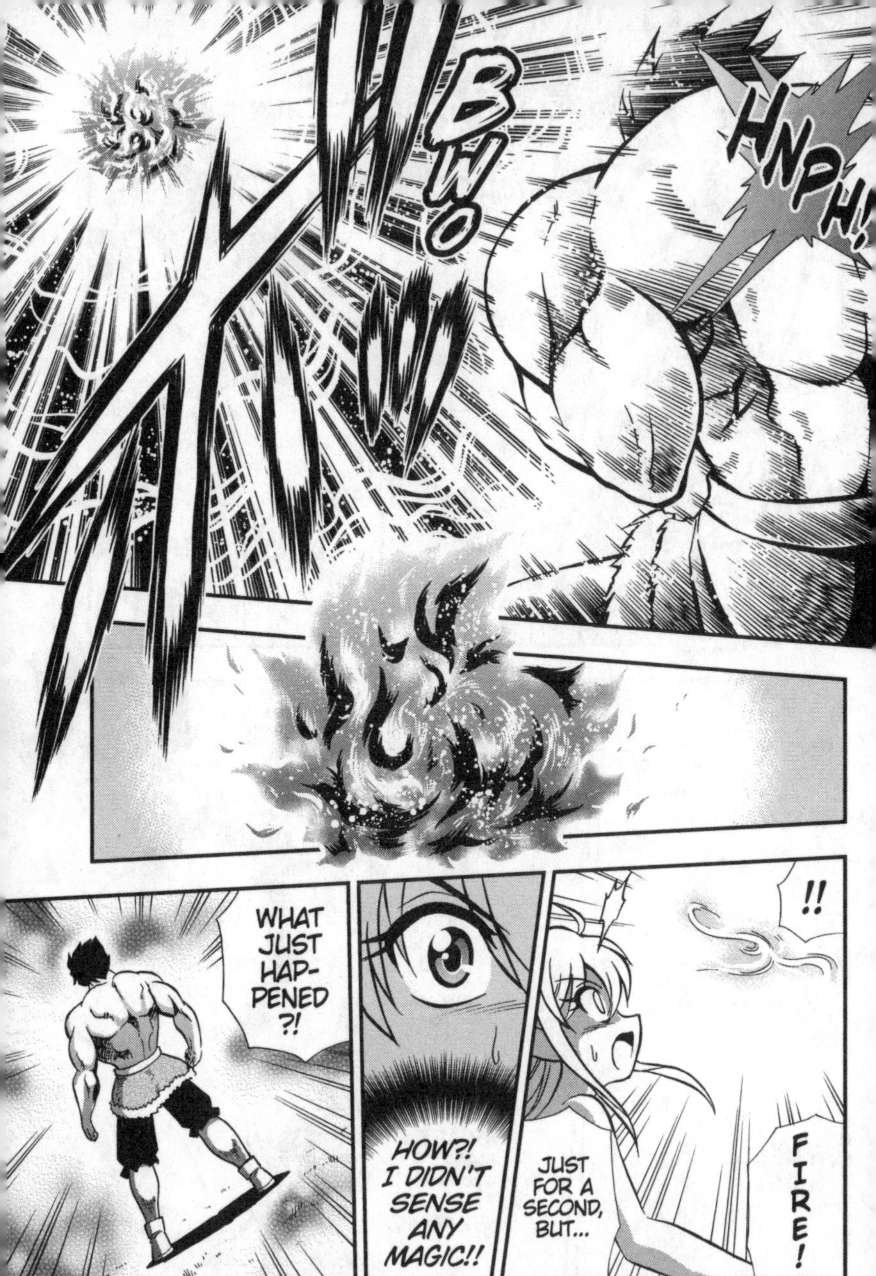
HNPH!
BWO
!!
FIRE!
JUST FOR A SECOND, BUT...
HOW?! I DIDN'T SENSE ANY MAGIC!!
WHAT JUST HAP-PENED?!

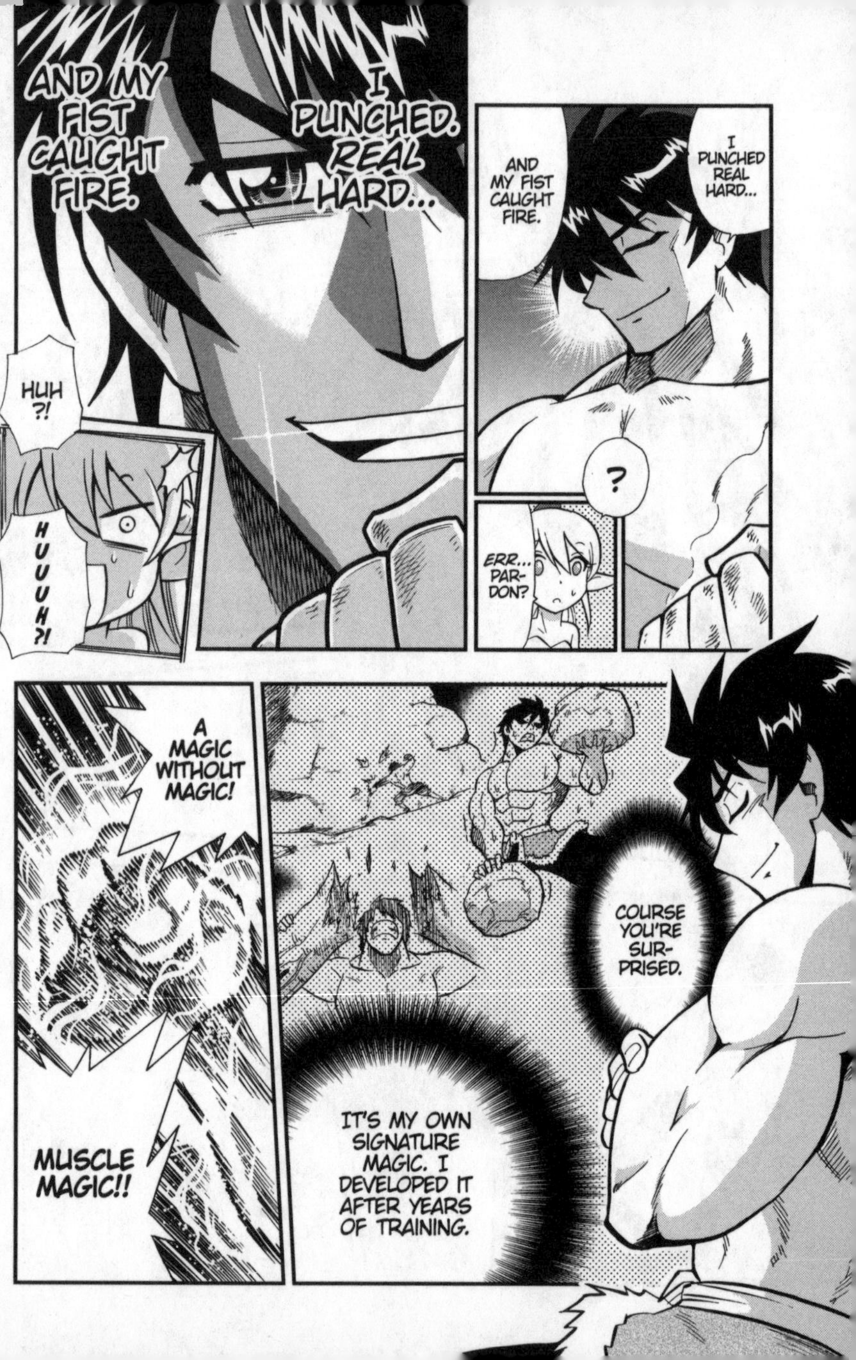
I PUNCHED REAL HARD...
AND MY FIST CAUGHT FIRE.
?
ERR... PARDON?
I PUNCHED. REAL HARD...
AND MY FIST CAUGHT FIRE.
HUH ?!
HUUUUH?!
COURSE YOU'RE SURPRISED.
IT'S MY OWN SIGNATURE MAGIC. I DEVELOPED IT AFTER YEARS OF TRAINING.
A MAGIC WITHOUT MAGIC!
MUSCLE MAGIC!!

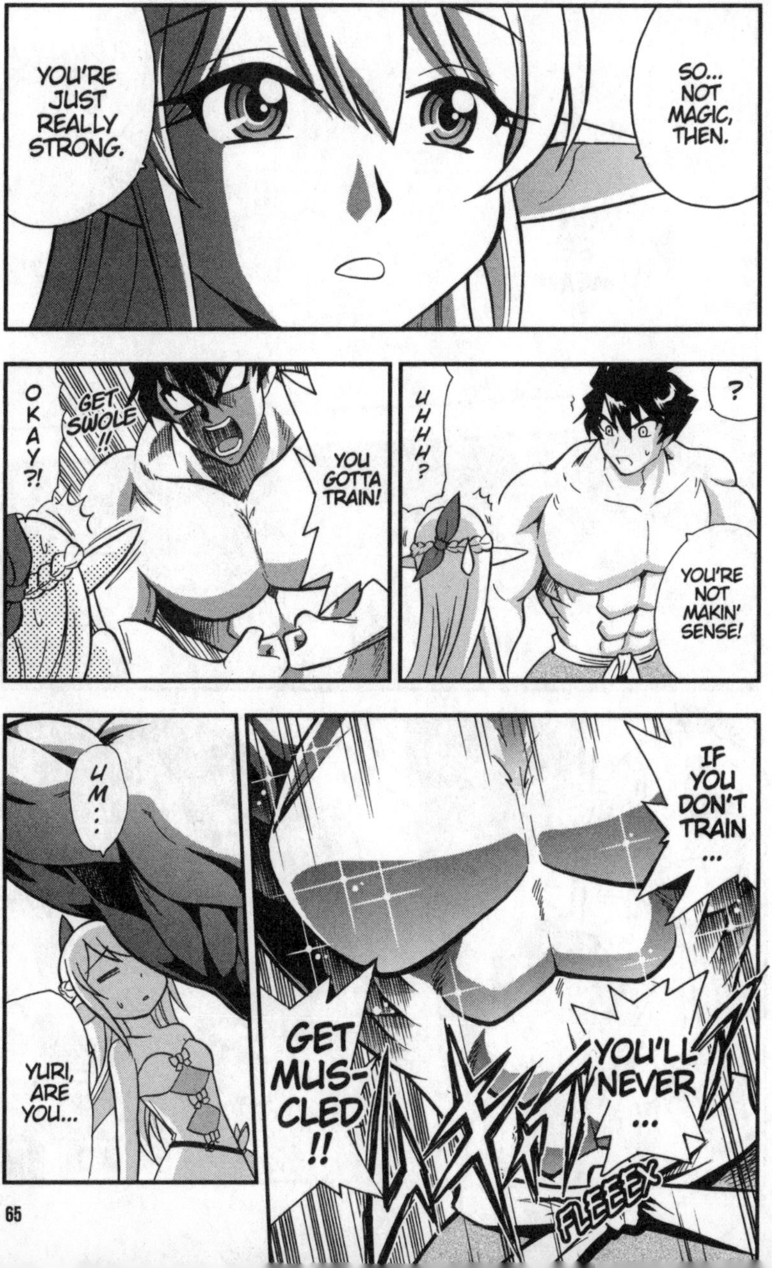
SO... NOT MAGIC, THEN.
YOU'RE JUST REALLY STRONG.
?
UHHHH?
YOU'RE NOT MAKIN' SENSE!
YOU GOTTA TRAIN!
GET SWOLE!!
OKAY?!
IF YOU DON'T TRAIN...
YOU'LL NEVER...
GET MUS-CLED!!
FLEEEX
UM...
YURI, ARE YOU...

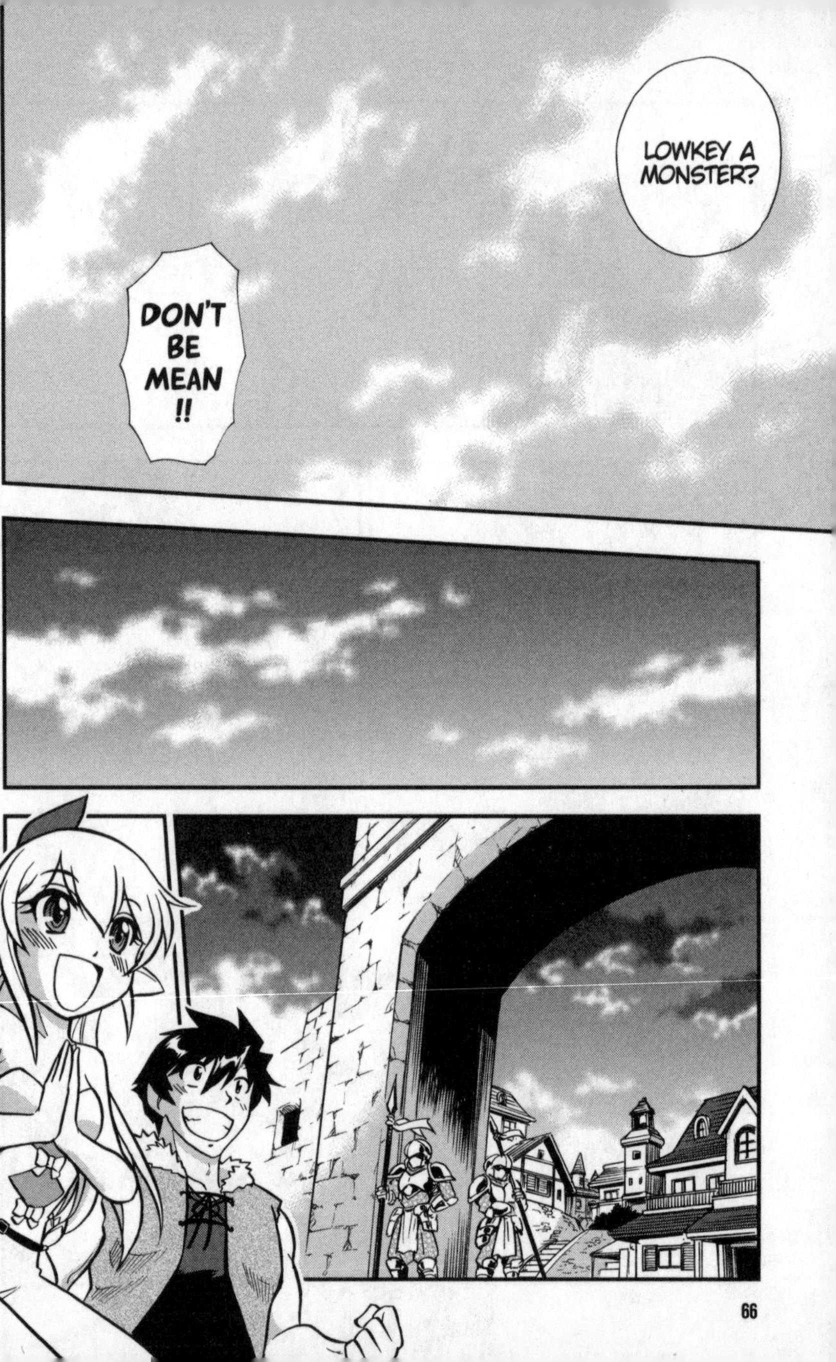
LOWKEY A MONSTER?
DON'T BE MEAN !!

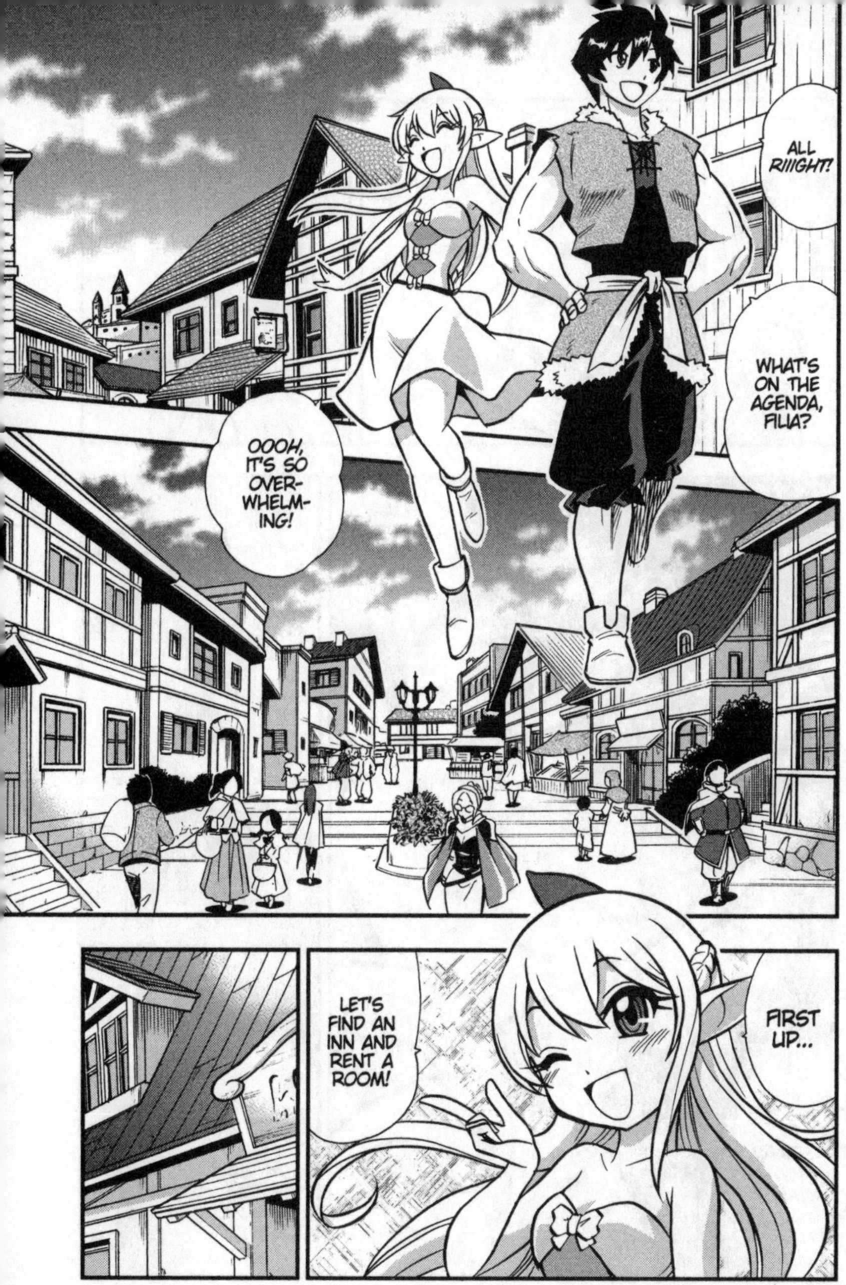
ALL RIIIGHT!
WHAT'S ON THE AGENDA, FILIA?
OOOH, IT'S SO OVER-WHELM-ING!
FIRST UP...
LET'S FIND AN INN AND RENT A ROOM!

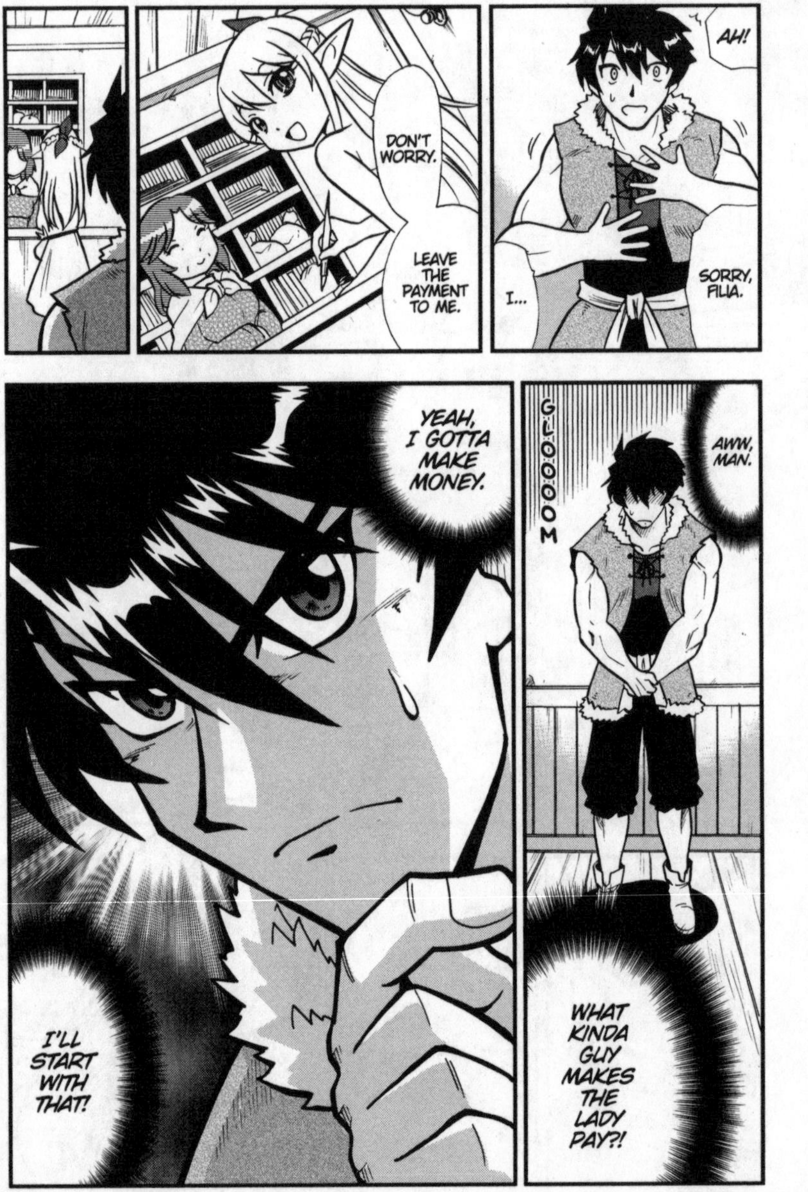
AH!
SORRY, FILIA.
I...
DON'T WORRY.
LEAVE THE PAYMENT TO ME.
GLOOOOOM
AWW, MAN.
WHAT KINDA GUY MAKES THE LADY PAY?!
YEAH, I GOTTA MAKE MONEY.
I'LL START WITH THAT!

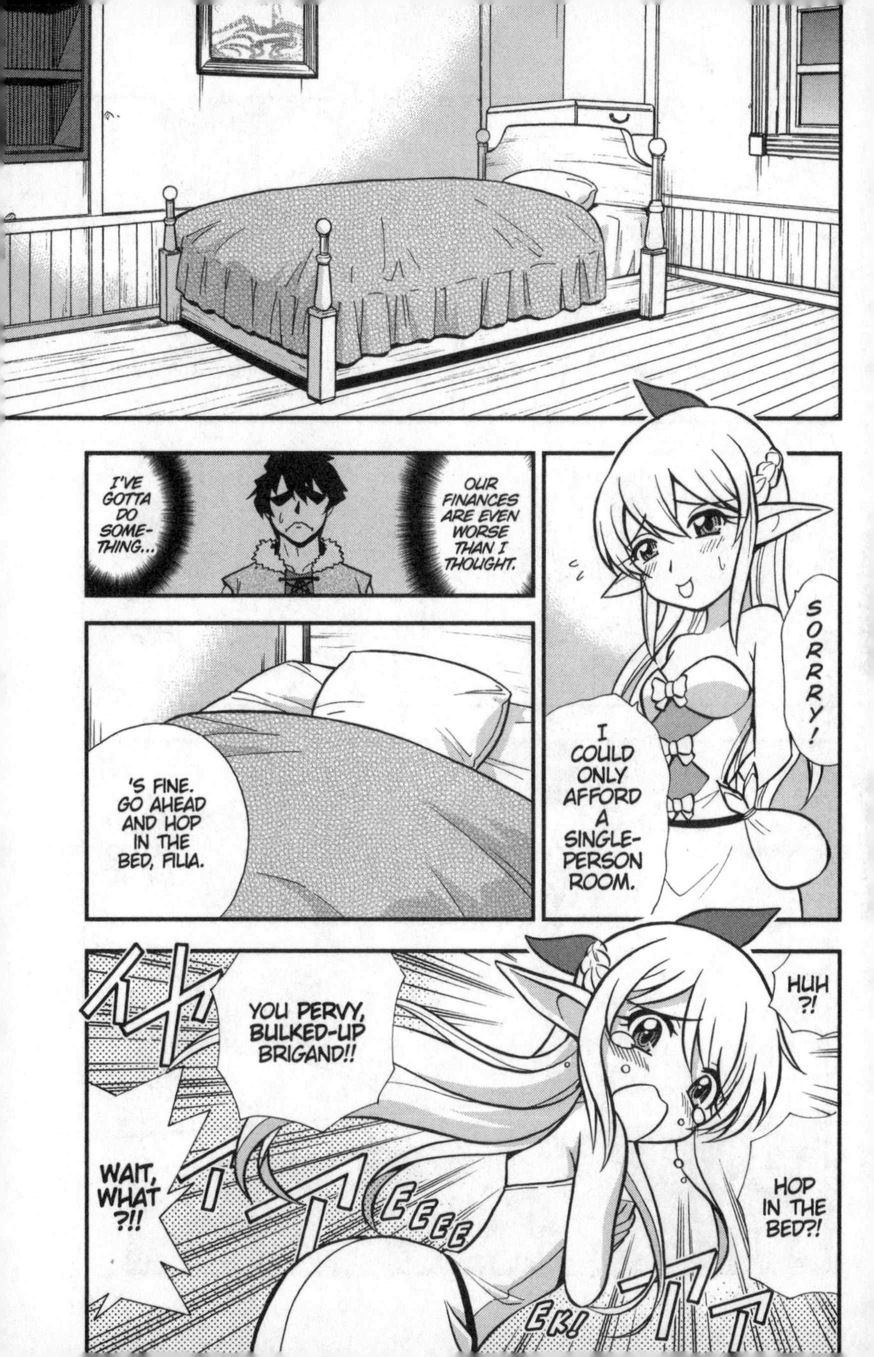
SORRRY!
I COULD ONLY AFFORD A SINGLE-PERSON ROOM.
OUR FINANCES ARE EVEN WORSE THAN I THOUGHT.
I'VE GOTTA DO SOME-THING...
'S FINE. GO AHEAD AND HOP IN THE BED, FILIA.
HUH?!
HOP IN THE BED?!
YOU PERVY, BULKED-UP BRIGAND!!
EEEE
EK!
WAIT, WHAT?!!

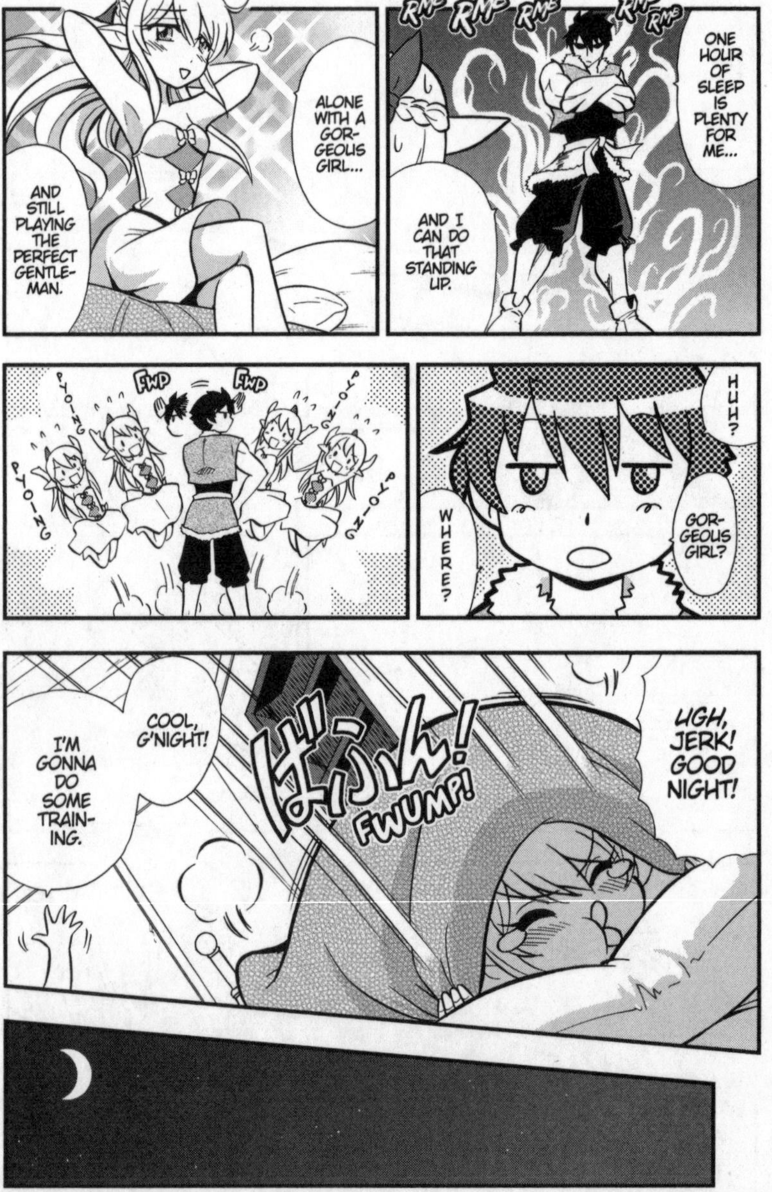
RMB RMB RMB RMB RMB
ONE HOUR OF SLEEP IS PLENTY FOR ME...
AND I CAN DO THAT STANDING UP.
ALONE WITH A GORGEOUS GIRL...
AND STILL PLAYING THE PERFECT GENTLEMAN.
HUH?
GORGEOUS GIRL?
WHERE?
FWP FWP
PYOING PYOING PYOING PYOING
UGH, JERK! GOOD NIGHT!
ばふん!
FWUMP!
COOL, G'NIGHT!
I'M GONNA DO SOME TRAINING.

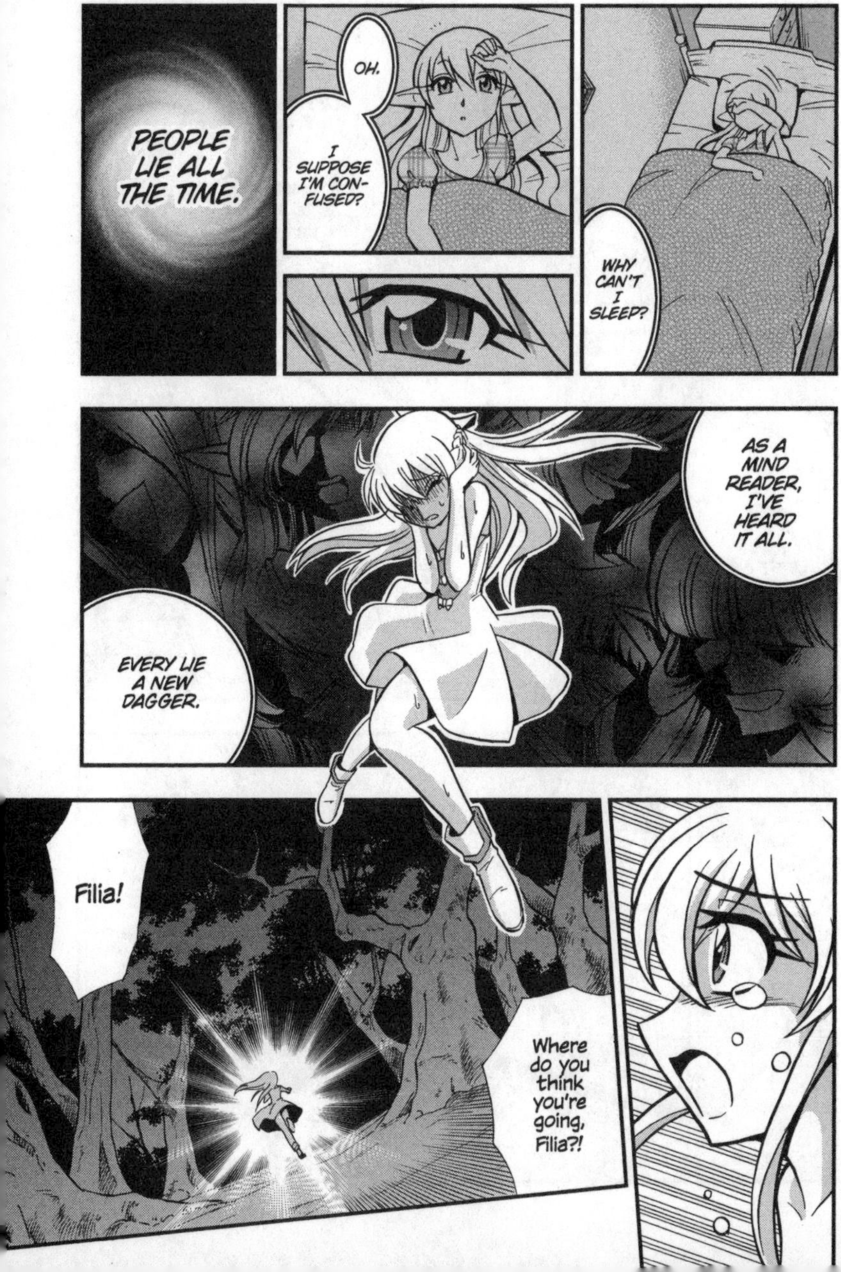
WHY CAN'T I SLEEP?
OH.
I SUPPOSE I'M CON-FUSED?
PEOPLE LIE ALL THE TIME.
AS A MIND READER, I'VE HEARD IT ALL.
EVERY LIE A NEW DAGGER.
Where do you think you're going, Filia?!
Filia!

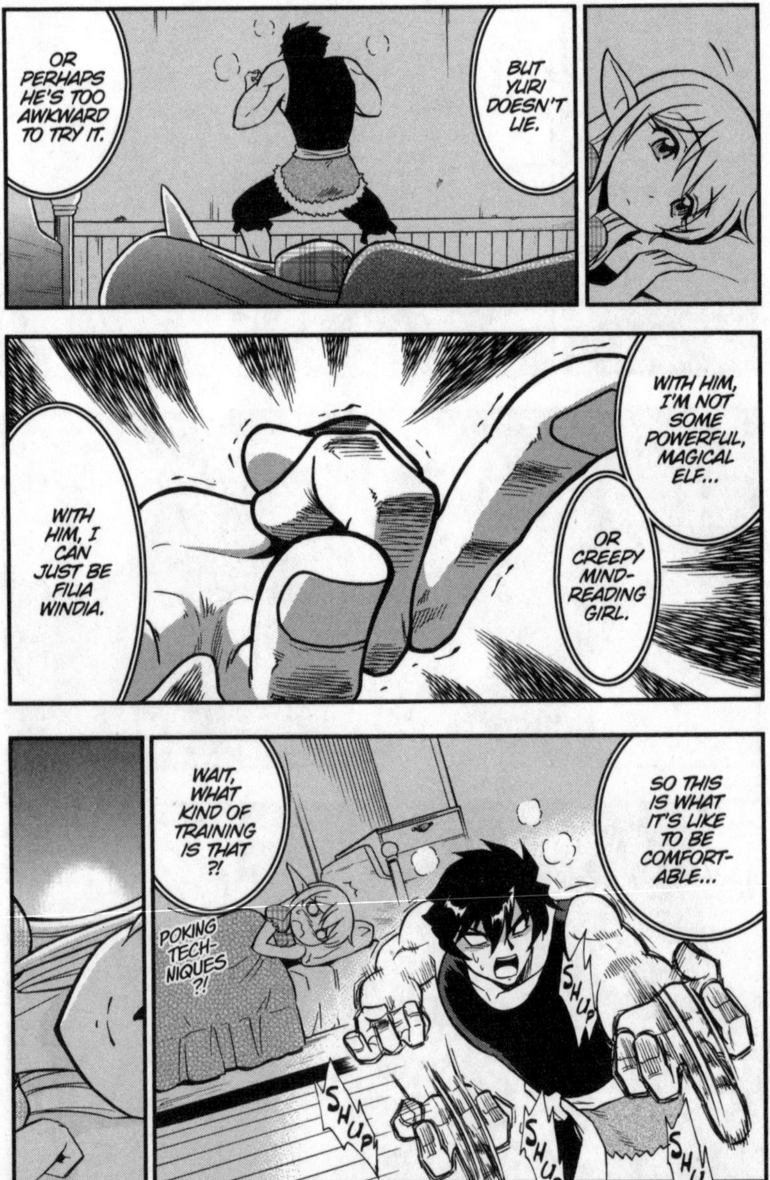
BUT YURI DOESN'T LIE.
OR PERHAPS HE'S TOO AWKWARD TO TRY IT.
WITH HIM, I'M NOT SOME POWERFUL, MAGICAL ELF...
OR CREEPY MIND-READING GIRL.
WITH HIM, I CAN JUST BE FILIA WINDIA.
SO THIS IS WHAT IT'S LIKE TO BE COMFORT-ABLE...
WAIT, WHAT KIND OF TRAINING IS THAT ?!
POKING TECH-NIQUES ?!
SHUP
SHUP
SHUP
SHUP

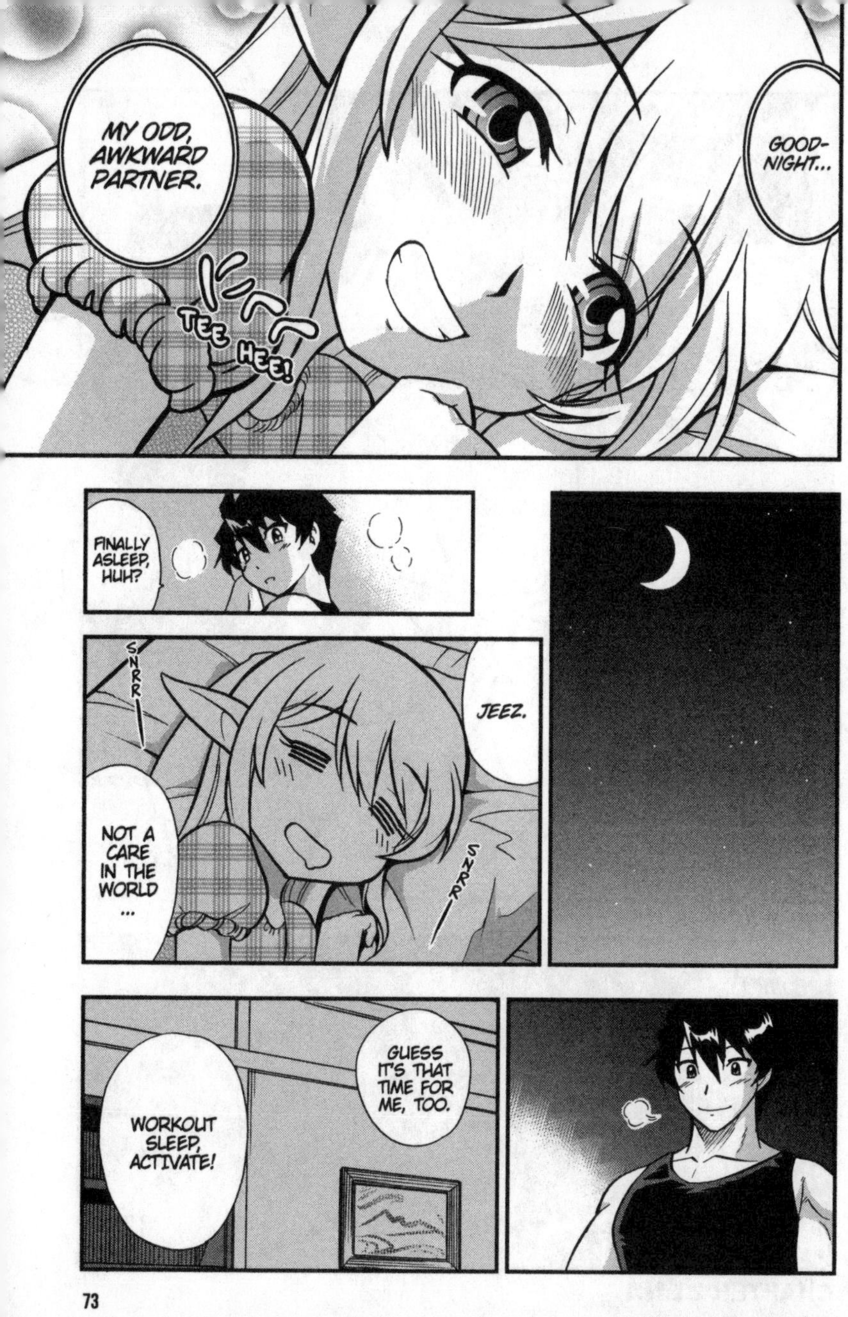
GOOD-NIGHT...
MY ODD, AWKWARD PARTNER.
TEE HEE!
FINALLY ASLEEP, HUH?
JEEZ.
SNRR—
NOT A CARE IN THE WORLD...
SNRR—
GUESS IT'S THAT TIME FOR ME, TOO.
WORKOUT SLEEP, ACTIVATE!

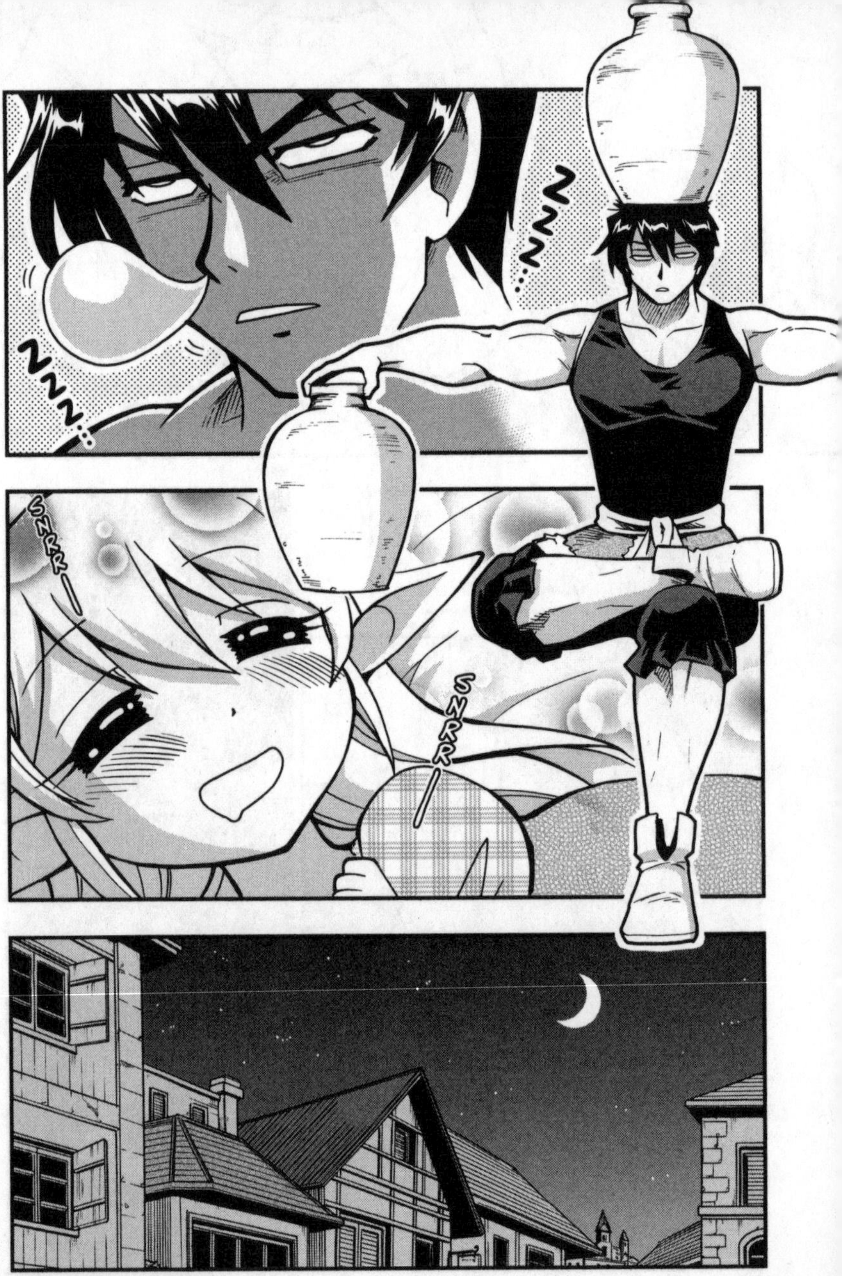
ZZZ...
ZZZ...
SNRR—
SNRR—

CHAPTER 2 END

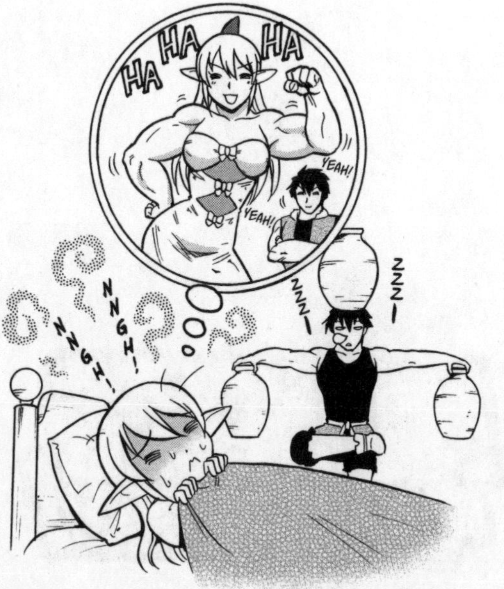
HA HA HA
YEAH!
YEAH!
ZZZ
ZZZ
NNGH!
NNGH!

MUSCLES ARE BETTER THAN MAGIC!

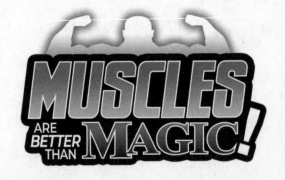

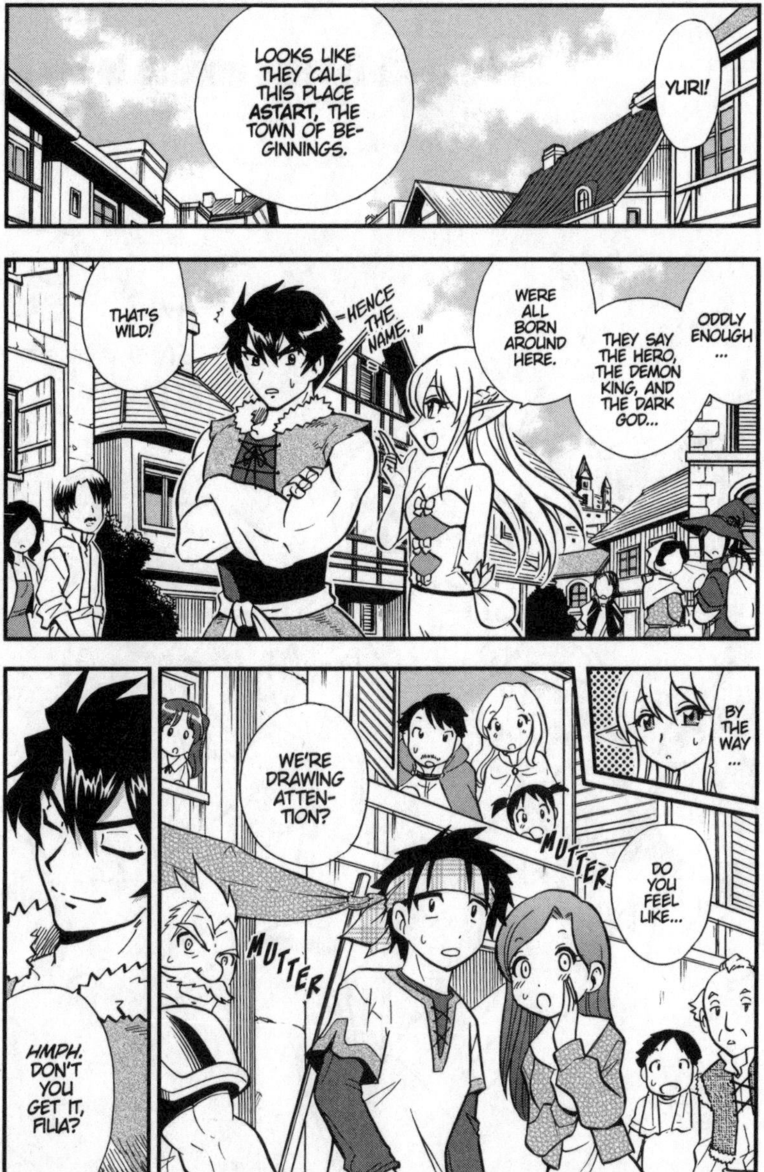
YURI!
LOOKS LIKE THEY CALL THIS PLACE ASTART, THE TOWN OF BE-GINNINGS.
ODDLY ENOUGH...
THEY SAY THE HERO, THE DEMON KING, AND THE DARK GOD...
WERE ALL BORN AROUND HERE.
=HENCE THE NAME.
THAT'S WILD!
BY THE WAY...
DO YOU FEEL LIKE...
WE'RE DRAWING ATTEN-TION?
MUTTER
MUTTER
HMPH. DON'T YOU GET IT, FILIA?

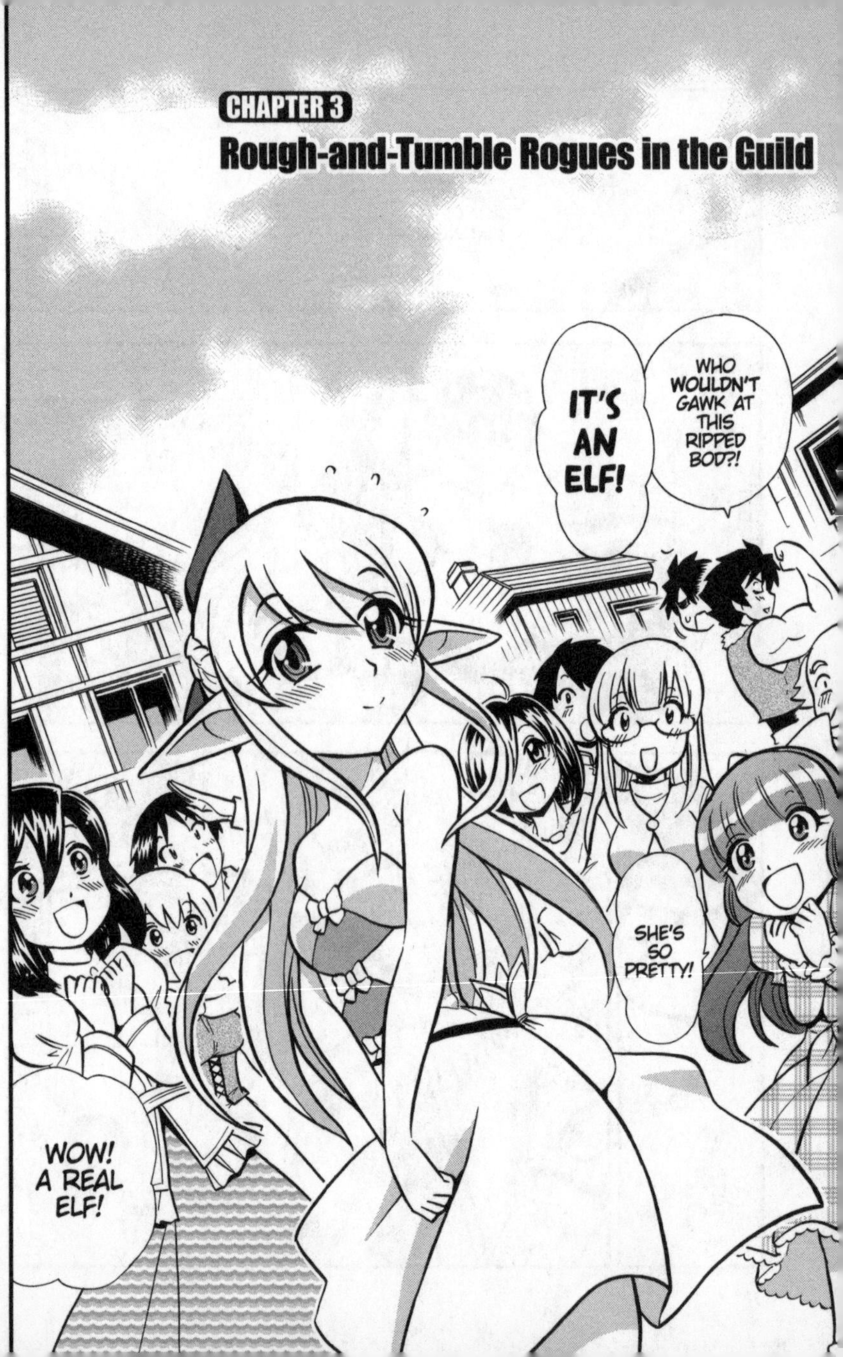
CHAPTER 3
Rough-and-Tumble Rogues in the Guild
WHO WOULDN'T GAWK AT THIS RIPPED BOD?!
IT'S AN ELF!
SHE'S SO PRETTY!
WOW! A REAL ELF!

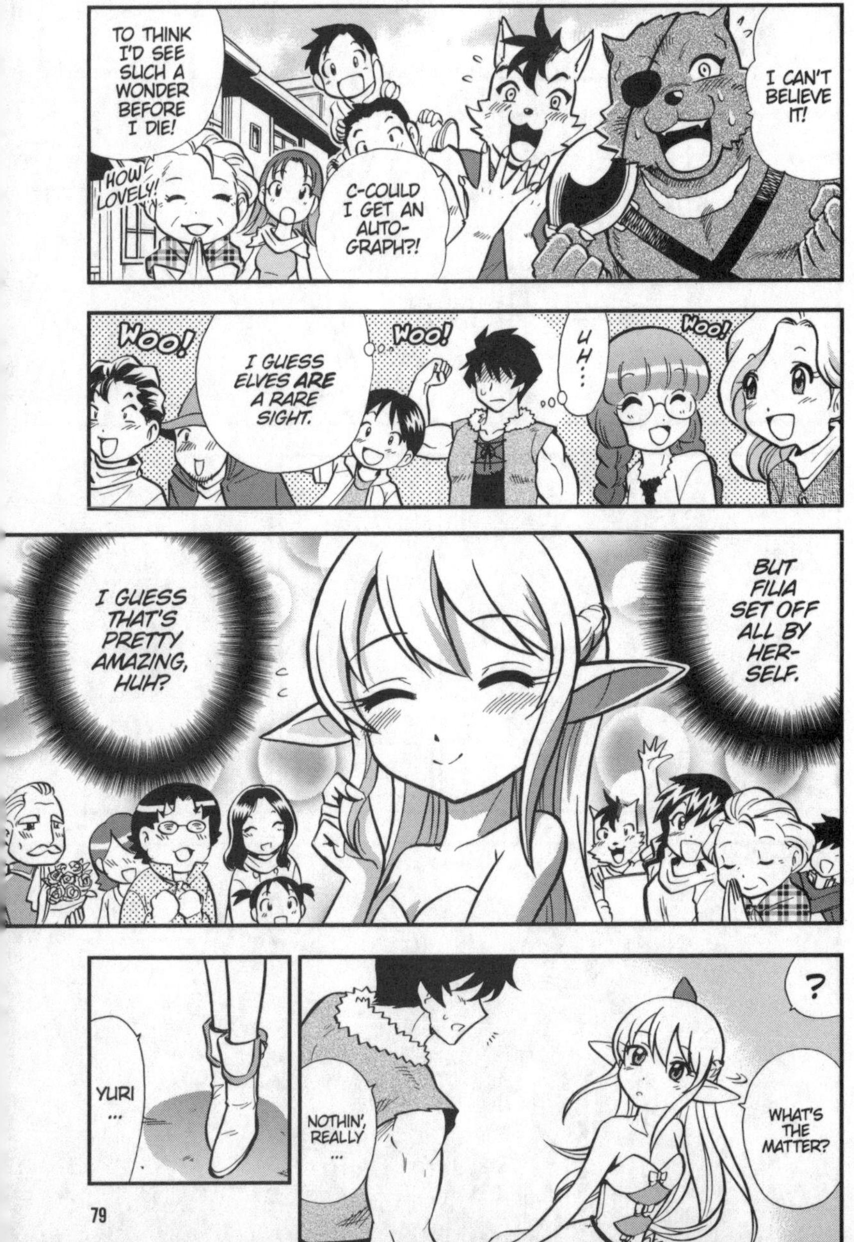
I CAN'T BELIEVE IT!
TO THINK I'D SEE SUCH A WONDER BEFORE I DIE!
C-COULD I GET AN AUTO-GRAPH?!
HOW LOVELY!
WOO!
UH...
WOO!
I GUESS ELVES ARE A RARE SIGHT.
WOO!
BUT FILIA SET OFF ALL BY HER-SELF.
I GUESS THAT'S PRETTY AMAZING, HUH?
?
WHAT'S THE MATTER?
NOTHIN', REALLY ...
YURI ...

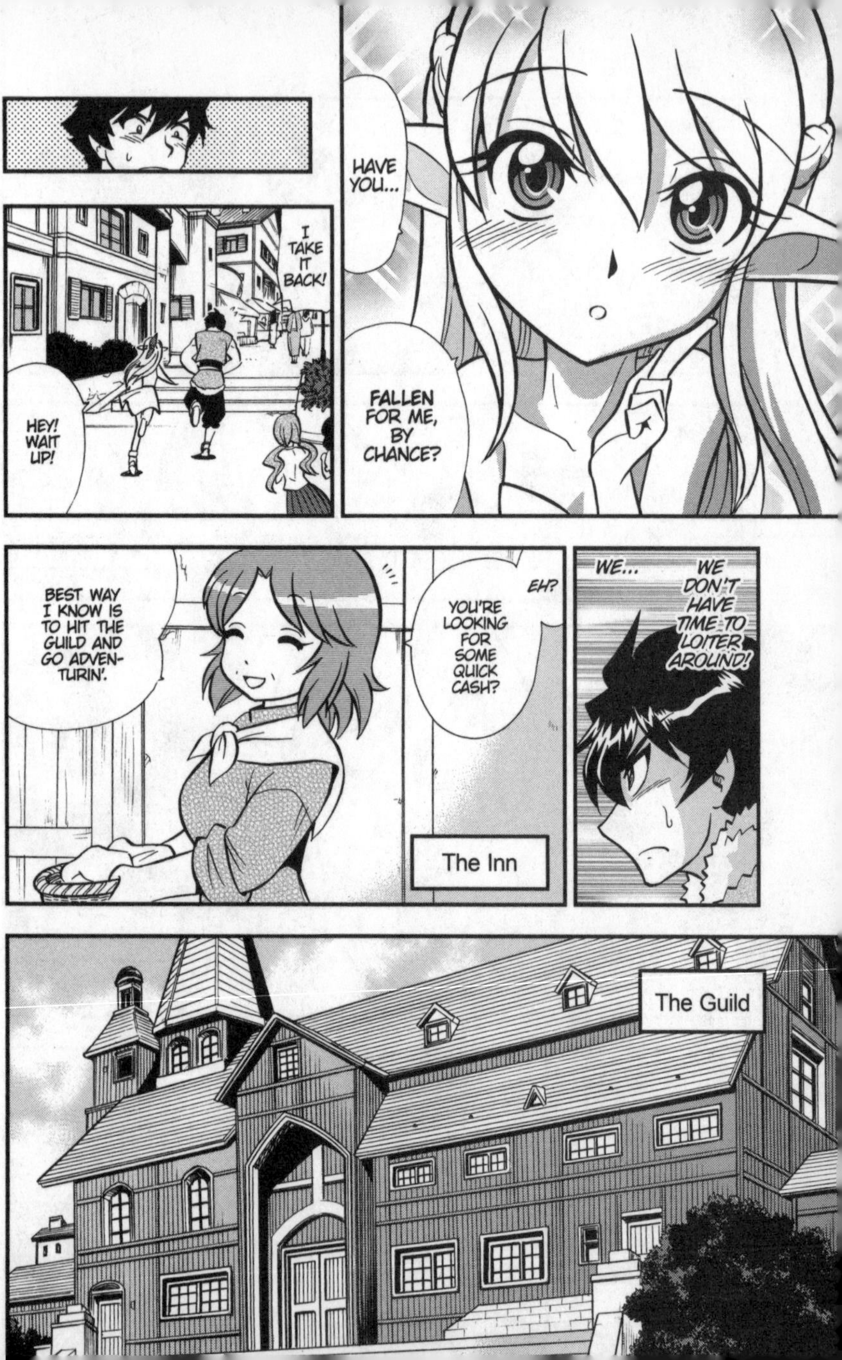
HAVE YOU...
FALLEN FOR ME, BY CHANCE?
I TAKE IT BACK!
HEY! WAIT UP!
WE...
WE DON'T HAVE TIME TO LOITER AROUND!
The Inn
EH?
YOU'RE LOOKING FOR SOME QUICK CASH?
BEST WAY I KNOW IS TO HIT THE GUILD AND GO ADVENTURIN'.
The Guild

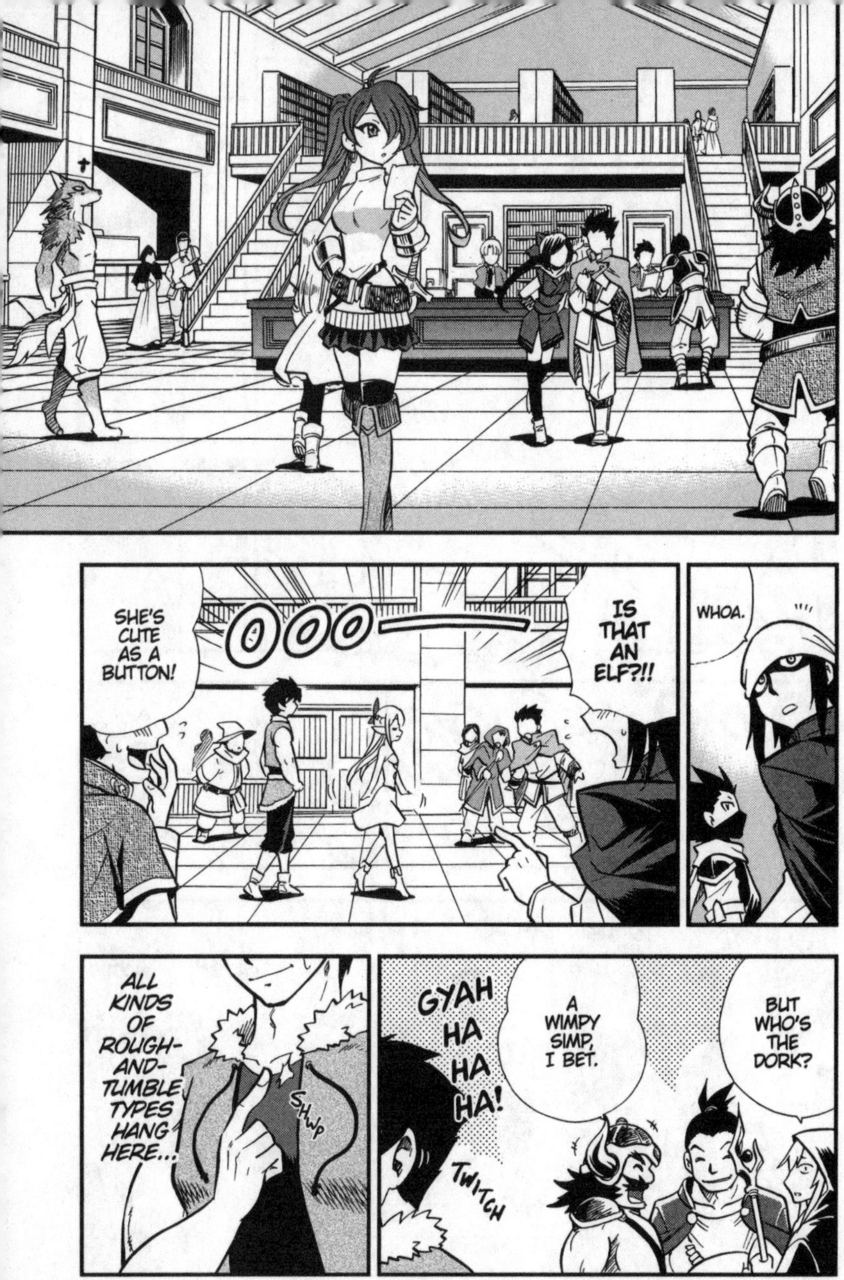
WHOA.
IS THAT AN ELF?!!
OOO—
SHE'S CUTE AS A BUTTON!
BUT WHO'S THE DORK?
A WIMPY SIMP, I BET.
GYAH HA HA HA!
TWITCH
ALL KINDS OF ROUGH-AND-TUMBLE TYPES HANG HERE...
SHWP

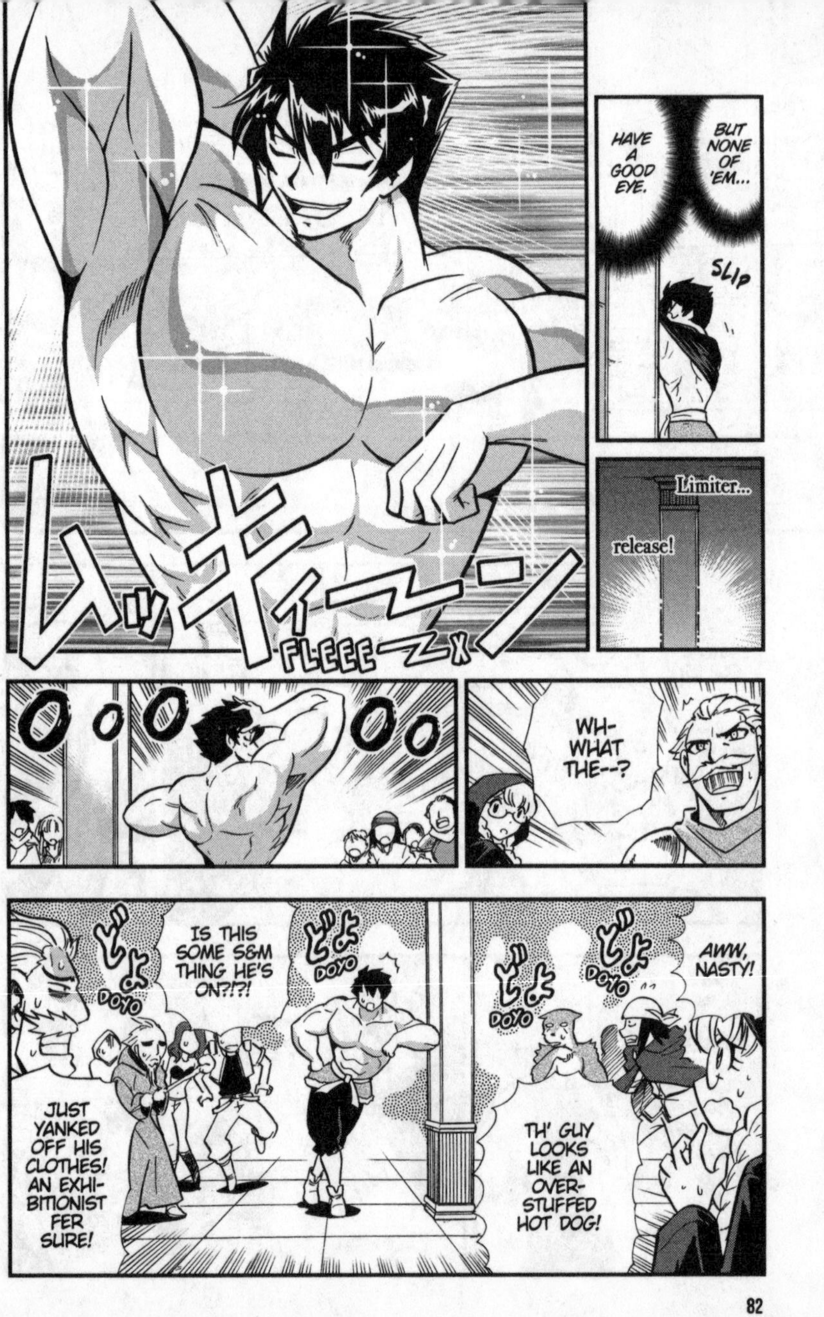
BUT NONE OF 'EM...
HAVE A GOOD EYE.
SLIP
Limiter...
release!
ムッキィーン
FLEEEZX
WH-WHAT THE--?
AWW, NASTY!
どよ
DOYO
TH' GUY LOOKS LIKE AN OVER-STUFFED HOT DOG!
どよ
DOYO
どよ
DOYO
IS THIS SOME S&M THING HE'S ON?!?!
どよ
DOYO
JUST YANKED OFF HIS CLOTHES! AN EXHIBITIONIST FER SURE!

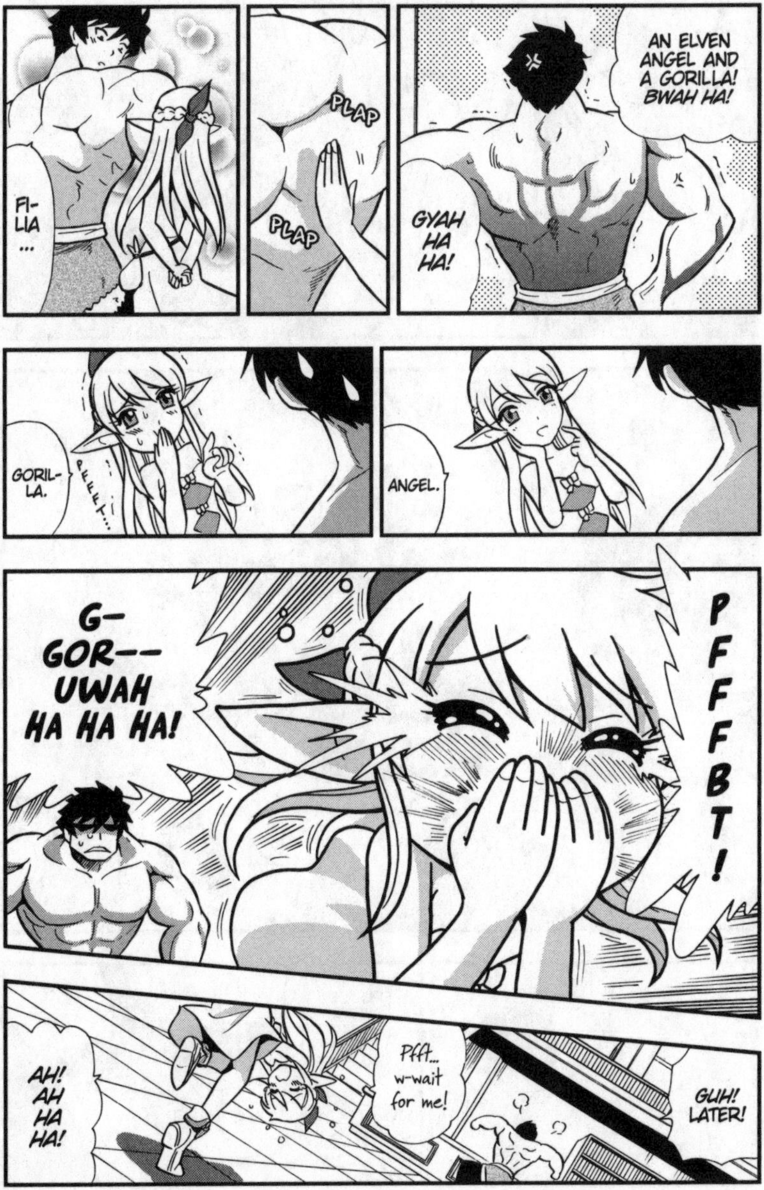
AN ELVEN ANGEL AND A GORILLA! BWAH HA!
GYAH HA HA!
PLAP
PLAP
FI-LIA...
ANGEL.
GORIL-LA.
PFFFT...
PFFFBT!
G-GOR--- UWAH HA HA HA!
GUH! LATER!
Pfft... w-wait for me!
AH! AH HA HA!

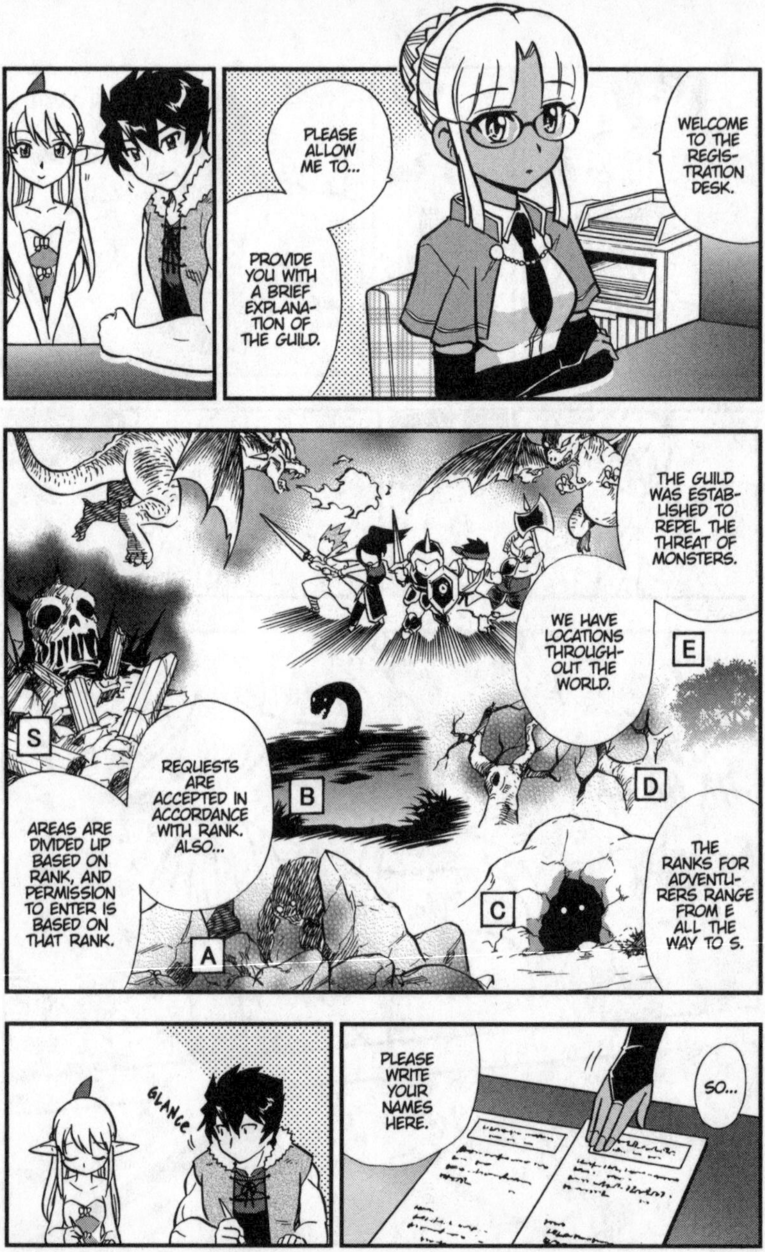
WELCOME TO THE REGIS-TRATION DESK.
PLEASE ALLOW ME TO...
PROVIDE YOU WITH A BRIEF EXPLANA-TION OF THE GUILD.
THE GUILD WAS ESTAB-LISHED TO REPEL THE THREAT OF MONSTERS.
WE HAVE LOCATIONS THROUGH-OUT THE WORLD.
E
D
THE RANKS FOR ADVENTU-RERS RANGE FROM E ALL THE WAY TO S.
C
REQUESTS ARE ACCEPTED IN ACCORDANCE WITH RANK. ALSO...
B
S
AREAS ARE DIVIDED UP BASED ON RANK, AND PERMISSION TO ENTER IS BASED ON THAT RANK.
A
SO...
PLEASE WRITE YOUR NAMES HERE.
GLANCE

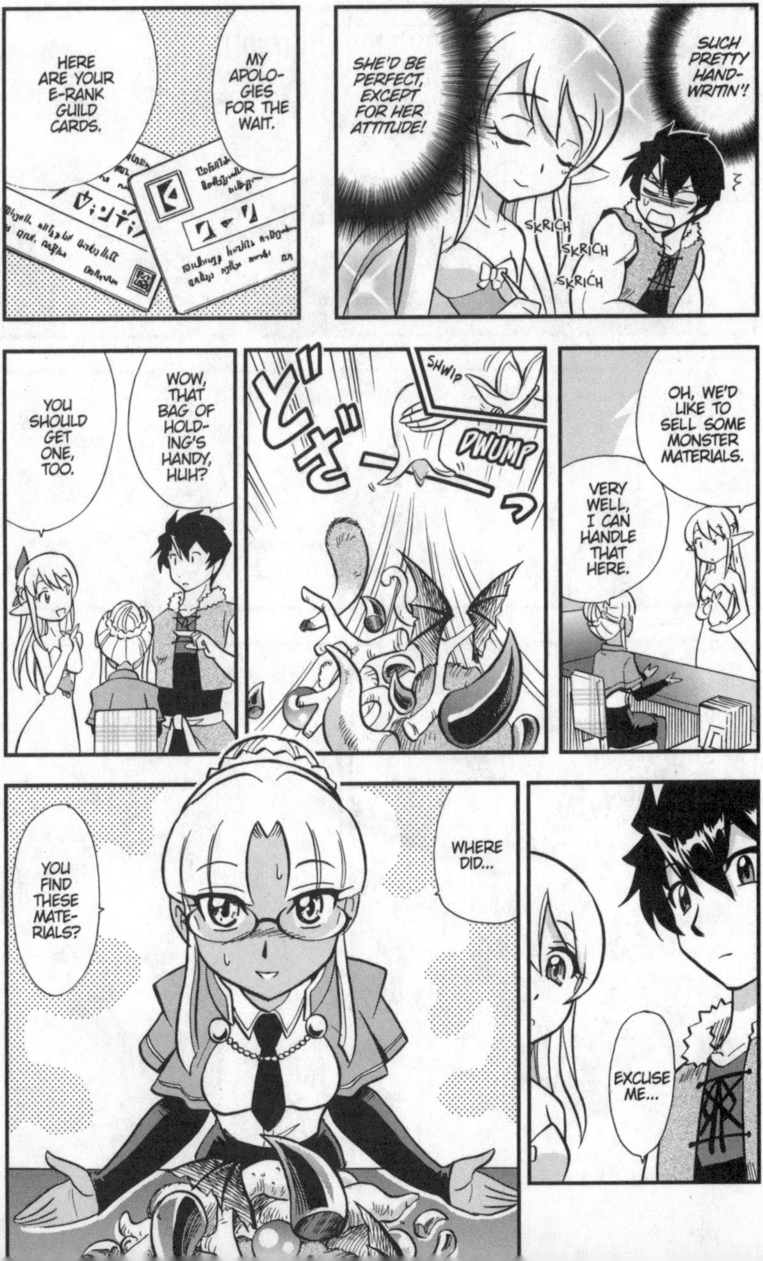
SUCH PRETTY HAND-WRITIN'!
SHE'D BE PERFECT, EXCEPT FOR HER ATTITUDE!
SKRICH
SKRICH
SKRICH
MY APOLOGIES FOR THE WAIT.
HERE ARE YOUR E-RANK GUILD CARDS.
OH, WE'D LIKE TO SELL SOME MONSTER MATERIALS.
VERY WELL, I CAN HANDLE THAT HERE.
SHWIP
DWUMP
どざーっ
WOW, THAT BAG OF HOLDING'S HANDY, HUH?
YOU SHOULD GET ONE, TOO.
EXCUSE ME...
WHERE DID...
YOU FIND THESE MATERIALS?

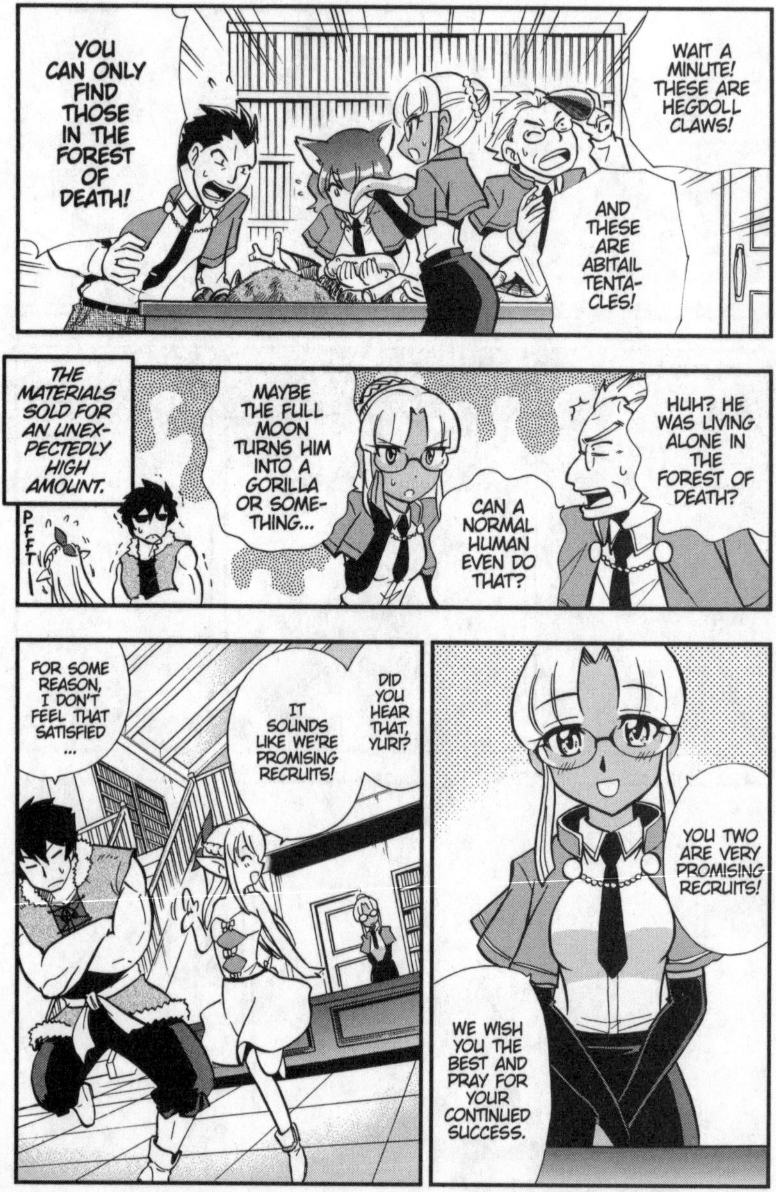
WAIT A MINUTE! THESE ARE HEGDOLL CLAWS!
AND THESE ARE ABITAIL TENTA-CLES!
YOU CAN ONLY FIND THOSE IN THE FOREST OF DEATH!
HUH? HE WAS LIVING ALONE IN THE FOREST OF DEATH?
CAN A NORMAL HUMAN EVEN DO THAT?
MAYBE THE FULL MOON TURNS HIM INTO A GORILLA OR SOME-THING...
THE MATERIALS SOLD FOR AN UNEX-PECTEDLY HIGH AMOUNT.
PFFT
YOU TWO ARE VERY PROMISING RECRUITS!
WE WISH YOU THE BEST AND PRAY FOR YOUR CONTINUED SUCCESS.
DID YOU HEAR THAT, YURI?
IT SOUNDS LIKE WE'RE PROMISING RECRUITS!
FOR SOME REASON, I DON'T FEEL THAT SATISFIED ...

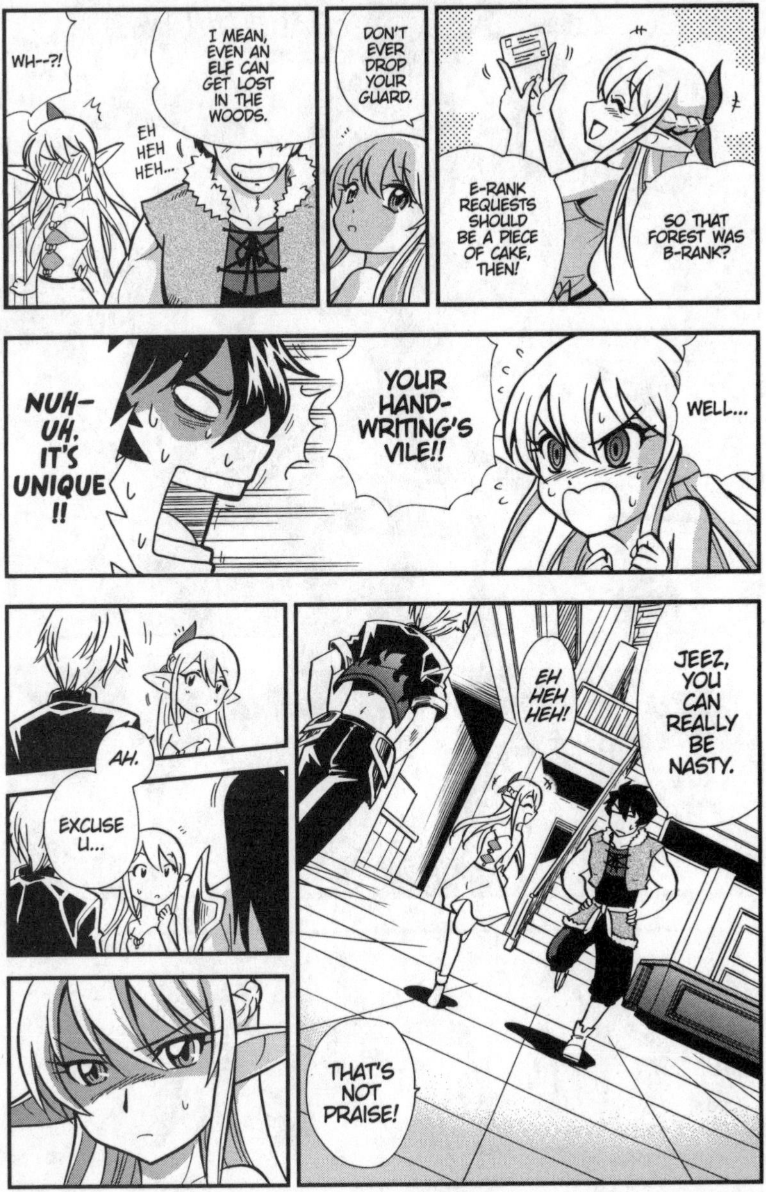
SO THAT FOREST WAS B-RANK?
E-RANK REQUESTS SHOULD BE A PIECE OF CAKE, THEN!
DON'T EVER DROP YOUR GUARD.
I MEAN, EVEN AN ELF CAN GET LOST IN THE WOODS.
EH HEH HEH...
WH--?!
WELL...
YOUR HAND-WRITING'S VILE!!
NUH-UH. IT'S UNIQUE!!
JEEZ, YOU CAN REALLY BE NASTY.
EH HEH HEH!
THAT'S NOT PRAISE!
AH.
EXCUSE U...

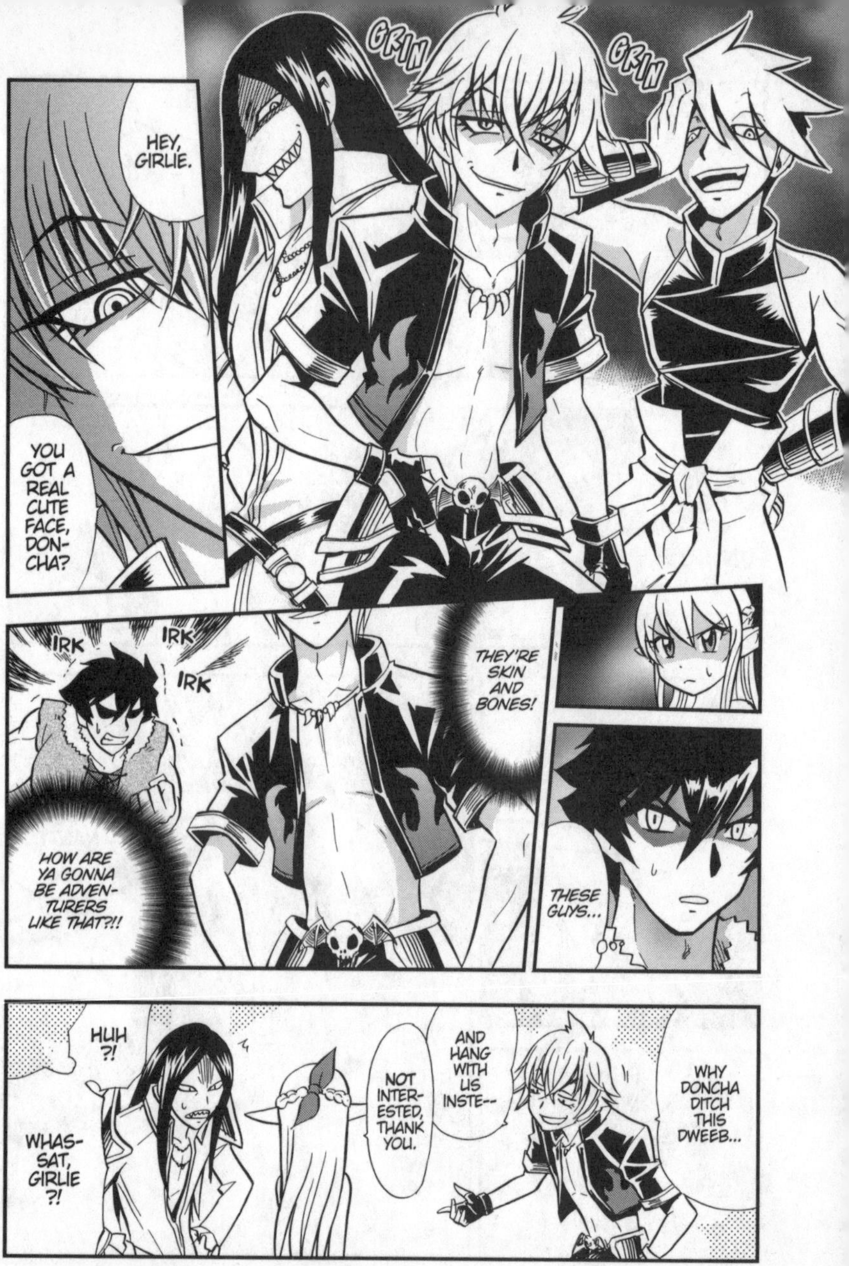
GRIN
GRIN
HEY, GIRLIE.
YOU GOT A REAL CUTE FACE, DON-CHA?
THESE GUYS...
THEY'RE SKIN AND BONES!
IRK
IRK
IRK
HOW ARE YA GONNA BE ADVEN-TURERS LIKE THAT?!!
WHY DONCHA DITCH THIS DWEEB...
AND HANG WITH US INSTE--
NOT INTER-ESTED, THANK YOU.
HUH?!
WHAS-SAT, GIRLIE?!

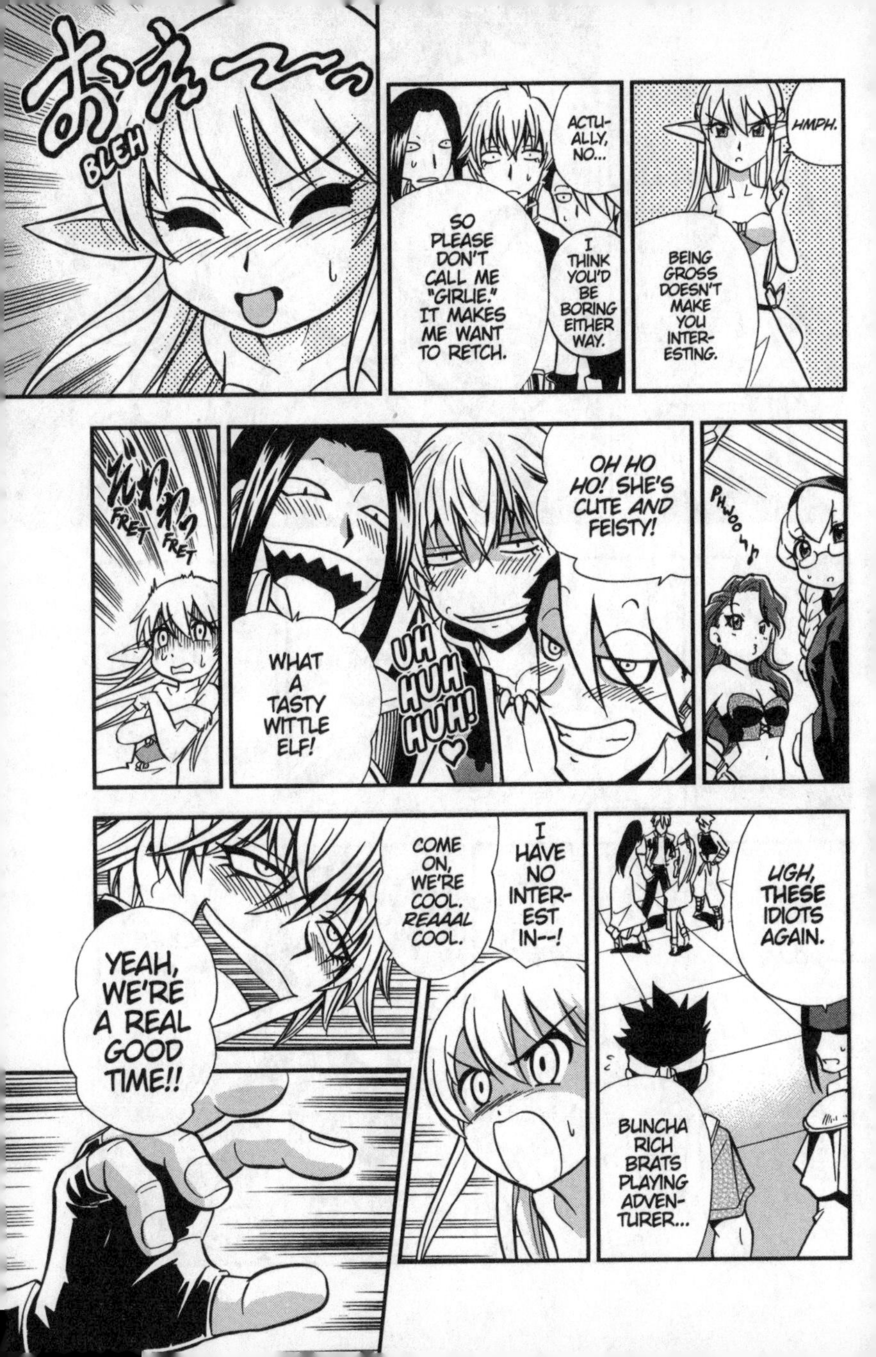
HMPH.
BEING GROSS DOESN'T MAKE YOU INTER-ESTING.
ACTU-ALLY, NO...
I THINK YOU'D BE BORING EITHER WAY.
SO PLEASE DON'T CALL ME "GIRLIE." IT MAKES ME WANT TO RETCH.
おえ〜〜
BLEH
PHWOO♪
OH HO HO! SHE'S CUTE AND FEISTY!
UH HUH HUH! ♡
WHAT A TASTY WITTLE ELF!
FRET FRET
UGH, THESE IDIOTS AGAIN.
BUNCHA RICH BRATS PLAYING ADVEN-TURER...
I HAVE NO INTER-EST IN--!
COME ON, WE'RE COOL. REAAAL COOL.
YEAH, WE'RE A REAL GOOD TIME!!

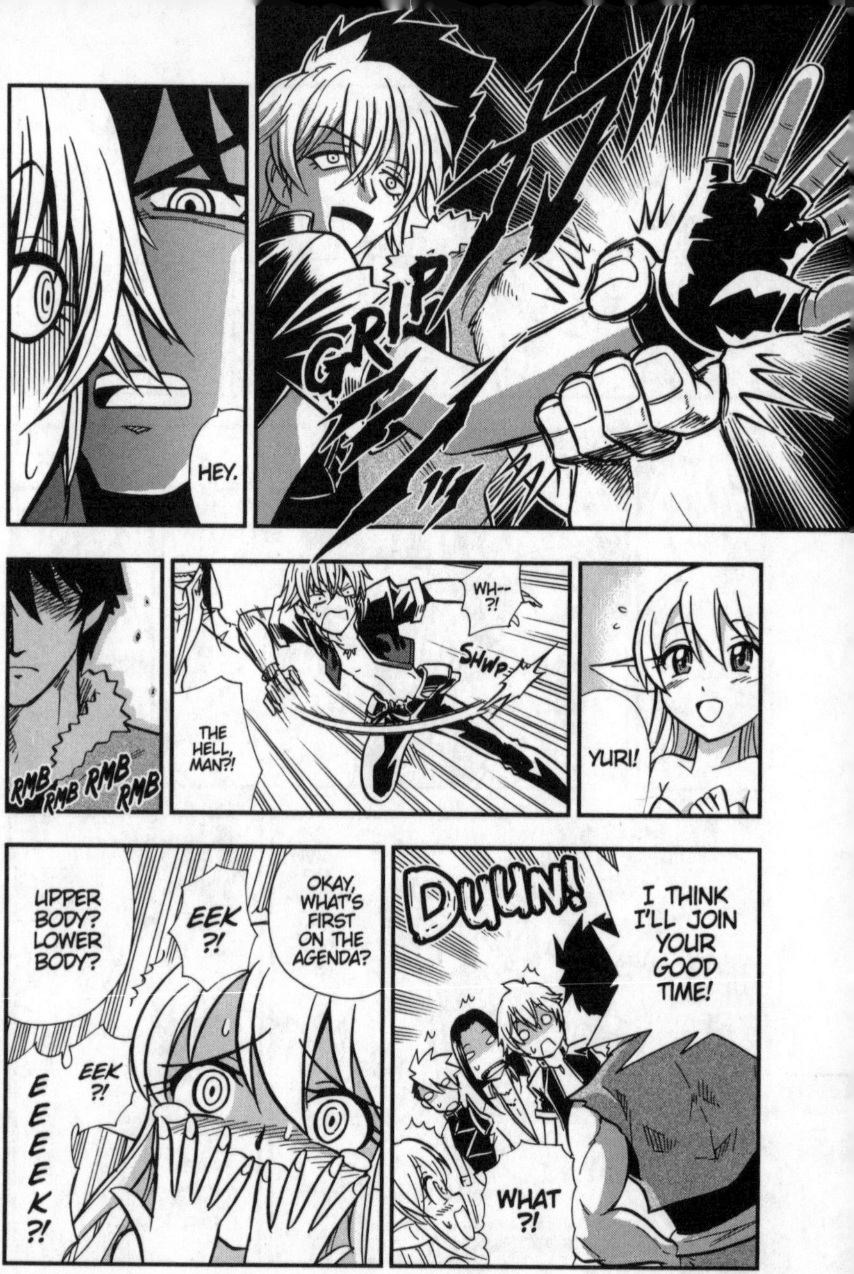

GRIP
HEY.
YURI!
WH--?!
SHWP
THE HELL, MAN?!
RMB RMB RMB RMB
DUUN!
I THINK I'LL JOIN YOUR GOOD TIME!
WHAT?!
OKAY, WHAT'S FIRST ON THE AGENDA?
EEK?!
UPPER BODY? LOWER BODY?
EEK?!
EEEEEK?!

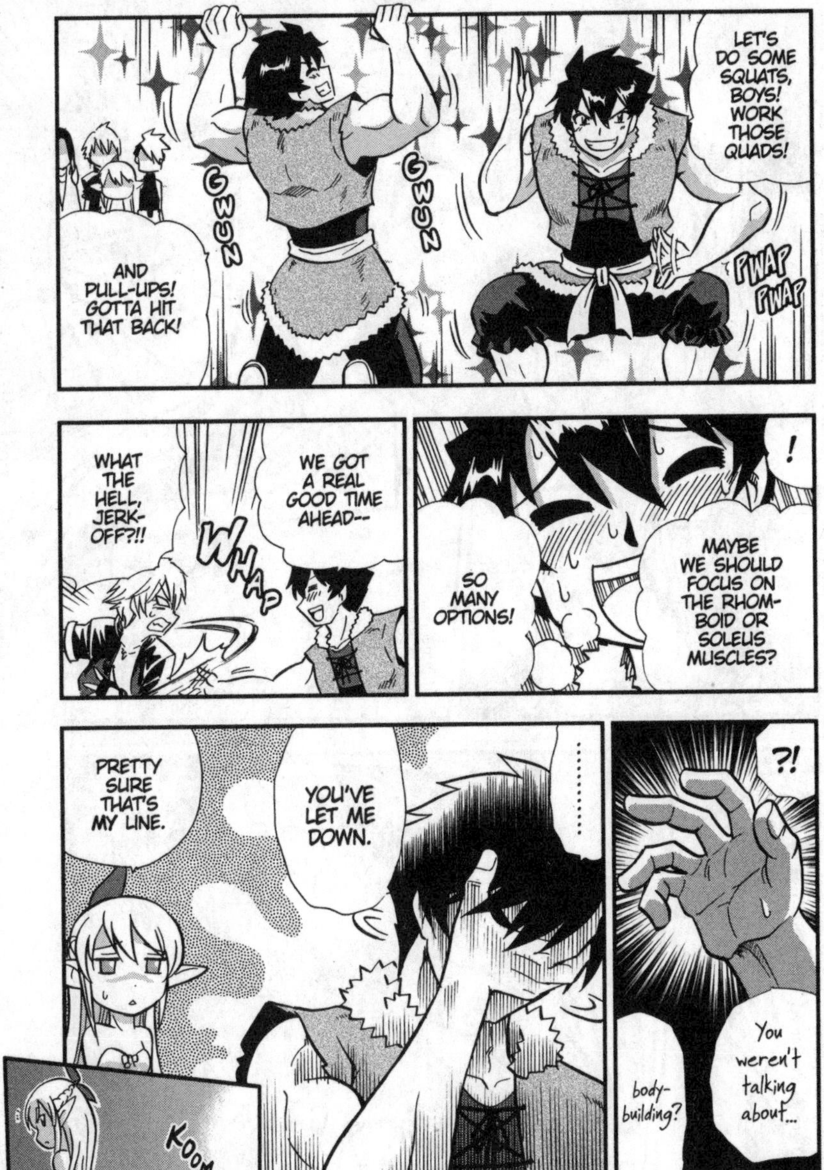
LET'S DO SOME SQUATS, BOYS! WORK THOSE QUADS!
PWAP PWAP
GWUN
GWUN
AND PULL-UPS! GOTTA HIT THAT BACK!
!
MAYBE WE SHOULD FOCUS ON THE RHOM-BOID OR SOLEUS MUSCLES?
SO MANY OPTIONS!
WE GOT A REAL GOOD TIME AHEAD--
WHAP
WHAT THE HELL, JERK-OFF?!!
?!
You weren't talking about...
body-building?
......
YOU'VE LET ME DOWN.
PRETTY SURE THAT'S MY LINE.
KOOM...

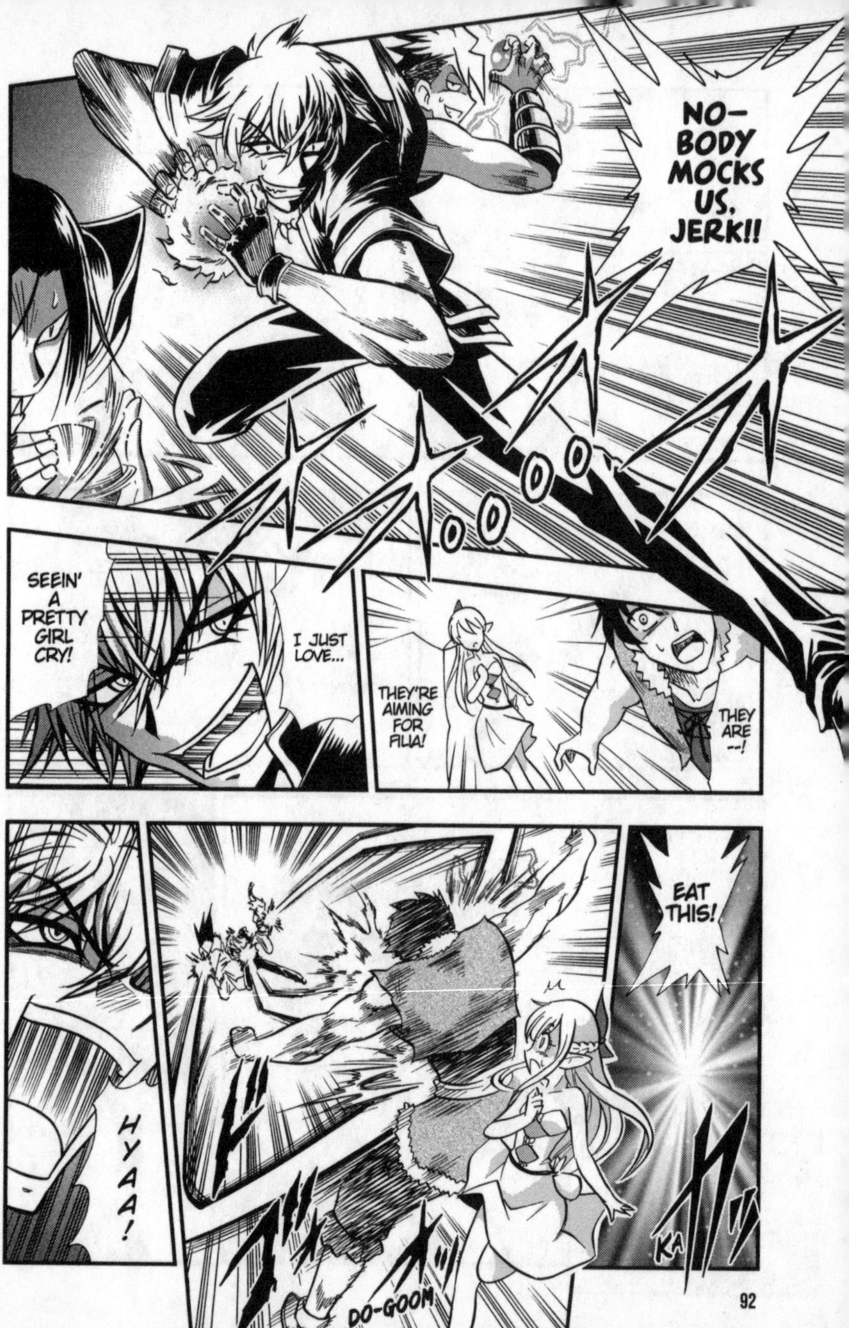
NO-BODY MOCKS US, JERK!!
OOOOO
THEY ARE --!
THEY'RE AIMING FOR FILIA!
I JUST LOVE...
SEEIN' A PRETTY GIRL CRY!
EAT THIS!
KA
DO-GOOM
HYAAA!

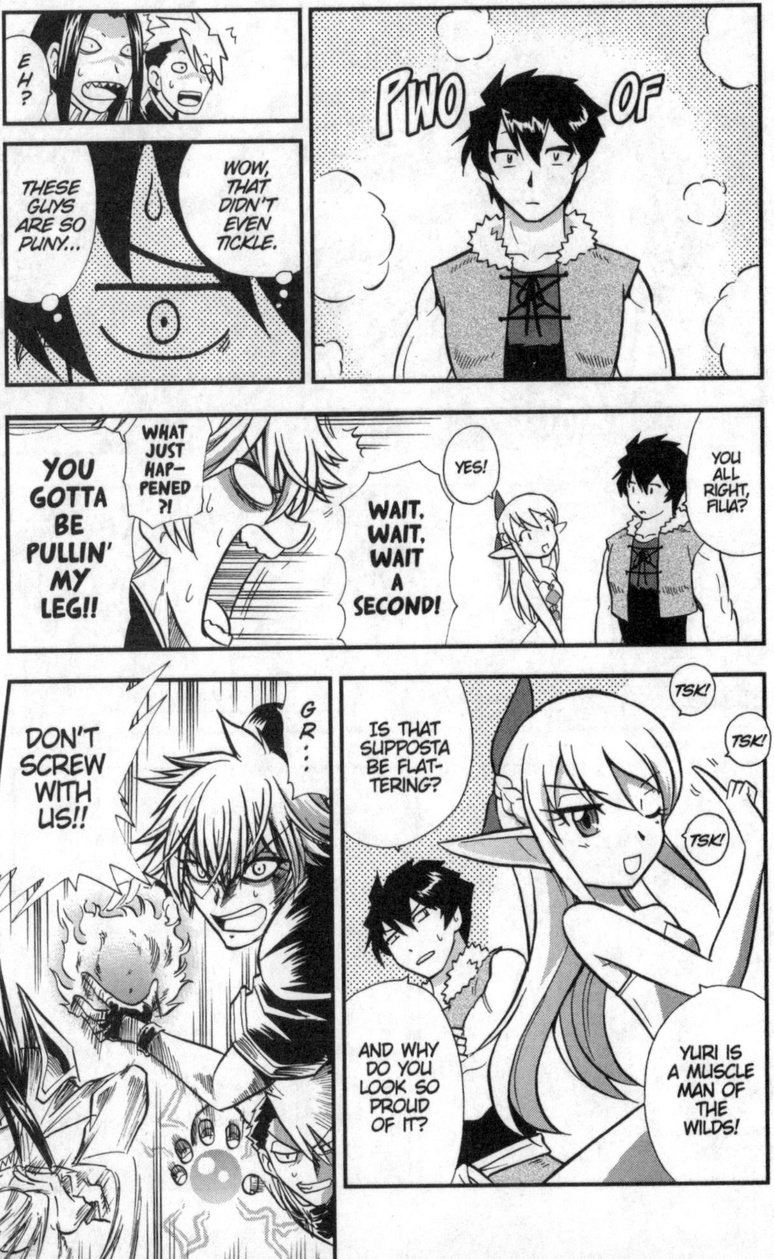
PWO OF
EH?
WOW, THAT DIDN'T EVEN TICKLE.
THESE GUYS ARE SO PUNY...
YOU ALL RIGHT, FILIA?
YES!
WAIT, WAIT, WAIT A SECOND!
WHAT JUST HAP-PENED?!
YOU GOTTA BE PULLIN' MY LEG!!
TSK!
TSK!
TSK!
YURI IS A MUSCLE MAN OF THE WILDS!
IS THAT SUPPOSTA BE FLAT-TERING?
AND WHY DO YOU LOOK SO PROUD OF IT?
GR...
DON'T SCREW WITH US!!

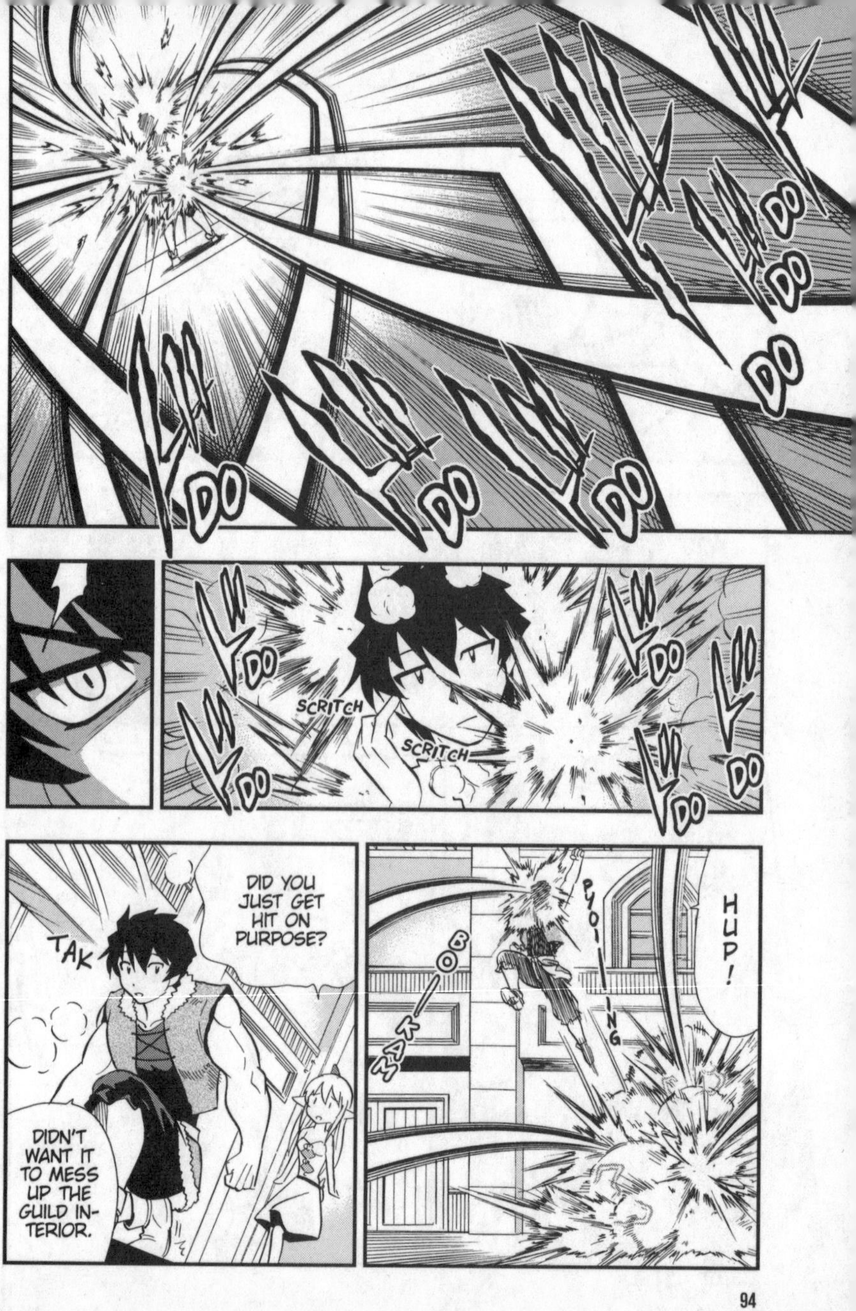
DO
DO
DO
DO
DO
DO
DO
DO
DO
DO
SCRITCH
SCRITCH
DO
DO
HUP!
PYOI--ING
BOI--KAM
DID YOU JUST GET HIT ON PURPOSE?
TAK
DIDN'T WANT IT TO MESS UP THE GUILD INTERIOR.

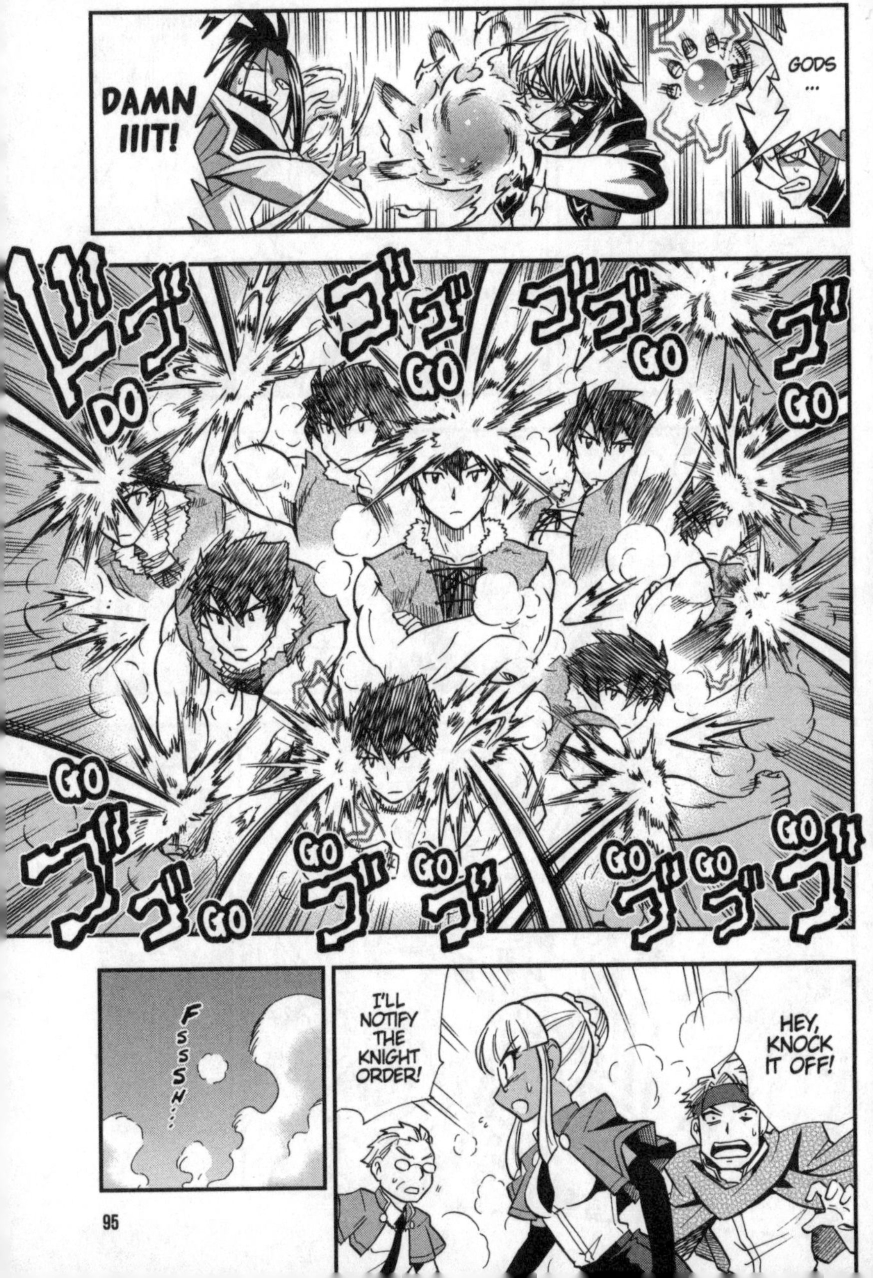
GODS ...
DAMN IIIT!
GO
GO
GO
DO
GO
GO
GO
GO
GO
GO
GO
HEY, KNOCK IT OFF!
I'LL NOTIFY THE KNIGHT ORDER!
FSSSSH...

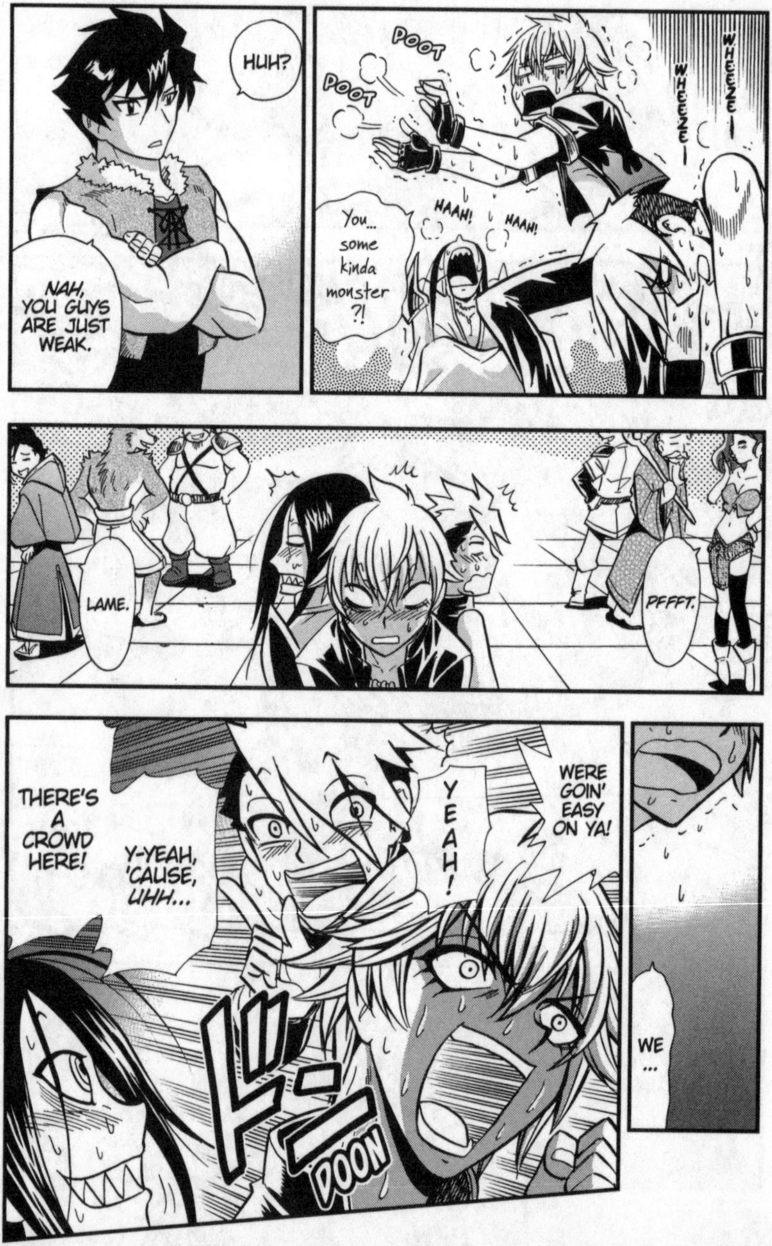
POOT
POOT
WHEEZE
WHEEZE
HAAH!
HAAH!
You... some kinda monster?!
HUH?
NAH, YOU GUYS ARE JUST WEAK.
PFFFT.
LAME.
WE ...
WERE GOIN' EASY ON YA!
YEAH!
Y-YEAH, 'CAUSE, UHH...
THERE'S A CROWD HERE!
DOON

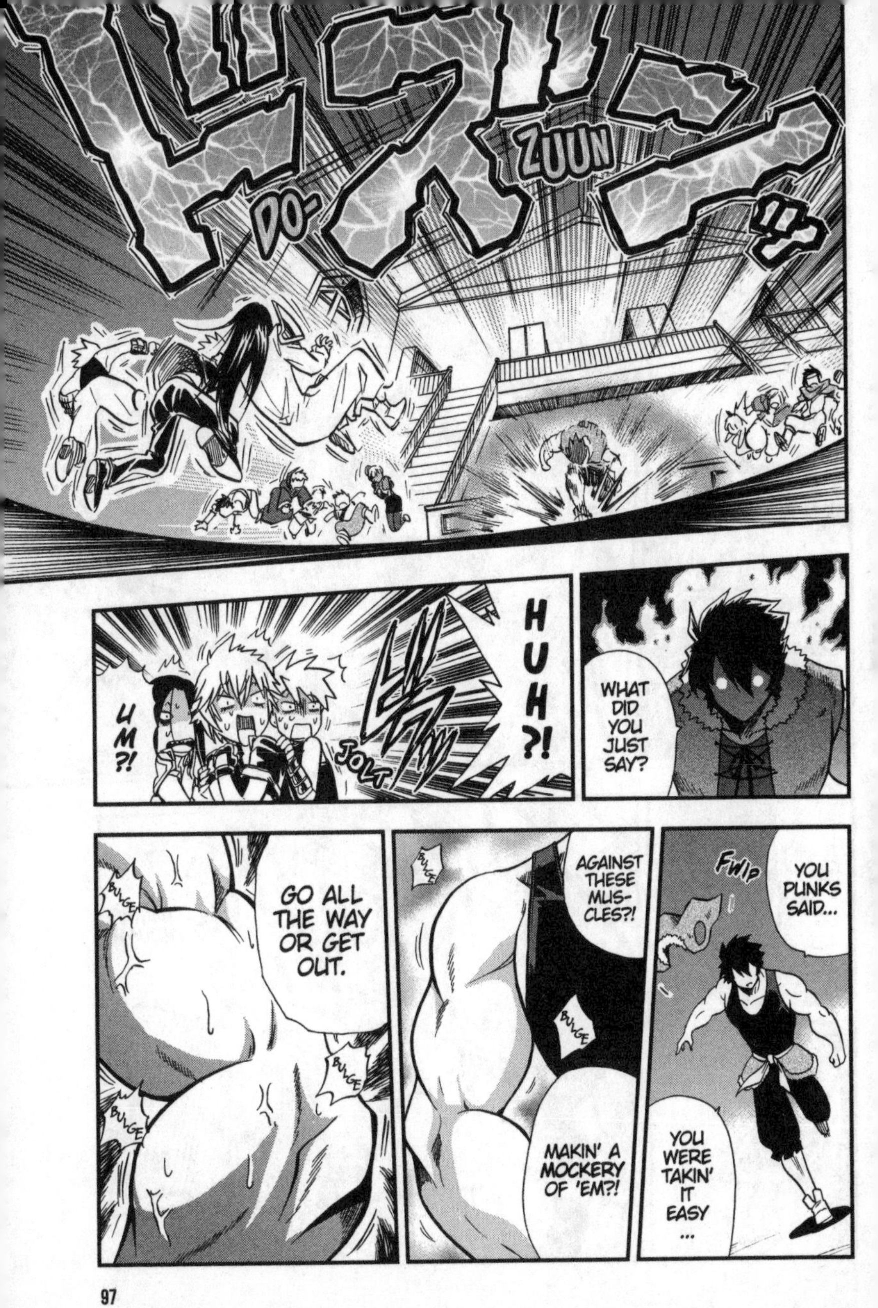

DO-
ZUUN
WHAT DID YOU JUST SAY?
HUH?!
JOLT
UM?!
YOU PUNKS SAID...
FWIP
YOU WERE TAKIN' IT EASY ...
AGAINST THESE MUS-CLES?!
BULGE
BULGE
MAKIN' A MOCKERY OF 'EM?!
GO ALL THE WAY OR GET OUT.
BULGE
BULGE
BULGE

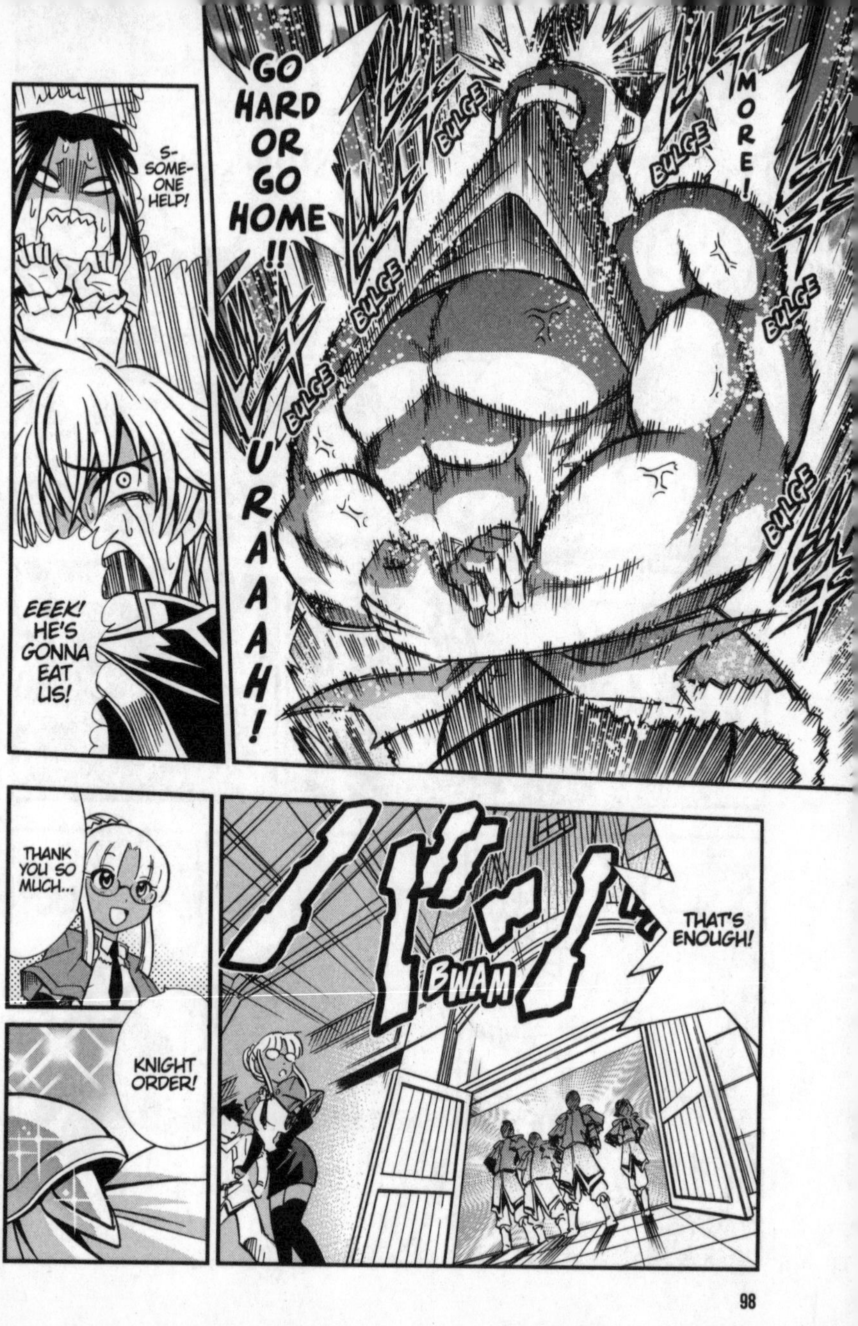
MORE!
GO HARD OR GO HOME!!
BULGE
BULGE
BULGE
BULGE
BULGE
BULGE
BULGE
URAAAAAH!
S-SOMEONE HELP!
EEEK! HE'S GONNA EAT US!
BWAM
THAT'S ENOUGH!
THANK YOU SO MUCH...
KNIGHT ORDER!

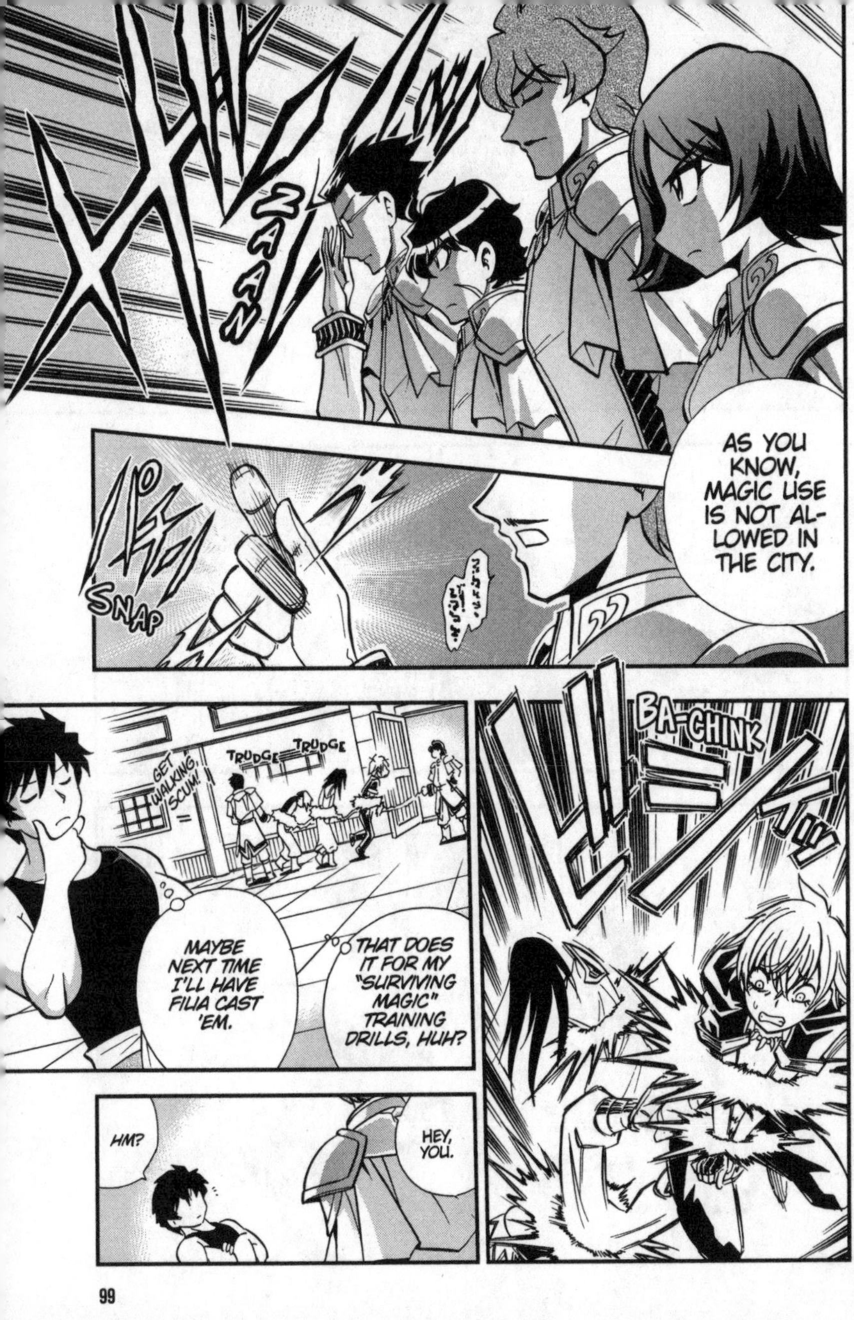
ZAAAN
AS YOU KNOW, MAGIC USE IS NOT AL-LOWED IN THE CITY.
SNAP
BA-CHINK
TRUDGE TRUDGE
GET WALKING, SCUM!
THAT DOES IT FOR MY "SURVIVING MAGIC" TRAINING DRILLS, HUH?
MAYBE NEXT TIME I'LL HAVE FILIA CAST 'EM.
HEY, YOU.
HM?

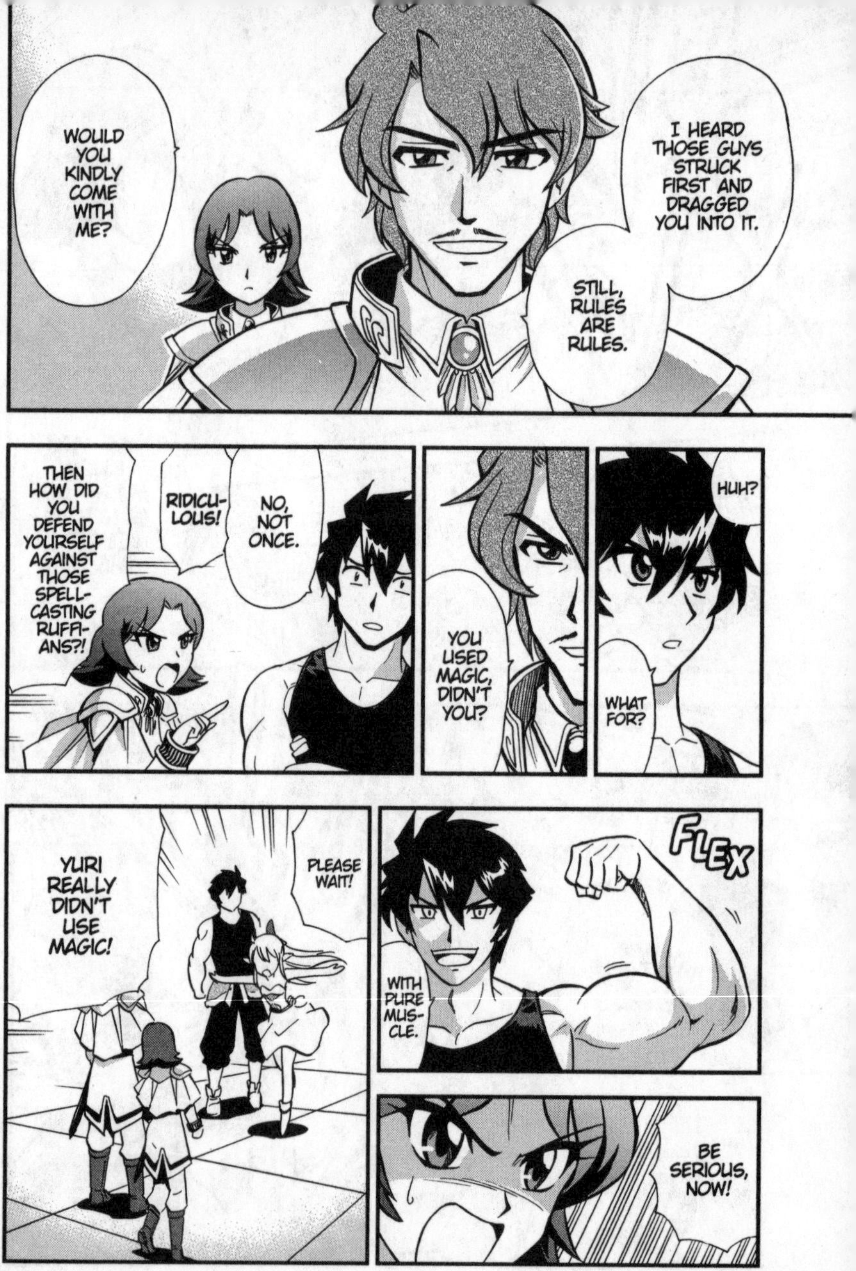
I HEARD THOSE GUYS STRUCK FIRST AND DRAGGED YOU INTO IT.
STILL, RULES ARE RULES.
WOULD YOU KINDLY COME WITH ME?
HUH?
WHAT FOR?
YOU USED MAGIC, DIDN'T YOU?
NO, NOT ONCE.
RIDICU-LOUS!
THEN HOW DID YOU DEFEND YOURSELF AGAINST THOSE SPELL-CASTING RUFFI-ANS?!
FLEX
WITH PURE MUS-CLE.
BE SERIOUS, NOW!
PLEASE WAIT!
YURI REALLY DIDN'T USE MAGIC!

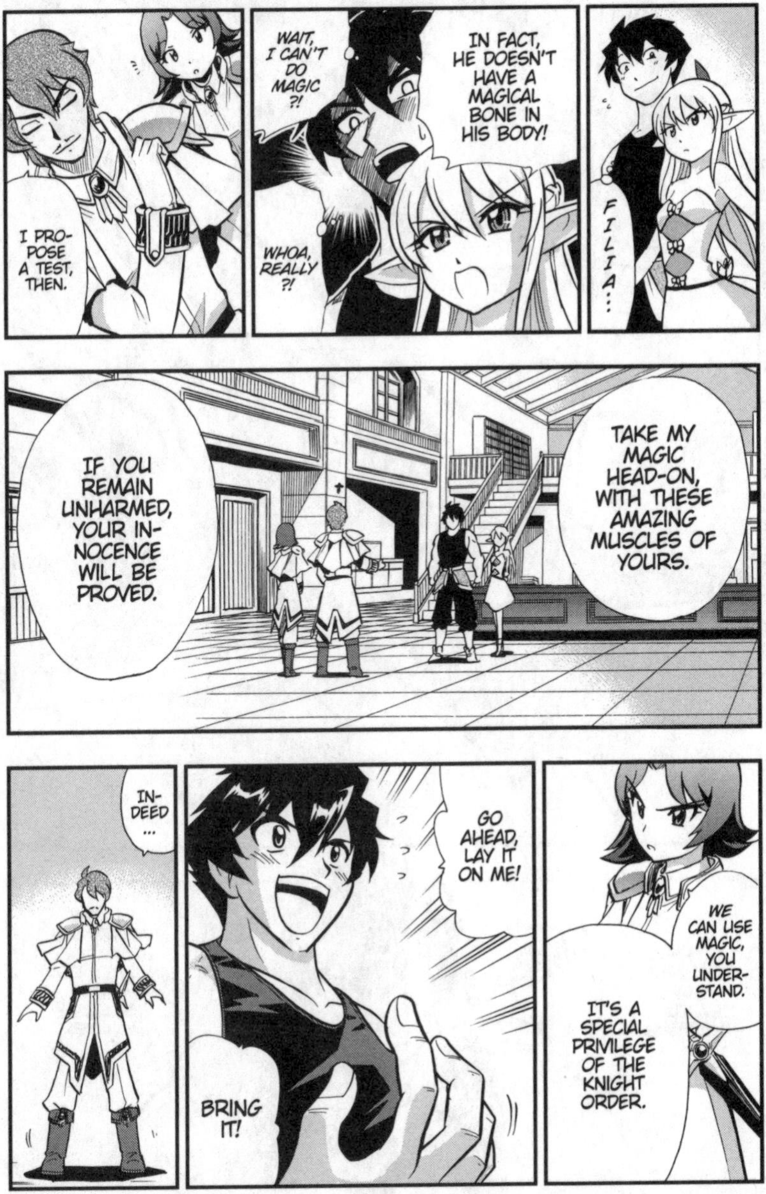
FILIA...
IN FACT, HE DOESN'T HAVE A MAGICAL BONE IN HIS BODY!
WAIT, I CAN'T DO MAGIC?!
WHOA, REALLY?!
I PROPOSE A TEST, THEN.
TAKE MY MAGIC HEAD-ON, WITH THESE AMAZING MUSCLES OF YOURS.
IF YOU REMAIN UNHARMED, YOUR INNOCENCE WILL BE PROVED.
WE CAN USE MAGIC, YOU UNDERSTAND.
IT'S A SPECIAL PRIVILEGE OF THE KNIGHT ORDER.
GO AHEAD, LAY IT ON ME!
BRING IT!
INDEED...

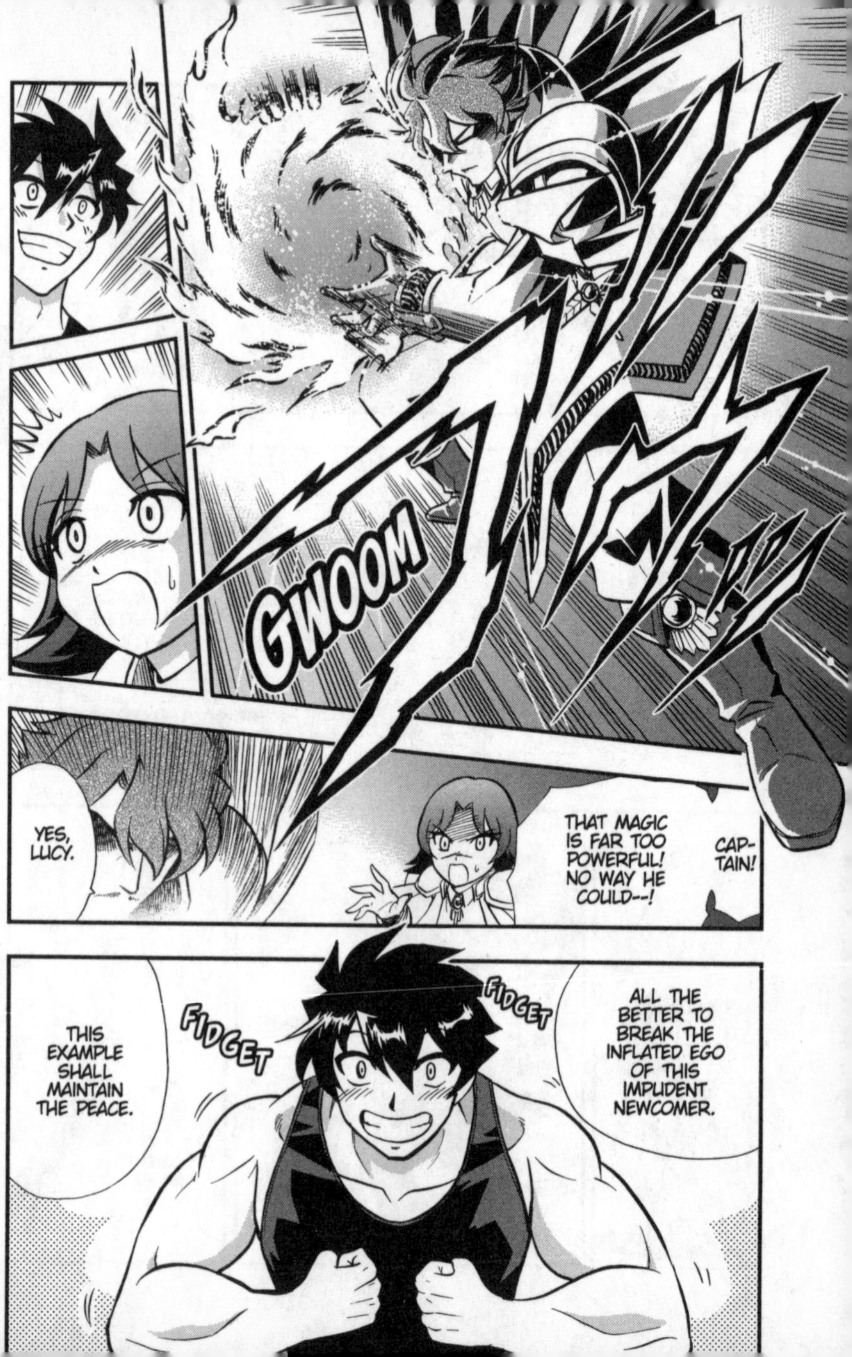
GWOOM
CAP-TAIN!
THAT MAGIC IS FAR TOO POWERFUL! NO WAY HE COULD--!
YES, LUCY.
ALL THE BETTER TO BREAK THE INFLATED EGO OF THIS IMPUDENT NEWCOMER.
FIDGET
FIDGET
THIS EXAMPLE SHALL MAINTAIN THE PEACE.

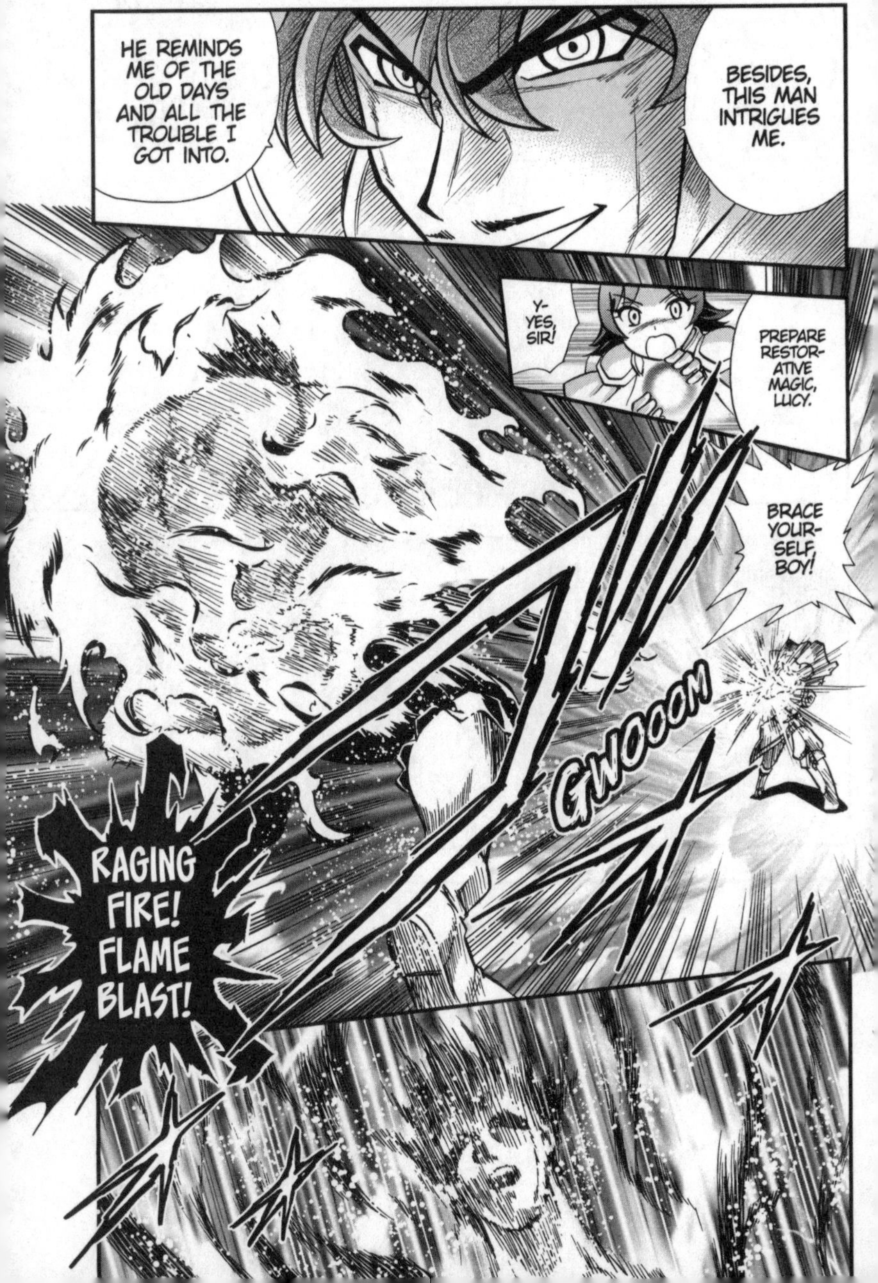
BESIDES, THIS MAN INTRIGUES ME.
HE REMINDS ME OF THE OLD DAYS AND ALL THE TROUBLE I GOT INTO.
PREPARE RESTOR-ATIVE MAGIC, LUCY.
Y-YES, SIR!
BRACE YOUR-SELF, BOY!
GWOOOM
RAGING FIRE! FLAME BLAST!

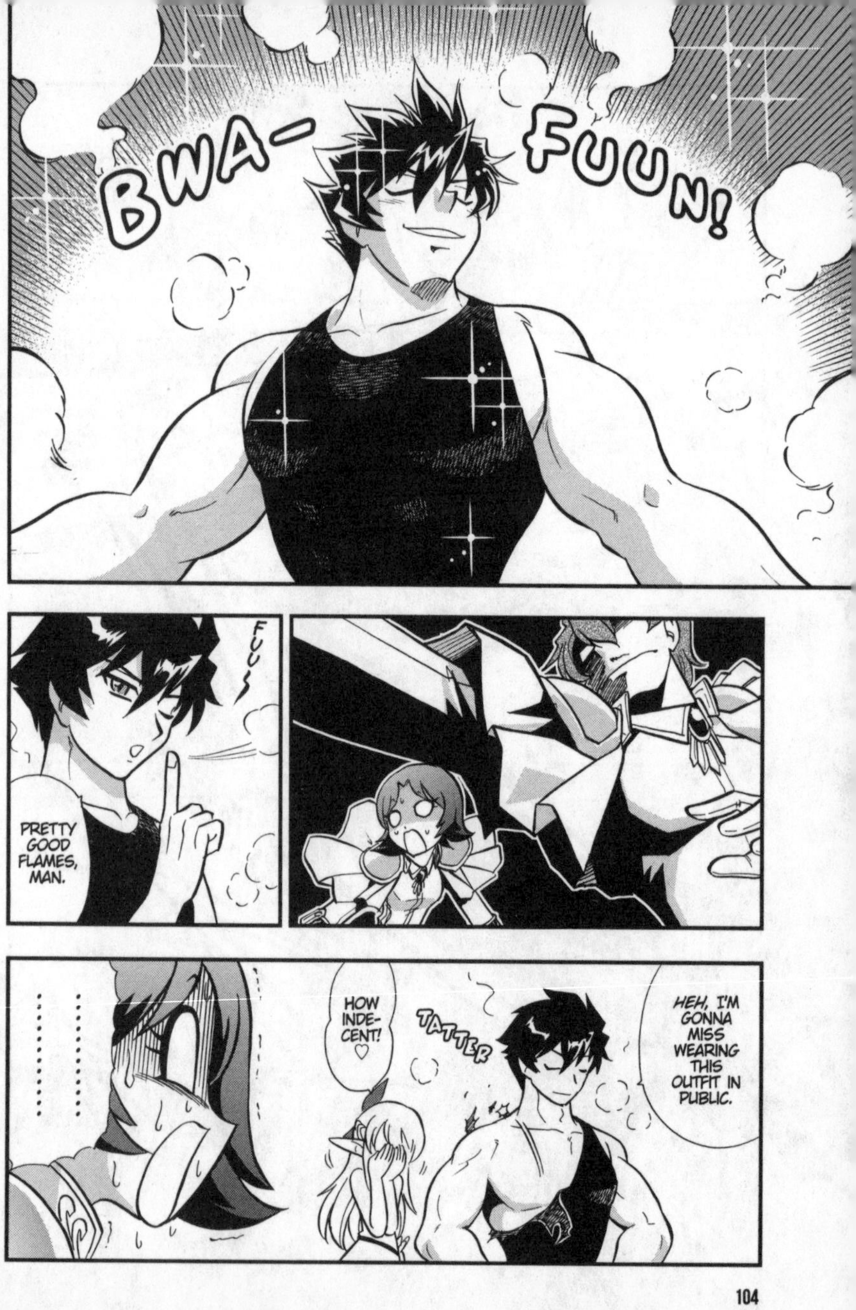
BWA- FUUN!
FUU
PRETTY GOOD FLAMES, MAN.
HEH, I'M GONNA MISS WEARING THIS OUTFIT IN PUBLIC.
TATTER
HOW INDECENT! ♡

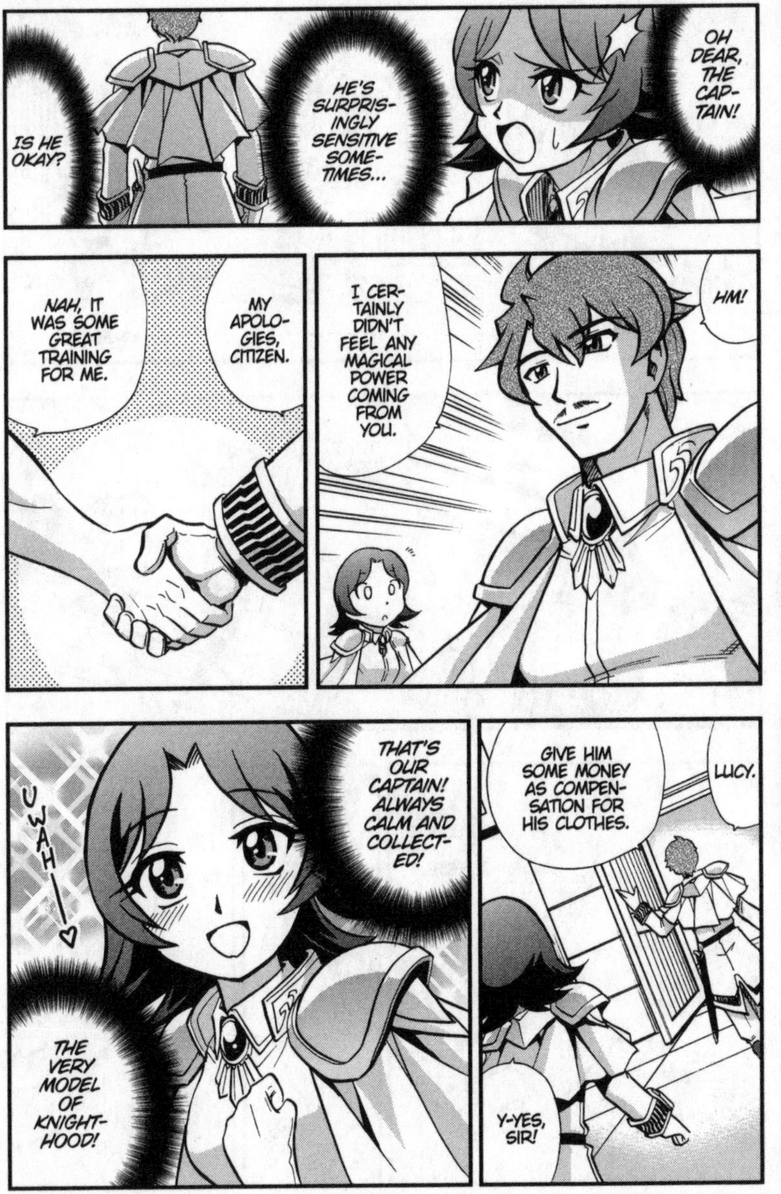
OH DEAR, THE CAPTAIN!
HE'S SURPRISINGLY SENSITIVE SOMETIMES...
IS HE OKAY?
HM!
I CERTAINLY DIDN'T FEEL ANY MAGICAL POWER COMING FROM YOU.
MY APOLOGIES, CITIZEN.
NAH, IT WAS SOME GREAT TRAINING FOR ME.
LUCY.
GIVE HIM SOME MONEY AS COMPENSATION FOR HIS CLOTHES.
Y-YES, SIR!
THAT'S OUR CAPTAIN! ALWAYS CALM AND COLLECTED!
UWAH—♥
THE VERY MODEL OF KNIGHTHOOD!

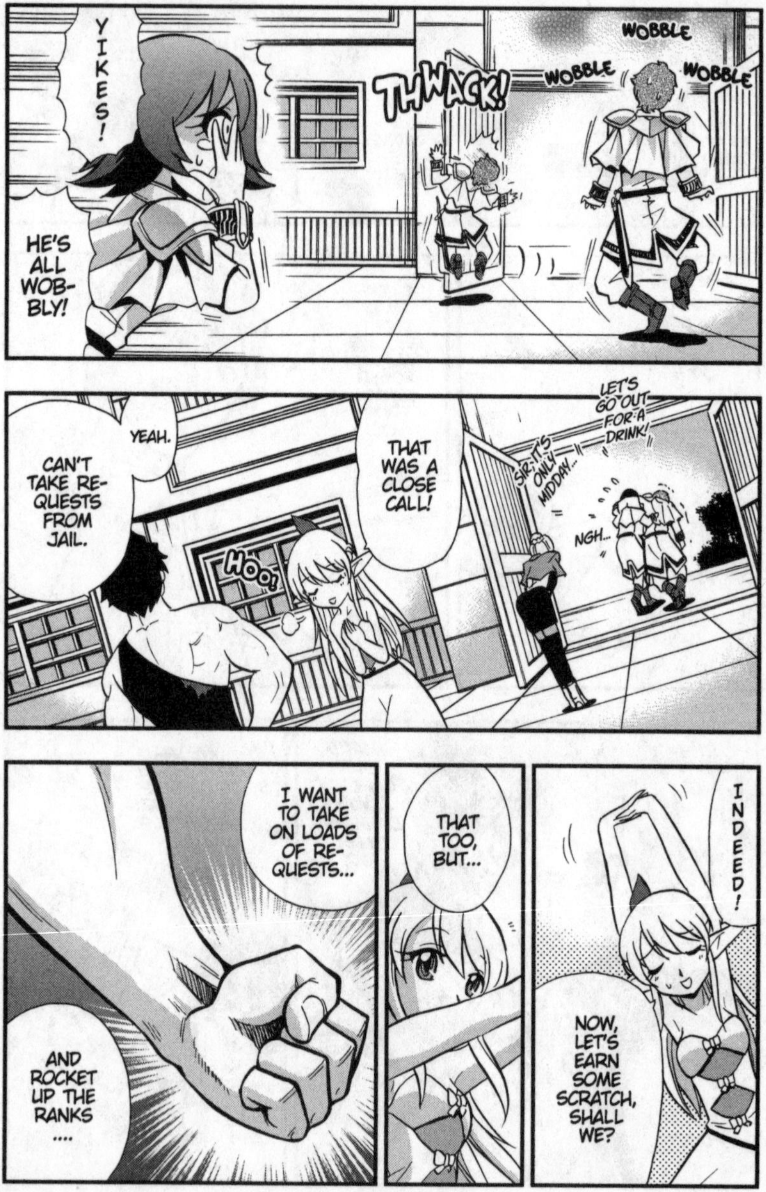
WOBBLE
WOBBLE
WOBBLE
THWACK!
YIKES!
HE'S ALL WOB-BLY!
LET'S GO OUT FOR A DRINK!
SIR, IT'S ONLY MIDDAY...
NGH...
THAT WAS A CLOSE CALL!
HOO!
YEAH.
CAN'T TAKE RE-QUESTS FROM JAIL.
INDEED!
NOW, LET'S EARN SOME SCRATCH, SHALL WE?
THAT TOO, BUT...
I WANT TO TAKE ON LOADS OF RE-QUESTS...
AND ROCKET UP THE RANKS ....

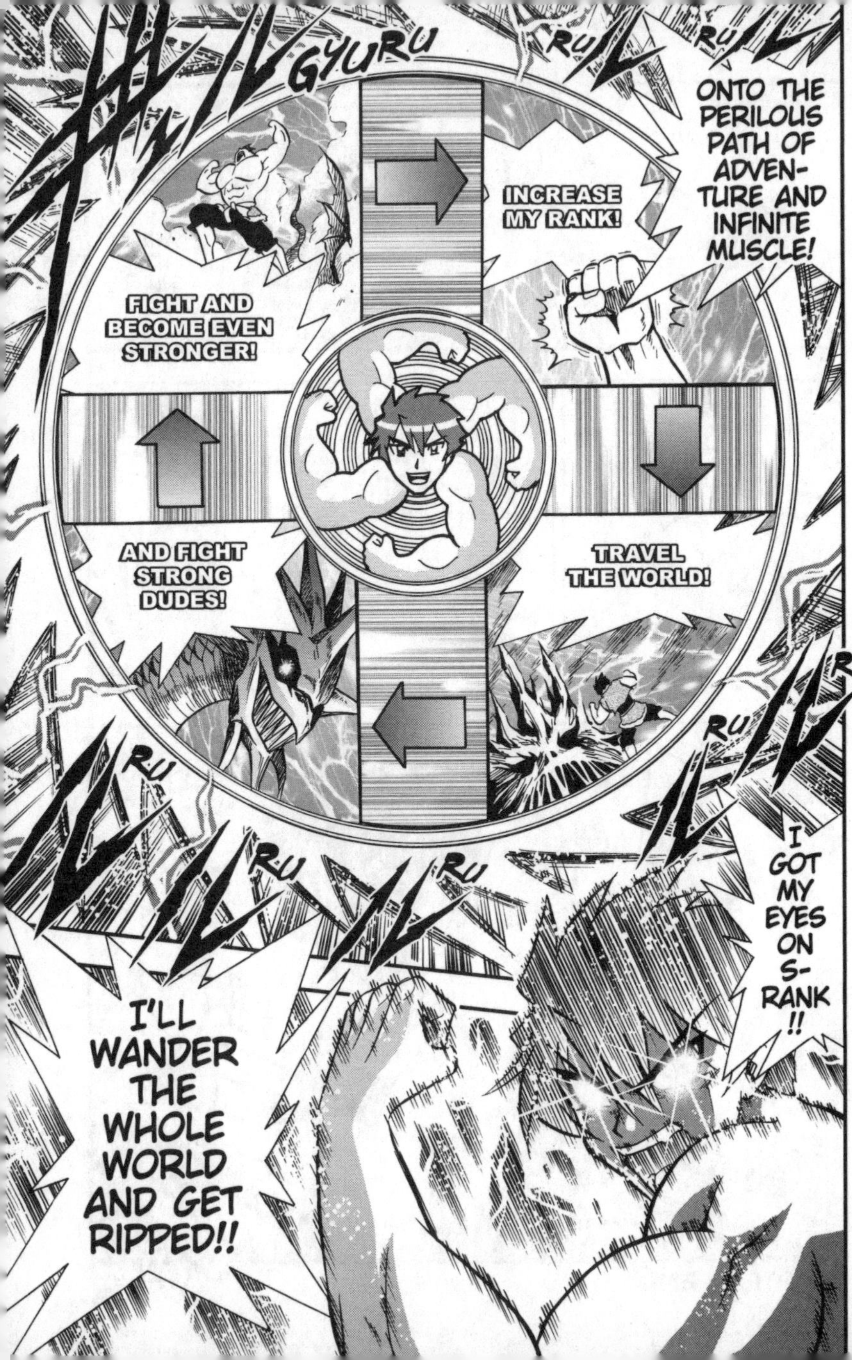

GYURU
RU
RU
ONTO THE PERILOUS PATH OF ADVENTURE AND INFINITE MUSCLE!
INCREASE MY RANK!
TRAVEL THE WORLD!
AND FIGHT STRONG DUDES!
FIGHT AND BECOME EVEN STRONGER!
RU
RU
RU
RU
RU
I GOT MY EYES ON S-RANK!!
I'LL WANDER THE WHOLE WORLD AND GET RIPPED!!

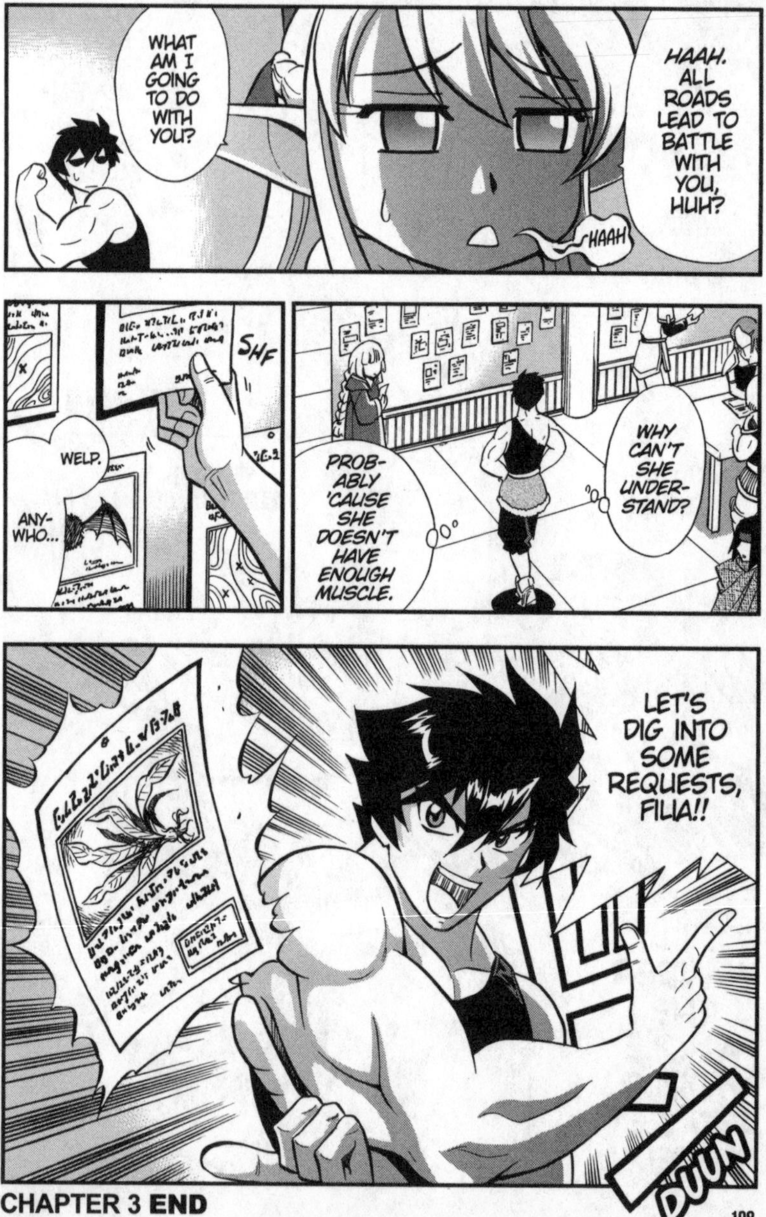
HAAH. ALL ROADS LEAD TO BATTLE WITH YOU, HUH?
HAAH
WHAT AM I GOING TO DO WITH YOU?
WHY CAN'T SHE UNDER-STAND?
PROB-ABLY 'CAUSE SHE DOESN'T HAVE ENOUGH MUSCLE.
SHF
WELP.
ANY-WHO...
LET'S DIG INTO SOME REQUESTS, FILIA!!
DUUN

CHAPTER 3 **END**

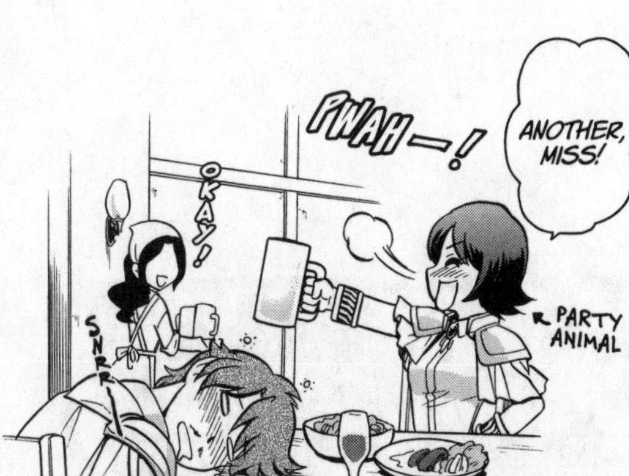
ANOTHER, MISS!
PWAH—!
PARTY ANIMAL
OKAY!
SNRR—
TOTAL LIGHTWEIGHT

MUSCLES
ARE BETTER THAN MAGIC!

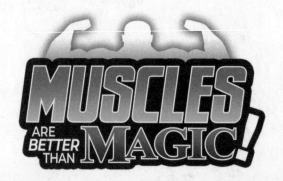

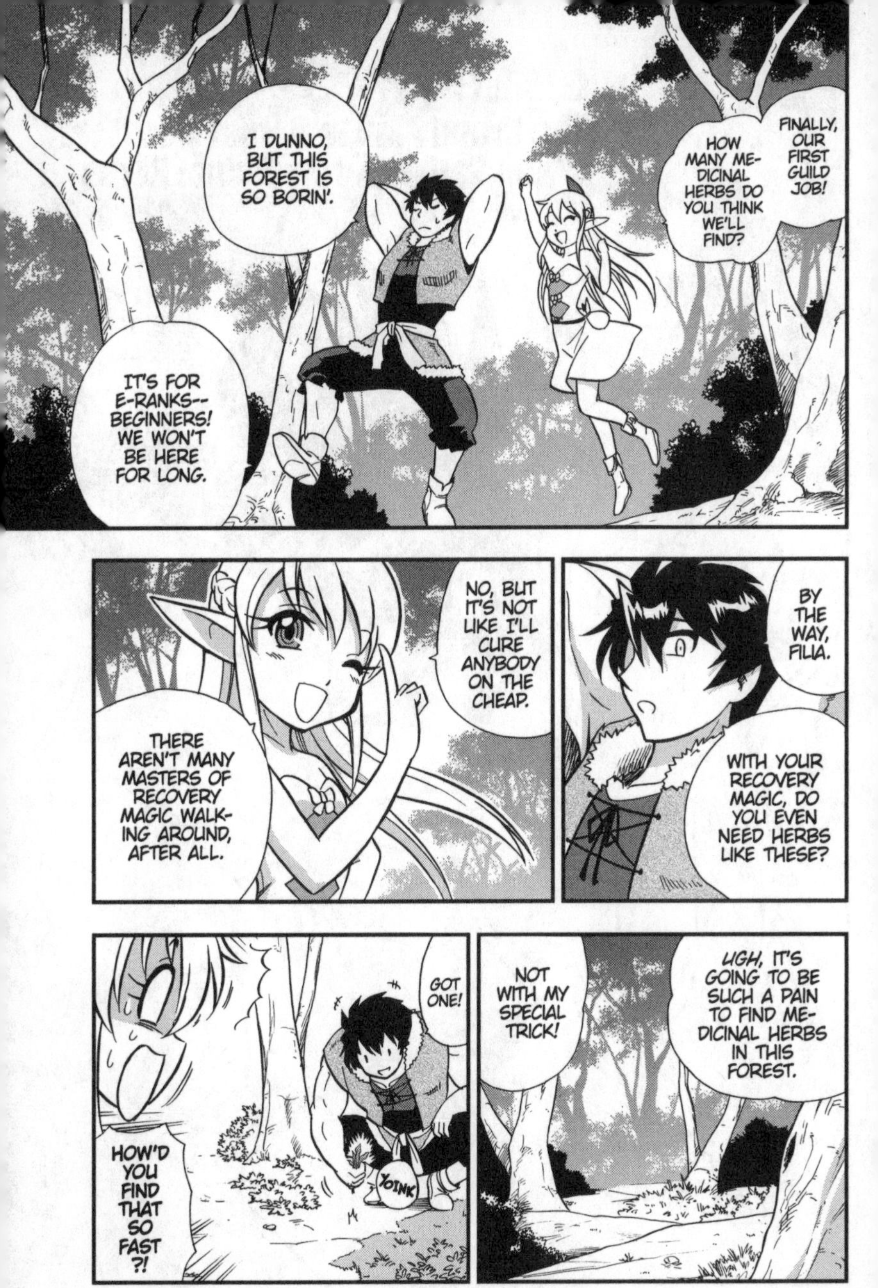
FINALLY, OUR FIRST GUILD JOB!
HOW MANY MEDICINAL HERBS DO YOU THINK WE'LL FIND?
I DUNNO, BUT THIS FOREST IS SO BORIN'.
IT'S FOR E-RANKS--BEGINNERS! WE WON'T BE HERE FOR LONG.
BY THE WAY, FILIA.
WITH YOUR RECOVERY MAGIC, DO YOU EVEN NEED HERBS LIKE THESE?
NO, BUT IT'S NOT LIKE I'LL CURE ANYBODY ON THE CHEAP.
THERE AREN'T MANY MASTERS OF RECOVERY MAGIC WALKING AROUND, AFTER ALL.
UGH, IT'S GOING TO BE SUCH A PAIN TO FIND MEDICINAL HERBS IN THIS FOREST.
NOT WITH MY SPECIAL TRICK!
GOT ONE!
YOINK
HOW'D YOU FIND THAT SO FAST?!

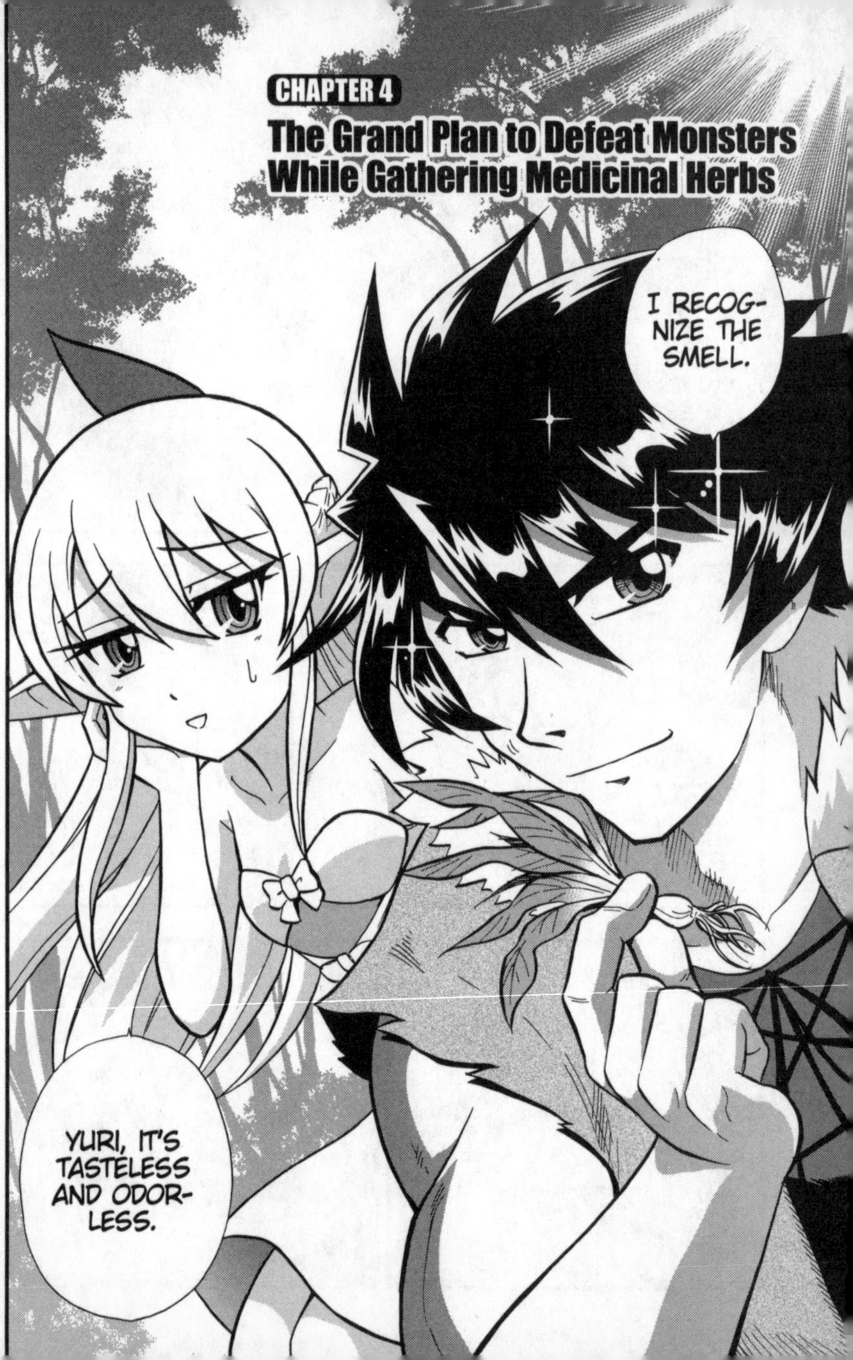
CHAPTER 4
The Grand Plan to Defeat Monsters While Gathering Medicinal Herbs
I RECOG-NIZE THE SMELL.
YURI, IT'S TASTELESS AND ODOR-LESS.

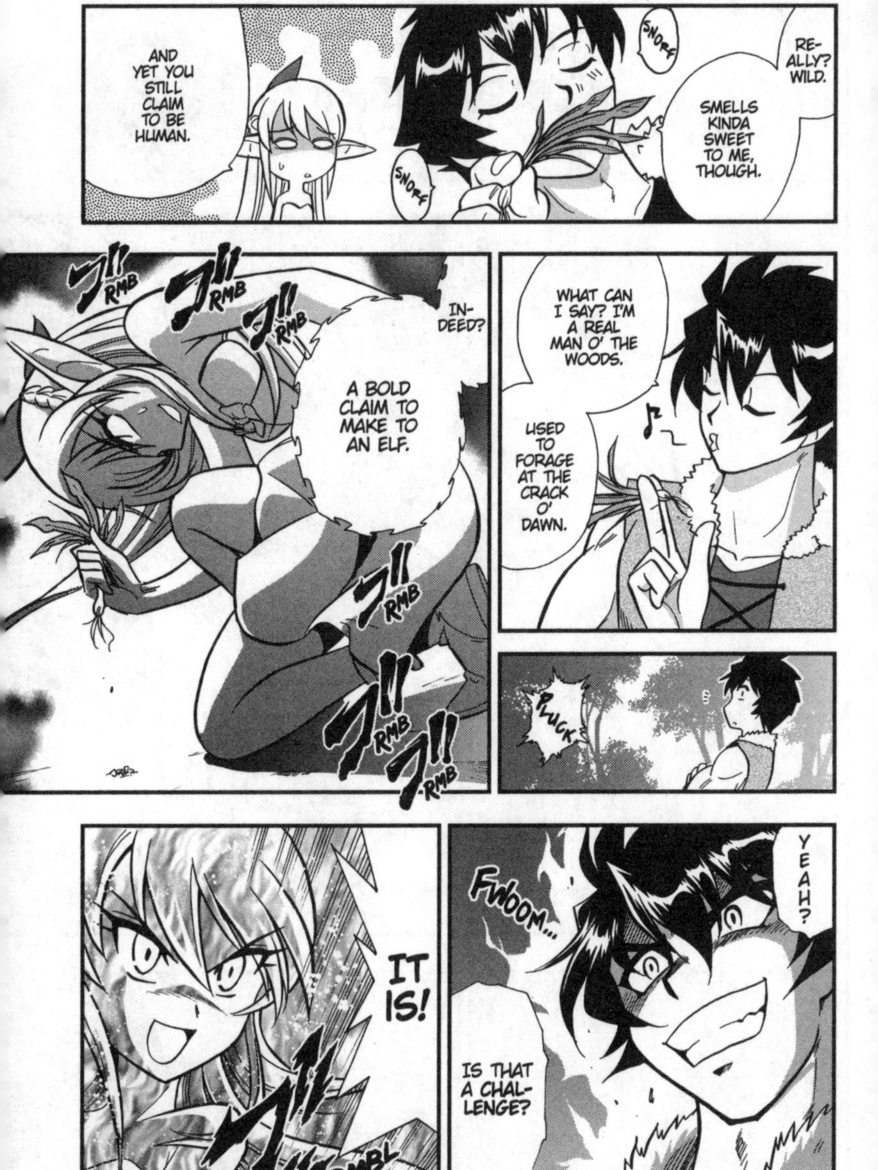
RE-ALLY? WILD.
SNORF
SMELLS KINDA SWEET TO ME, THOUGH.
SNORF
AND YET YOU STILL CLAIM TO BE HUMAN.
WHAT CAN I SAY? I'M A REAL MAN O' THE WOODS.
USED TO FORAGE AT THE CRACK O' DAWN.
PLUCK
IN-DEED?
A BOLD CLAIM TO MAKE TO AN ELF.
RMB
RMB
RMB
RMB
RMB
RMB
YEAH?
FWOOM...
IS THAT A CHAL-LENGE?
IT IS!
RMBL

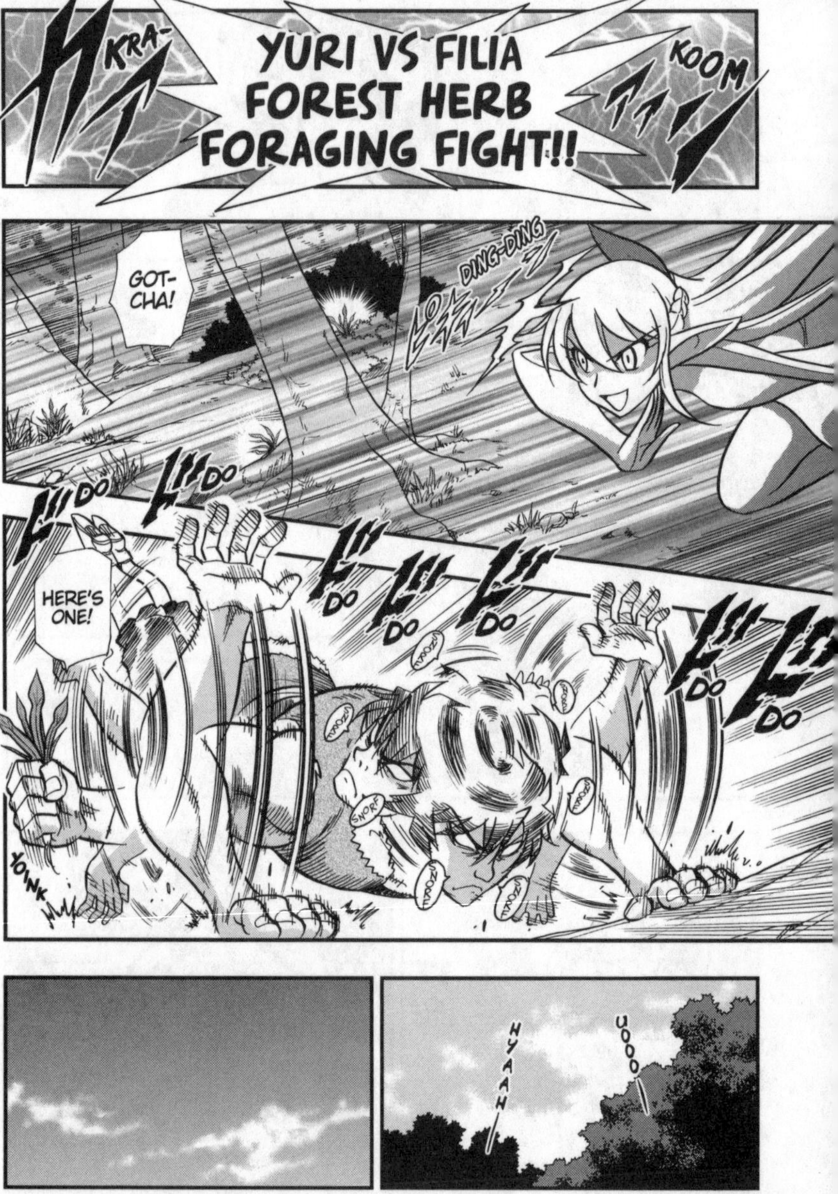
KRA-
KOOM
YURI VS FILIA
FOREST HERB
FORAGING FIGHT!!
DING-DING
GOT-CHA!
DO
DO
DO
DO
DO
DO
DO
HERE'S ONE!
SNORF
SNORF
SNORF
SNORF
YOINK
UOOO—!
HYAAAH—!

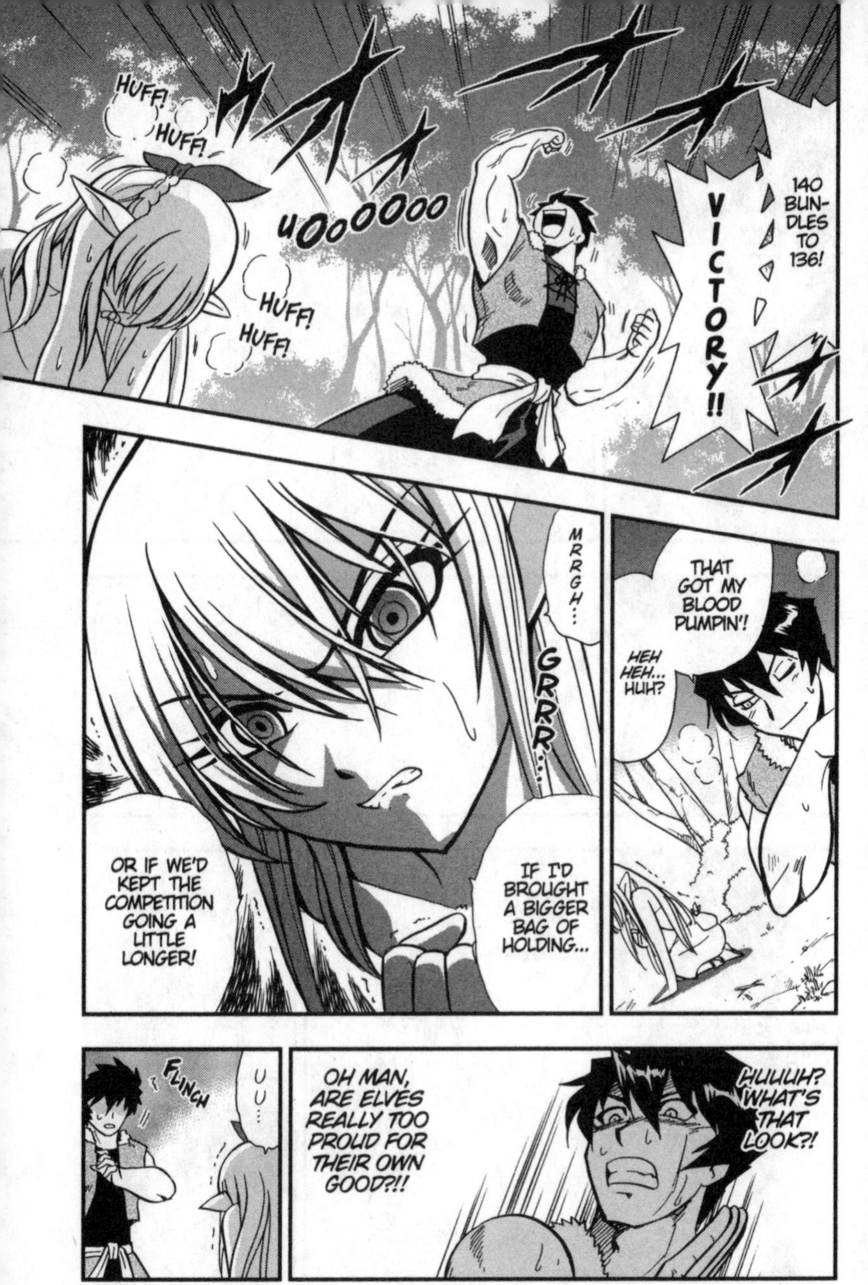
140 BUNDLES TO 136!
VICTORY!!
UOOOOOOO
HUFF! HUFF!
HUFF! HUFF!
THAT GOT MY BLOOD PUMPIN'!
HEH HEH... HUH?
MRRGH...
GRRR...
IF I'D BROUGHT A BIGGER BAG OF HOLDING...
OR IF WE'D KEPT THE COMPETITION GOING A LITTLE LONGER!
HUUUH? WHAT'S THAT LOOK?!
OH MAN, ARE ELVES REALLY TOO PROUD FOR THEIR OWN GOOD?!!
FLINCH
UU...

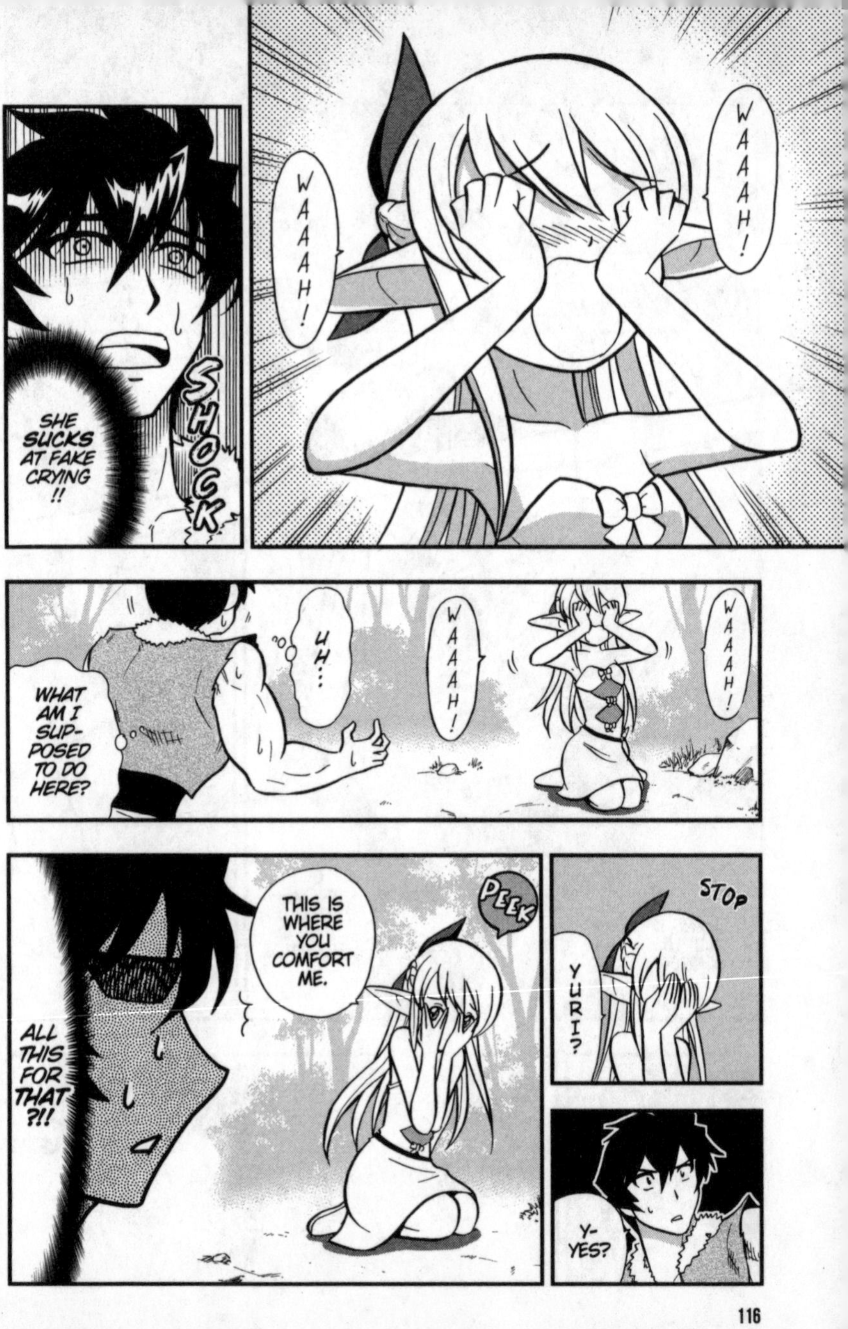
WAAAAH!
WAAAAH!
SHOCK
SHE SUCKS AT FAKE CRYING!!
WAAAAH!
WAAAAH!
UH...
WHAT AM I SUP-POSED TO DO HERE?
STOP
YURI?
Y-YES?
PEEK
THIS IS WHERE YOU COMFORT ME.
ALL THIS FOR THAT?!!

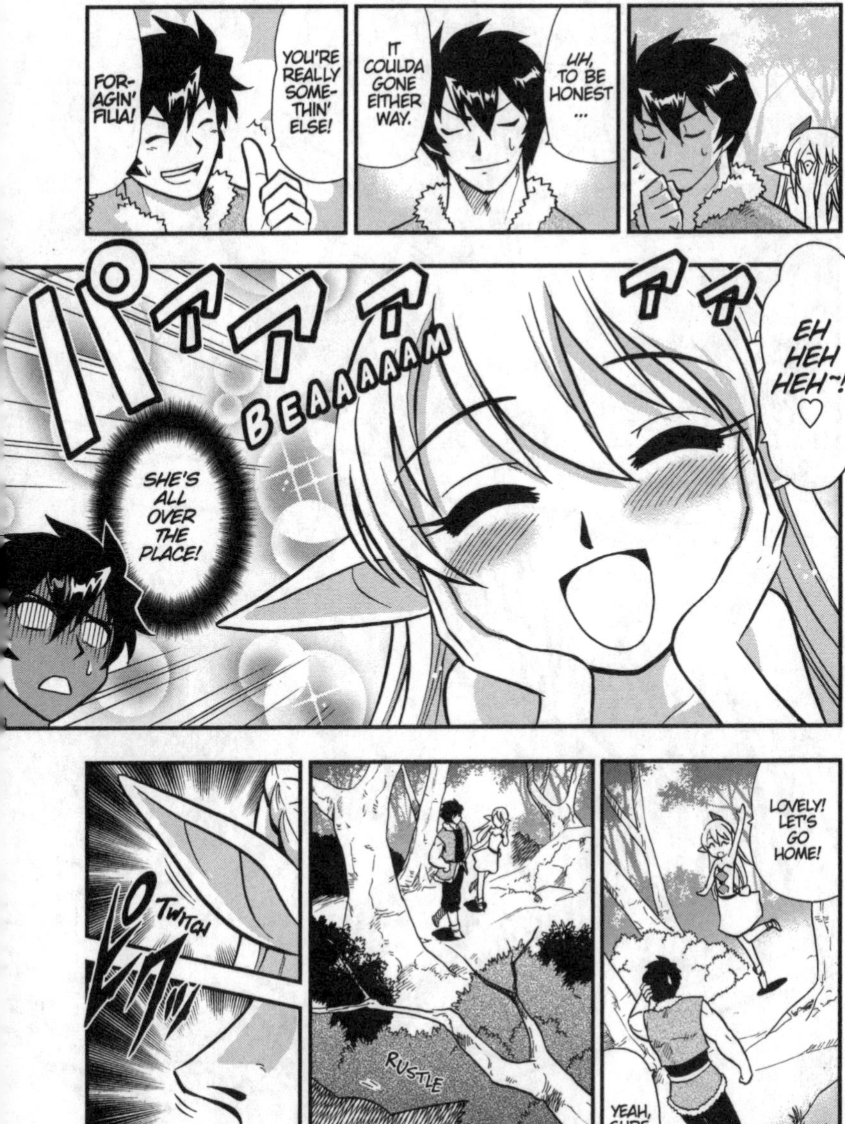
UH, TO BE HONEST ...
IT COULDA GONE EITHER WAY.
YOU'RE REALLY SOME-THIN' ELSE!
FOR-AGIN' FILIA!
EH HEH HEH~! ♡
パアアアアア
BEAAAAAM
SHE'S ALL OVER THE PLACE!
LOVELY! LET'S GO HOME!
YEAH, SURE.
RUSTLE
TWITCH

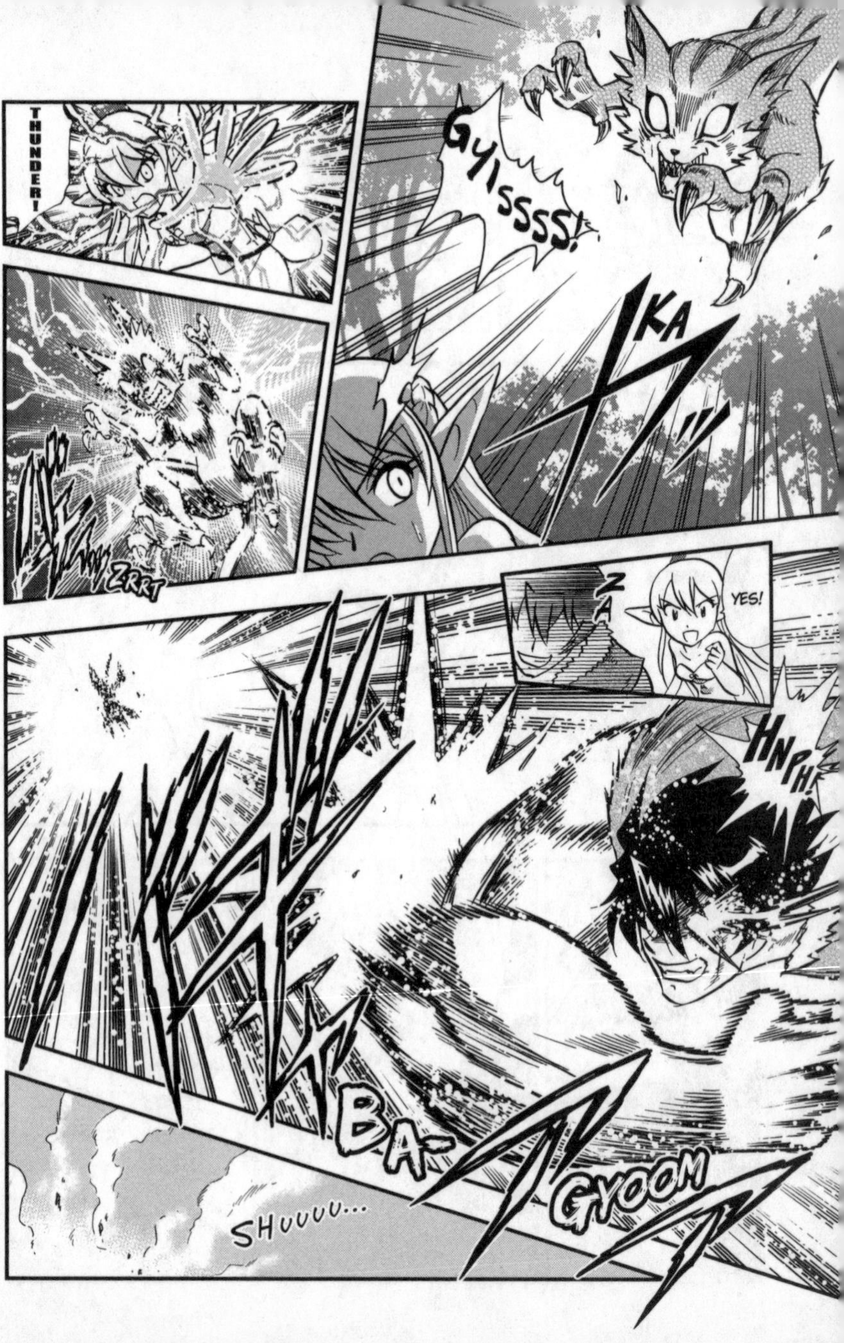
GYISSSS!
KA
THUNDER!
ZRRT
YES!
ZA
HNPH!
BA-
GYOOM
SHUUUU...

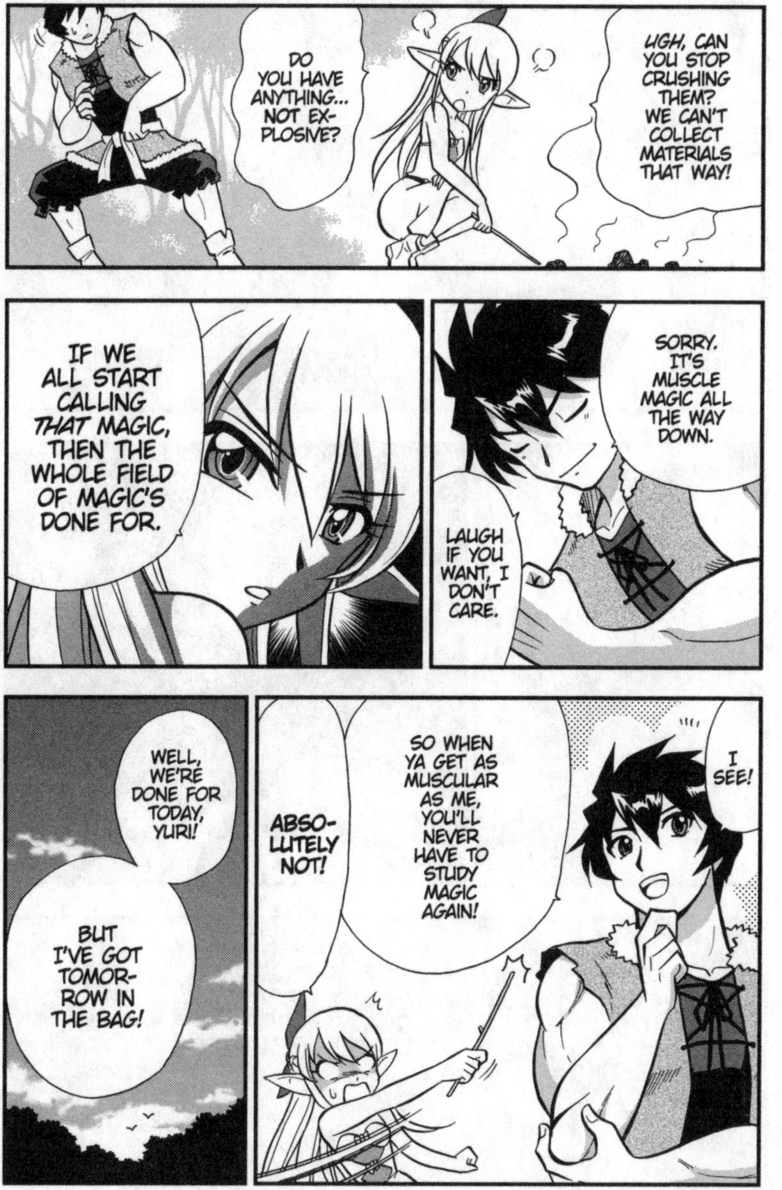
UGH, CAN YOU STOP CRUSHING THEM? WE CAN'T COLLECT MATERIALS THAT WAY!
DO YOU HAVE ANYTHING... NOT EX-PLOSIVE?
SORRY. IT'S MUSCLE MAGIC ALL THE WAY DOWN.
LAUGH IF YOU WANT, I DON'T CARE.
IF WE ALL START CALLING *THAT* MAGIC, THEN THE WHOLE FIELD OF MAGIC'S DONE FOR.
I SEE!
SO WHEN YA GET AS MUSCULAR AS ME, YOU'LL NEVER HAVE TO STUDY MAGIC AGAIN!
ABSO-LUTELY NOT!
WELL, WE'RE DONE FOR TODAY, YURI!
BUT I'VE GOT TOMOR-ROW IN THE BAG!

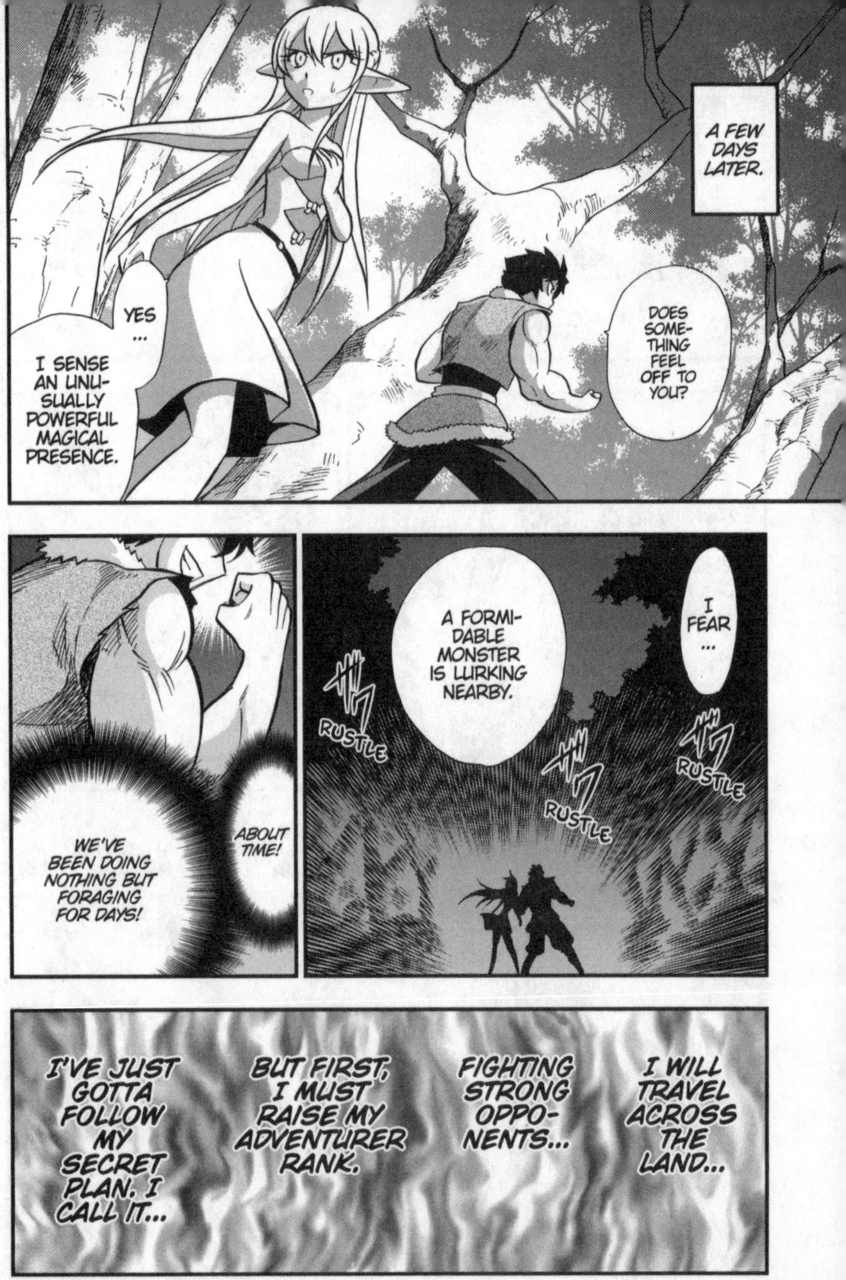
A FEW DAYS LATER.
DOES SOME-THING FEEL OFF TO YOU?
YES ...
I SENSE AN UNU-SUALLY POWERFUL MAGICAL PRESENCE.
I FEAR ...
A FORMI-DABLE MONSTER IS LURKING NEARBY.
RUSTLE
RUSTLE
RUSTLE
ABOUT TIME!
WE'VE BEEN DOING NOTHING BUT FORAGING FOR DAYS!
I WILL TRAVEL ACROSS THE LAND...
FIGHTING STRONG OPPO-NENTS...
BUT FIRST, I MUST RAISE MY ADVENTURER RANK.
I'VE JUST GOTTA FOLLOW MY SECRET PLAN. I CALL IT...

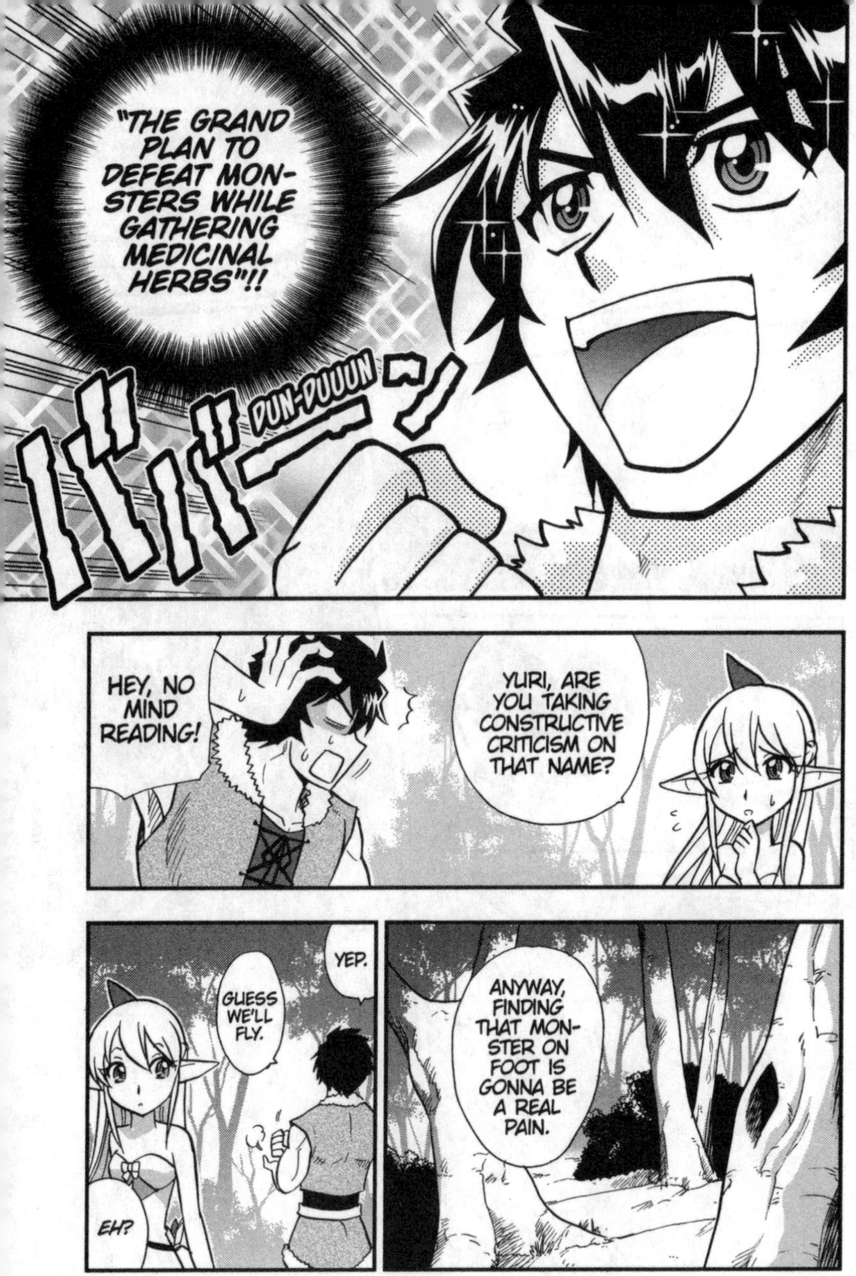
"THE GRAND PLAN TO DEFEAT MONSTERS WHILE GATHERING MEDICINAL HERBS"!!
DUN-DUUUN
YURI, ARE YOU TAKING CONSTRUCTIVE CRITICISM ON THAT NAME?
HEY, NO MIND READING!
ANYWAY, FINDING THAT MONSTER ON FOOT IS GONNA BE A REAL PAIN.
YEP.
GUESS WE'LL FLY.
EH?

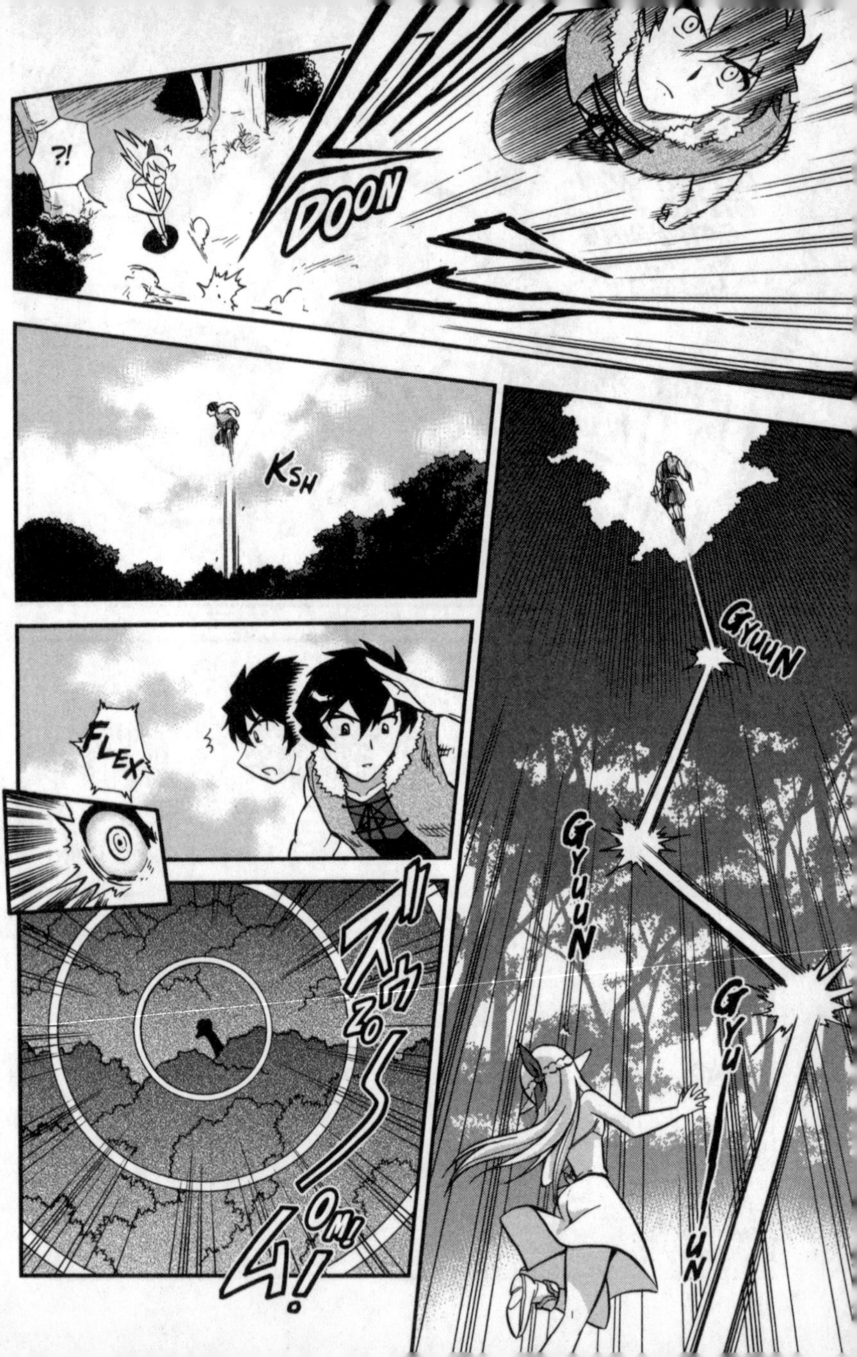
DOON
?!
GYUUN
GYUUN
GYUUN
KSH
FLEX
ZOOM!

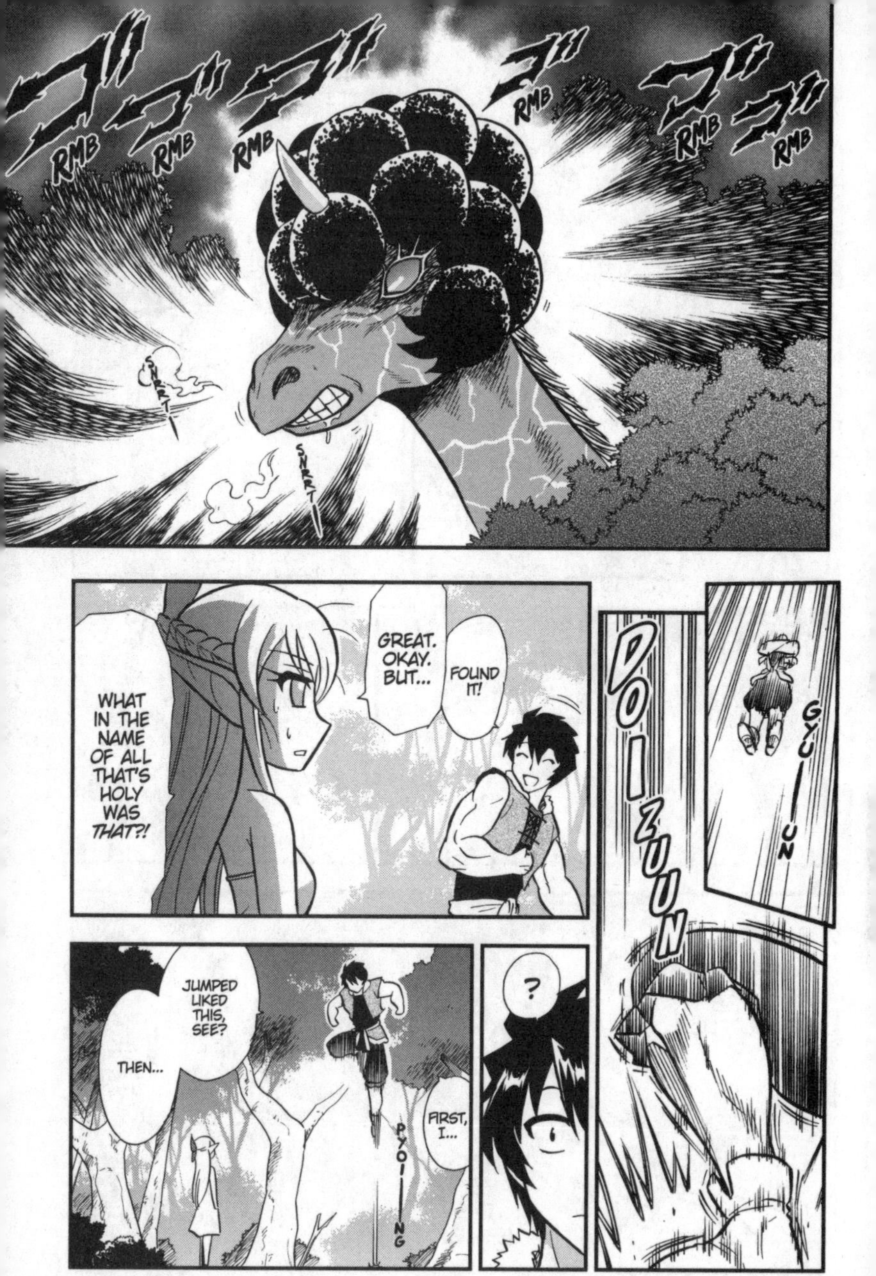
RMB
RMB
RMB
RMB
RMB
RMB
SNRRT
SNRRT
GYU-I-I-UN
DOIIZUUN
FOUND IT!
GREAT. OKAY. BUT...
WHAT IN THE NAME OF ALL THAT'S HOLY WAS *THAT*?!
?
FIRST, I...
PYOIIIING
JUMPED LIKED THIS, SEE?
THEN...

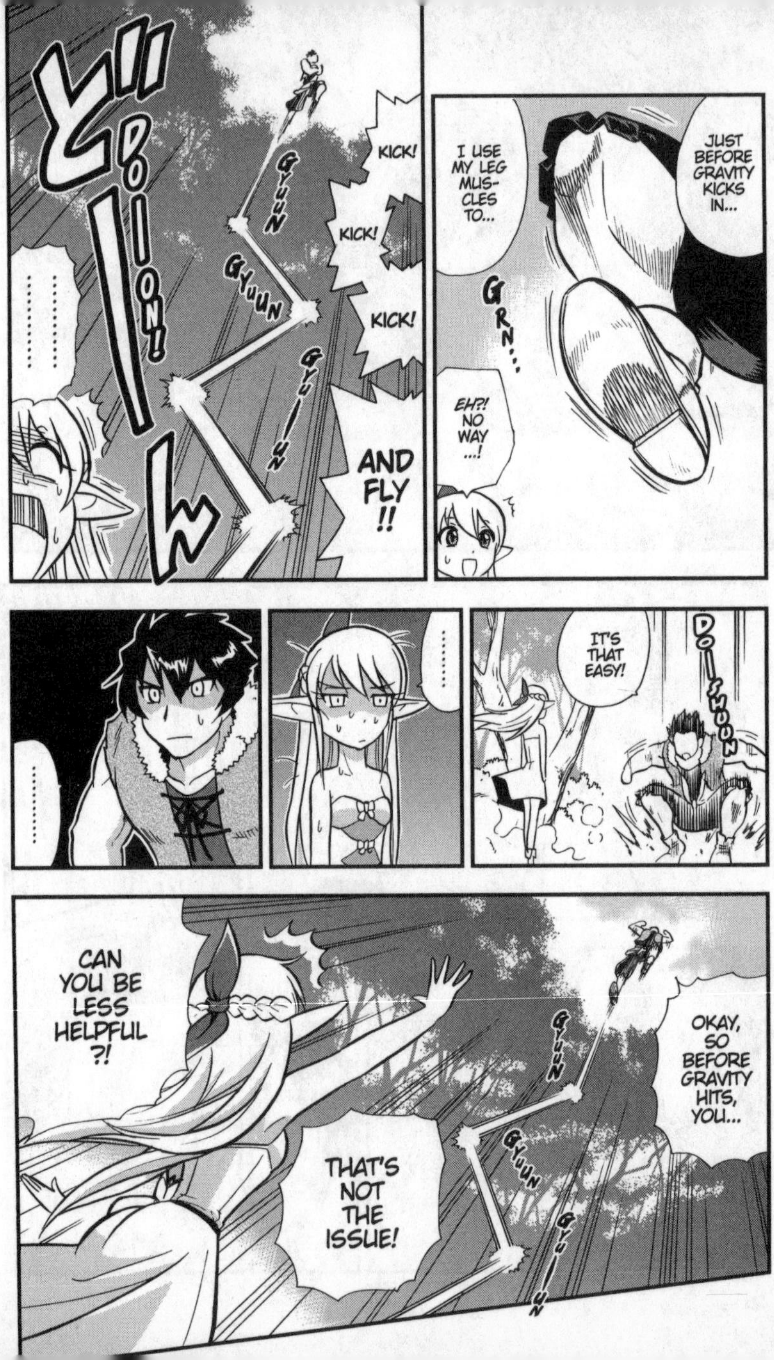
JUST BEFORE GRAVITY KICKS IN...
I USE MY LEG MUS-CLES TO...
GRN...
EH?! NO WAY...!
KICK!
KICK!
KICK!
AND FLY!!
GYUUN
GYUUN
GYUIUN
DOIIION!
......
IT'S THAT EASY!
DOISHOON
......
......
OKAY, SO BEFORE GRAVITY HITS, YOU...
GYUUN
GYUUN
GYUIUN
THAT'S NOT THE ISSUE!
CAN YOU BE LESS HELPFUL?!

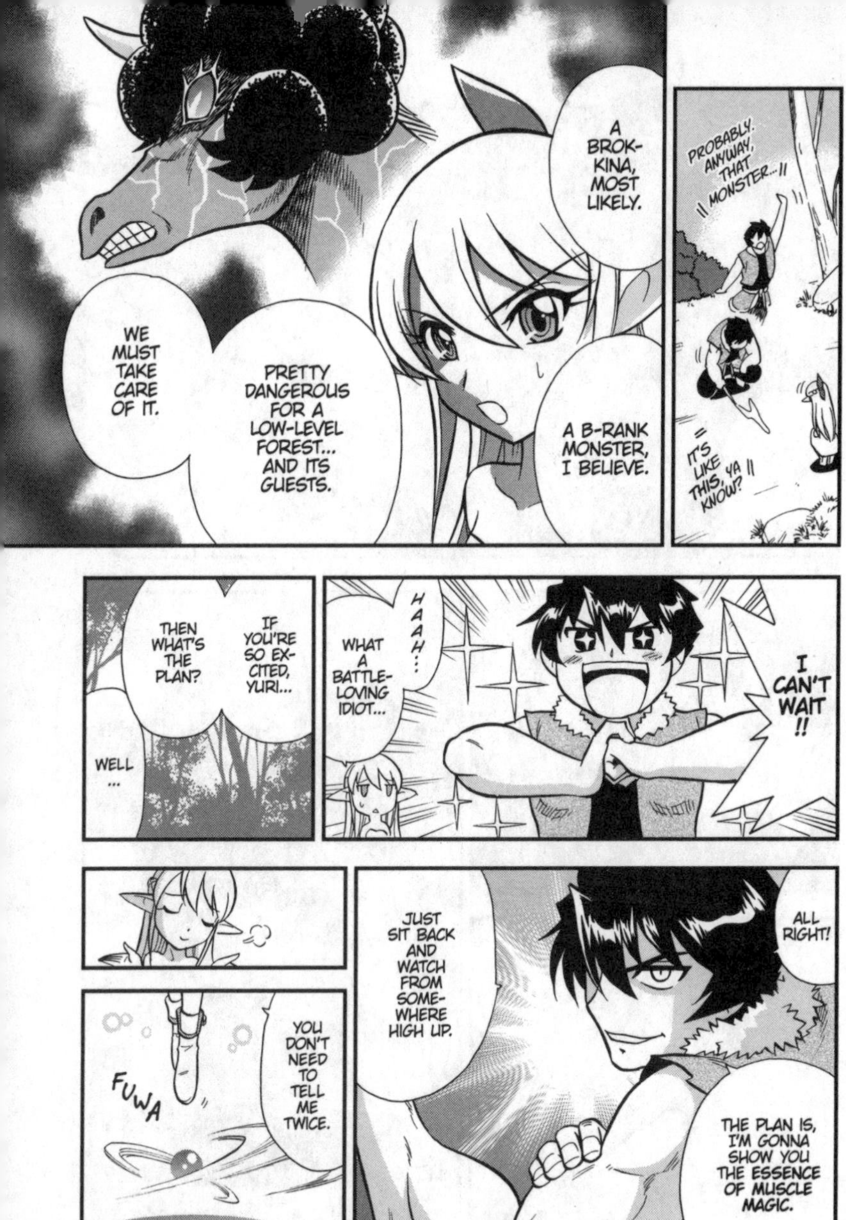
PROBABLY. ANYWAY, THAT MONSTER...
IT'S LIKE THIS, YA KNOW?
A BROKKINA, MOST LIKELY.
A B-RANK MONSTER, I BELIEVE.
PRETTY DANGEROUS FOR A LOW-LEVEL FOREST... AND ITS GUESTS.
WE MUST TAKE CARE OF IT.
I CAN'T WAIT!!
HAAH...
WHAT A BATTLE-LOVING IDIOT...
IF YOU'RE SO EXCITED, YURI...
THEN WHAT'S THE PLAN?
WELL...
ALL RIGHT!
THE PLAN IS, I'M GONNA SHOW YOU THE ESSENCE OF MUSCLE MAGIC.
JUST SIT BACK AND WATCH FROM SOMEWHERE HIGH UP.
YOU DON'T NEED TO TELL ME TWICE.
FUWA

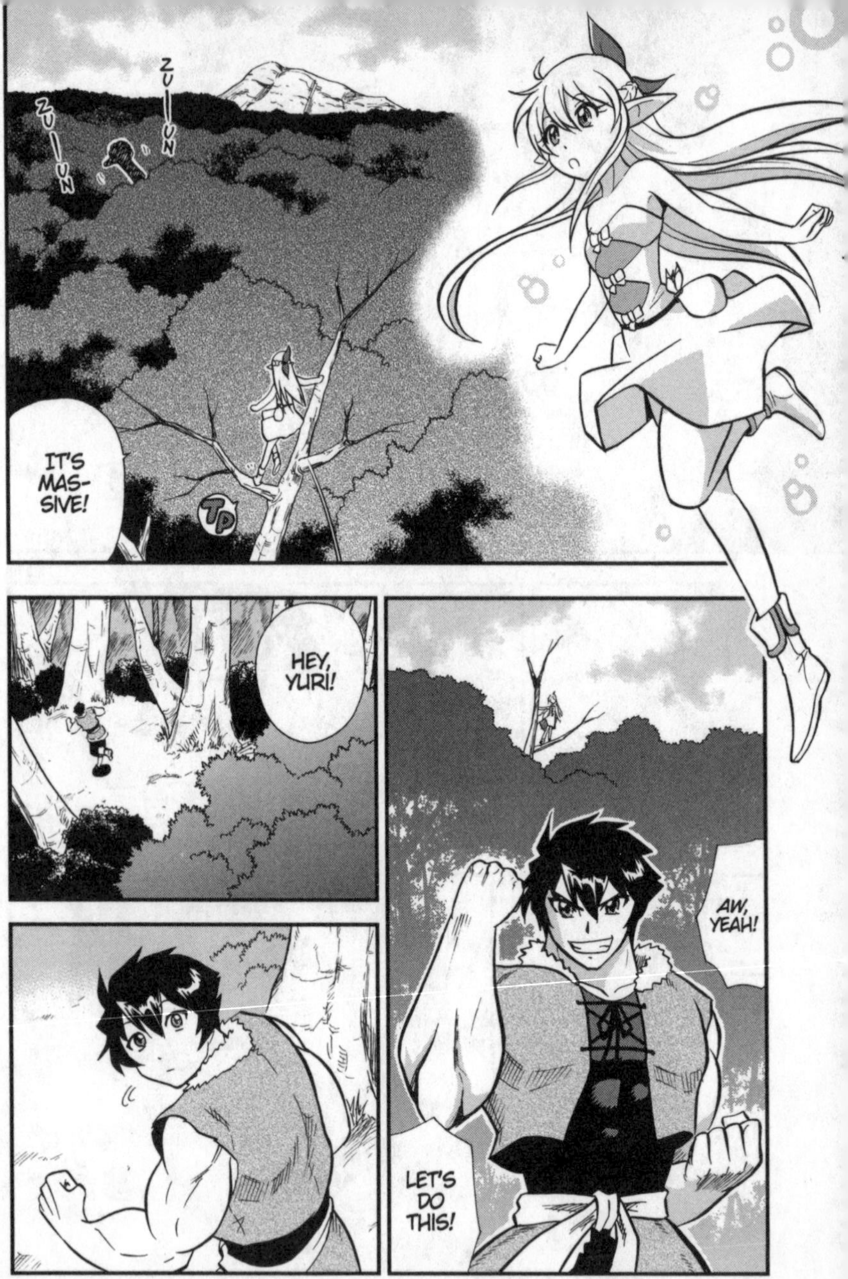
ZU-I-I-UN
ZU-I-I-UN
IT'S MAS-SIVE!
TP
AW, YEAH!
LET'S DO THIS!
HEY, YURI!

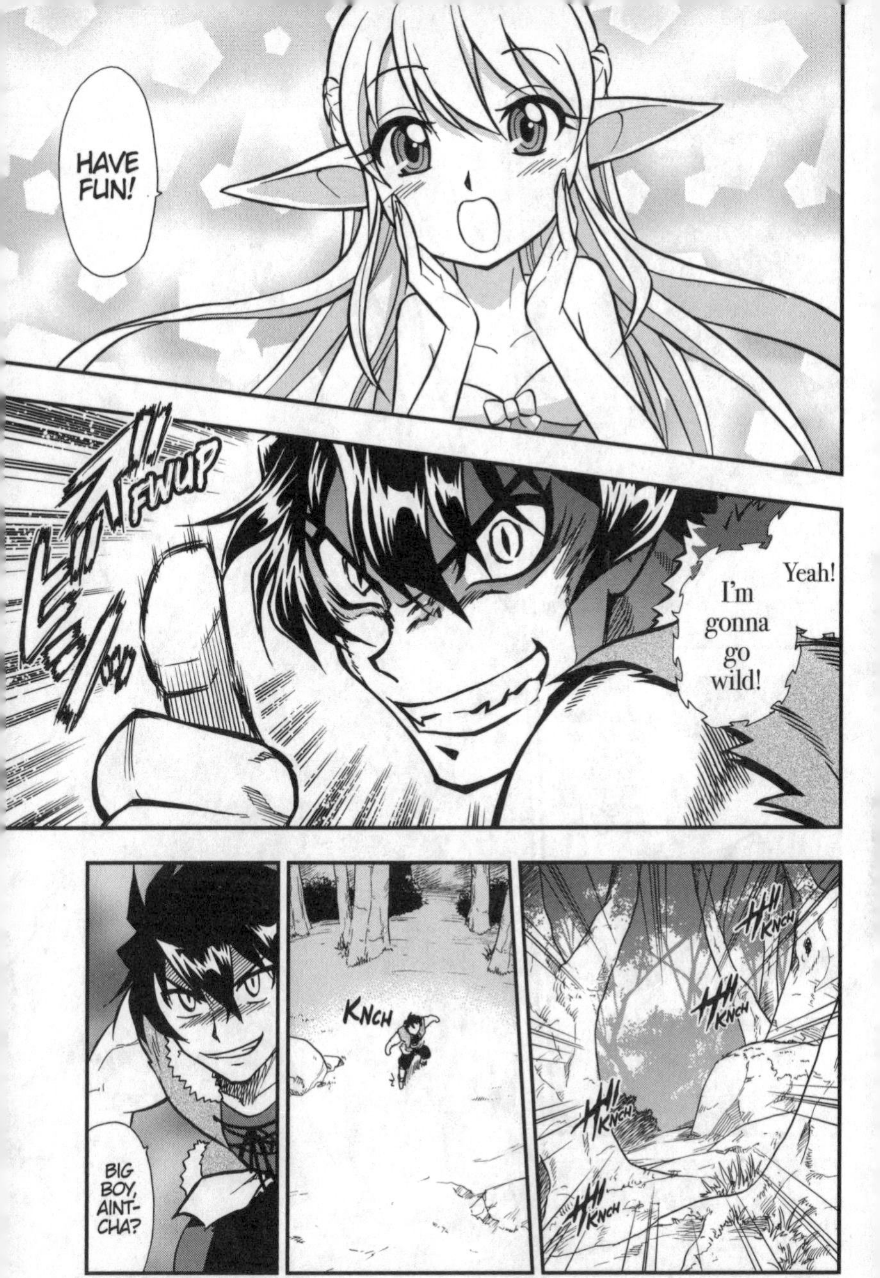
HAVE FUN!
Yeah! I'm gonna go wild!
FWUP
KNCH
KNCH
KNCH
KNCH
KNCH
BIG BOY, AINT-CHA?

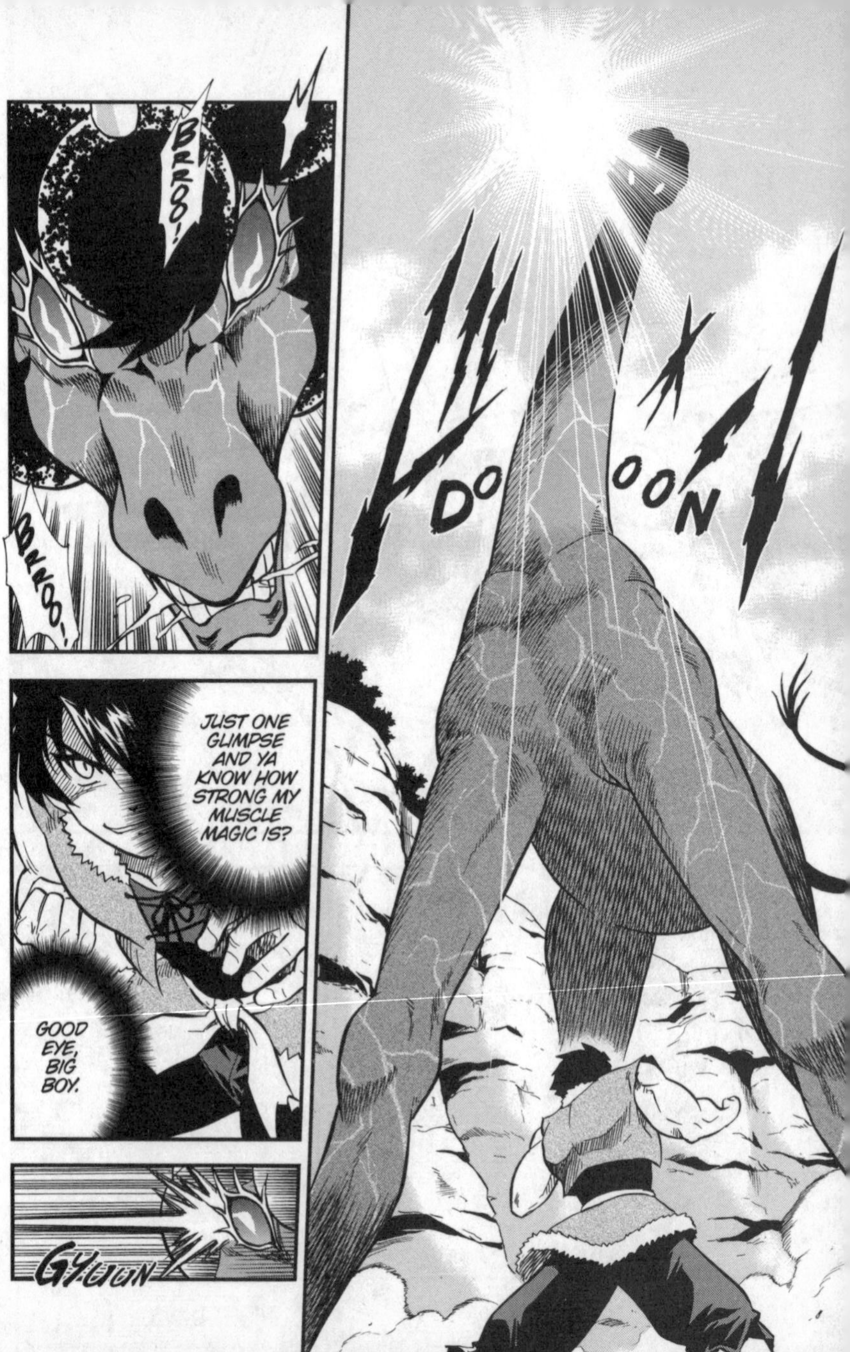
DOOON
BRROO!
BRROO...
JUST ONE GLIMPSE AND YA KNOW HOW STRONG MY MUSCLE MAGIC IS?
GOOD EYE, BIG BOY.
GYUUN

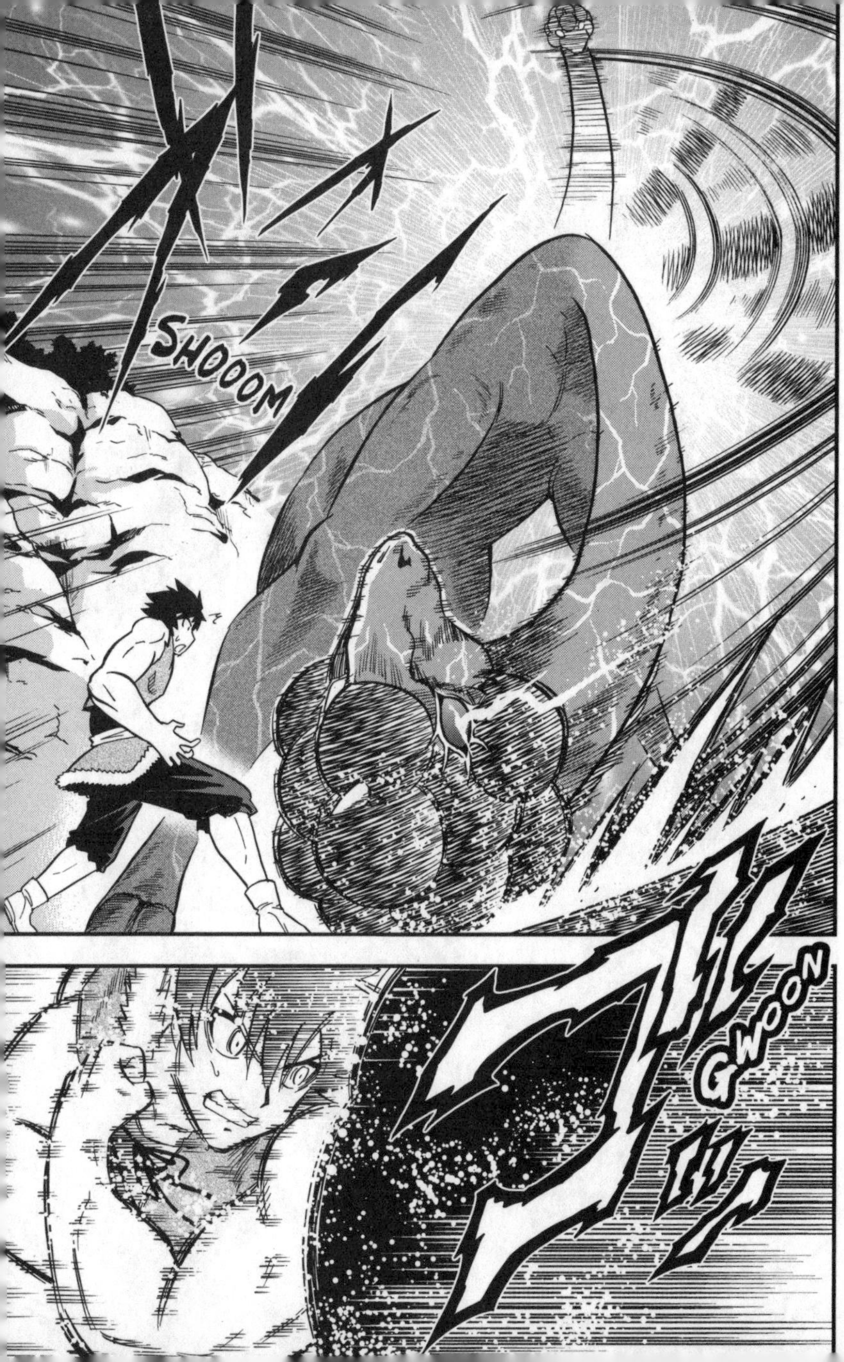
SHOOOM
GWOON

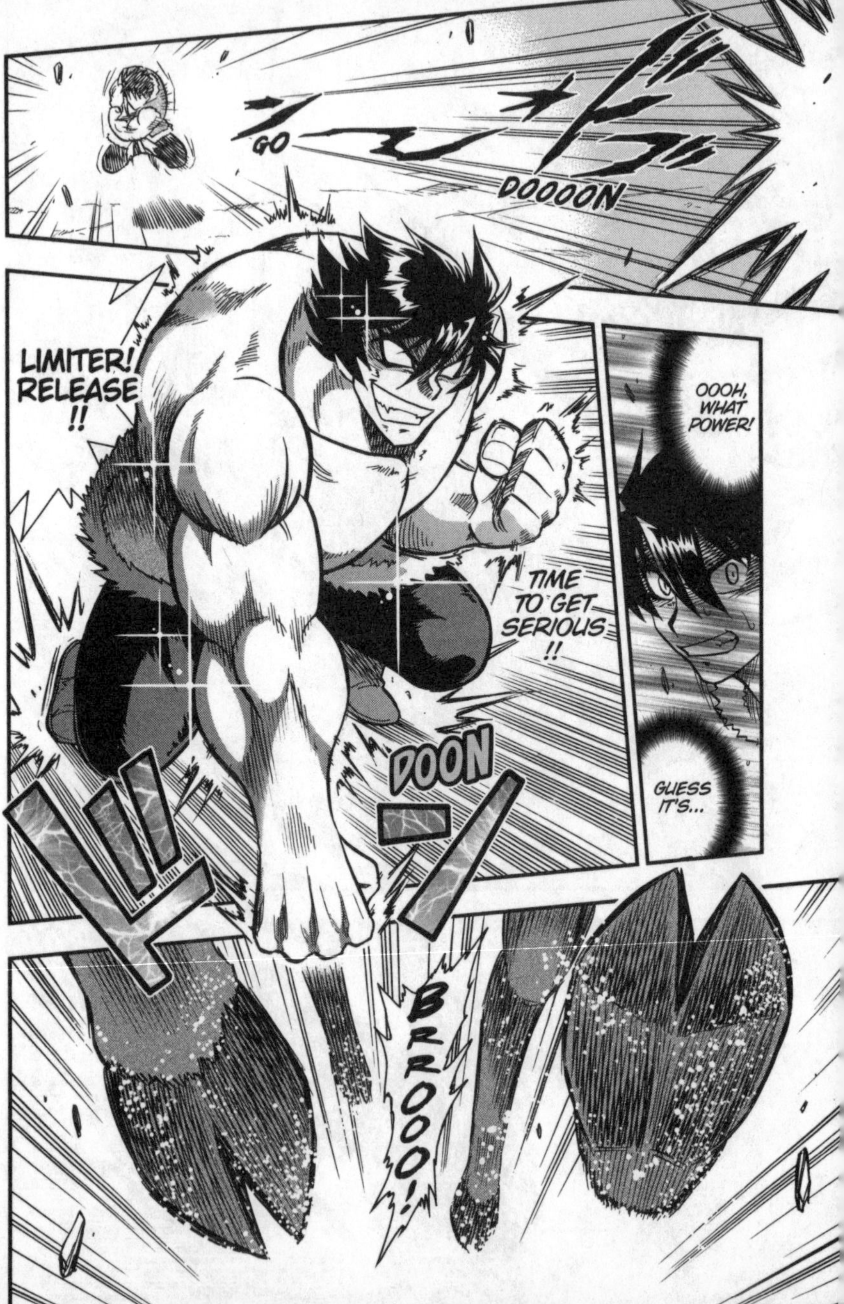
GO
DOOOOON
OOOH, WHAT POWER!
GUESS IT'S...
TIME TO GET SERIOUS !!
LIMITER! RELEASE !!
DOON
BRROOOO!

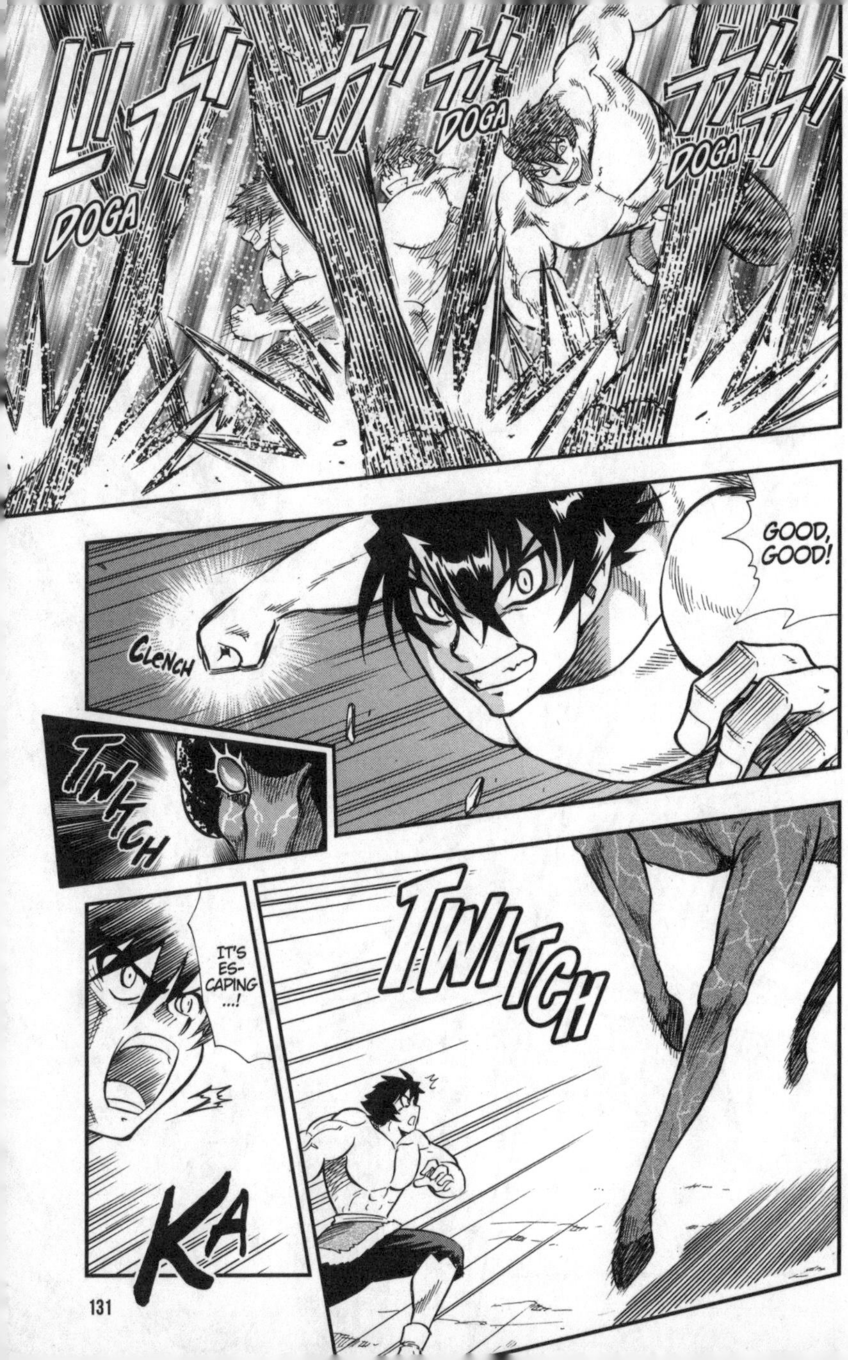
DOGA
DOGA
DOGA
DOGA
GOOD, GOOD!
CLENCH
TWITCH
TWITCH
IT'S ES-CAPING ...!
KA

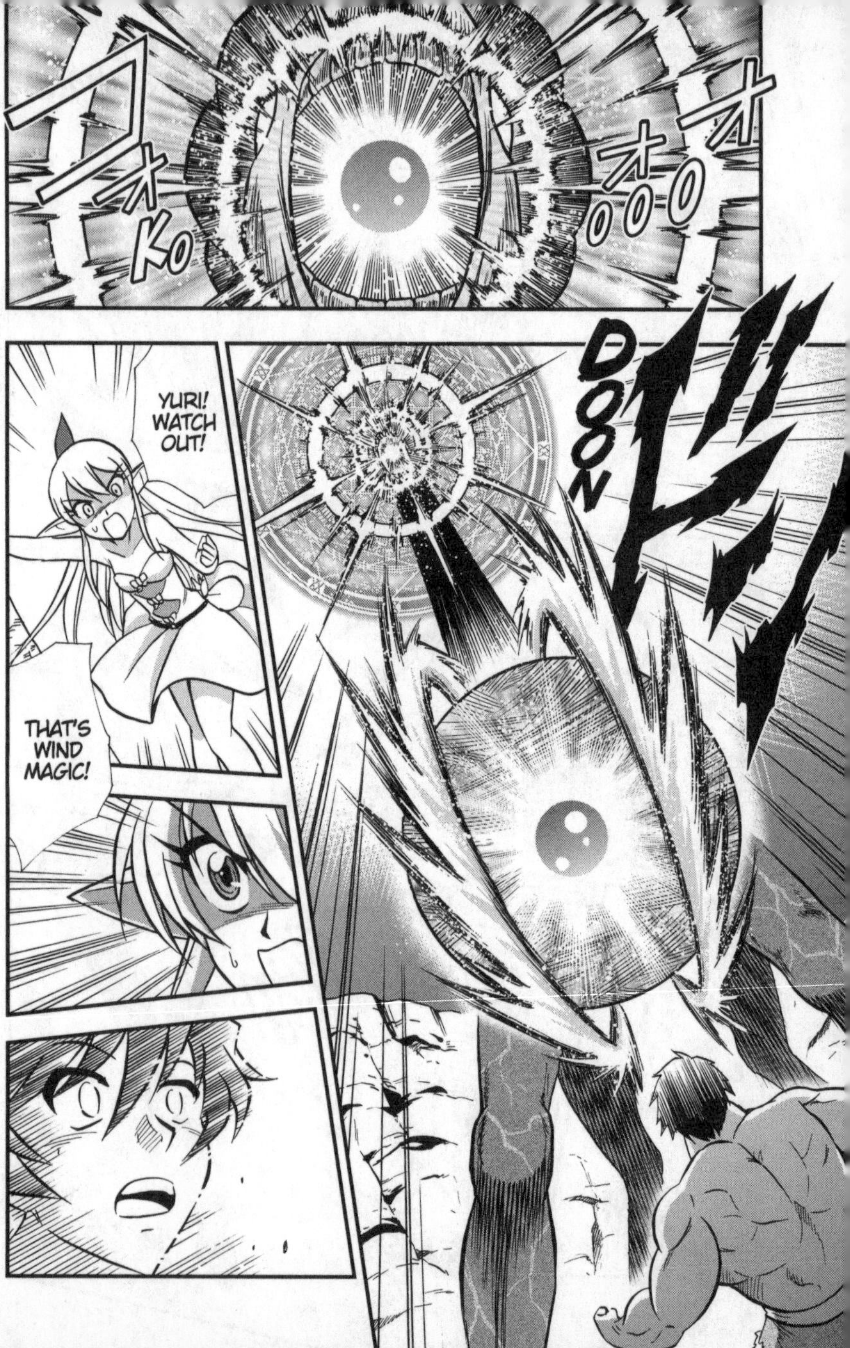
KO
OOOO
DOOON
YURI! WATCH OUT!
THAT'S WIND MAGIC!

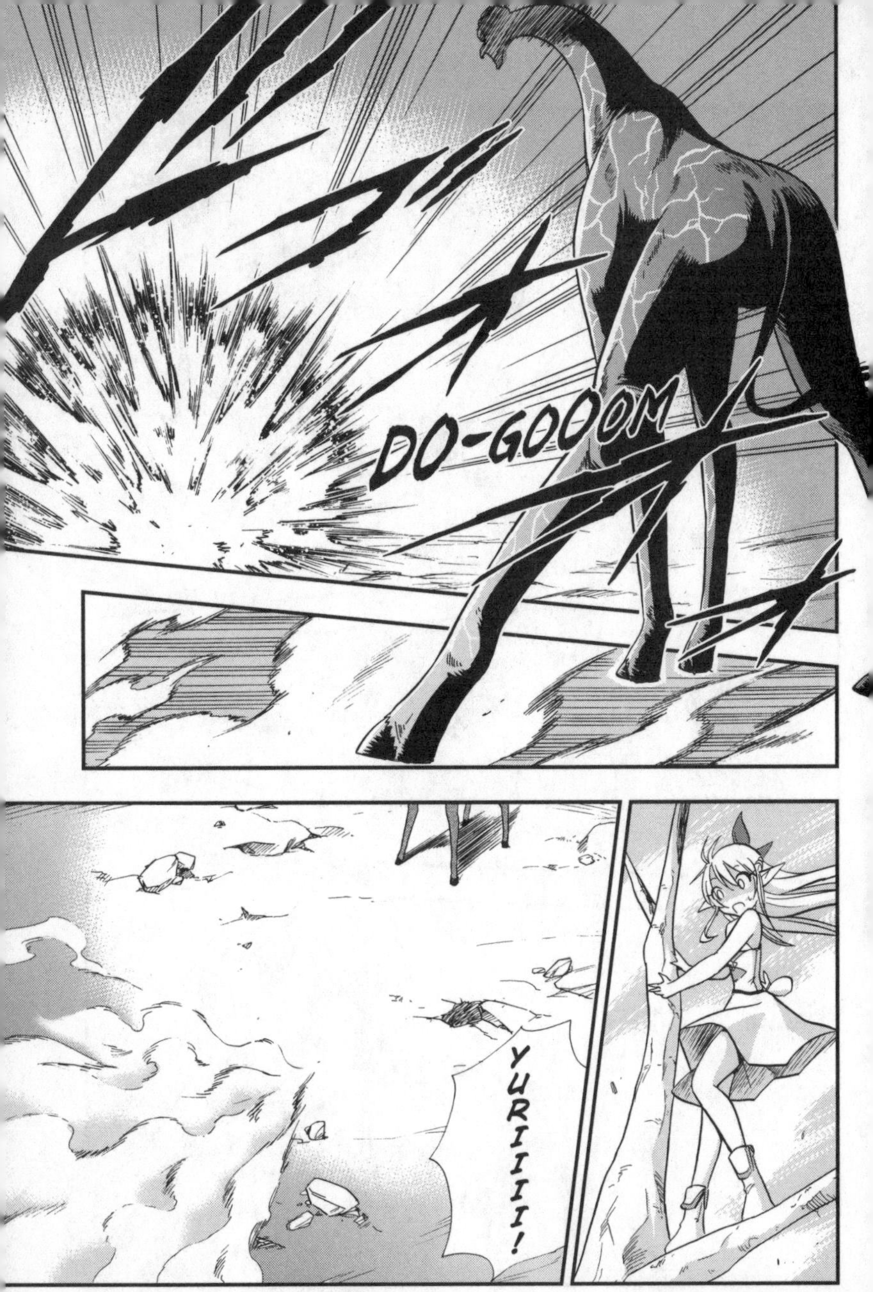
DO-GOOOM
YURIIIII!

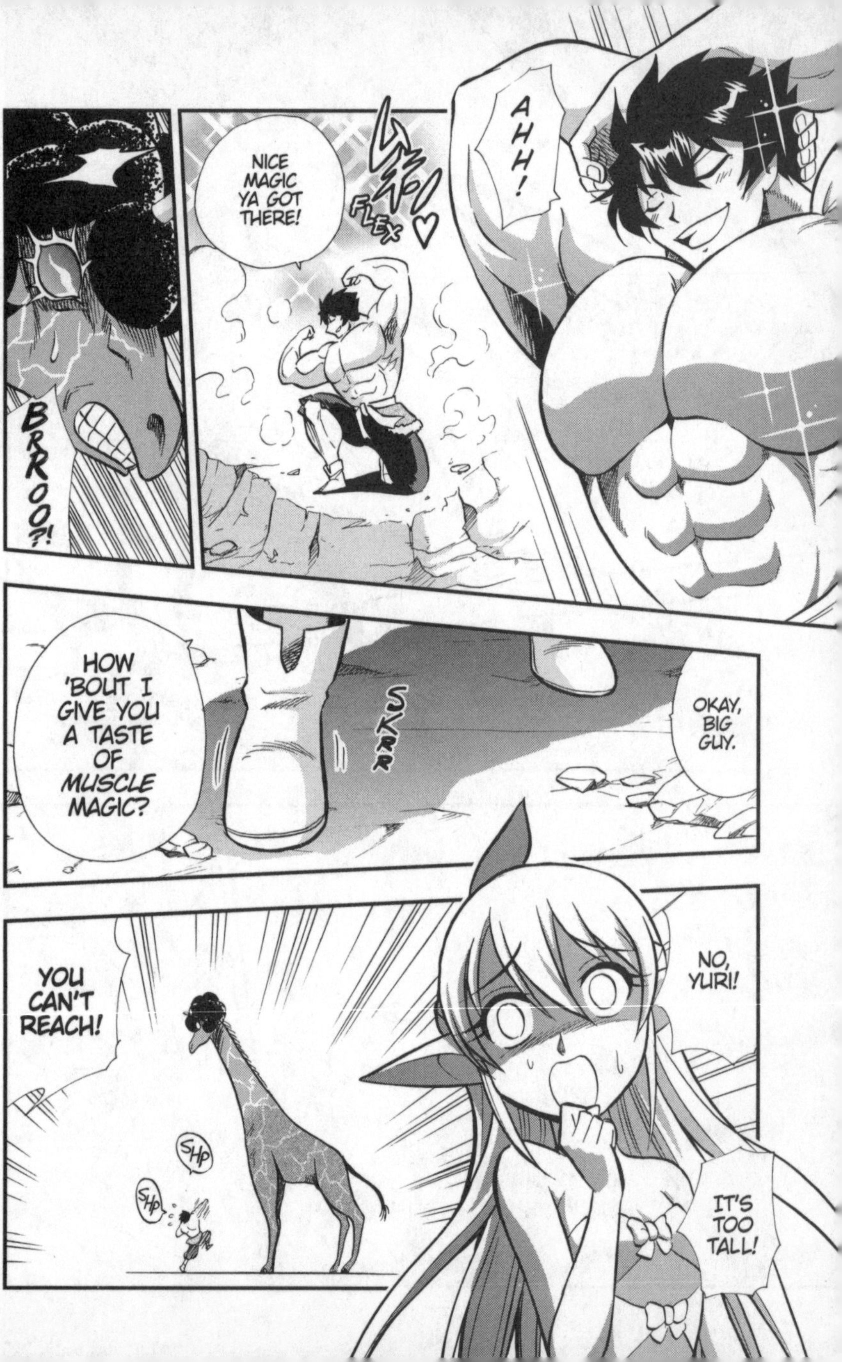
AHH!
NICE MAGIC YA GOT THERE!
FLEX
BRROO?!
OKAY, BIG GUY.
SKRR
HOW 'BOUT I GIVE YOU A TASTE OF MUSCLE MAGIC?
NO, YURI!
IT'S TOO TALL!
YOU CAN'T REACH!
SHP
SHP

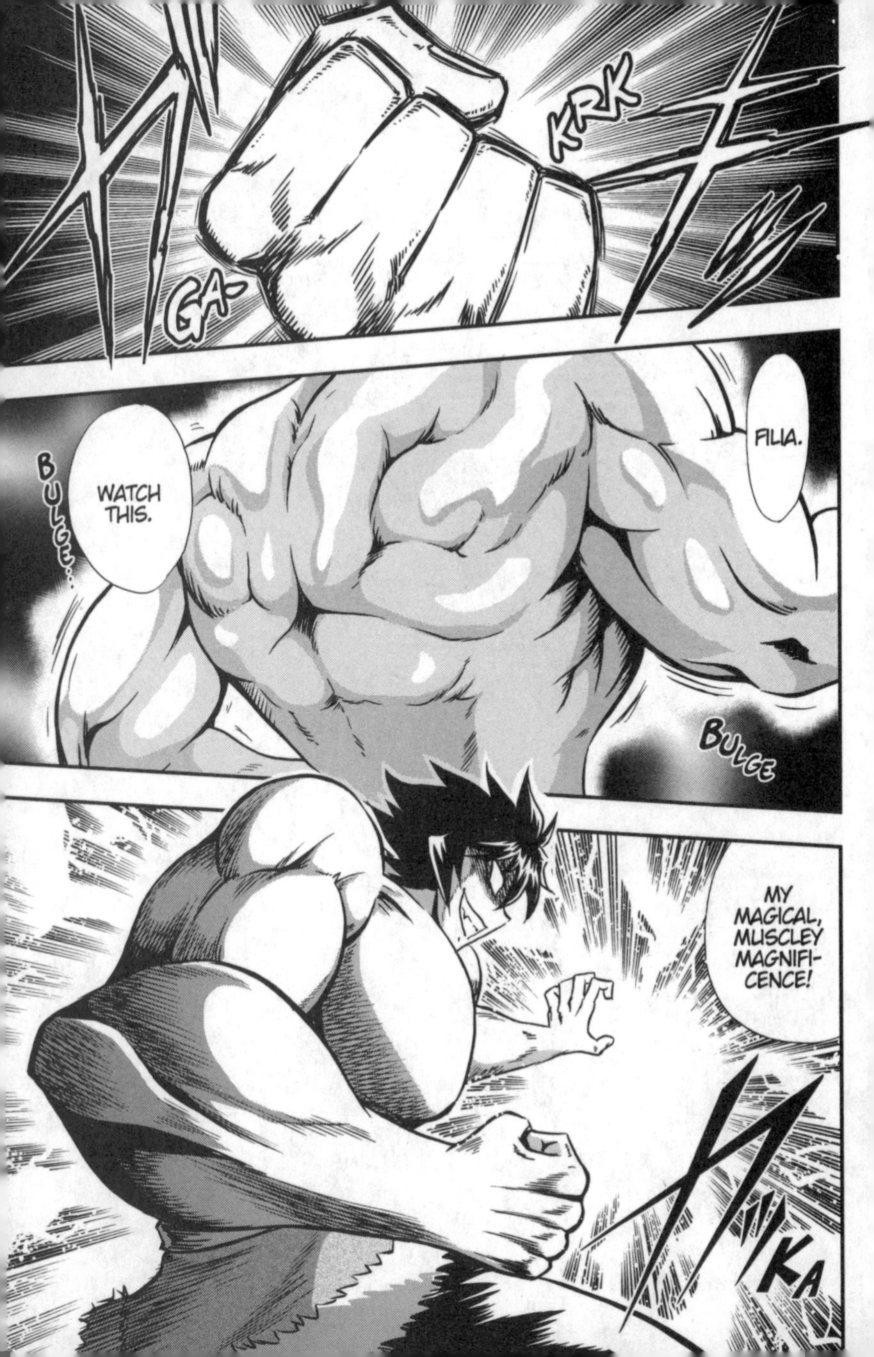
KRK
GA-
FILIA.
WATCH THIS.
BULGE...
BULGE
MY MAGICAL, MUSCLEY MAGNIFI-CENCE!
KA

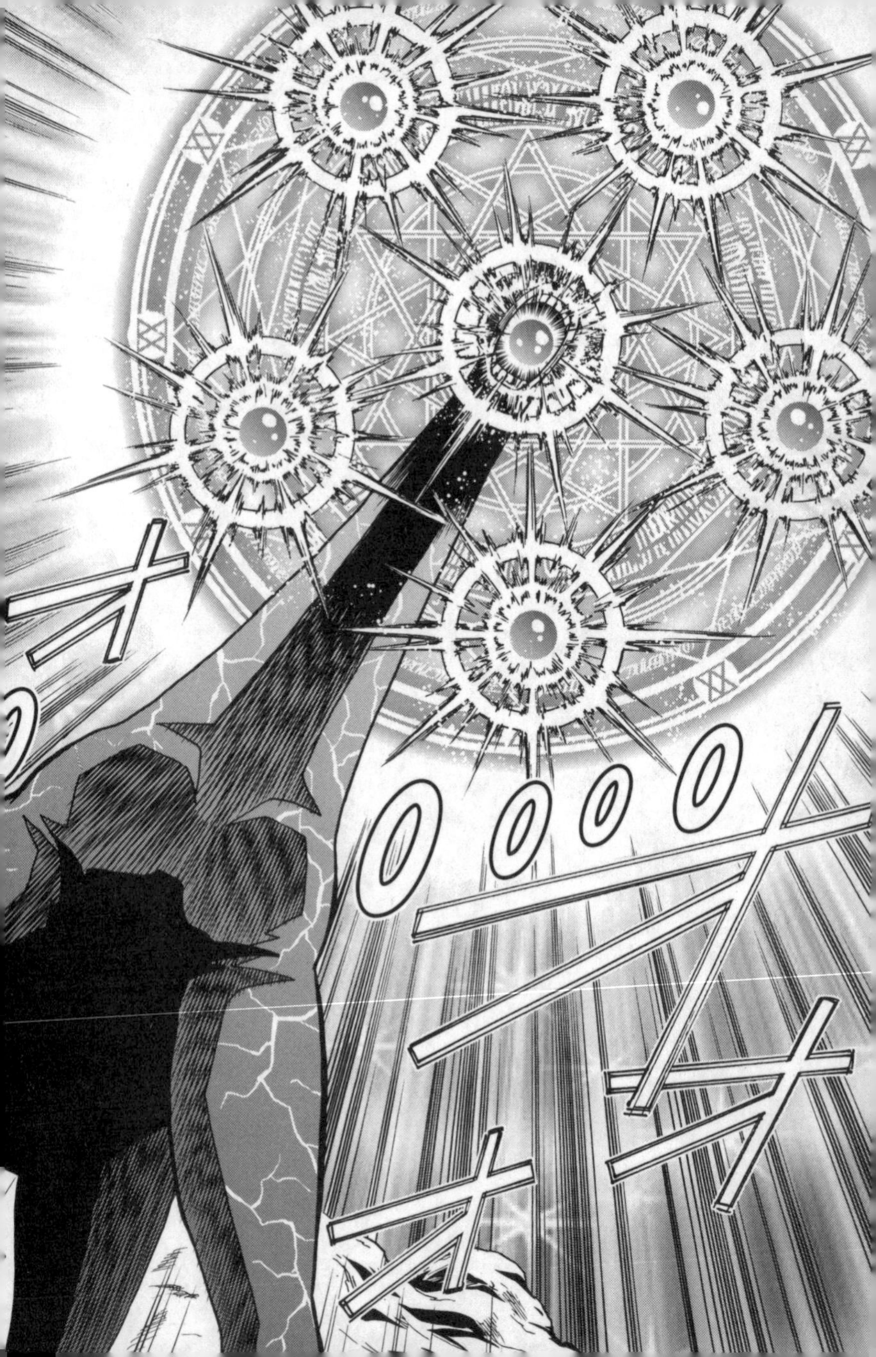

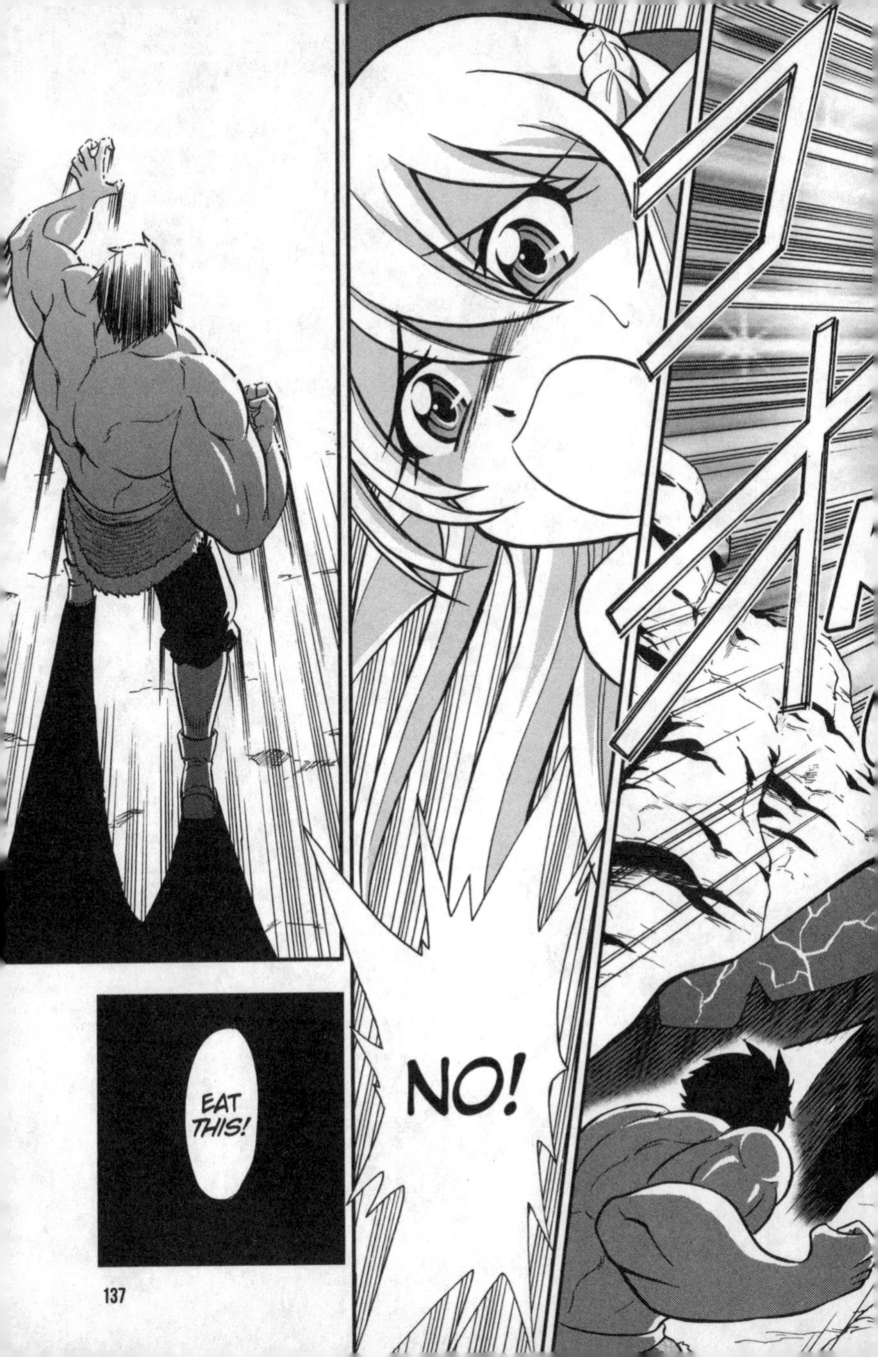
NO!
EAT THIS!

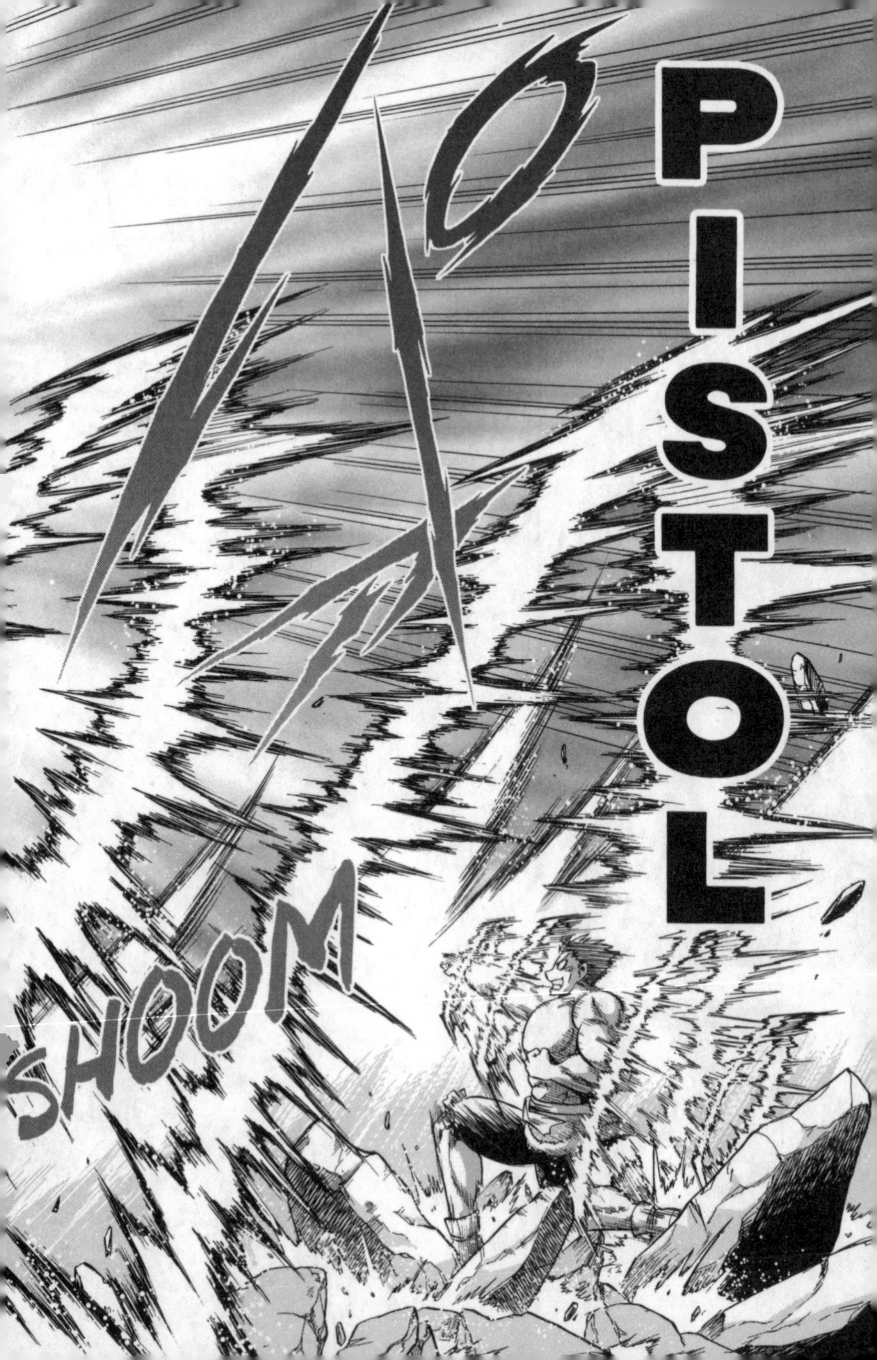
PISTOL
SHOOM

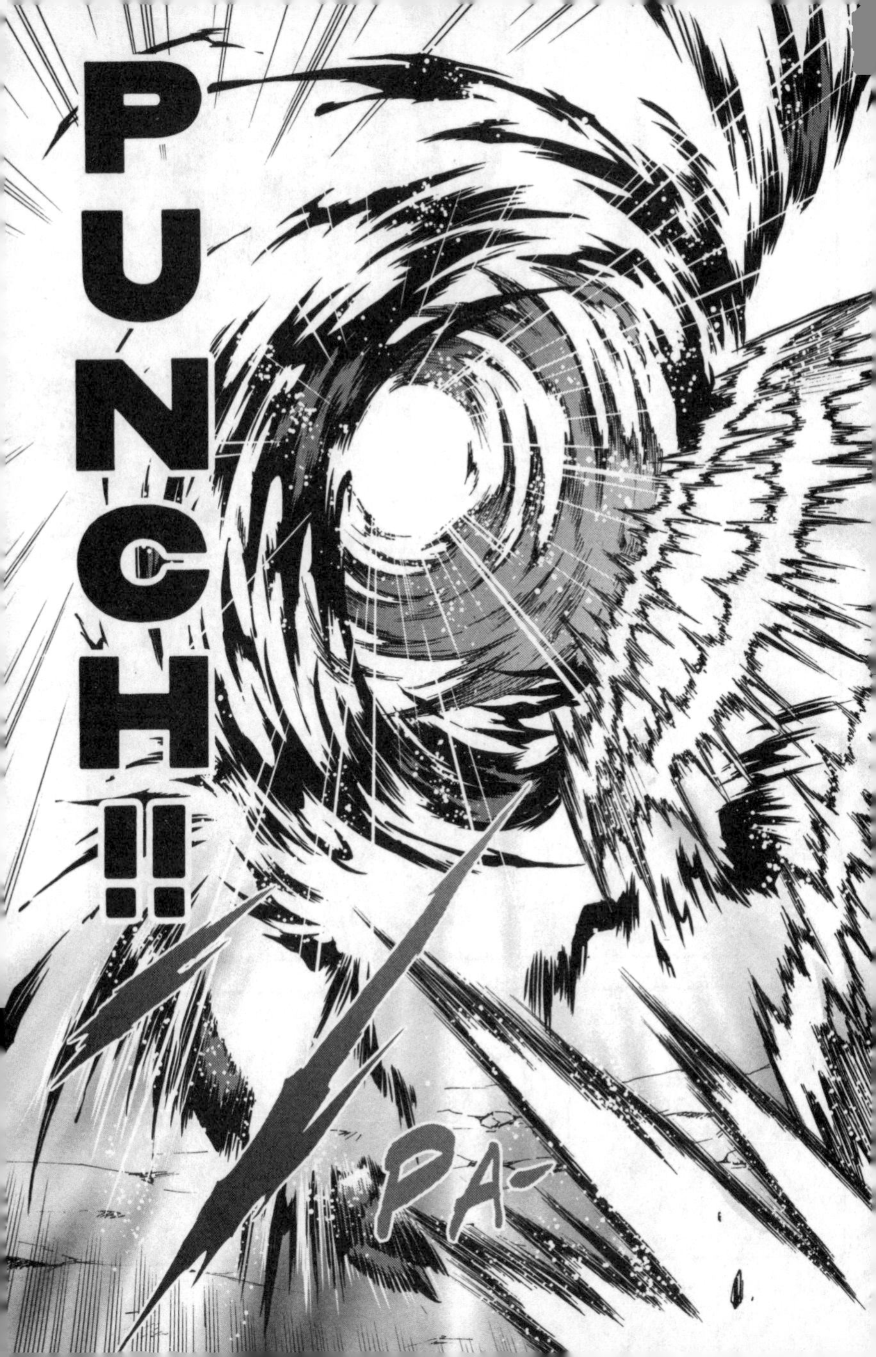
PUNCH!!
PA-

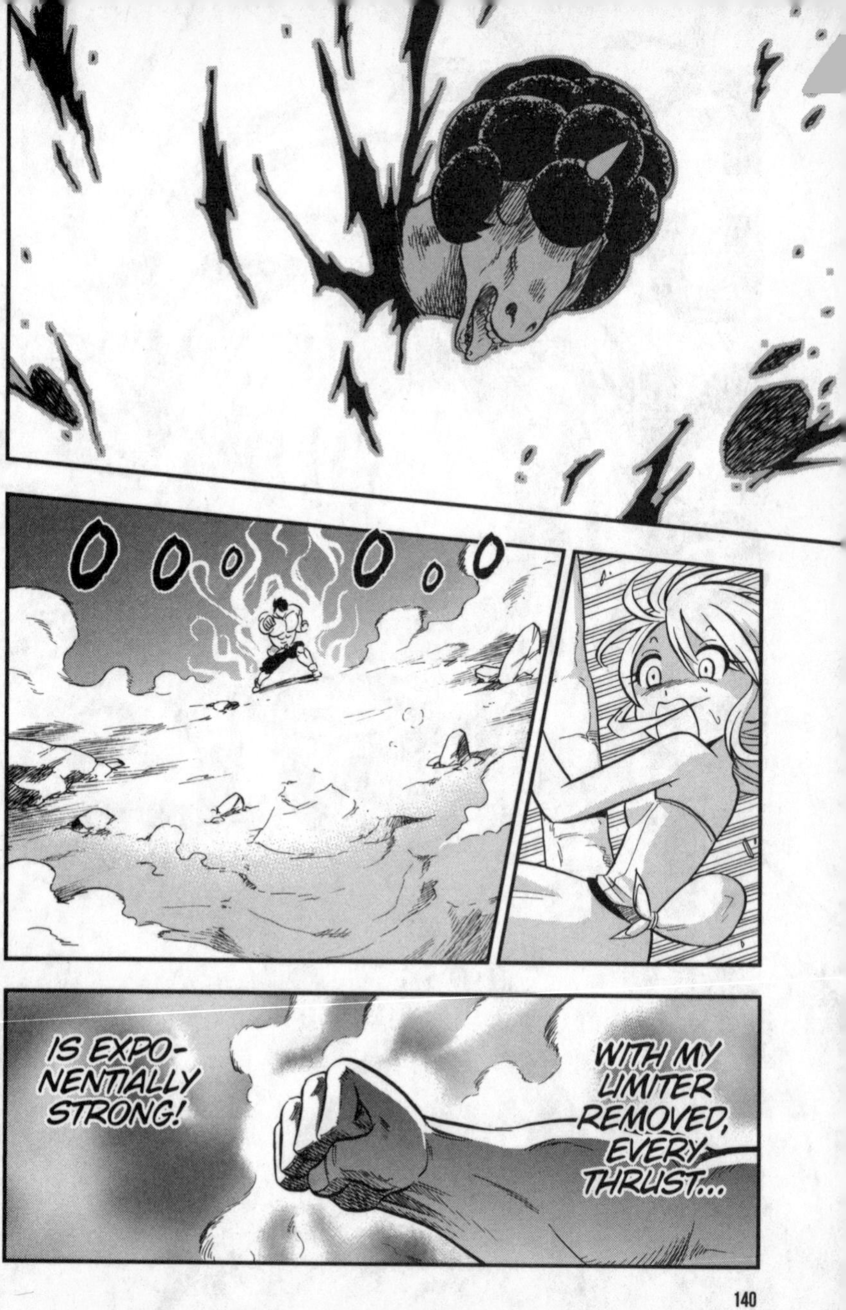
WITH MY LIMITER REMOVED, EVERY THRUST...
IS EXPONENTIALLY STRONG!

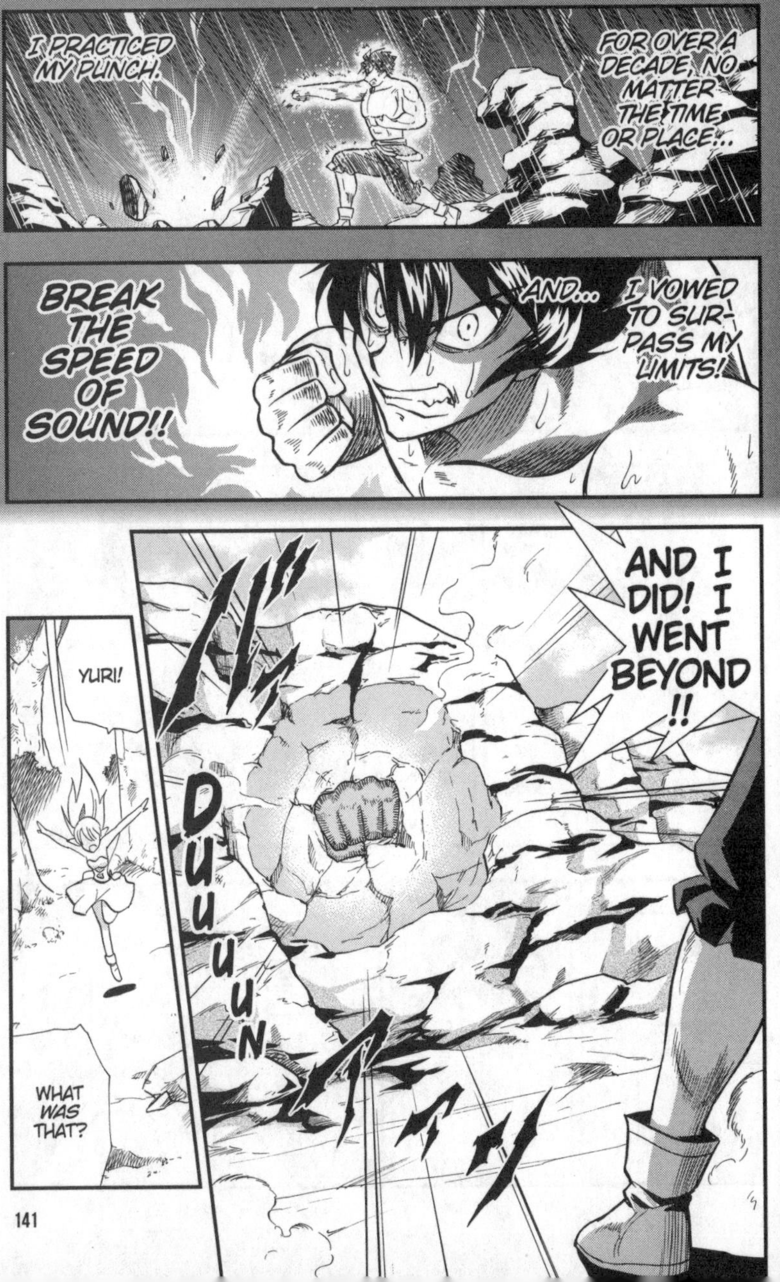
FOR OVER A DECADE, NO MATTER THE TIME OR PLACE...
I PRACTICED MY PUNCH.
AND...
I VOWED TO SUR-PASS MY LIMITS!
BREAK THE SPEED OF SOUND!!
AND I DID! I WENT BEYOND!!
DUUUUUN
YURI!
WHAT WAS THAT?

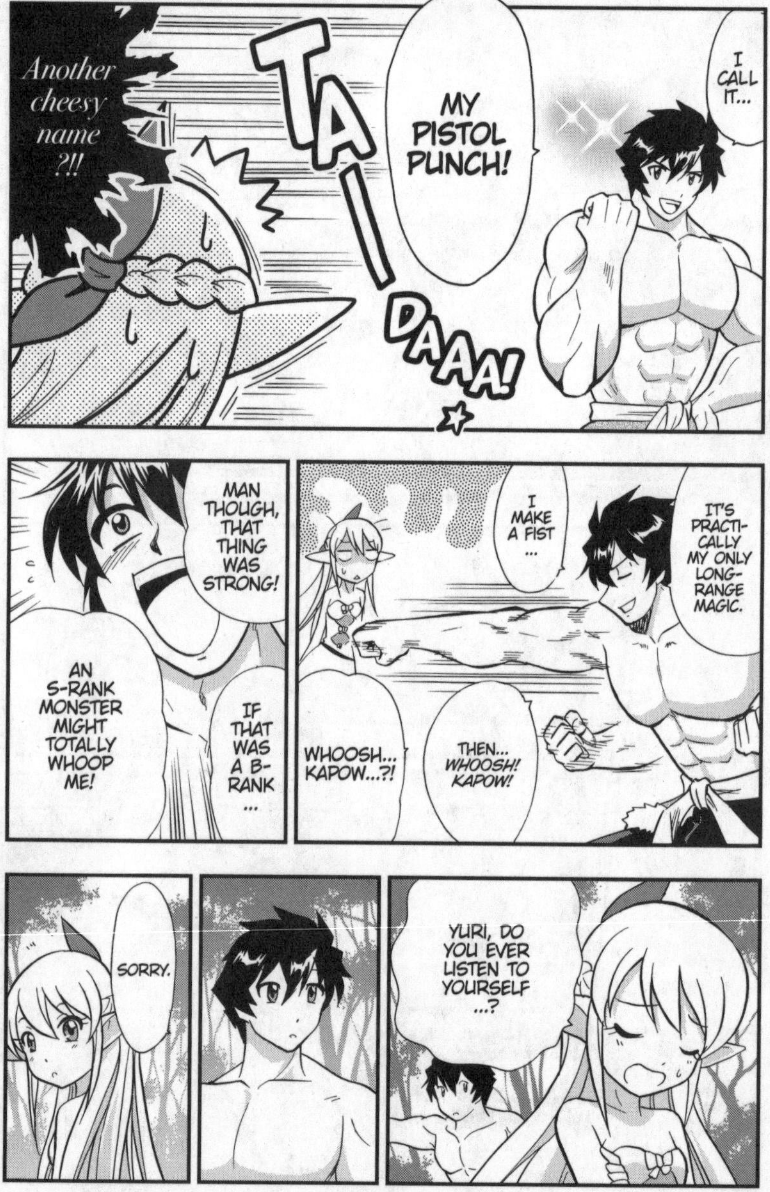

I CALL IT...
MY PISTOL PUNCH!
TA-I-DAAAA!
Another cheesy name ?!!
IT'S PRACTICALLY MY ONLY LONG-RANGE MAGIC.
I MAKE A FIST ...
THEN... WHOOSH! KAPOW!
WHOOSH... KAPOW...?!
MAN THOUGH, THAT THING WAS STRONG!
IF THAT WAS A B-RANK ...
AN S-RANK MONSTER MIGHT TOTALLY WHOOP ME!
YURI, DO YOU EVER LISTEN TO YOURSELF ...?
SORRY.

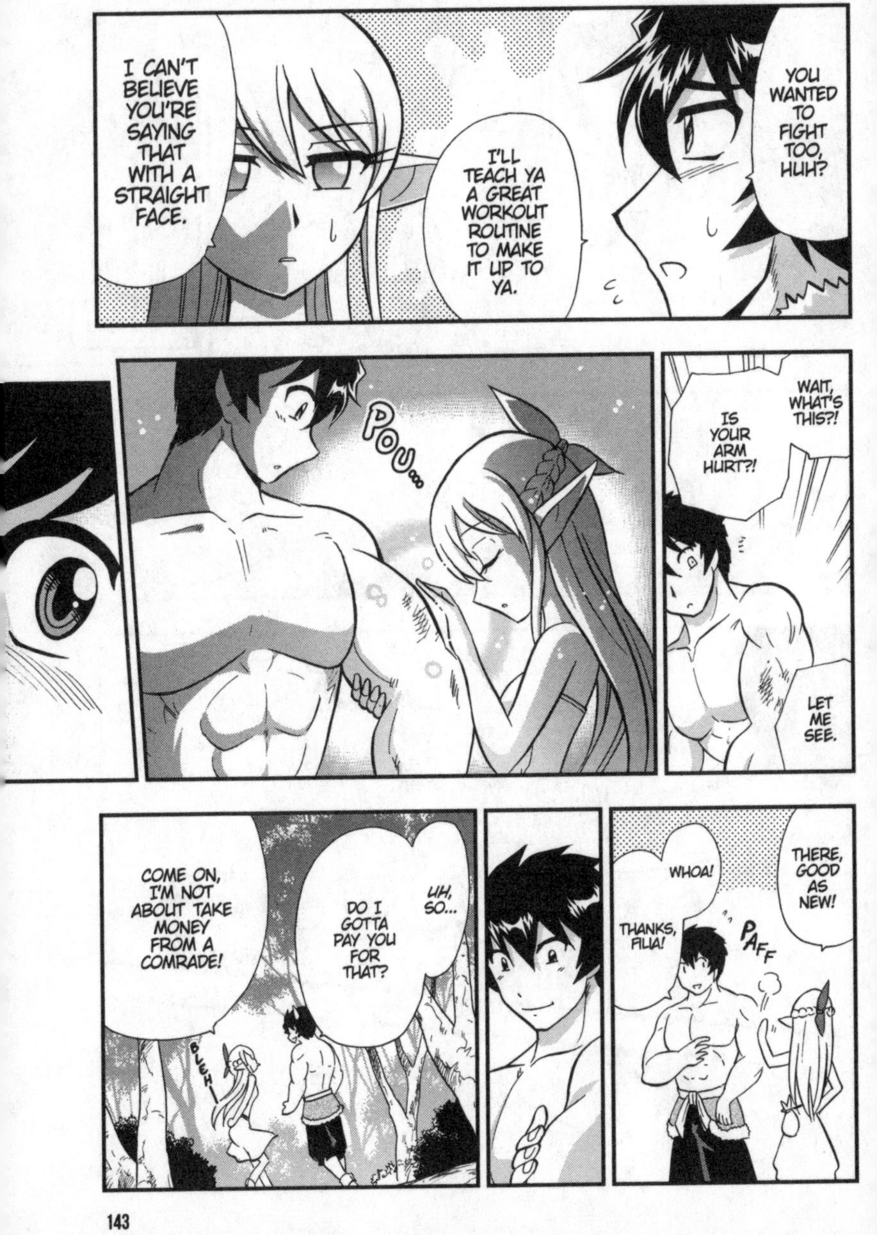
YOU WANTED TO FIGHT TOO, HUH?
I'LL TEACH YA A GREAT WORKOUT ROUTINE TO MAKE IT UP TO YA.
I CAN'T BELIEVE YOU'RE SAYING THAT WITH A STRAIGHT FACE.
WAIT, WHAT'S THIS?!
IS YOUR ARM HURT?!
LET ME SEE.
POU...
THERE, GOOD AS NEW!
WHOA!
PAFF
THANKS, FILIA!
UH, SO...
DO I GOTTA PAY YOU FOR THAT?
COME ON, I'M NOT ABOUT TAKE MONEY FROM A COMRADE!
BLEH!

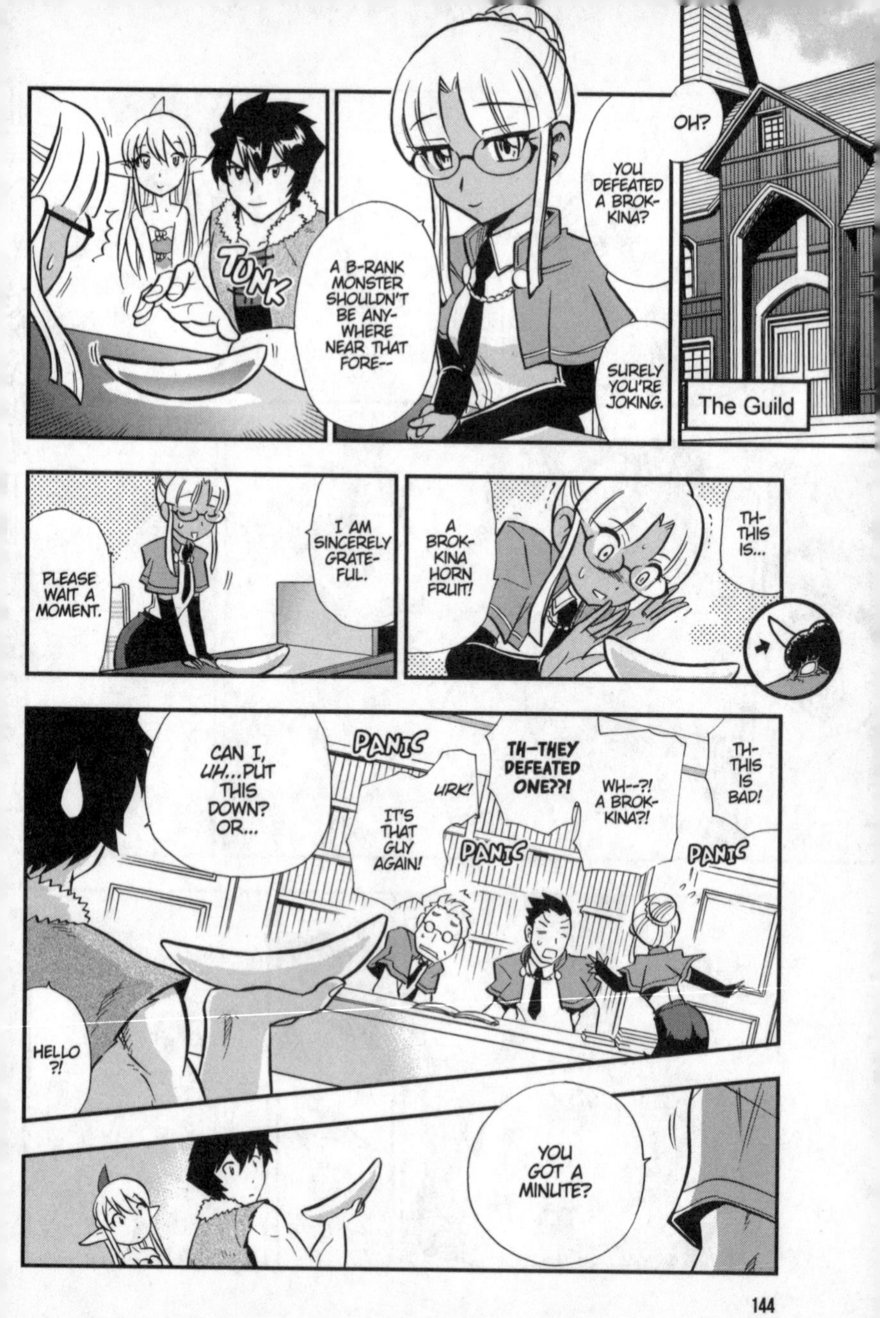

The Guild
OH?
YOU DEFEATED A BROK-KINA?
SURELY YOU'RE JOKING.
A B-RANK MONSTER SHOULDN'T BE ANY-WHERE NEAR THAT FORE--
TUNK
TH-THIS IS...
A BROK-KINA HORN FRUIT!
I AM SINCERELY GRATE-FUL.
PLEASE WAIT A MOMENT.
TH-THIS IS BAD!
WH--?! A BROK-KINA?!
TH-THEY DEFEATED ONE??!
PANIC
URK!
IT'S THAT GUY AGAIN!
PANIC
PANIC
CAN I, UH...PUT THIS DOWN? OR...
HELLO ?!
YOU GOT A MINUTE?

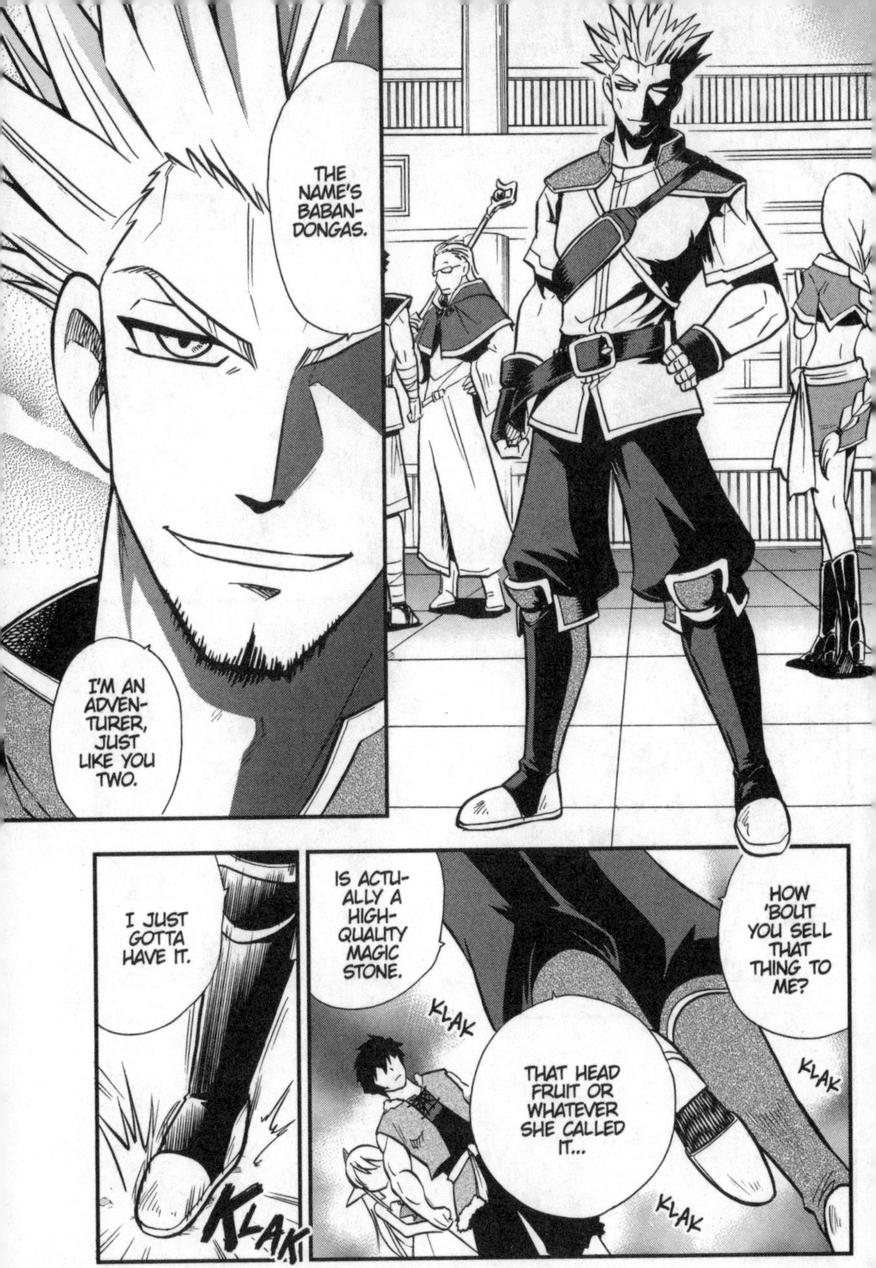
THE NAME'S BABAN-DONGAS.
I'M AN ADVEN-TURER, JUST LIKE YOU TWO.
HOW 'BOUT YOU SELL THAT THING TO ME?
KLAK
THAT HEAD FRUIT OR WHATEVER SHE CALLED IT...
IS ACTU-ALLY A HIGH-QUALITY MAGIC STONE.
KLAK
KLAK
I JUST GOTTA HAVE IT.
KLAK

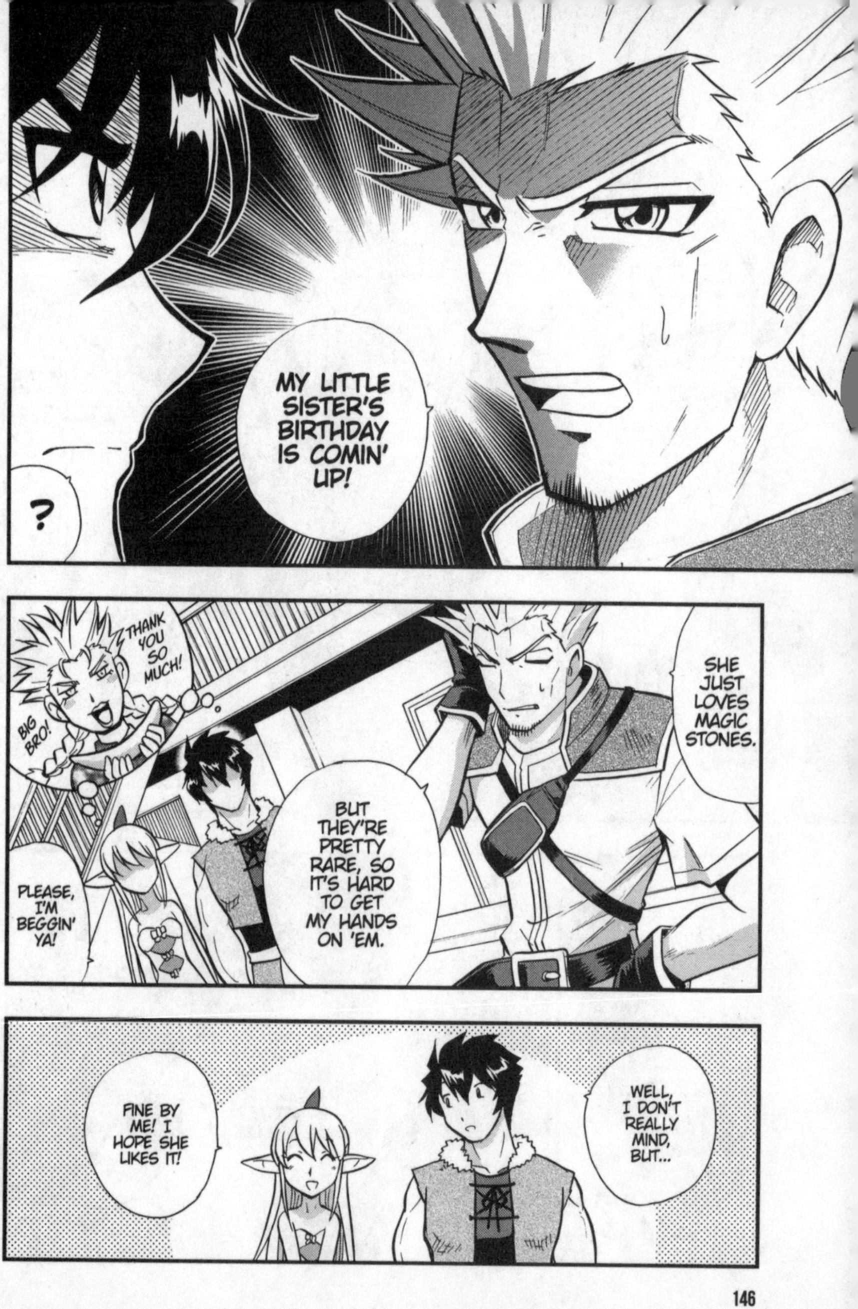
MY LITTLE SISTER'S BIRTHDAY IS COMIN' UP!
?
SHE JUST LOVES MAGIC STONES.
BUT THEY'RE PRETTY RARE, SO IT'S HARD TO GET MY HANDS ON 'EM.
THANK YOU SO MUCH!
BIG BRO!
PLEASE, I'M BEGGIN' YA!
WELL, I DON'T REALLY MIND, BUT...
FINE BY ME! I HOPE SHE LIKES IT!

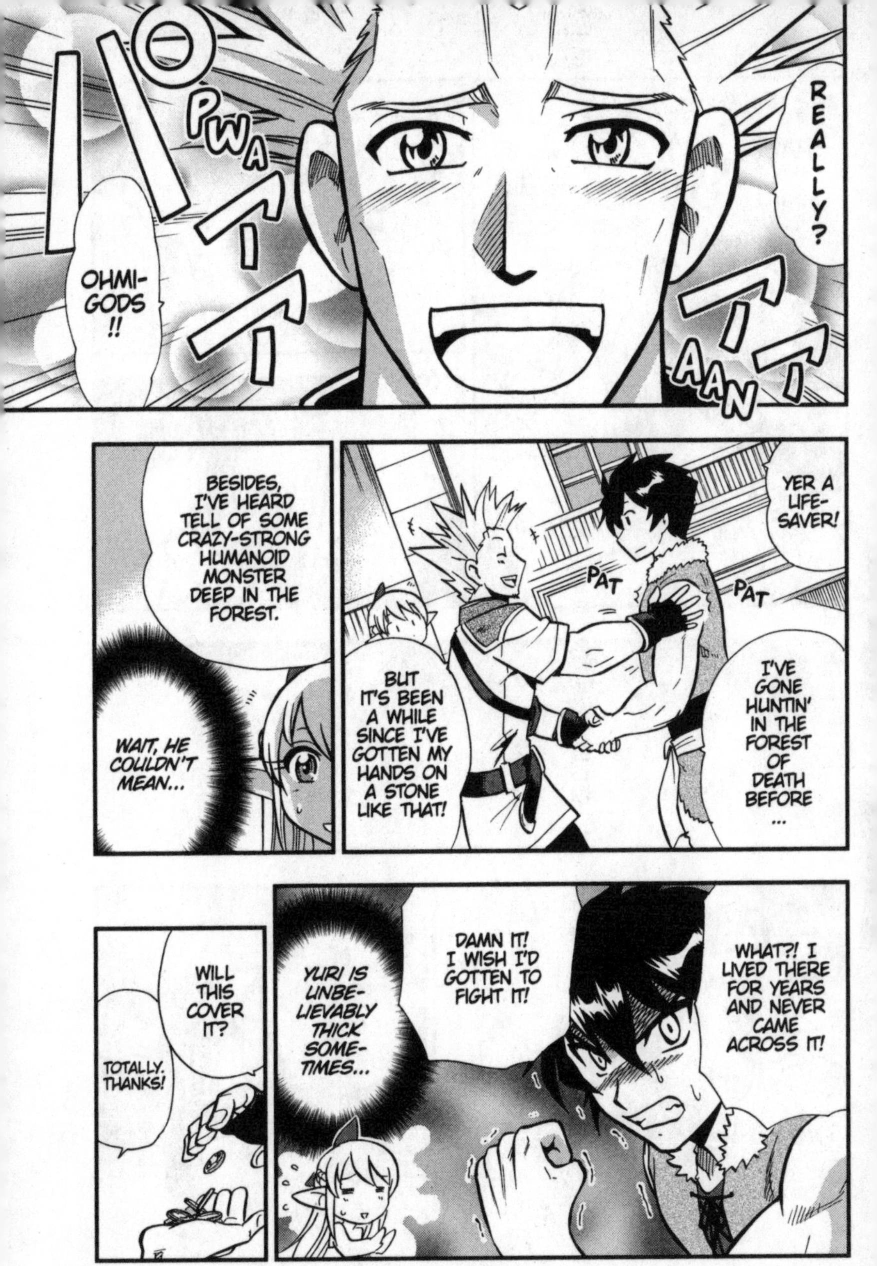
REALLY?
PWA
AAN
OHMI-GODS!!
YER A LIFE-SAVER!
PAT
PAT
I'VE GONE HUNTIN' IN THE FOREST OF DEATH BEFORE...
BUT IT'S BEEN A WHILE SINCE I'VE GOTTEN MY HANDS ON A STONE LIKE THAT!
BESIDES, I'VE HEARD TELL OF SOME CRAZY-STRONG HUMANOID MONSTER DEEP IN THE FOREST.
WAIT, HE COULDN'T MEAN...
WHAT?! I LIVED THERE FOR YEARS AND NEVER CAME ACROSS IT!
DAMN IT! I WISH I'D GOTTEN TO FIGHT IT!
YURI IS UNBE-LIEVABLY THICK SOME-TIMES...
WILL THIS COVER IT?
TOTALLY. THANKS!

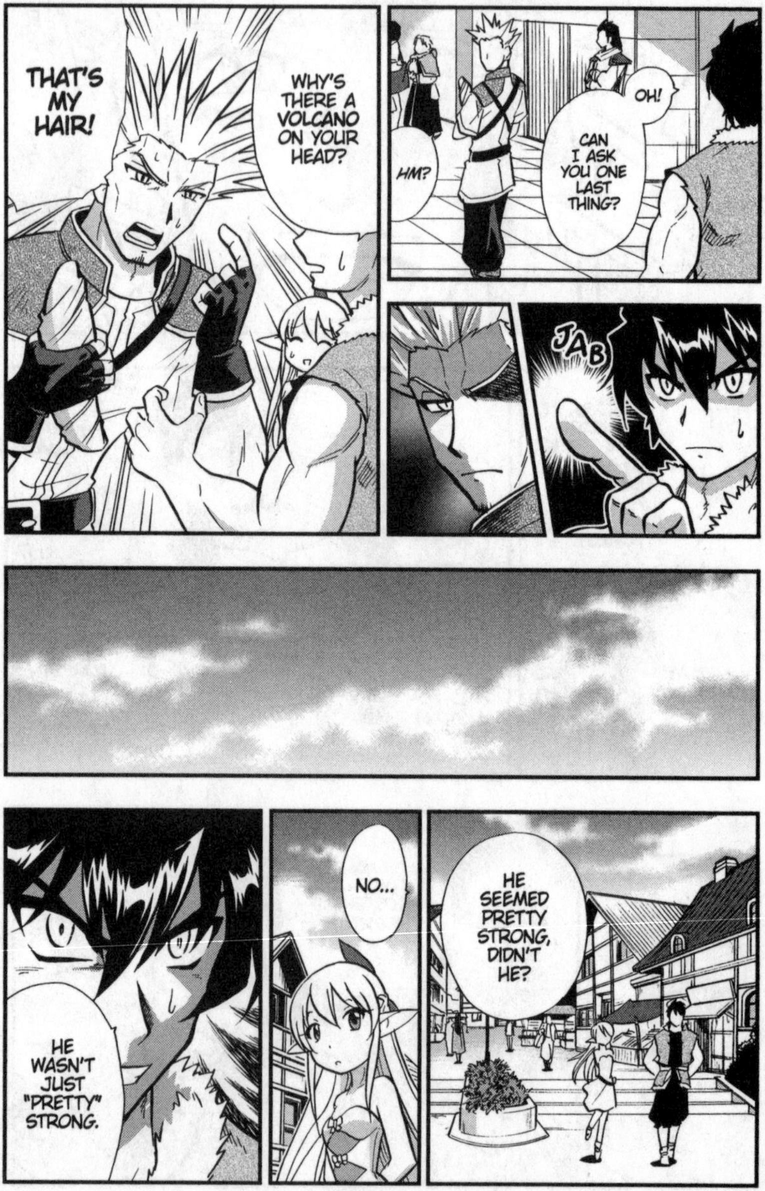
OH!
CAN I ASK YOU ONE LAST THING?
HM?
JAB
WHY'S THERE A VOLCANO ON YOUR HEAD?
THAT'S MY HAIR!
HE SEEMED PRETTY STRONG, DIDN'T HE?
NO...
HE WASN'T JUST "PRETTY" STRONG.

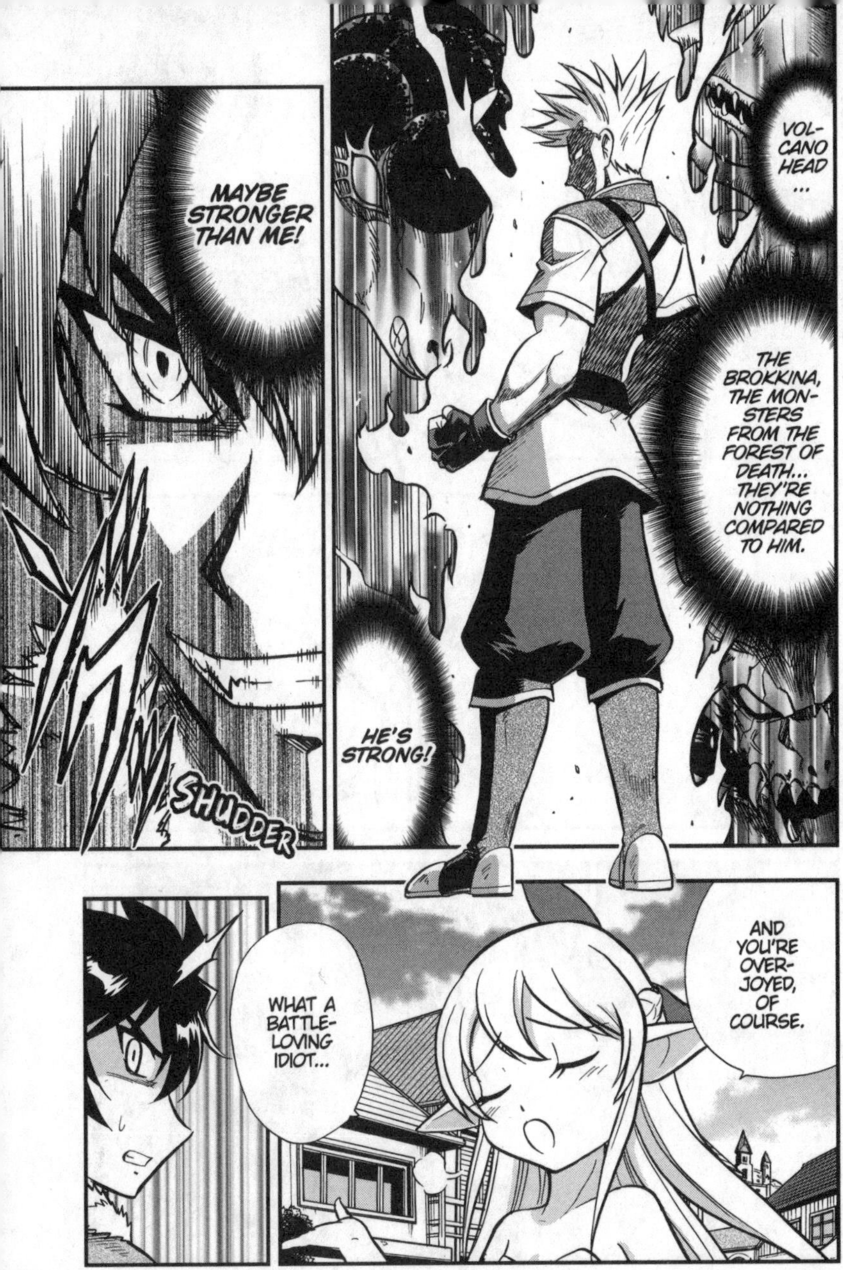
VOL-
CANO
HEAD
...
THE BROKKINA, THE MON-STERS FROM THE FOREST OF DEATH... THEY'RE NOTHING COMPARED TO HIM.
HE'S STRONG!
MAYBE STRONGER THAN ME!
SHUDDER
AND YOU'RE OVER-JOYED, OF COURSE.
WHAT A BATTLE-LOVING IDIOT...

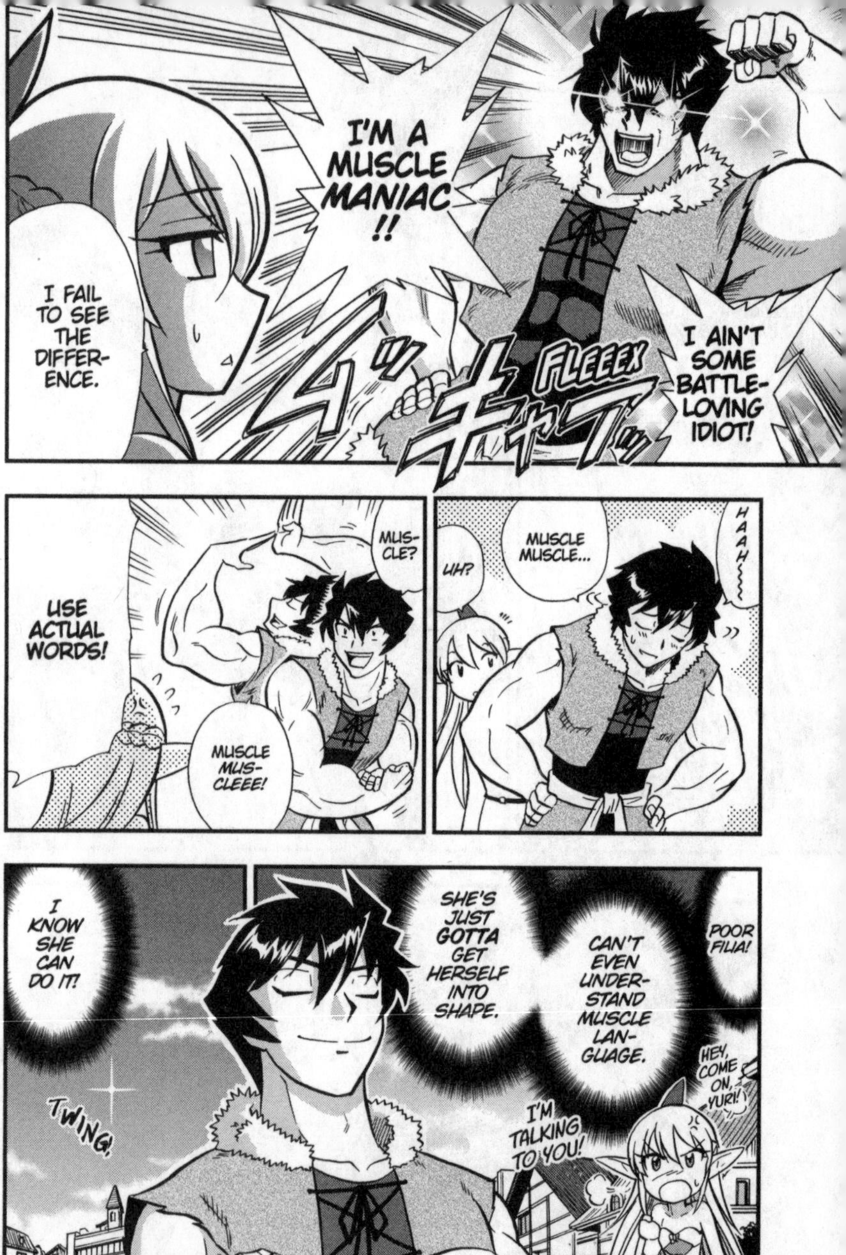
I AIN'T SOME BATTLE-LOVING IDIOT!
I'M A MUSCLE MANIAC!!
FLEEEX
I FAIL TO SEE THE DIFFERENCE.
HAAAH~~
MUSCLE MUSCLE...
UH?
MUSCLE?
MUSCLE MUSCLEEE!
USE ACTUAL WORDS!
POOR FILIA!
CAN'T EVEN UNDERSTAND MUSCLE LANGUAGE.
SHE'S JUST GOTTA GET HERSELF INTO SHAPE.
I KNOW SHE CAN DO IT!
TWING!
HEY, COME ON, YURI!
I'M TALKING TO YOU!
CHAPTER 4 END

"Pistol" is the name of a magical tool.

BA-KIIIN

It uses wind magic to shoot lead balls!!

MUSCLES ARE BETTER THAN MAGIC!

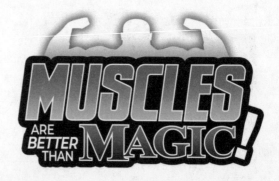

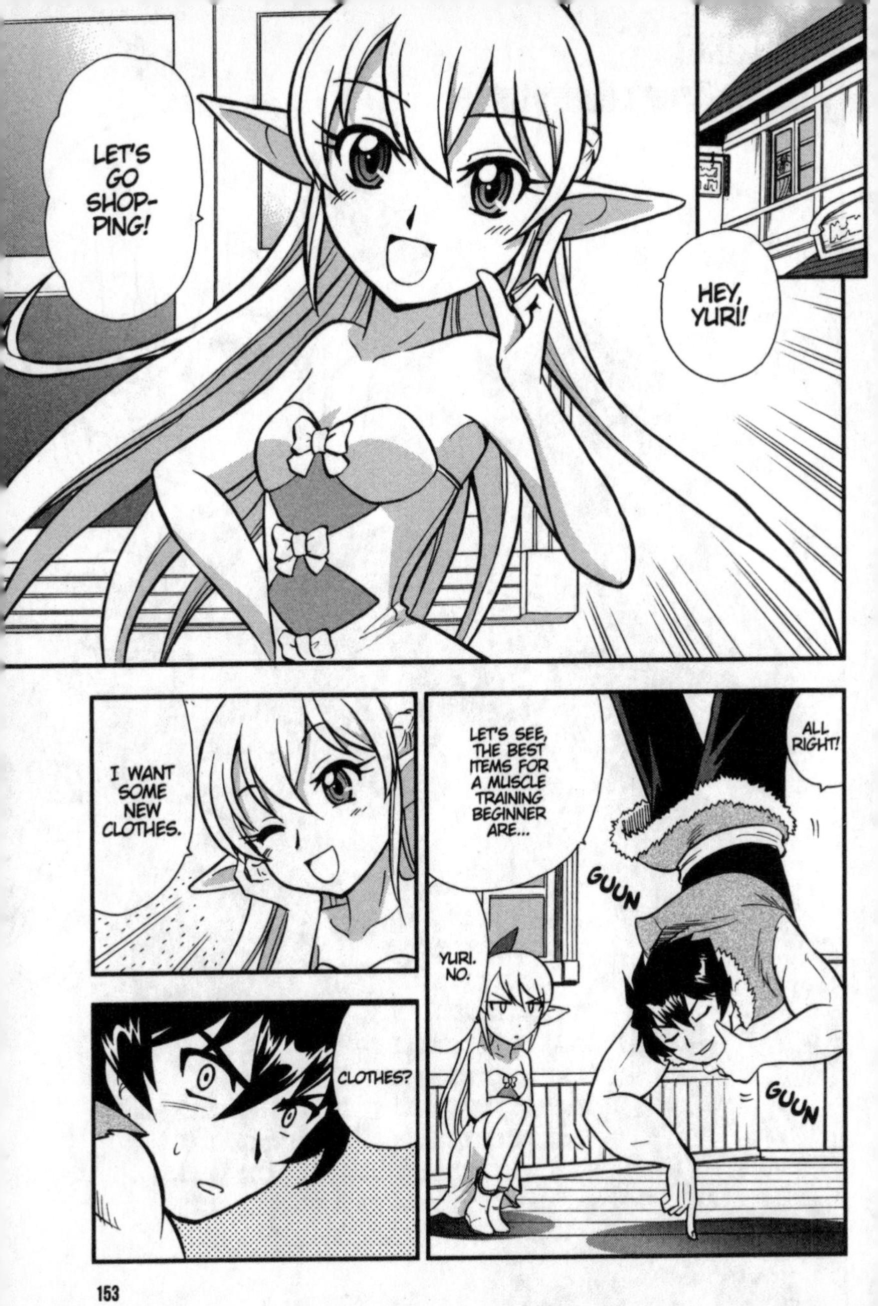

HEY, YURI!
LET'S GO SHOP-PING!
ALL RIGHT!
LET'S SEE, THE BEST ITEMS FOR A MUSCLE TRAINING BEGINNER ARE...
GUUN
GUUN
YURI. NO.
I WANT SOME NEW CLOTHES.
CLOTHES?

CHAPTER 5

Looks Aren't Everything

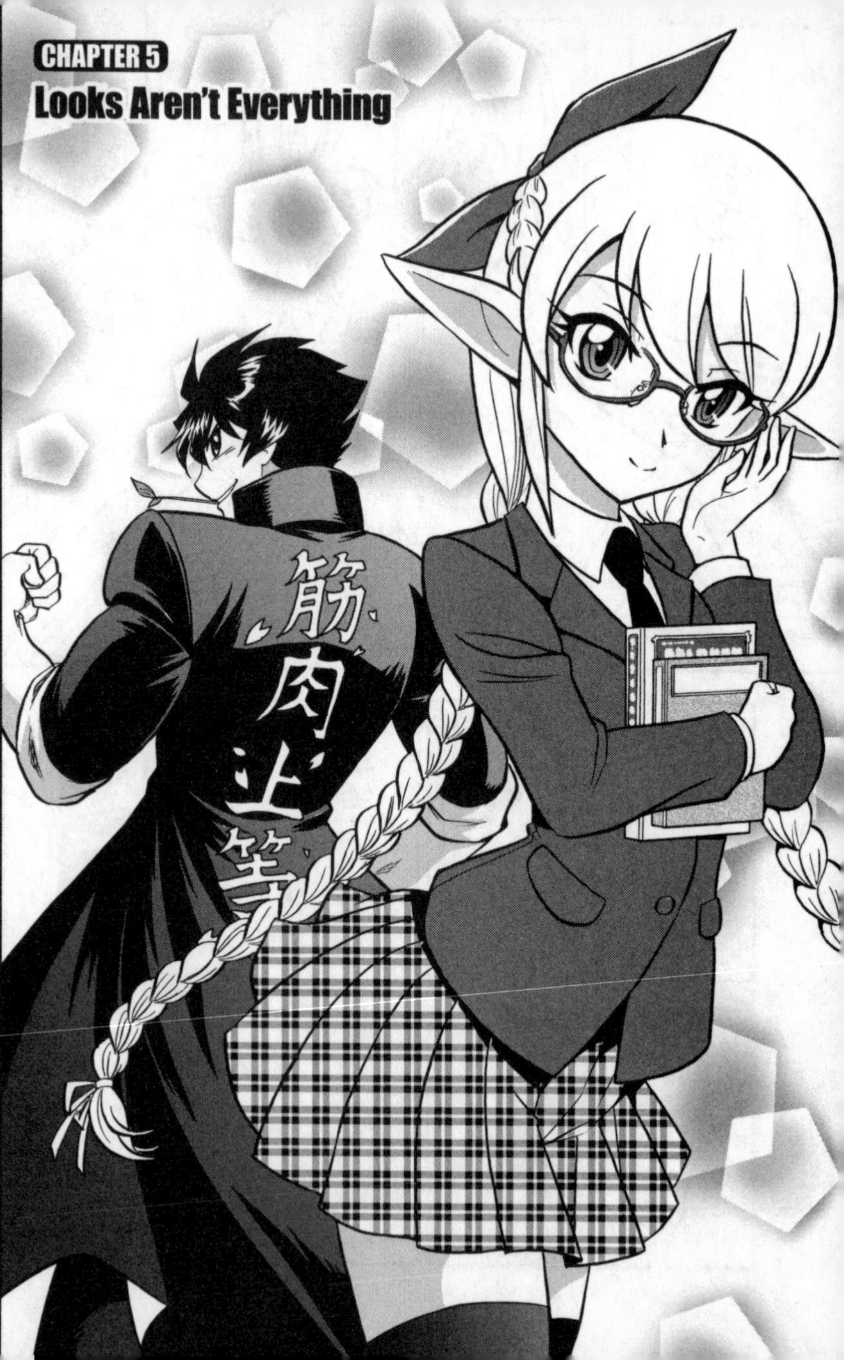
筋肉上等
Jacket: Supreme Muscle

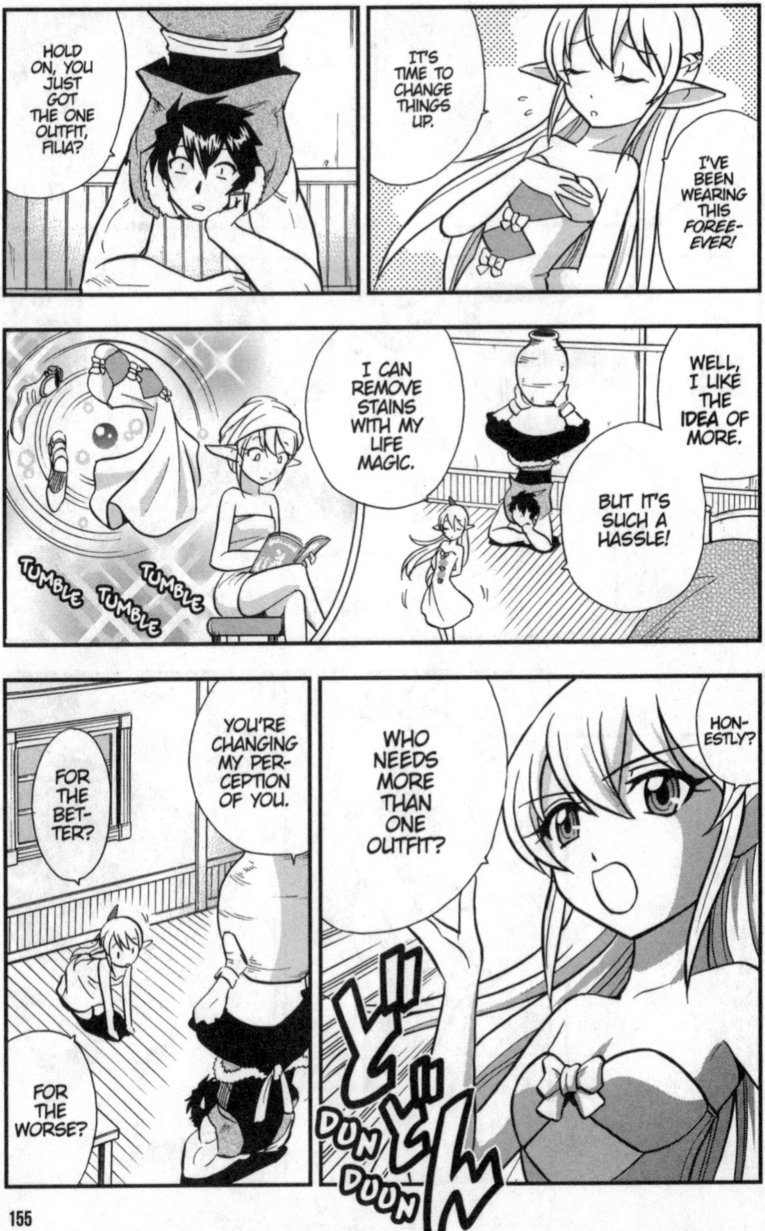
IT'S TIME TO CHANGE THINGS UP.
I'VE BEEN WEARING THIS FOREE-EVER!
HOLD ON, YOU JUST GOT THE ONE OUTFIT, FILIA?
WELL, I LIKE THE IDEA OF MORE.
BUT IT'S SUCH A HASSLE!
I CAN REMOVE STAINS WITH MY LIFE MAGIC.
TUMBLE TUMBLE TUMBLE
HON-ESTLY?
WHO NEEDS MORE THAN ONE OUTFIT?
DUN DUUN
YOU'RE CHANGING MY PER-CEPTION OF YOU.
FOR THE BET-TER?
FOR THE WORSE?

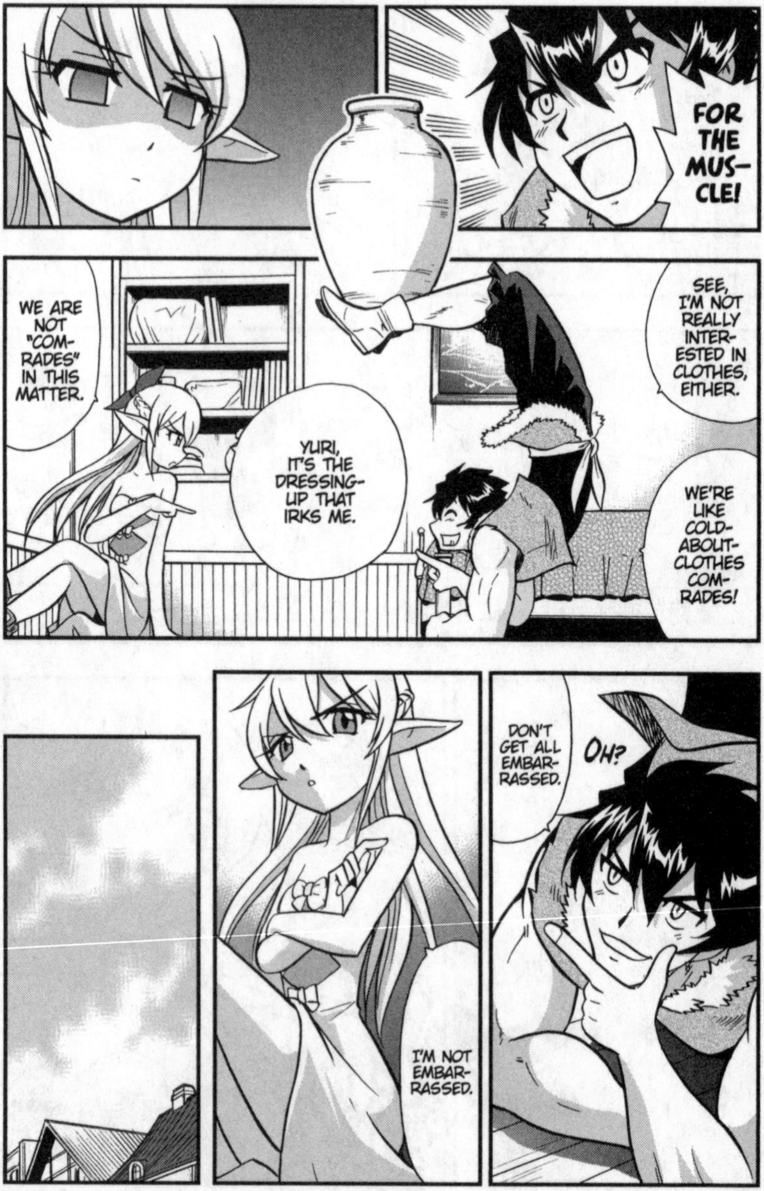
FOR THE MUSCLE!
SEE, I'M NOT REALLY INTERESTED IN CLOTHES, EITHER.
WE'RE LIKE COLD-ABOUT-CLOTHES COMRADES!
WE ARE NOT "COMRADES" IN THIS MATTER.
YURI, IT'S THE DRESSING-UP THAT IRKS ME.
OH?
DON'T GET ALL EMBARRASSED.
I'M NOT EMBARRASSED.

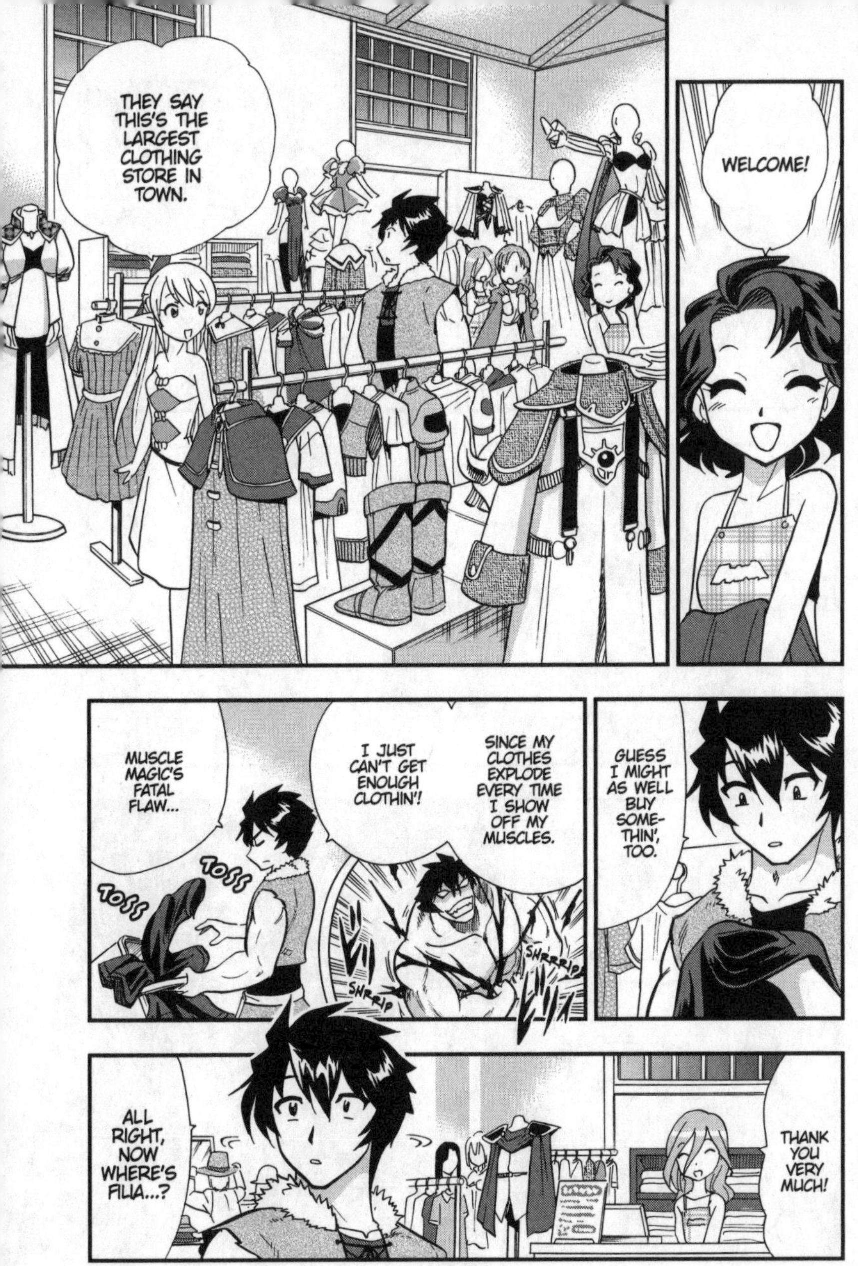
WELCOME!
THEY SAY THIS'S THE LARGEST CLOTHING STORE IN TOWN.
GUESS I MIGHT AS WELL BUY SOME-THIN', TOO.
SINCE MY CLOTHES EXPLODE EVERY TIME I SHOW OFF MY MUSCLES.
I JUST CAN'T GET ENOUGH CLOTHIN'!
SHRRRIP
SHRRIP
MUSCLE MAGIC'S FATAL FLAW...
TOSS
TOSS
THANK YOU VERY MUCH!
ALL RIGHT, NOW WHERE'S FILIA...?

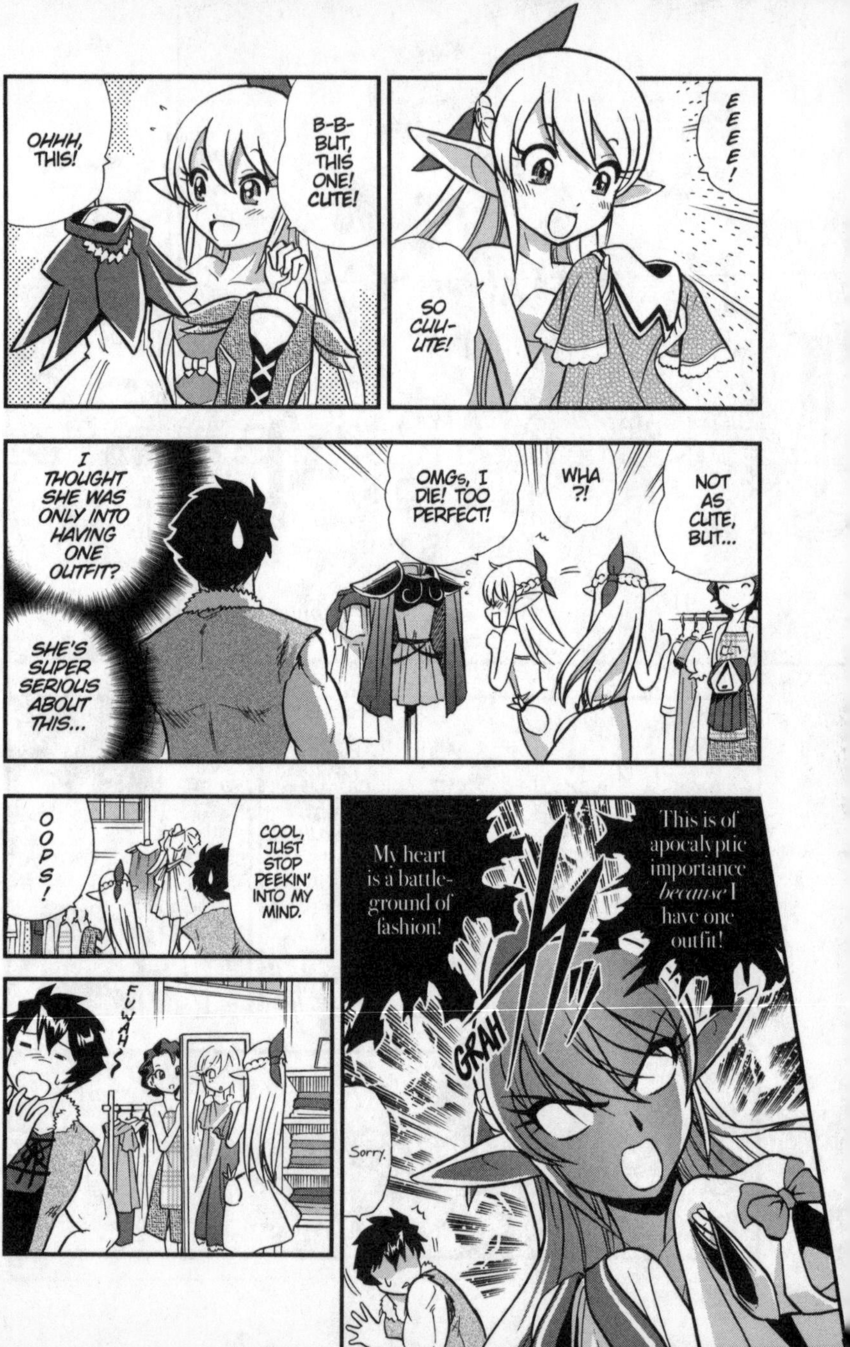
EEEE!
SO CUUU-UTE!
B-B-BUT, THIS ONE! CUTE!
OHHH, THIS!
NOT AS CUTE, BUT...
WHA ?!
OMGs, I DIE! TOO PERFECT!
I THOUGHT SHE WAS ONLY INTO HAVING ONE OUTFIT?
SHE'S SUPER SERIOUS ABOUT THIS...
This is of apocalyptic importance *because* I have one outfit!
My heart is a battle-ground of fashion!
GRAH
Sorry.
COOL, JUST STOP PEEKIN' INTO MY MIND.
OOPS!
FUWAH~

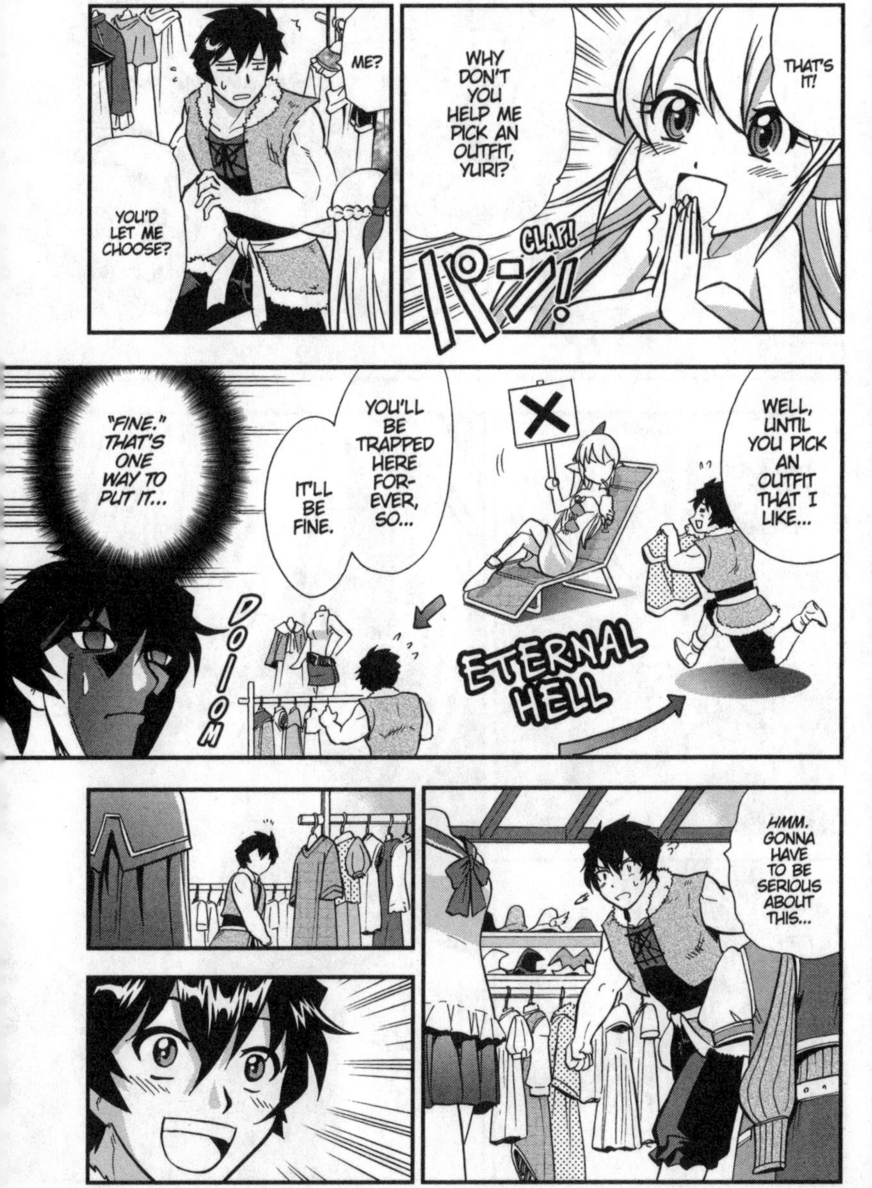
THAT'S IT!
WHY DON'T YOU HELP ME PICK AN OUTFIT, YURI?
CLAP!
パーン!
ME?
YOU'D LET ME CHOOSE?
WELL, UNTIL YOU PICK AN OUTFIT THAT I LIKE...
ETERNAL HELL
YOU'LL BE TRAPPED HERE FOR-EVER, SO...
IT'LL BE FINE.
DOOOM
"FINE." THAT'S ONE WAY TO PUT IT...
HMM. GONNA HAVE TO BE SERIOUS ABOUT THIS...

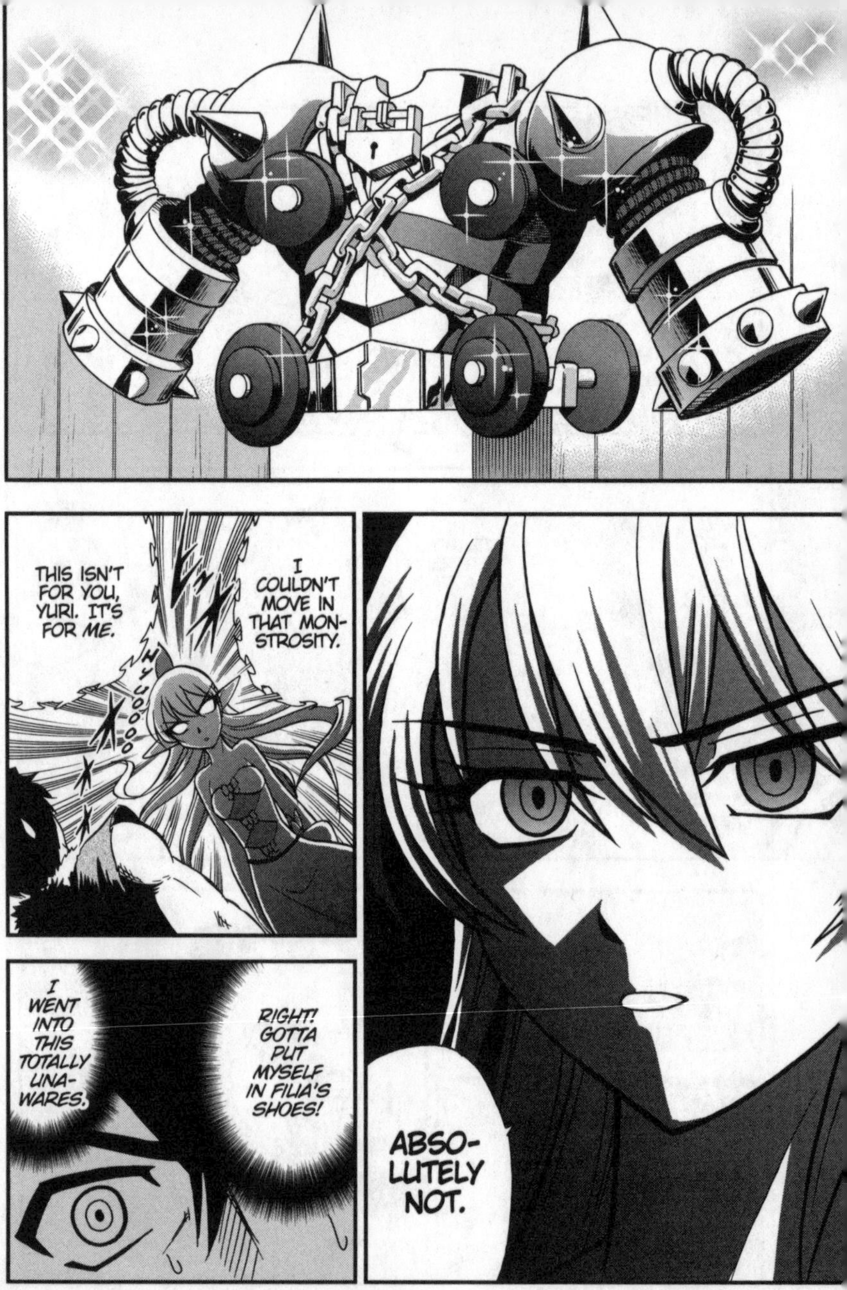
ABSO-LUTELY NOT.
I COULDN'T MOVE IN THAT MON-STROSITY.
THIS ISN'T FOR YOU, YURI. IT'S FOR ME.
HYUOOOOO
RIGHT! GOTTA PUT MYSELF IN FILIA'S SHOES!
I WENT INTO THIS TOTALLY UNA-WARES.

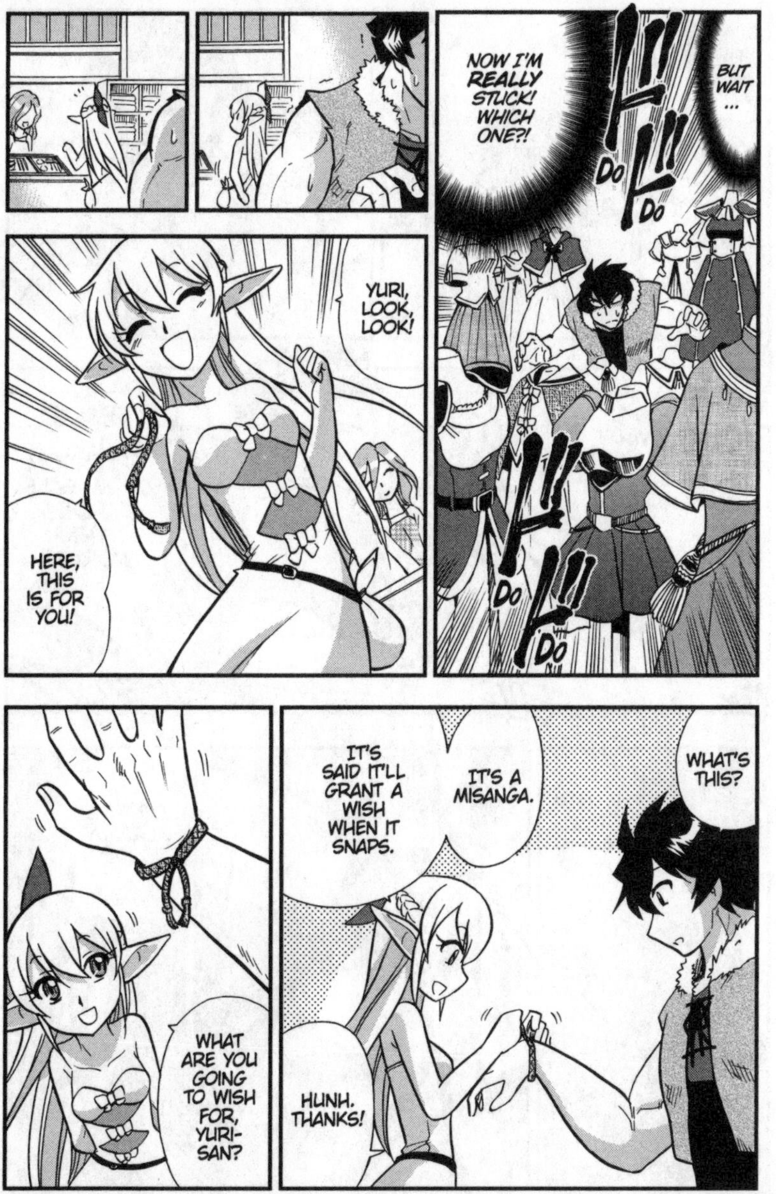
BUT WAIT ...
NOW I'M REALLY STUCK! WHICH ONE?!
DO DO
DO DO
YURI, LOOK, LOOK!
HERE, THIS IS FOR YOU!
WHAT'S THIS?
IT'S A MISANGA.
IT'S SAID IT'LL GRANT A WISH WHEN IT SNAPS.
HUNH. THANKS!
WHAT ARE YOU GOING TO WISH FOR, YURI-SAN?

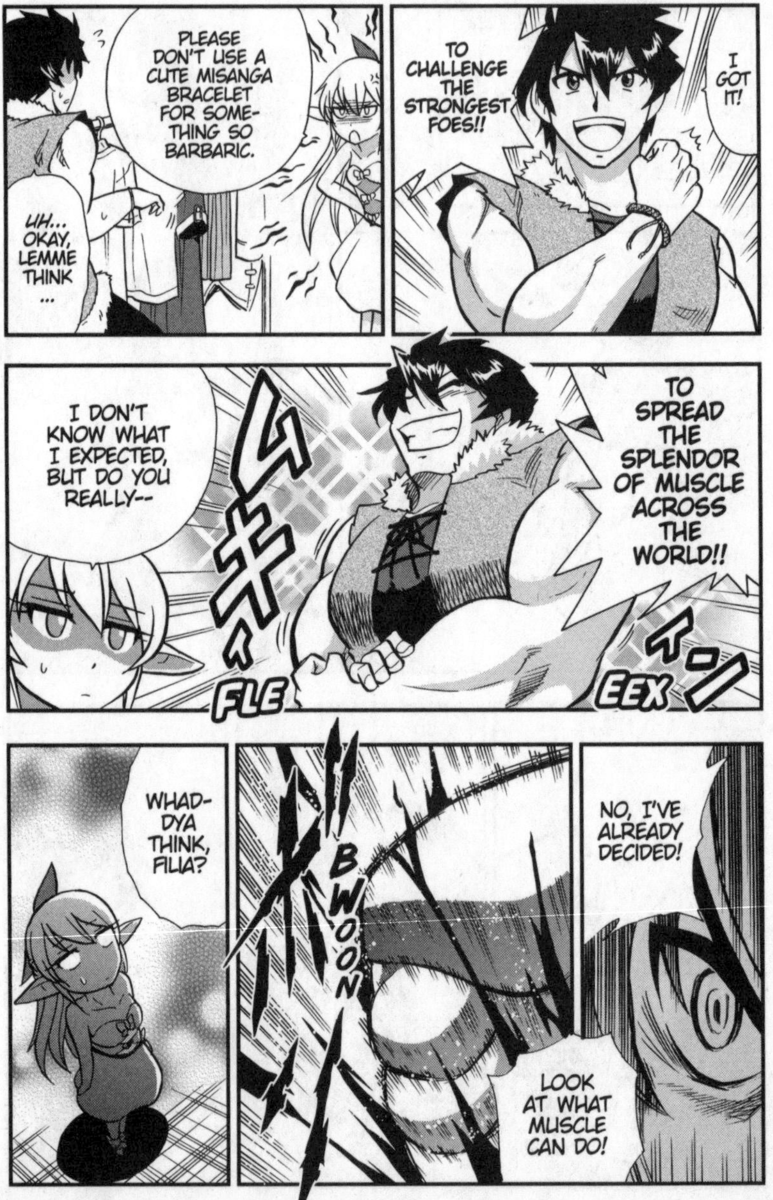
I GOT IT!
TO CHALLENGE THE STRONGEST FOES!!
PLEASE DON'T USE A CUTE MISANGA BRACELET FOR SOME-THING SO BARBARIC.
UH... OKAY, LEMME THINK ...
TO SPREAD THE SPLENDOR OF MUSCLE ACROSS THE WORLD!!
ムキィーン
EEX
FLE
I DON'T KNOW WHAT I EXPECTED, BUT DO YOU REALLY--
NO, I'VE ALREADY DECIDED!
LOOK AT WHAT MUSCLE CAN DO!
BWOOON
WHAD-DYA THINK, FILIA?

Wild, huh?!

NYU~UN

HM?

YURI!

YOU BROKE IT!

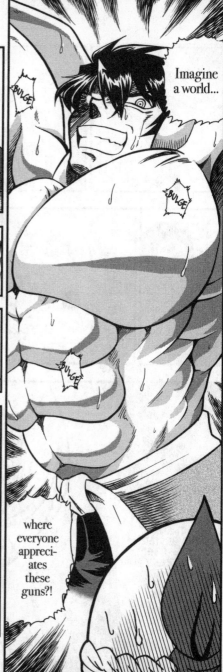

Imagine a world...

BULGE

BULGE

BULGE

where everyone appreciates these guns?!

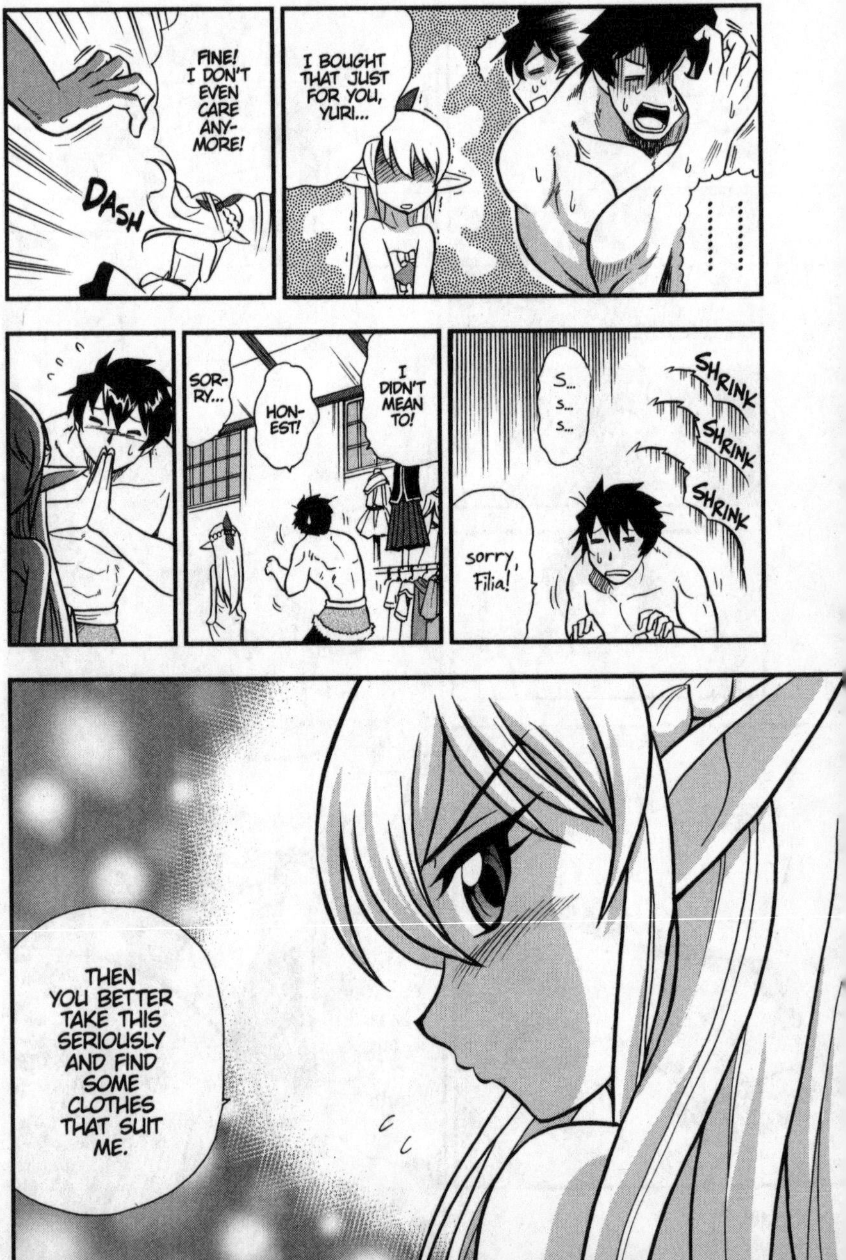
......
I BOUGHT THAT JUST FOR YOU, YURI...
FINE! I DON'T EVEN CARE ANYMORE!
DASH
SHRINK
SHRINK
SHRINK
S... s... s...
sorry, Filia!
I DIDN'T MEAN TO!
HON-EST!
SOR-RY...
THEN YOU BETTER TAKE THIS SERIOUSLY AND FIND SOME CLOTHES THAT SUIT ME.

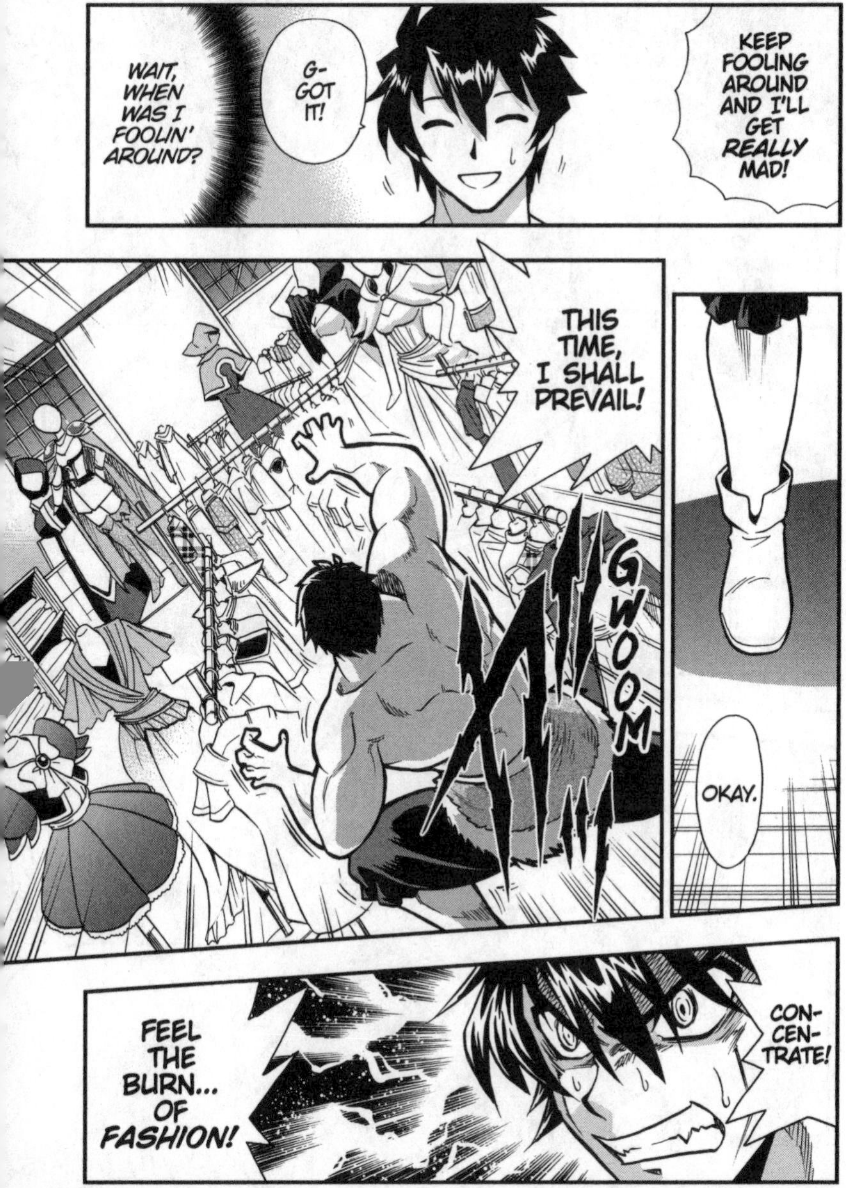
KEEP FOOLING AROUND AND I'LL GET REALLY MAD!
G-GOT IT!
WAIT, WHEN WAS I FOOLIN' AROUND?
OKAY.
THIS TIME, I SHALL PREVAIL!
GWOOM
CON-CEN-TRATE!
FEEL THE BURN... OF FASHION!

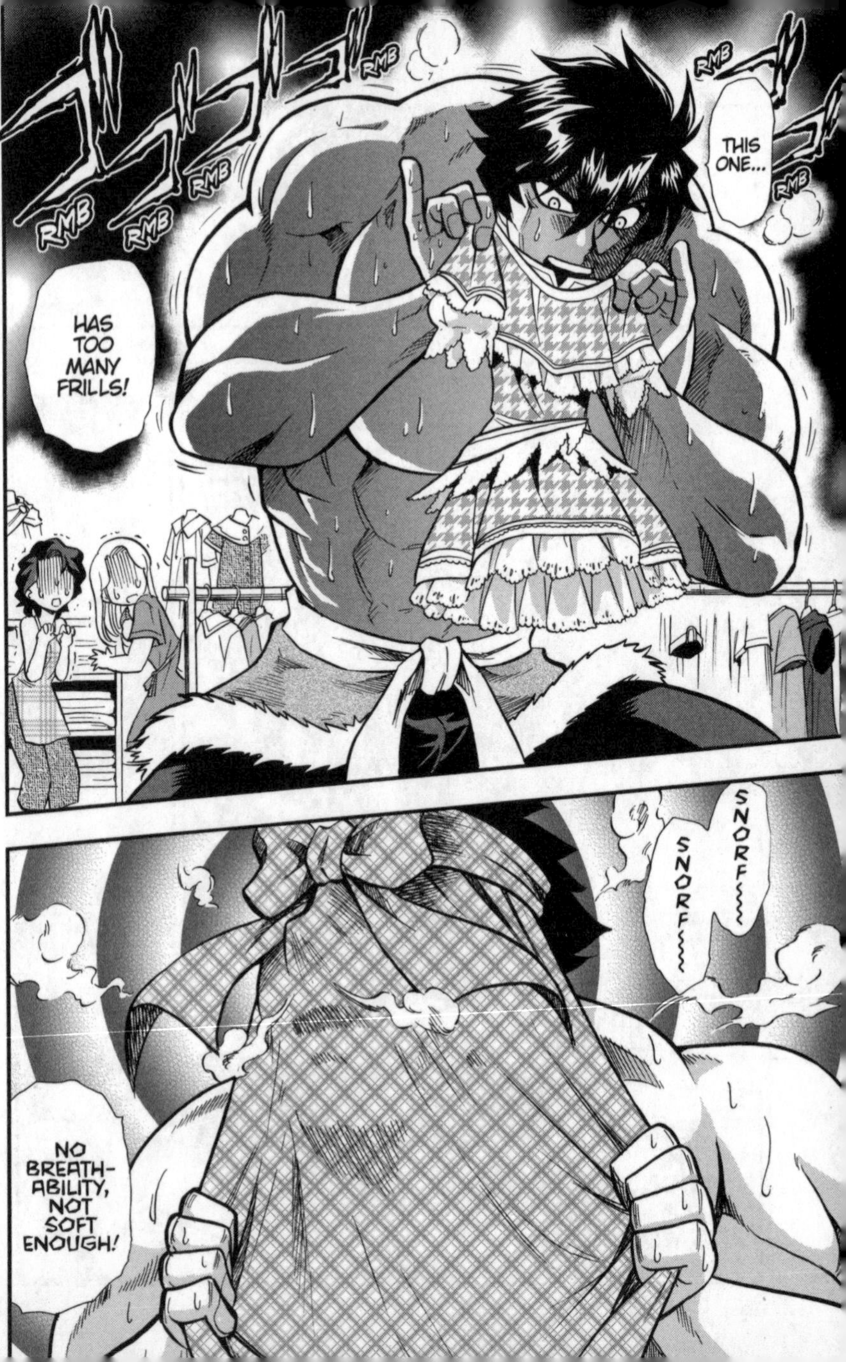
RMB
RMB
THIS ONE...
RMB
RMB
RMB
RMB
RMB
HAS TOO MANY FRILLS!
SNORF~~
SNORF~~
NO BREATH-ABILITY, NOT SOFT ENOUGH!

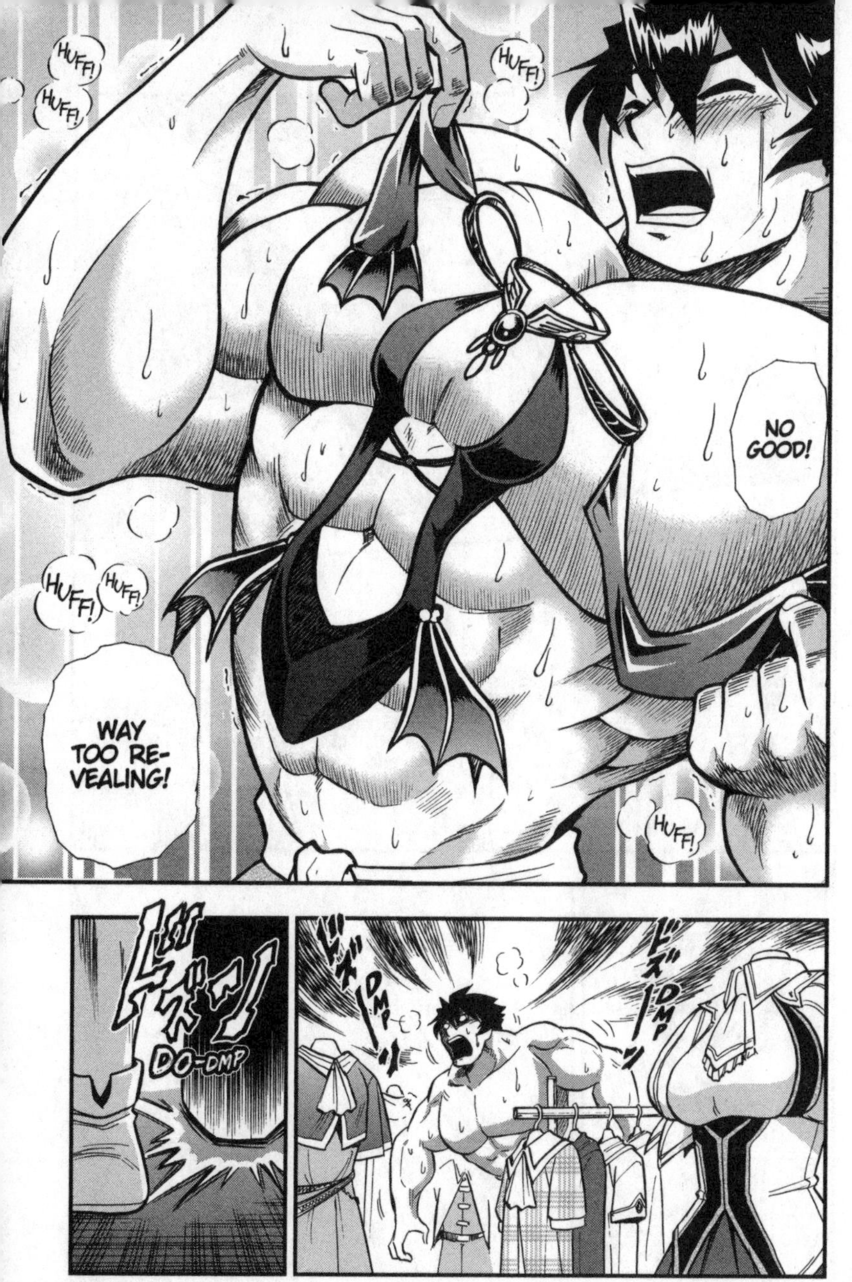
HUFF!
NO GOOD!
HUFF!
HUFF!
HUFF!
HUFF!
WAY TOO RE-VEALING!
HUFF!
DMP
DMP
DO-DMP

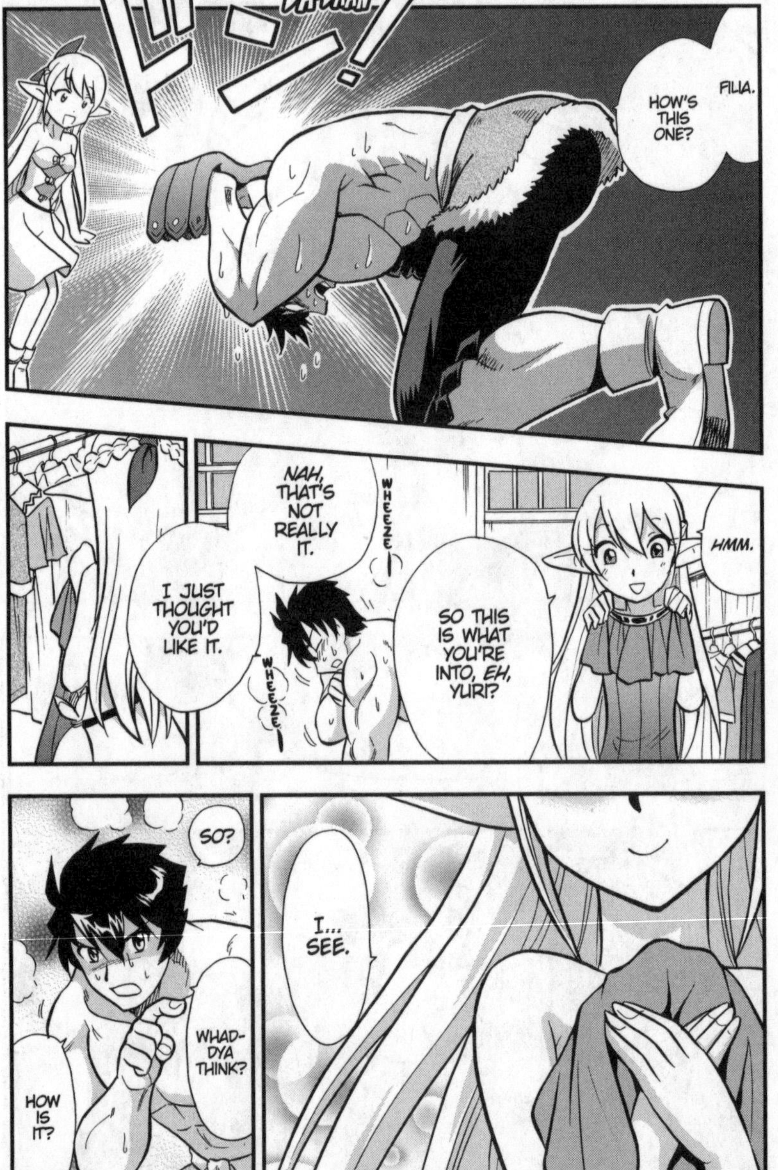
DA-DAAN
FILIA.
HOW'S THIS ONE?
HMM.
SO THIS IS WHAT YOU'RE INTO, EH, YURI?
NAH, THAT'S NOT REALLY IT.
WHEEZE
I JUST THOUGHT YOU'D LIKE IT.
WHEEZE
I... SEE.
SO?
WHAD-DYA THINK?
HOW IS IT?

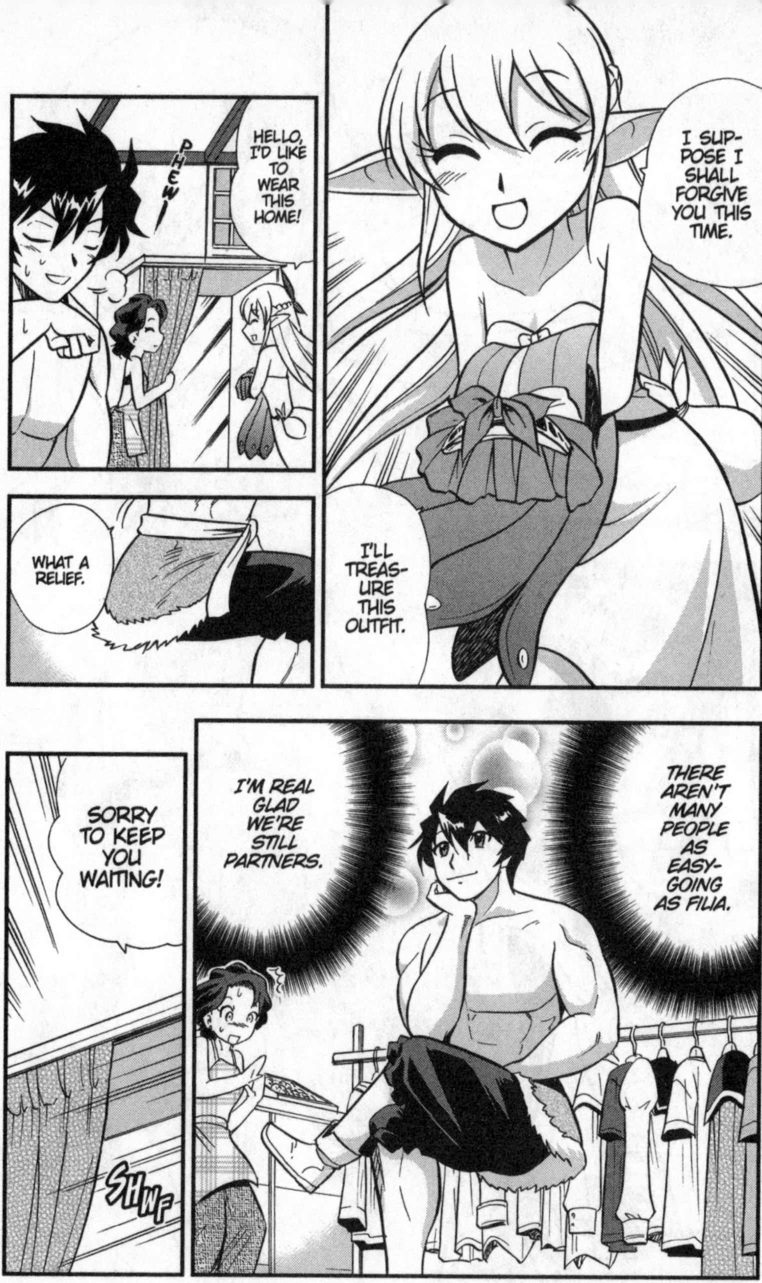
I SUP-POSE I SHALL FORGIVE YOU THIS TIME.
I'LL TREASURE THIS OUTFIT.
HELLO, I'D LIKE TO WEAR THIS HOME!
PHEW!
WHAT A RELIEF.
THERE AREN'T MANY PEOPLE AS EASY-GOING AS FILIA.
I'M REAL GLAD WE'RE STILL PARTNERS.
SORRY TO KEEP YOU WAITING!
SHWF

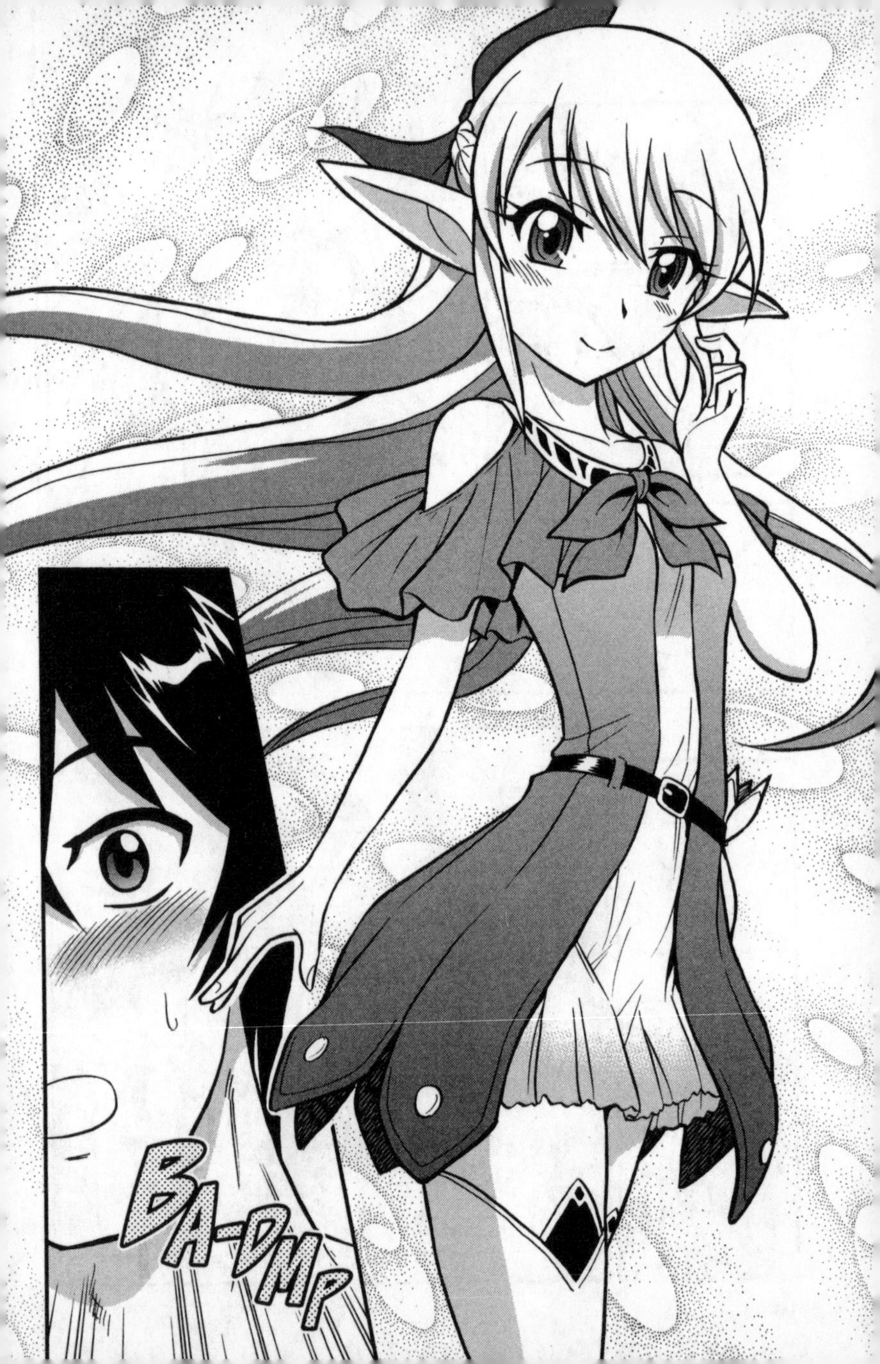
BA-DMP

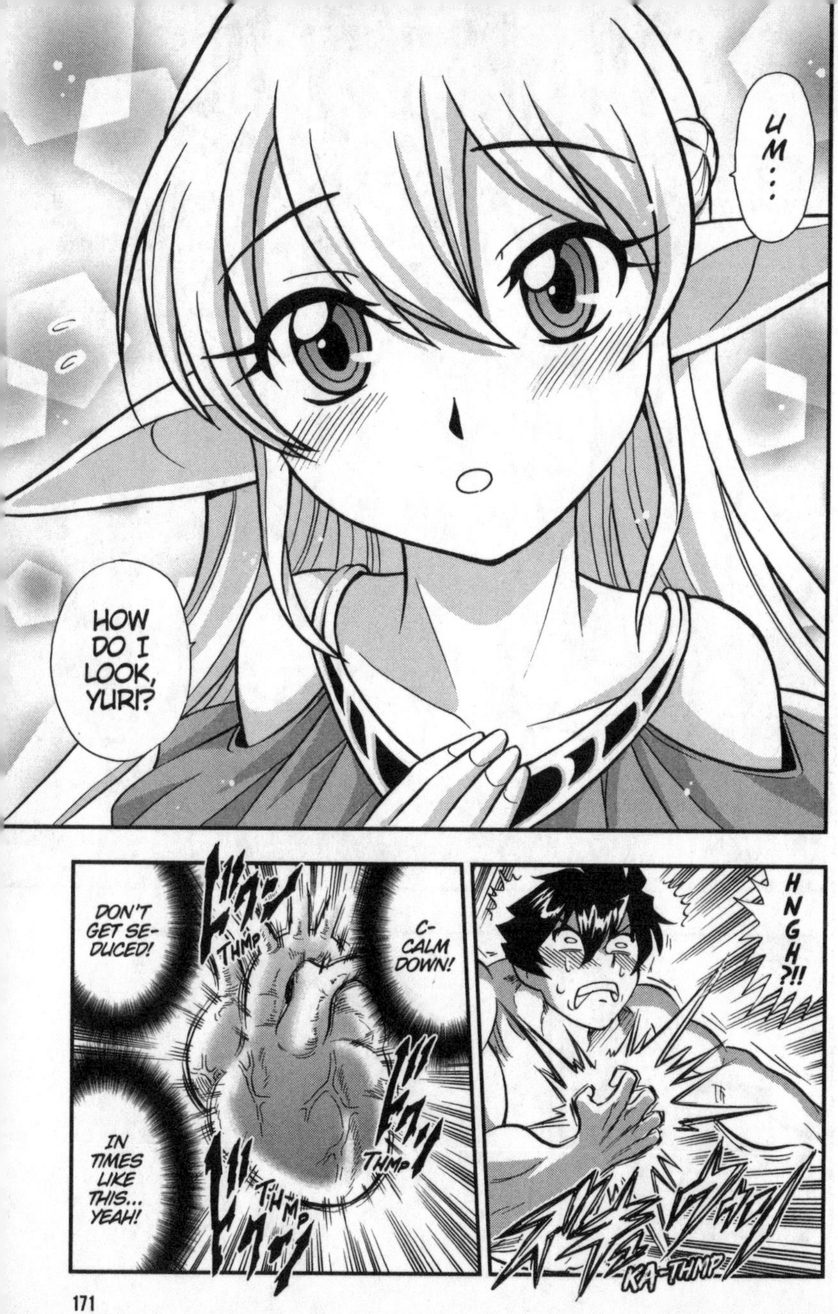
UM...
HOW DO I LOOK, YURI?
HNGH?!!
KA-THMP
C-CALM DOWN!
DON'T GET SE-DUCED!
THMP
THMP
IN TIMES LIKE THIS... YEAH!
THMP

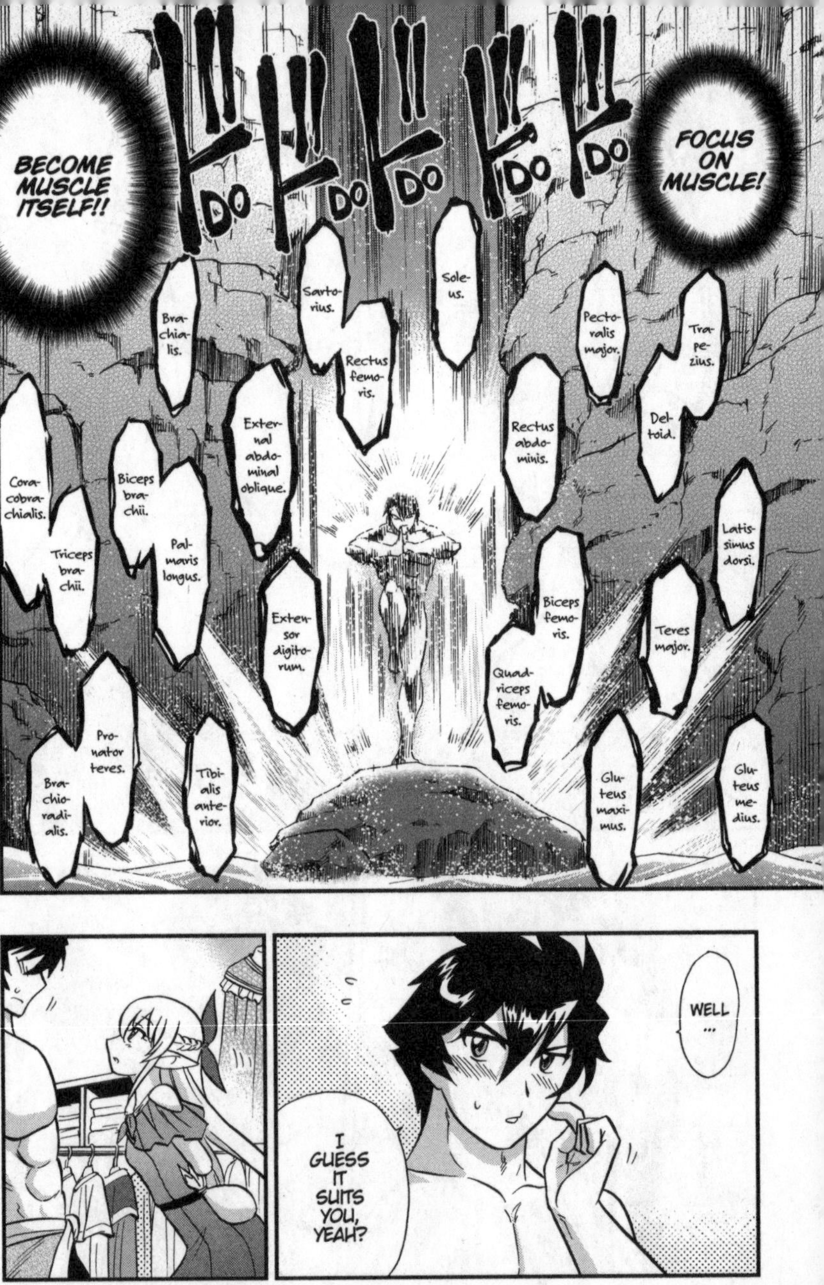
FOCUS ON MUSCLE!
DO DO DO DO DO DO
BECOME MUSCLE ITSELF!!
Trapezius.
Pectoralis major.
Deltoid.
Rectus abdominis.
Soleus.
Rectus femoris.
Sartorius.
External abdominal oblique.
Brachialis.
Biceps brachii.
Coracobrachialis.
Latissimus dorsi.
Teres major.
Biceps femoris.
Quadriceps femoris.
Extensor digitorum.
Palmaris longus.
Triceps brachii.
Gluteus medius.
Gluteus maximus.
Tibialis anterior.
Pronator teres.
Brachioradialis.
WELL ...
I GUESS IT SUITS YOU, YEAH?

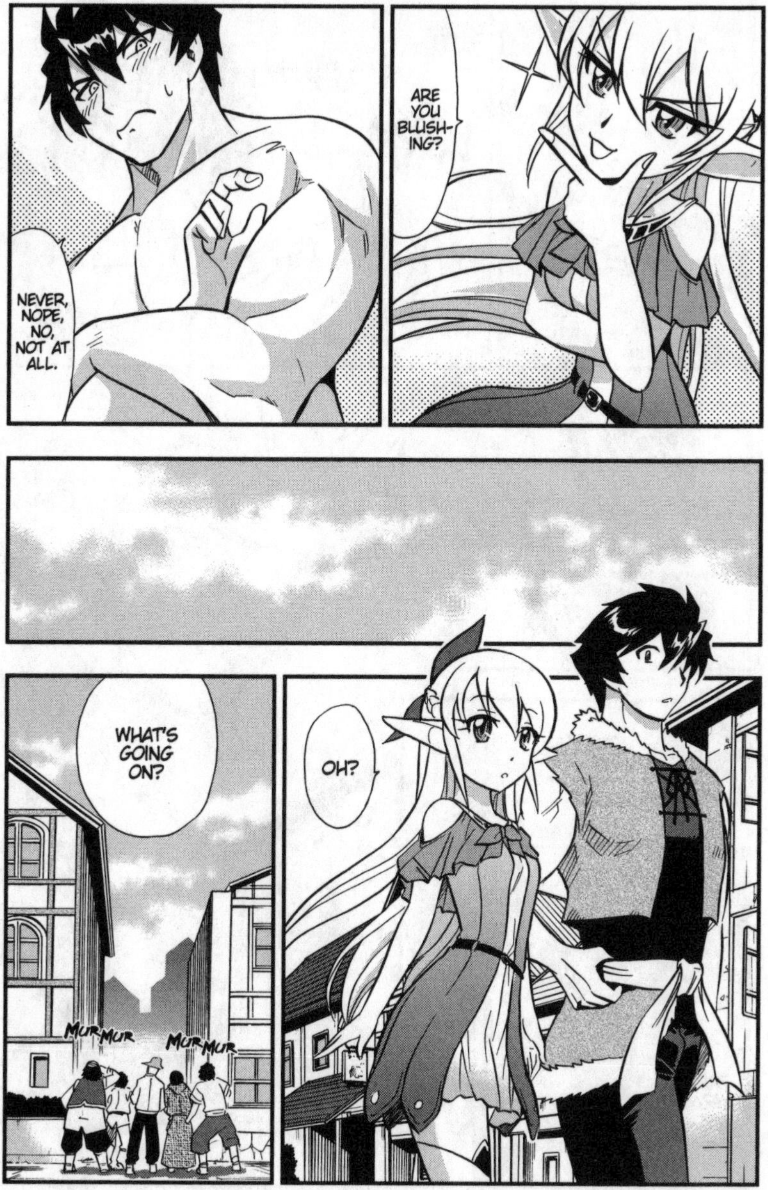
ARE YOU BLUSH-ING?
NEVER, NOPE, NO, NOT AT ALL.
OH?
WHAT'S GOING ON?
MUR MUR
MUR MUR

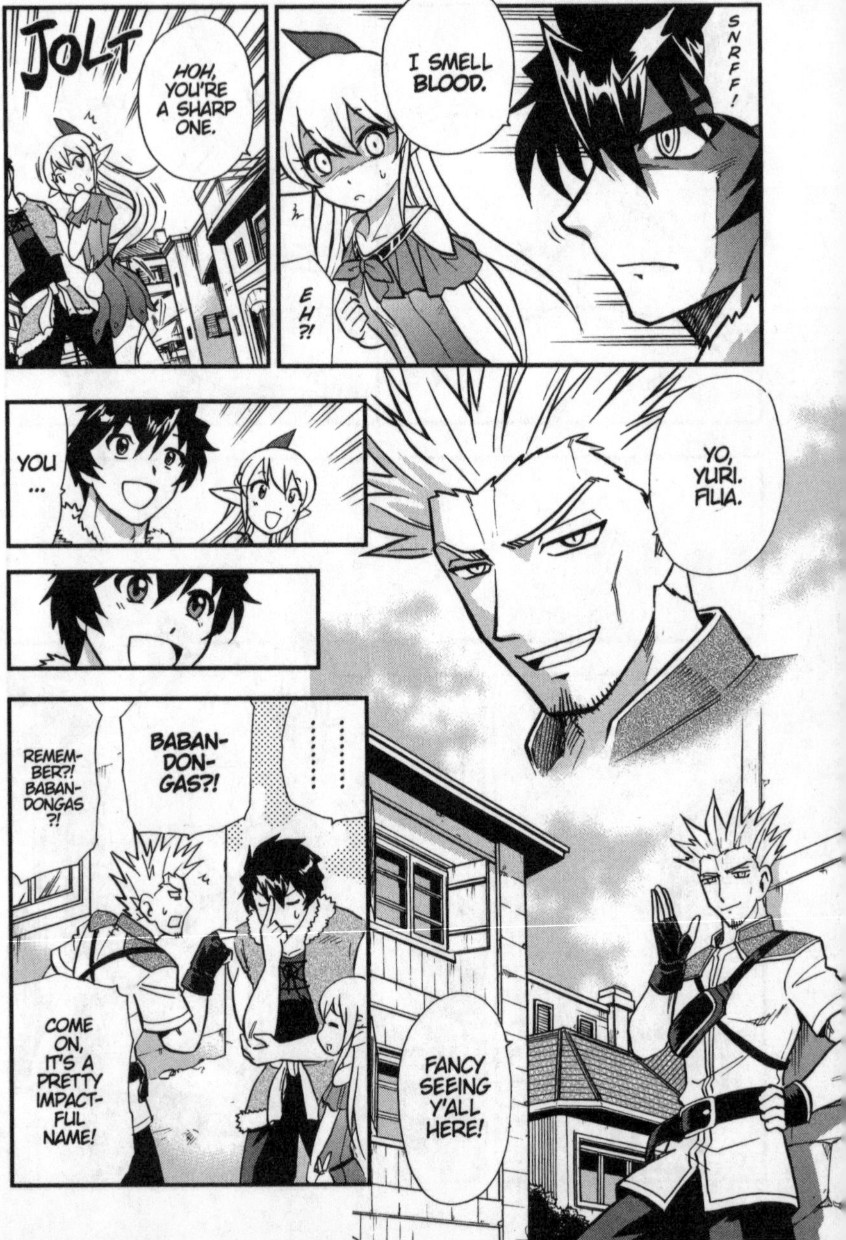
SNRFF!
I SMELL BLOOD.
EH?!
JOLT
HOH, YOU'RE A SHARP ONE.
YO, YURI. FILIA.
FANCY SEEING Y'ALL HERE!
YOU ...
......
BABAN-DONGAS?!
REMEMBER?! BABANDONGAS?!
COME ON, IT'S A PRETTY IMPACTFUL NAME!

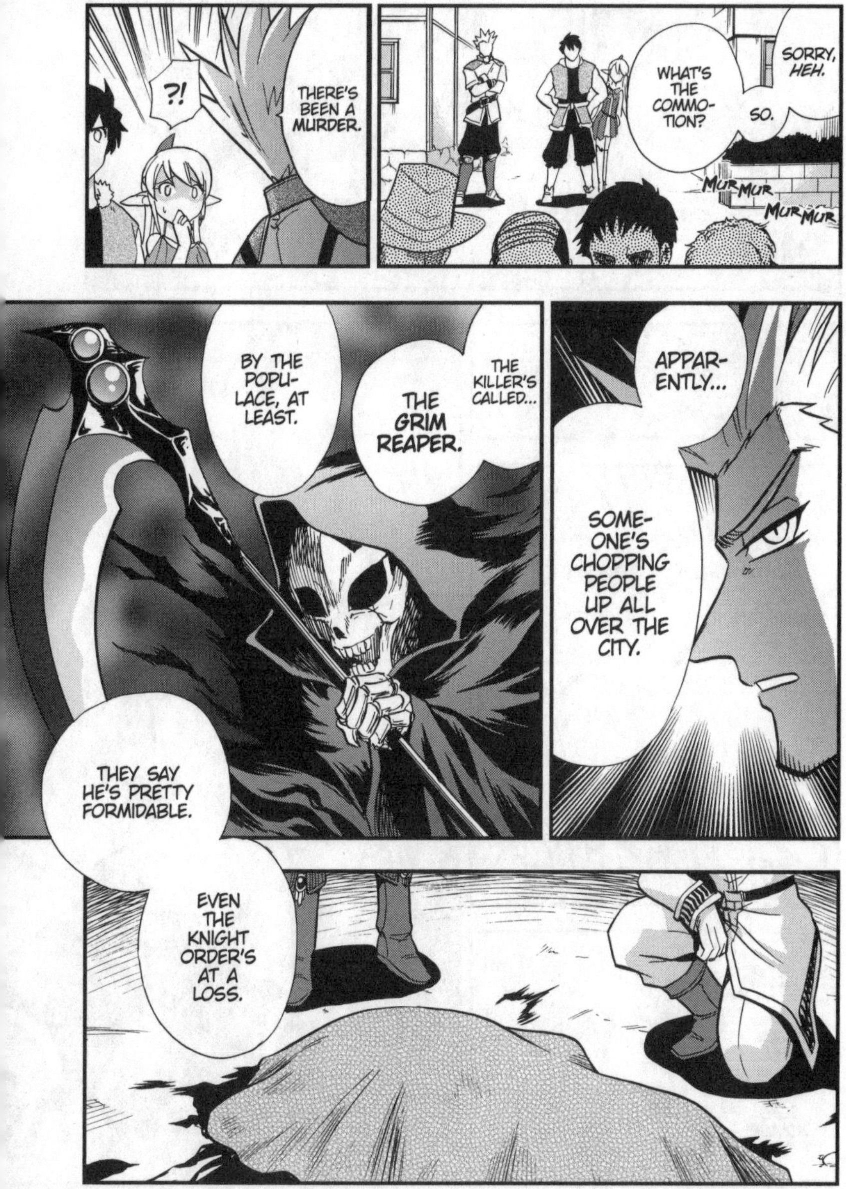
SORRY, HEH.
SO.
WHAT'S THE COMMOTION?
MUR MUR
MUR MUR
THERE'S BEEN A MURDER.
?!
APPARENTLY...
SOMEONE'S CHOPPING PEOPLE UP ALL OVER THE CITY.
THE KILLER'S CALLED...
THE GRIM REAPER.
BY THE POPULACE, AT LEAST.
THEY SAY HE'S PRETTY FORMIDABLE.
EVEN THE KNIGHT ORDER'S AT A LOSS.

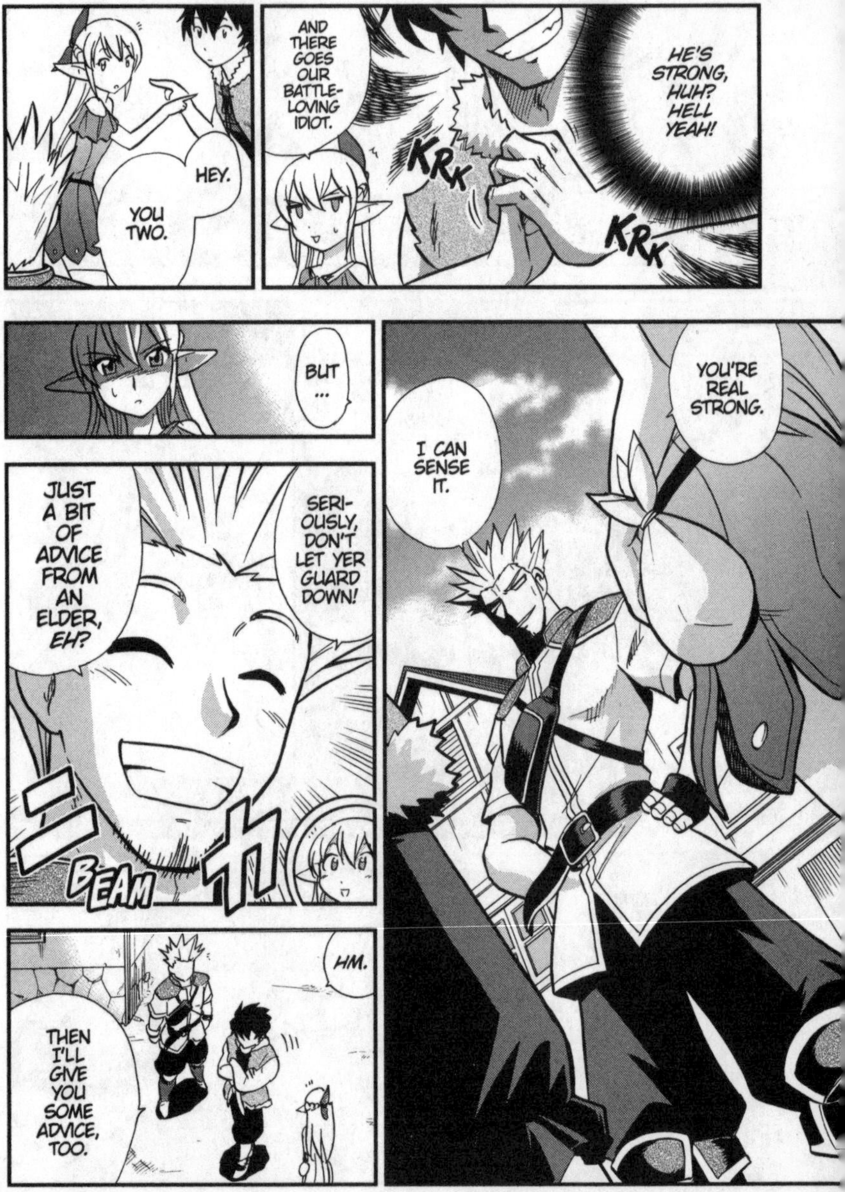
HE'S STRONG, HUH? HELL YEAH!
KRK
KRK
AND THERE GOES OUR BATTLE-LOVING IDIOT.
HEY.
YOU TWO.
YOU'RE REAL STRONG.
I CAN SENSE IT.
BUT ...
SERIOUSLY, DON'T LET YER GUARD DOWN!
JUST A BIT OF ADVICE FROM AN ELDER, *EH?*
BEAM
HM.
THEN I'LL GIVE YOU SOME ADVICE, TOO.

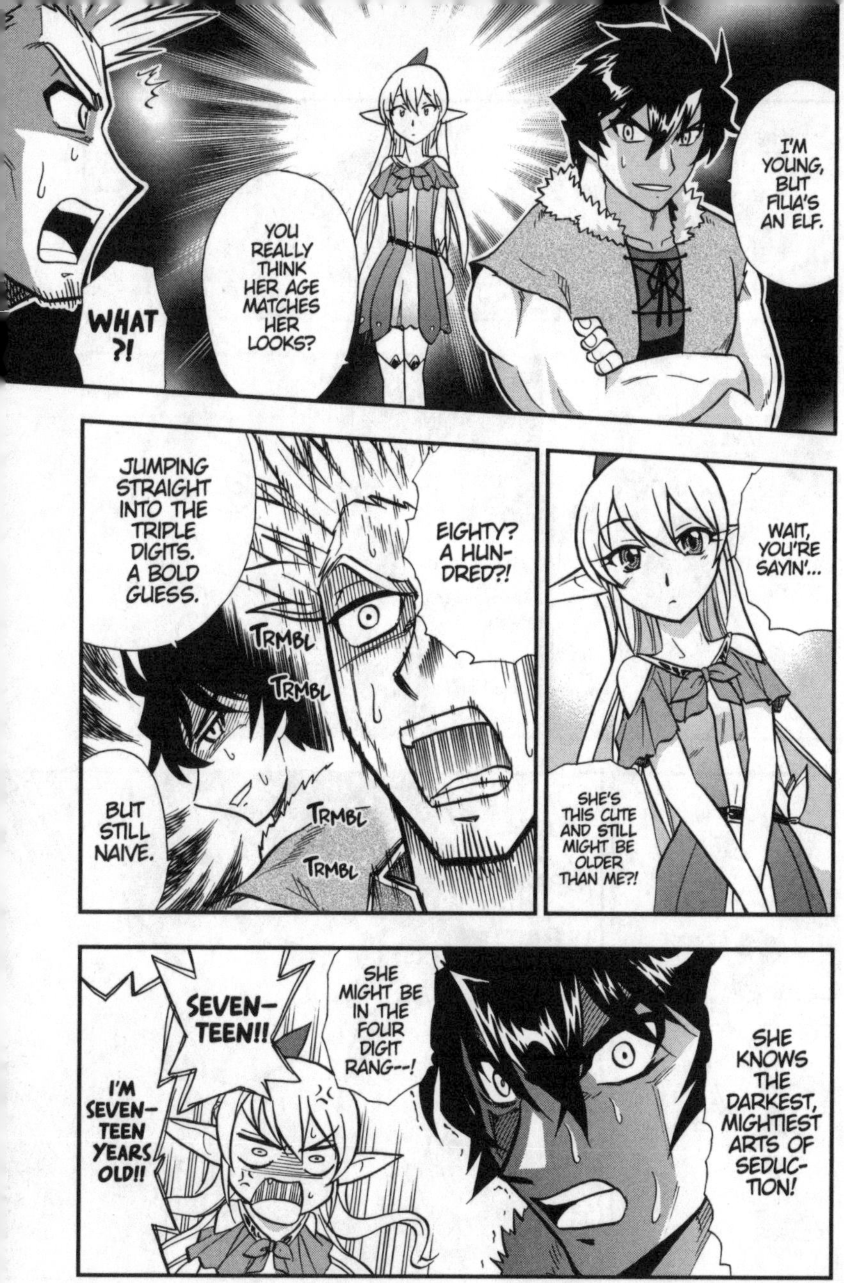
I'M YOUNG, BUT FILIA'S AN ELF.
YOU REALLY THINK HER AGE MATCHES HER LOOKS?
WHAT?!
WAIT, YOU'RE SAYIN'...
SHE'S THIS CUTE AND STILL MIGHT BE OLDER THAN ME?!
EIGHTY? A HUN-DRED?!
JUMPING STRAIGHT INTO THE TRIPLE DIGITS. A BOLD GUESS.
TRMBL
TRMBL
TRMBL
TRMBL
BUT STILL NAIVE.
SHE KNOWS THE DARKEST, MIGHTIEST ARTS OF SEDUC-TION!
SHE MIGHT BE IN THE FOUR DIGIT RANG--!
SEVEN-TEEN!!
I'M SEVEN-TEEN YEARS OLD!!

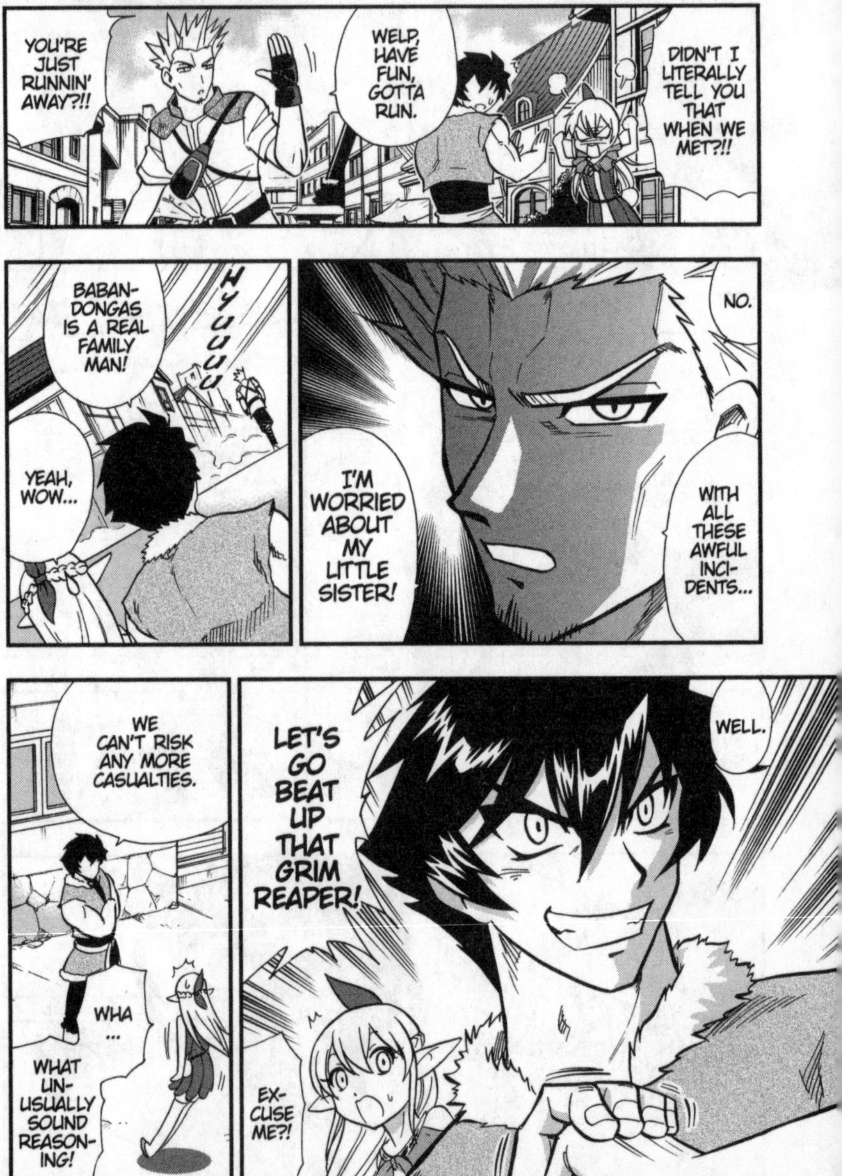
DIDN'T I LITERALLY TELL YOU THAT WHEN WE MET?!!
WELP, HAVE FUN, GOTTA RUN.
YOU'RE JUST RUNNIN' AWAY?!!
NO.
WITH ALL THESE AWFUL INCIDENTS...
I'M WORRIED ABOUT MY LITTLE SISTER!
HYUUUUU
BABANDONGAS IS A REAL FAMILY MAN!
YEAH, WOW...
WELL.
LET'S GO BEAT UP THAT GRIM REAPER!
EXCUSE ME?!
WE CAN'T RISK ANY MORE CASUALTIES.
WHA...
WHAT UNUSUALLY SOUND REASONING!

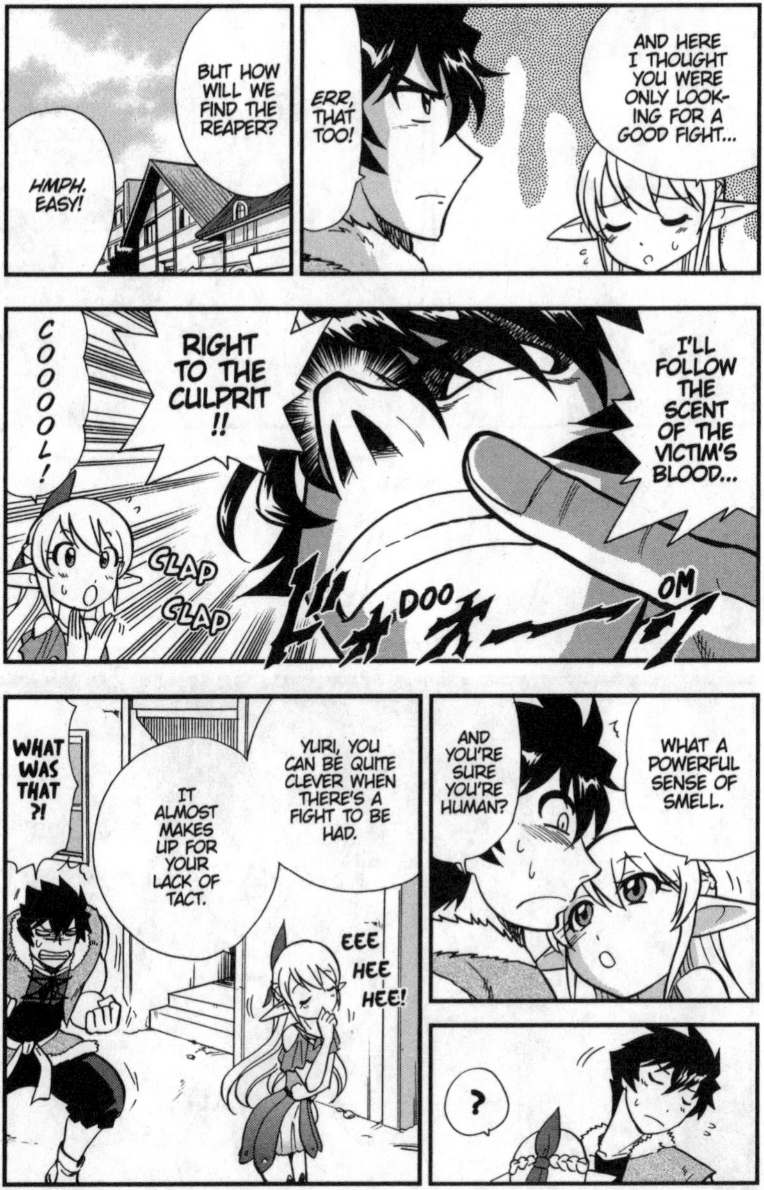

AND HERE I THOUGHT YOU WERE ONLY LOOK-ING FOR A GOOD FIGHT...
ERR, THAT TOO!
BUT HOW WILL WE FIND THE REAPER?
HMPH. EASY!
I'LL FOLLOW THE SCENT OF THE VICTIM'S BLOOD...
RIGHT TO THE CULPRIT !!
DOO
OM
COOOOOL!
CLAP
CLAP
WHAT A POWERFUL SENSE OF SMELL.
AND YOU'RE SURE YOU'RE HUMAN?
?
YURI, YOU CAN BE QUITE CLEVER WHEN THERE'S A FIGHT TO BE HAD.
IT ALMOST MAKES UP FOR YOUR LACK OF TACT.
WHAT WAS THAT ?!
EEE HEE HEE!

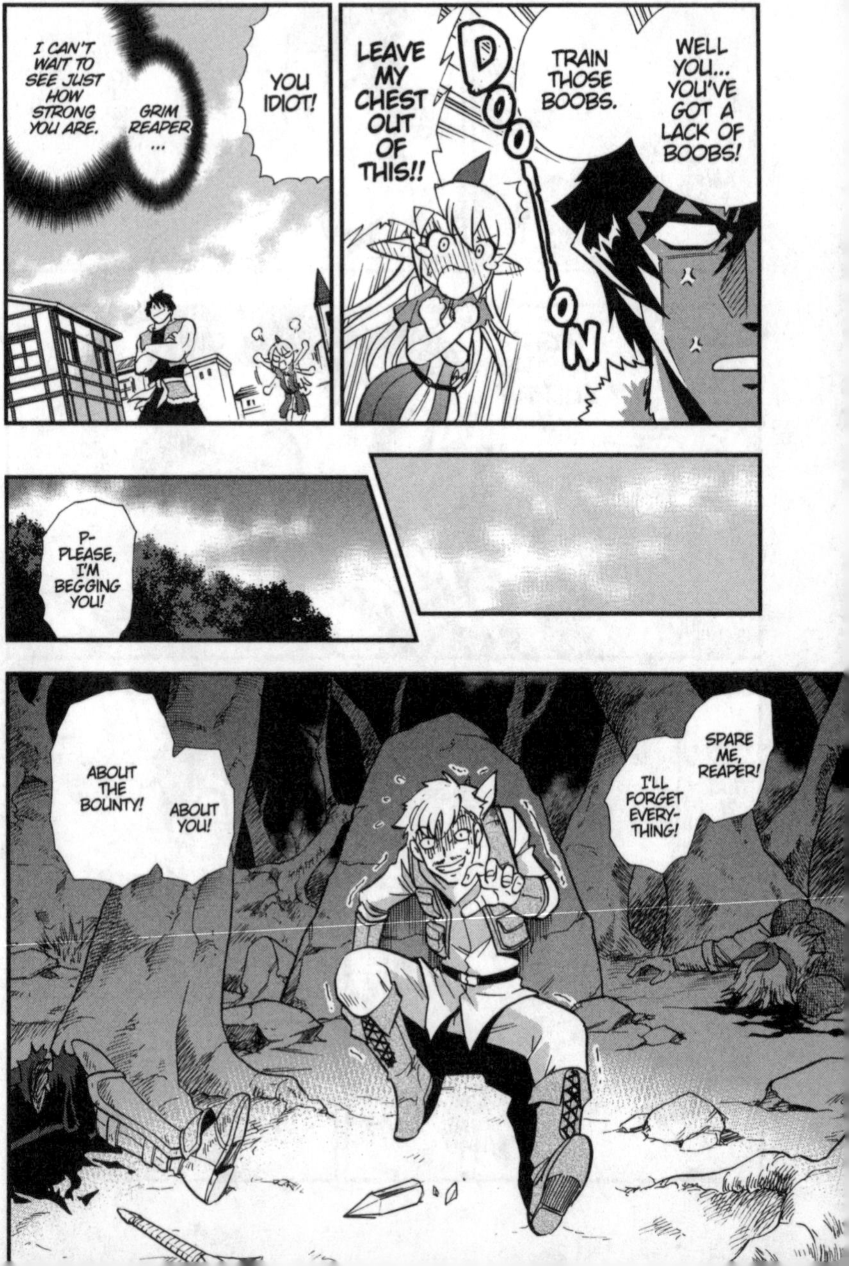
WELL YOU... YOU'VE GOT A LACK OF BOOBS!
TRAIN THOSE BOOBS.
DOO-ON
LEAVE MY CHEST OUT OF THIS!!
YOU IDIOT!
GRIM REAPER ...
I CAN'T WAIT TO SEE JUST HOW STRONG YOU ARE.
P-PLEASE, I'M BEGGING YOU!
SPARE ME, REAPER!
I'LL FORGET EVERYTHING!
ABOUT YOU!
ABOUT THE BOUNTY!

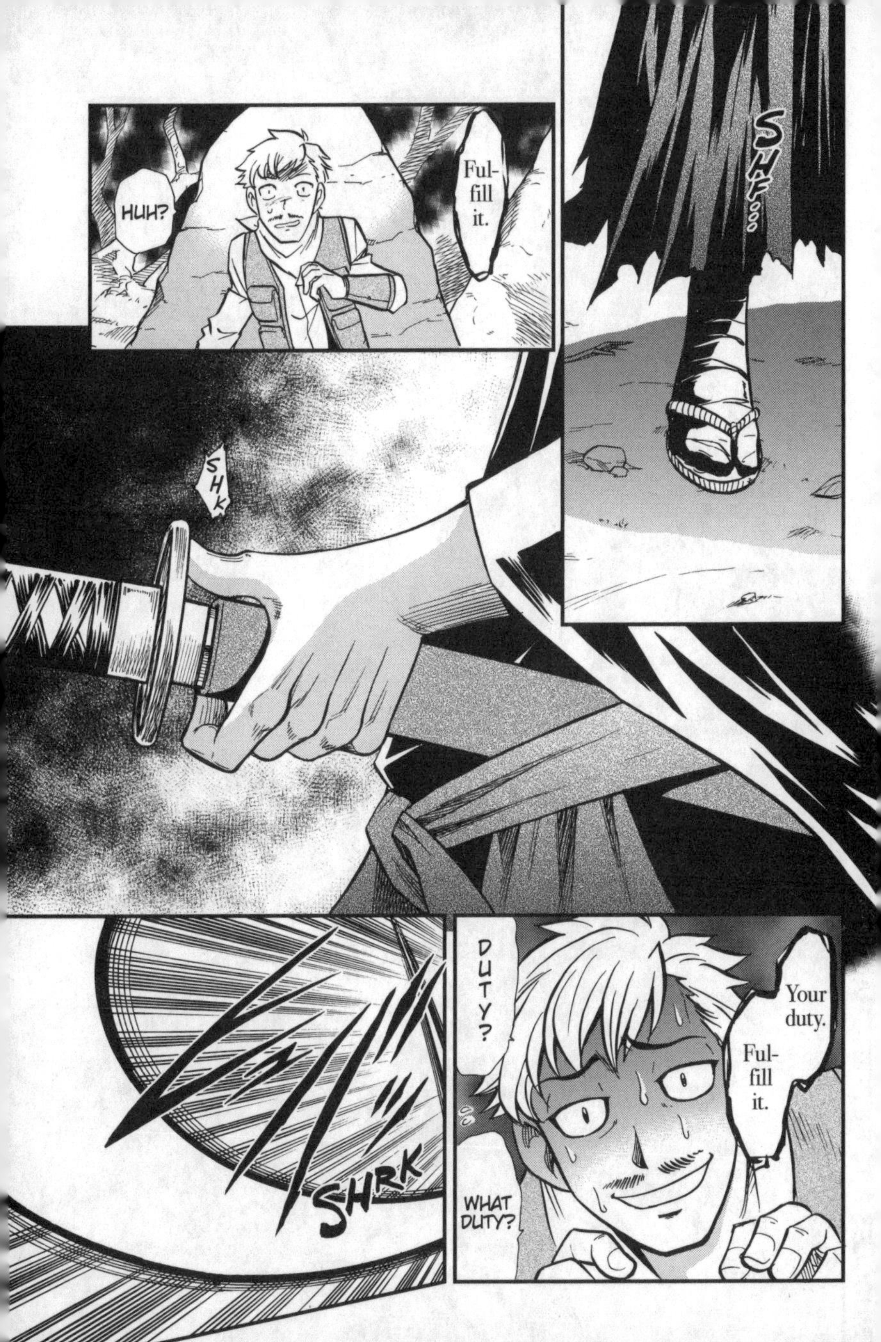
SHF...
Ful-fill it.
HUH?
SHK
Your duty.
Ful-fill it.
DUTY?
WHAT DUTY?
SHRK

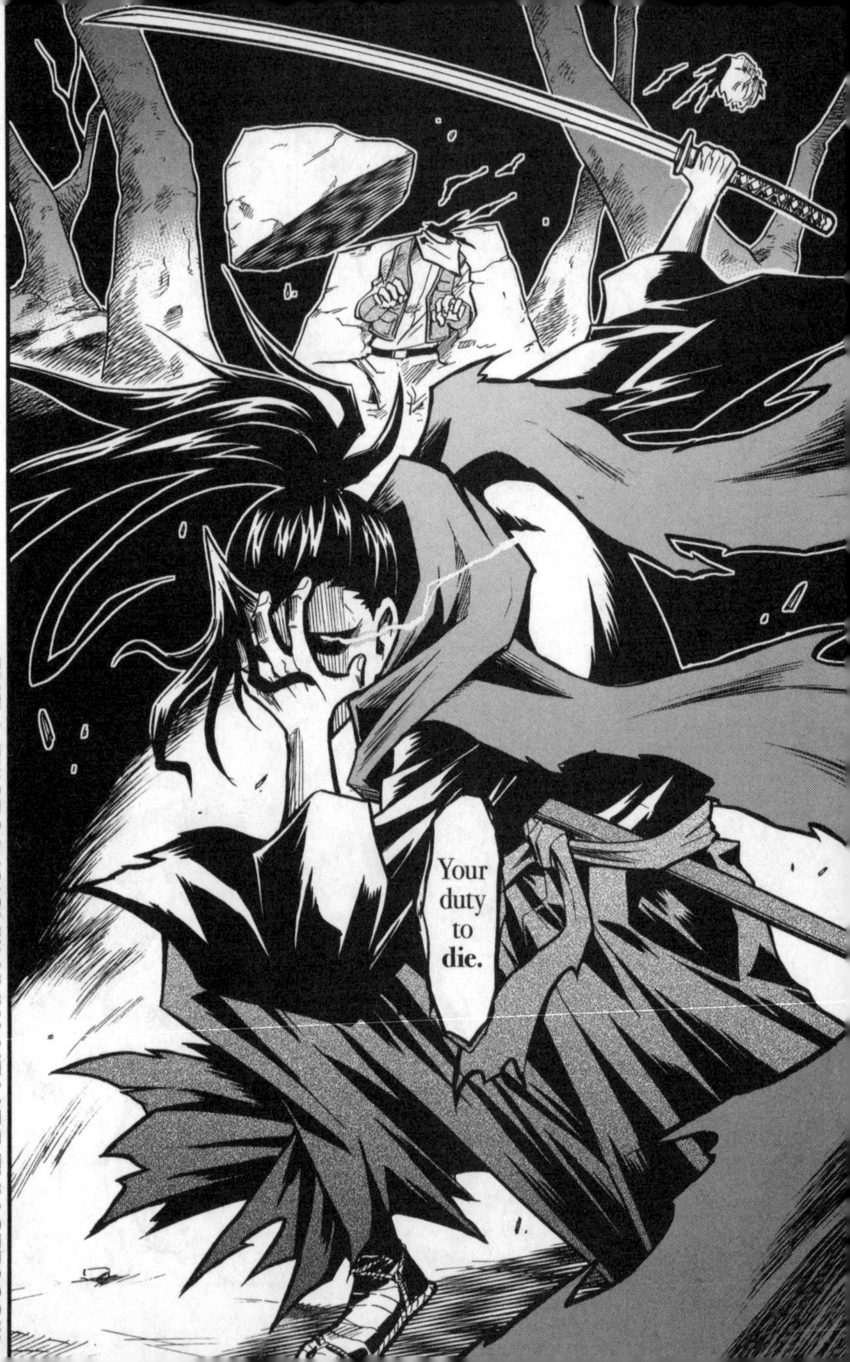
Your duty to die.

MUSCLES ARE BETTER THAN MAGIC! VOLUME 1 END

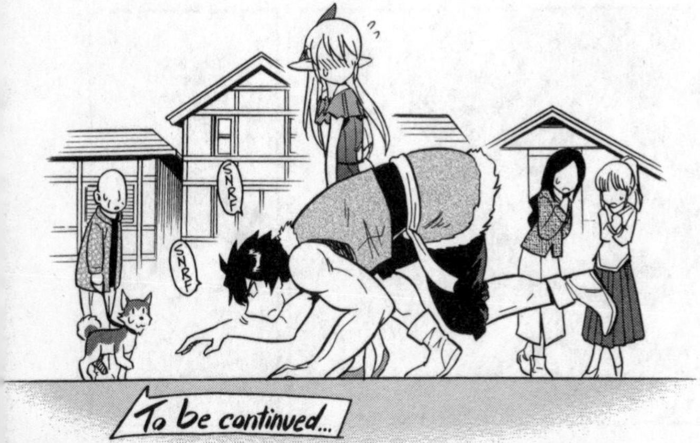
SNRF
SNRF
To be continued...

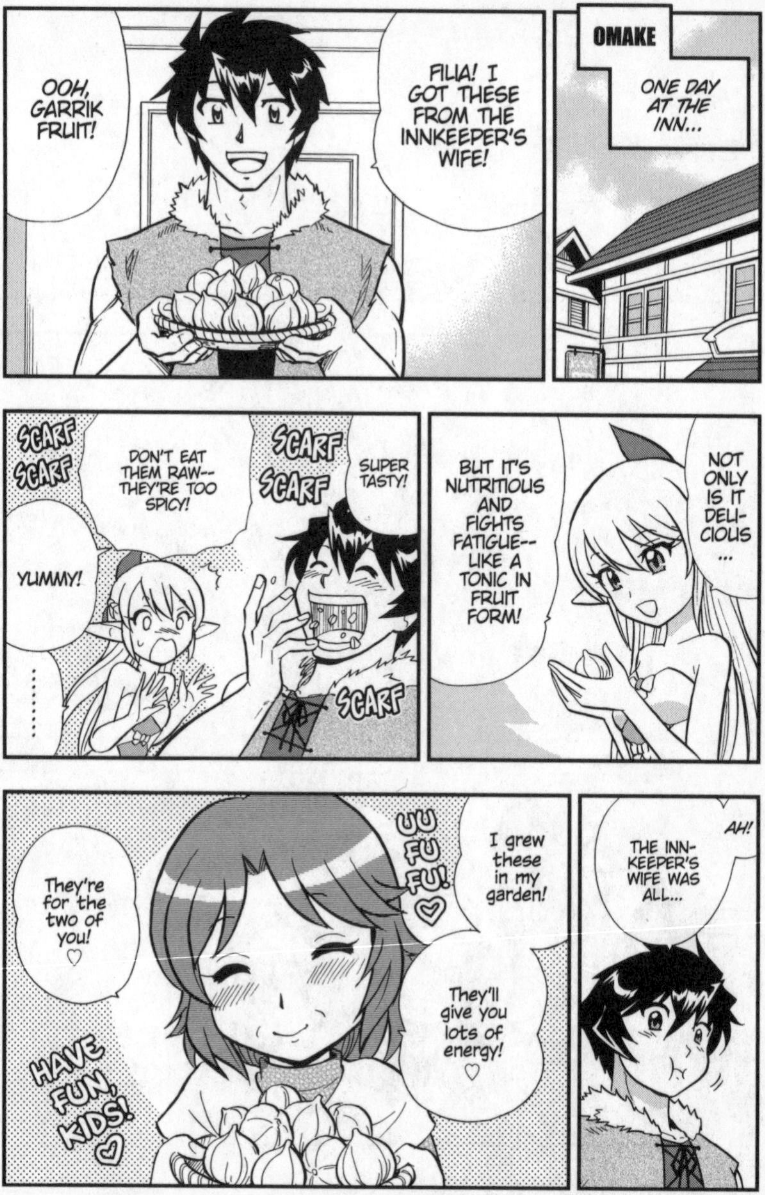
OMAKE
ONE DAY AT THE INN...
FILIA! I GOT THESE FROM THE INNKEEPER'S WIFE!
OOH, GARRIK FRUIT!
NOT ONLY IS IT DELICIOUS...
BUT IT'S NUTRITIOUS AND FIGHTS FATIGUE-- LIKE A TONIC IN FRUIT FORM!
SUPER TASTY!
SCARF SCARF
DON'T EAT THEM RAW-- THEY'RE TOO SPICY!
SCARF SCARF
YUMMY!
SCARF
......
AH!
THE INN-KEEPER'S WIFE WAS ALL...
I grew these in my garden!
UU FU FU! ♡
They'll give you lots of energy! ♡
They're for the two of you! ♡
HAVE FUN, KIDS! ♡

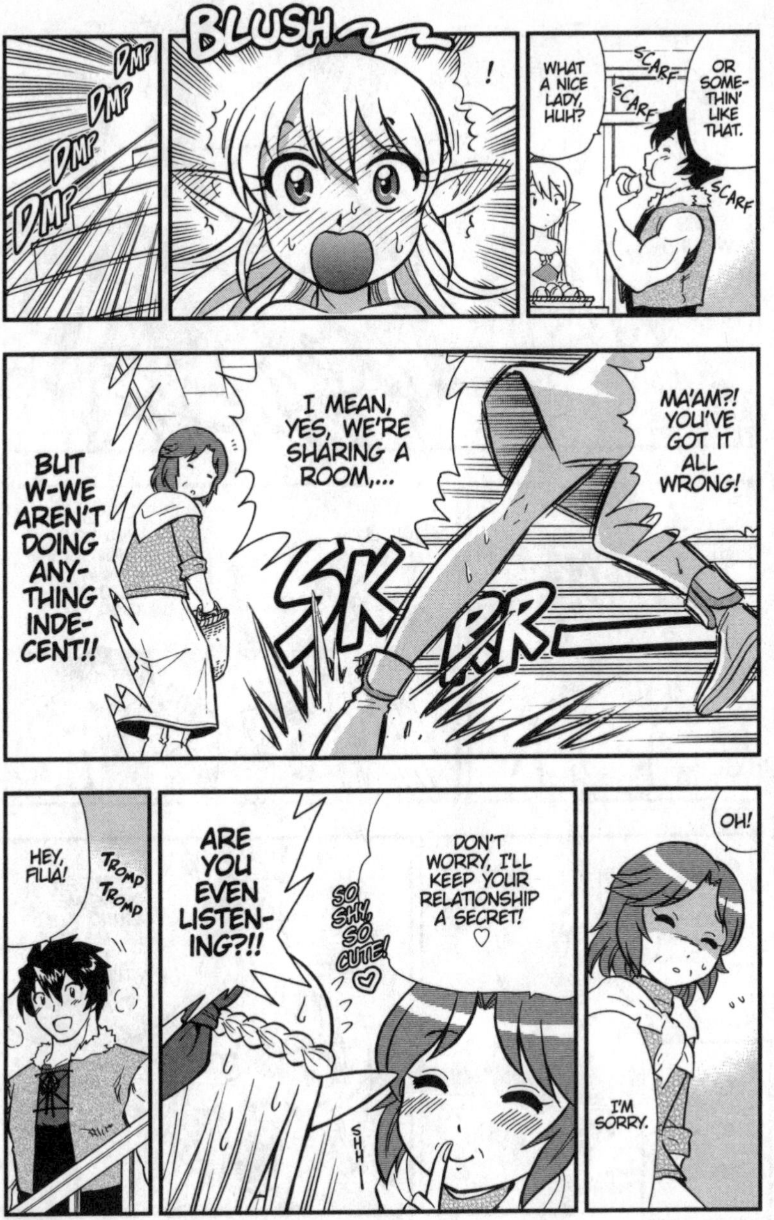
WHAT A NICE LADY, HUH?
OR SOMETHIN' LIKE THAT.
SCARF SCARF SCARF
BLUSH
!
DMP DMP DMP DMP DMP
MA'AM?! YOU'VE GOT IT ALL WRONG!
I MEAN, YES, WE'RE SHARING A ROOM,...
BUT W-WE AREN'T DOING ANYTHING INDECENT!!
SKRR
OH!
I'M SORRY.
DON'T WORRY, I'LL KEEP YOUR RELATIONSHIP A SECRET! ♡
SO SHY, SO CUTE!
ARE YOU EVEN LISTENING?!!
SHH
HEY, FILIA!
TROMP TROMP

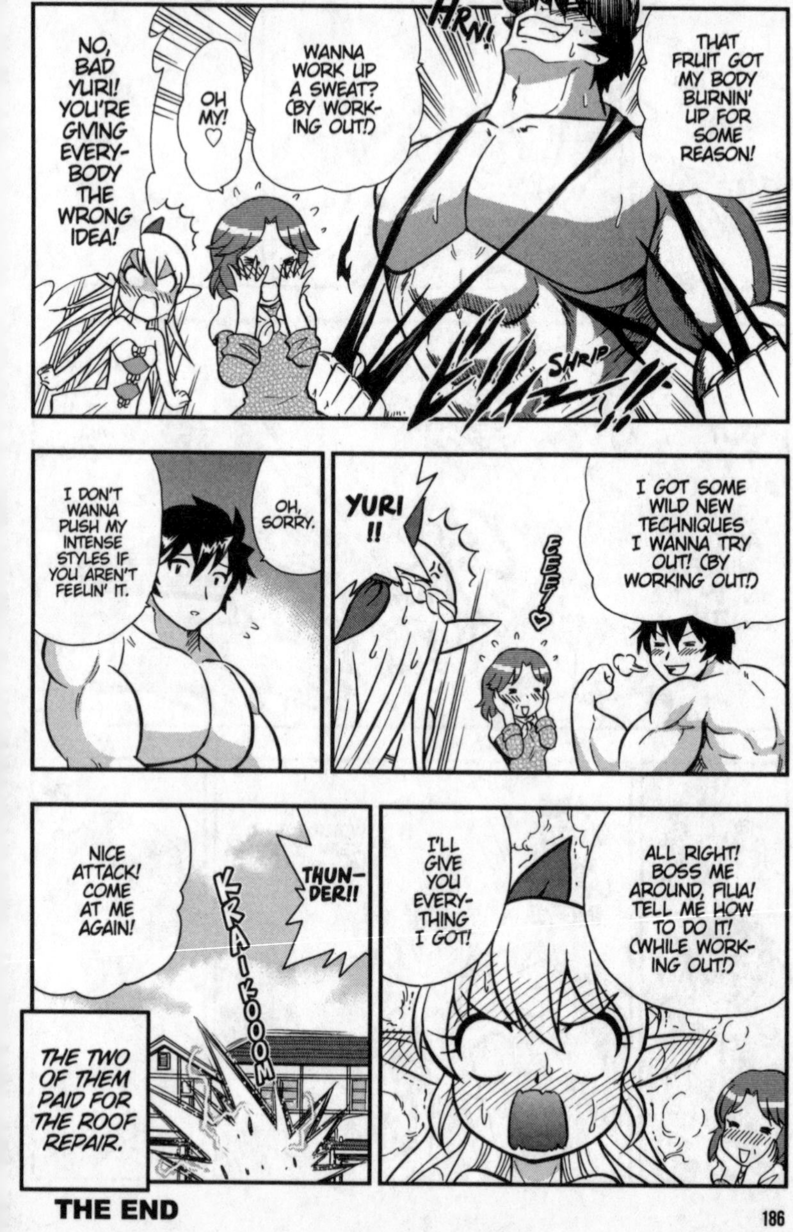
THAT FRUIT GOT MY BODY BURNIN' UP FOR SOME REASON!
HRN!
WANNA WORK UP A SWEAT? (BY WORKING OUT!)
OH MY! ♡
NO, BAD YURI! YOU'RE GIVING EVERYBODY THE WRONG IDEA!
SHRIP
I GOT SOME WILD NEW TECHNIQUES I WANNA TRY OUT! (BY WORKING OUT!)
EEEE! ♡
YURI!!
OH, SORRY.
I DON'T WANNA PUSH MY INTENSE STYLES IF YOU AREN'T FEELIN' IT.
ALL RIGHT! BOSS ME AROUND, FILIA! TELL ME HOW TO DO IT! (WHILE WORKING OUT!)
I'LL GIVE YOU EVERYTHING I GOT!
THUNDER!!
NICE ATTACK! COME AT ME AGAIN!
KRAIKOOOM
THE TWO OF THEM PAID FOR THE ROOF REPAIR.

THE END

AFTERWORD

"Do you want to work on a manga version of this novel?"

When my editor asked me that question, I was just baffled. "Huh? Why? Wouldn't someone who draws prettier pictures be better?"

But then my editor showed me the book, *Muscles Are Better than Magic!* When I saw the title, I was totally convinced. I mean, what a dumb title! (That's praise from me.) And the content is super ridiculous, too! (Also big praise from me.)

Long story short—yep! I had to do it!!

Thus, the book you're reading now, dear reader, was born. Thank you all very much! Another big thank you goes to the author of the original work, Doraneko-sensei, for (almost) always smiling and giving us the okay whenever we arranged the storyboards in a weird way (so as not to be outdone by the hilarious original work).

Anyway, I hope you're looking forward to seeing how the battle against the Grim Reaper goes in the next volume!

Until then, keep on
training those muscles!
Muscle!!

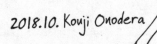

2018.10. Kouji Onodera

Congratulations on the release of the first tankoubon volume! When I heard that my story was going to be a manga, I was so shocked and delighted I felt like I was being lifted up to the heavens. I loved manga so much when I was a kid that spent nearly all of my allowance on it. When I heard the news, my heart started pounding so hard it felt like it was going to jump out of my chest. An excitement to rival that of my first love!

When I finally saw Volume 1, I was even more impressed. It was beyond anything I could have imagined. I jumped around the room, totally blissed out. Onodera-sensei's passionate and energetic art couldn't possibly be more macho, and it had this kind of synergy that made Yuri stand out even more—simply untouchable. As the author of the original, I couldn't be happier.

Onodera-sensei's drawings of Yuri and Filia are so vivid that I'm honestly enjoying them more as a "first-time reader" than I am as the "original author."

I'm looking forward to seeing more adventures about this ridiculously uneven duo!

Doraneko

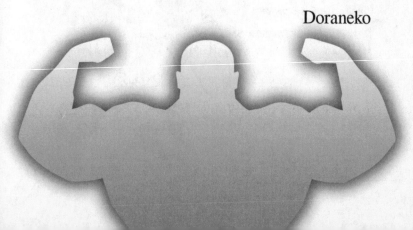

MUSCLES ARE BETTER THAN MAGIC!

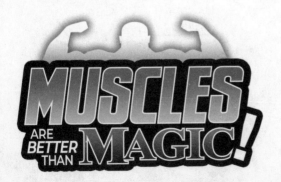

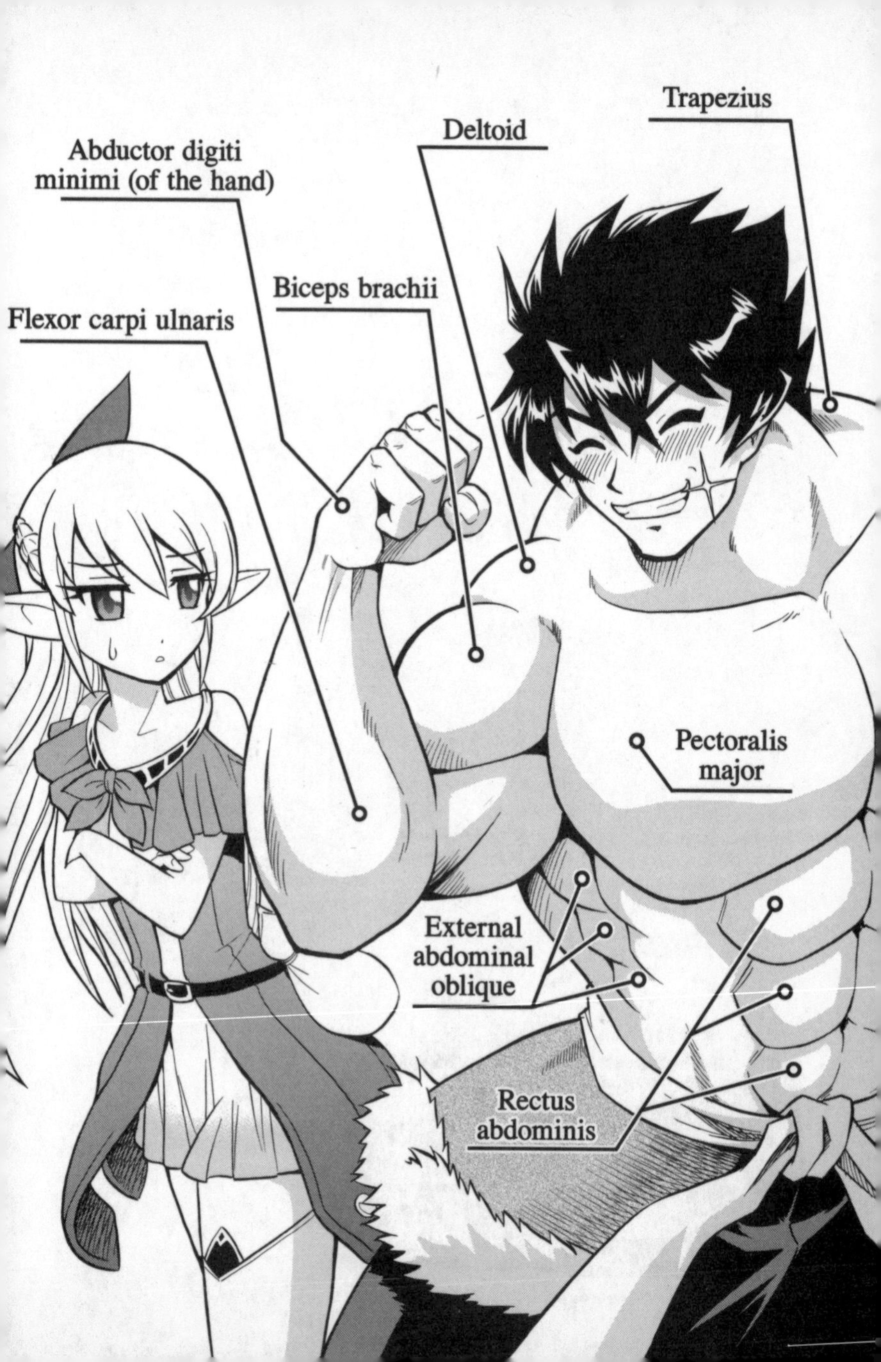
Trapezius
Deltoid
Abductor digiti minimi (of the hand)
Biceps brachii
Flexor carpi ulnaris
Pectoralis major
External abdominal oblique
Rectus abdominis

MUSCLES ARE BETTER THAN MAGIC!

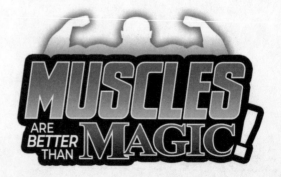

SEVEN SEAS ENTERTAINMENT PRESENTS

MUSCLES ARE BETTER THAN MAGIC!

VOLUME 1

story by **DORANEKO**   art by **KOUJI ONODERA**   character designs by **RELUCY**

TRANSLATION
Timothy MacKenzie

ADAPTATION
M.B. Hare

LETTERING
Ochie Caraan

COVER DESIGN
Nicky Lim

LOGO DESIGN
George Panella

PROOFREADER
Stephanie Cohen

COPY EDITOR
Dawn Davis

EDITOR
Matthew Birkenhauer

PREPRESS TECHNICIAN
hiannon Rasmussen–Silverstein

PRODUCTION ASSISTANT
Christa Miesner

PRODUCTION MANAGER
Lissa Pattillo

MANAGING EDITOR
Julie Davis

ASSOCIATE PUBLISHER
Adam Arnold

PUBLISHER
Jason DeAngelis

MAHO? SONNAKOTO YORI KINNIKU DA! VOL. 1
©Kouji Onodera 2018, DORANEKO 2018
First published in Japan in 2018 by KADOKAWA CORPORATION, Tokyo.
English translation rights arranged with KADOKAWA CORPORATION, Tokyo.

Seven Seas press and purchase enquiries can be sent to Marketing Manager Lianne Sentar at press@gomanga.com. Information regarding the distribution and purchase of digital editions is available from Digital Manager CK Russell at digital@gomanga.com.

ISBN: 978-1-64505-956-1
Printed in Canada
First Printing: April 2021
10 9 8 7 6 5 4 3 2 1

READING DIRECTIONS

This book reads from *right to left*, Japanese style. If this is your first time reading manga, you start reading from the top right panel on each page and take it from there. If you get lost, just follow the numbered diagram here. It may seem backwards at first, but you'll get the hang of it! Have fun!!

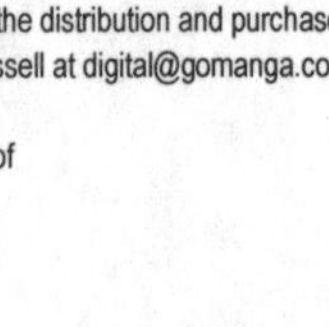

Follow us online: www.SevenSeasEntertainment.com